MEDICAL SOCIOLOGY

second edition

William C. Cockerham

University of Illinois

PRENTICE-HALL, INC., ENGLEWOOD CLIFFS, NEW JERSEY 07632

Library of Congress Cataloging in Publication Data

COCKERHAM, WILLIAM C.
  Medical sociology.

  Bibliography.
  Includes index.
  1. Social medicine.   I. Title.
[DNLM: 1. Sociology, Medical. Wa 31 C666m]
RA418.C657   1982   362.1   81–11850
ISBN 0–13–573410–X   AACR2

Editorial/production supervision: Tom Pendleton
Interior Design: Tom Pendleton
Cover Design: Mario Piazza
Cover Photo by Marc Anderson
Manufacturing Buyer: John Hall

Prentice-Hall Series in Sociology
Neil J. Smelser, *Editor*

© 1982, 1978 by Prentice-Hall, Inc., Englewood Cliffs, N.J. 07632

Printed in the United States of America

10   9   8   7   6   5   4   3   2

ISBN 0-13-573410-X

PRENTICE-HALL INTERNATIONAL, INC., *London*
PRENTICE-HALL OF AUSTRALIA PTY. LIMITED, *London*
PRENTICE-HALL OF CANADA, LTD., *Toronto*
PRENTICE-HALL OF INDIA PRIVATE LIMITED, *London*
PRENTICE-HALL OF JAPAN, INC., *Tokyo*
PRENTICE-HALL OF SOUTHEAST ASIA PTE. LIMITED, *Singapore*
WHITEHALL BOOKS LIMITED, *Wellington, New Zealand*

TO MY CHILDREN

Laura, Geoffrey, and Sean

CONTENTS

PREFACE AND ACKNOWLEDGMENTS

When the first edition of this textbook appeared in 1978, there were few recent textbooks available for students interested in medical sociology. Since that time, however, there has been a virtual explosion in the publication of text material dealing with the social aspects of medicine. The availability of a variety of textbooks, along with the continuing development and expansion of courses and programs in medical sociology, points toward both the relevance and popularity of the subject matter, and its maturity as a major subfield within the discipline of sociology. Thus, medical sociology itself appears to be in a very healthy state, not only in the United States but elsewhere in the world as demonstrated by the vast amount of work being done on this subject in several different countries.

The purpose of the second edition is to add new material and reflect the many trends and changes that have taken place in medical sociology since the first edition. This edition, for example, analyses the increasing impact of consumerism on the patient-physician relationship, the women's health movement, holistic health, faith-healing, systems of health care delivery in other nations, current trends in social policy, and other topics important in understanding the full spectrum of the relationship between health and society. As more and more evidence becomes available that identifies the importance of the relationship between health and the social environment, the more important it becomes to be familiar with the knowledge that characterizes medical sociology. The intent of this book is to help fill that need.

The material contained in the pages of this book are my own responsibility in terms of perspective, scope, and style of presentation. Nevertheless, I am deeply grateful to several people for their assistance in helping this book become a reality. First, I would like to thank Tom Pendleton and

Jeanne Hoeting who served as production editors for this edition at Prentice-Hall, Inc. Next, I would like to acknowledge the insightful comments of those colleagues who reviewed all or part of either the first or second editions of this work. My appreciation for sharing their views and helping to improve the quality of this book goes to Neil Smelser, University of California, Berkeley; Spencer Condie, Brigham Young University; Norman Denzin, University of Illinois; Morton Creditor, University of Illinois Medical Center; Jeffrey Salloway, Rush University School of Medicine; John Collette, University of Utah; Sharon Guten, Case Western Reserve University; Herbert Bynder, University of Colorado; Paul Brezina, County College of Morris; Alexander Rysman, Northeastern University; Eliot Freidson, New York University; and Sol Levine, Boston University.

William Cockerham
Urbana, Illinois

PART I

HEALTH
AND SOCIETY

chapter **1**

MEDICAL SOCIOLOGY

The relationship between social conditions and factors that influence health and the development of disease has long been a major interest of humankind. Throughout history people have generally tended to view health problems from the perspective of their own particular societies and cultures. As a result, they have usually responded to the threat of disease in predictable ways. Knowledge about norms, values, beliefs, social structures, and lifestyles has provided insight not only about the social organization of human resources designed to cope with health hazards, but also about the nature and causes of illness. The recognition, therefore, of the significance of the complex relationship between social factors and the level of health characteristic of specific social groups has led to the development of medical sociology as an important substantive area within the general field of sociology. As an academic discipline, sociology is concerned with the function, structure, and roles of social institutions and social processes, and with the social behavior of groups. Thus it follows that medical sociology is concerned with the social facets of health and illness, the social functions of health institutions and organizations, the relationship of systems of health care delivery to other social systems, and the social behavior of health personnel and those people who are consumers of health care.

Robert Straus (1957) has made a significant observation about medical sociology that helps to explain its current orientation. Straus suggested that medical sociology was divided into two separate but closely interrelated areas: sociology *in* medicine and sociology *of* medicine.

The sociologist in medicine is a sociologist who collaborates directly with the physician and other health personnel in studying the social factors that are relevant to a particular health disorder. The work of the sociologist in medicine is intended to be directly applicable to patient care or to the solving of a public health problem. Some of the tasks of the sociologist in medicine are to analyze the etiology or causes of health disorders, the differences in social attitudes as they relate to health, and the way in which the incidence and prevalence of a specific health disorder is related to such social variables as age, sex, socioeconomic status, racial/ethnic group identity, education, and occupation. Such an analysis is then intended to be made available to health practitioners to assist them in treating health problems. Thus, sociology in medicine can be characterized as *applied research and analysis primarily motivated by a medical problem* rather than a sociological problem. Sociologists in medicine usually work in medical schools, nursing schools, public health schools, teaching hospitals, public health agencies, and other health organizations. They may also work for a governmental agency like the U.S. Department of Health and Human Services in the capacity of biostatisticians, health planners, administrators, and advisors.

The sociology *of* medicine, on the other hand, has a different emphasis. It deals with such factors as the organization, role relationships, norms, values, and beliefs of medical practice as a form of human behavior. The emphasis is upon the social processes that occur in the medical setting and how these contribute to our understanding of medical sociology in particular and to our understanding of social life in general. With few exceptions, there are no unique or special theories that pertain exclusively to the sociology of medicine; instead, the sociology of medicine shares the same goals as all other areas of sociology and may consequently be characterized as *research and analysis of the medical environment from a sociological perspective.* Although some sociologists of medicine are employed in health institutions, the majority work as professors in the sociology departments of universities and colleges.

THE EMERGING RELATIONSHIP
BETWEEN MEDICINE AND SOCIOLOGY

Good health is a prerequisite for the adequate functioning of any individual or society. If our health is sound we can engage in numerous types of activities. But if we are ill or injured, we may face the curtailment of our usual round of daily life and we may also become so preoccupied with our state of health that other pursuits are of secondary importance or quite meaningless. Obviously, nobody likes to feel unequal to his or her daily schedule. This natural concern with the healthy functioning of our bodies has probably been with us throughout our existence on this planet. René DuBos has suggested in *Man, Medicine, and Environment* (1969) that primitive human beings were closer to the animals in that they, too, relied upon their instincts to stay healthy. Yet some primitive humans recognized a cause and effect relationship between doing certain things and alleviating symptoms of a disease or improving the condition of a wound.

Since there was so much that primitive humans did not understand about the functioning of the body, *magic* became an integral component of the beliefs about the causes and cures of health disorders. Actually, an uncritical acceptance of magic and the supernatural pervaded practically every aspect of primitive life. So it is not surprising that early humans thought that illness was caused by evil spirits. Primitive medicines made from vegetables or animals were invariably used in combination with some form of ritual to expel the harmful spirit from a diseased body. During the Neolithic age, some 4,000 to 5,000 years ago, people living in what is today the Eastern Mediterranean and North Africa are known to have even engaged in a surgical procedure called *trepanation* or trephining, which consists of a hole being bored in the skull in order to liberate the evil spirit supposedly contained in a person's head. The finding by anthropologists of more than one hole in some skulls and the lack of signs of osteomyelitis (erosion of bone tissue) suggest that the operation was not always fatal. Some estimates indicate that the mortality rate from trepanation was as low as 10 percent, an amazing accomplishment considering the difficulty of the procedure and the crude conditions under which it must have been performed (Mora, 1975).

Therefore, as DuBos explains, medicine has had a dual nature from its very inception in that it included knowledge about definite medical procedures and a belief in some magic or religious power involving forces beyond human comprehension. This dual nature of medicine is still with us today, as a patient's family and friends will attempt to supplement the modern physician's skill and experience with prayer. The prevailing structure of medical science, regardless of a society's level of medical knowledge and technology, still functions within the context of the values, attitudes, and beliefs of the people who comprise that society.

Ancient Greece

One of the earliest attempts in the Western world to formulate principles of health care based upon rational thought and the rejection of supernatural phenomena is found in the work of the Greek physician Hippocrates. Little is known of Hippocrates the man, who lived around 400 B.C., not even whether he actually authored the collection of books that bears his name. Nevertheless, the writings attributed to him have provided a number of principles underlying modern medical practice. One of his most famous contributions, the Hippocratic Oath, is the foundation of contemporary medical morality and ethics. Among other things, it requires the physician to swear that he or she will help the sick, refrain from intentional wrongdoing or harm, and keep confidential all matters pertaining to the doctor-patient relationship.

Hippocrates also argued that medical knowledge should be derived from an understanding of the natural sciences and the logic of cause and effect relationships. In his classic treatise, *On Airs, Waters, and Places,* Hippocrates pointed out that human well-being is influenced by the totality of environmental factors: living habits or lifestyle, climate, topography of the land, and the quality of air, water, and food. Interestingly enough, concerns about our health and the quality of airs, waters, and places are still very much with us in the twentieth century.

Another influential Hippocratic work was *The Book of Prognostics,* in which the author set forth his theory of medicine. Hippocrates believed that good health resulted from the equilibrium within the body of four humors (blood, phlegm, black bile, and yellow bile) and the harmony of the body itself with living habits and the environment. As long as the four humors were in balance, the body was healthy. If an imbalance occurred, that is, if there was more of one type of humor than another, a person was sick. Although wrong, Hippocrates' humoral theory of disease has persisted even to this day as a basic belief in the folk medicine of many cultures. For example, the practice of traditional folk medicine among Mexican-Americans in the twentieth-century United States is clearly based upon Hippocrates' notions of equilibrium and involves, among other remedies, the use of hot foods for a chill and cold foods for a fever. But what is more relevant for modern medicine is the Hippocratic demand for a *rational and systematic approach to patient care.* This approach, to be based upon thorough observation of the patient's symptoms and a logical plan of treatment according to proven procedures, remains central to contemporary medical practice.

Besides his other contributions, Hippocrates maintained that both the mind and the body profoundly affect each other and cannot be considered as independent entities. Health consisted of a healthy mind in a healthy body. Thus, a basic precept of the Hippocratic orientation was the recognition that the social environment was an important factor in understanding illness. In the treatment of patients, it was necessary to consider the "whole" person under the Hippocratic system.

The Middle Ages and Renaissance

In their intellectual orientation toward disease, the ancient Greeks displayed a frame of reference that was more similar to contemporary medicine than to the subsequent practices of the Middle Ages and the Renaissance. Much of the medical knowledge of the ancient world was lost during the Dark Ages after the fall of Rome and what knowledge remained was preserved by the Roman Catholic Church. It was the position of the Church that it, not medicine, was responsible for the study of the mind and the treatment of social problems. The role of the physician was to focus exclusively on treating ailments of the human body. A few physicians, such as Paracelsus, a famous Swiss doctor who lived in the early sixteenth century, did continue to show concern with health and social conditions. Paracelsus demonstrated that diseases common to certain occupations (such as mining) were related to the work environment. He also argued that mentally ill people were neither criminals nor sinners but sick people in need of medical assistance. However, the Middle Ages and the Renaissance saw few systematic measures undertaken to explain the relationship between the mind and the body and the effect of adverse social conditions upon health in general.

The Post–Renaissance

The lack of understanding of social and psychological factors in illness continued during the seventeenth century. The French philosopher René Descartes, considered the most outstanding representative of seventeenth-century rationalism, helped to shape the direction of philosophical thought for nearly three centuries, profoundly influencing the direction of both psychology and medicine (DuBos, 1969; Mora, 1975). Descartes laid the basis for a philosophical orientation consisting of mathematical axioms and correlates that failed to take human emotions into account. He also reinforced the mind-body dichotomy by insisting that each was an entirely different type of entity. The mind, identified by Descartes as being in the pineal gland, was supposedly an expression of God, too mysterious to be approached as the object of scientific study. By contrast, Descartes defined the body as a physical machine whose operation was within the scope of human knowledge and therefore could be studied. The implication of Descartes' work for medicine was that physicians should not attempt to understand the person as a whole, but should concentrate exclusively upon the physical functioning of the body. DuBos states:

> Descartes' philosophy led scientists to neglect questions pertaining to the nature of the mind and the soul and encouraged them to focus their efforts on the much simpler, more concrete, problems of body structure and operation. They could apply knowledge of physics and chemistry, derived from the study of inanimate matter, to the problems of the body without fear of debasing the more lofty manifestations of man's nature, those of his soul. The self-imposed limitations and intellectual freedom that biologists derived from Cartesian dualism gave them a general tendency to study man as a nonthinking, nonfeeling entity.[1]

The approach of Descartes and his followers was in keeping with the Christian notion of the human body as a weak and imperfect vessel intended to transfer the soul from this world to the next. As long as there was a tacit understanding that the investigation of the mind was a religious matter, the Church did not object to the scientific study of the body. The result was that both Western religion and science sponsored the idea "of the body as a machine, of disease as a breakdown of the machine, and of the doctor's task as repair of the machine" (Engle, 1977:131).

Progress in Public Health

Although many of Descartes' theories were discarded in the twentieth century, they nonetheless provided a philosophical framework for the emphasis two centuries of scientists placed upon understanding the physical and chemical processes of the human body. The mind–body relationship was not a fruitful topic of scientific investigation until well into the nineteenth century. However, occasional observations continued to link social and cultural factors to the general state of health of a particular community. An awareness of the social etiology of disease dawned through common sense and practical experience. A most significant development occurred when it was realized that uncontaminated food, water, and air, as well as sanitary living conditions, could reduce the onset and spread of communicable diseases. Prior to the advent of modern medicine, high mortality rates from communicable diseases such as typhus, tuberculosis, scarlet fever,

---

[1] René DuBos, *Man, Medicine, and Environment* (New York: Mentor, 1969), p. 77.

measles, and cholera were significantly lowered in both Europe and North America through improved hygiene and sanitation. Thus the late eighteenth and early nineteenth centuries are conspicuous for the systematic implementation of public health measures.

Noting the link between life style and health, some nineteenth-century European physicians argued that improvement was necessary in the living conditions of the poor. They advocated governmental recognition of the social as well as medical nature of measures undertaken to promote health. Rudolf Virchow, for instance, a prominent physician known in clinical medicine for the development of cellular pathology, insisted that medicine was a social science. Virchow, a German, argued strongly that the poor should have not only quality medical care, but also that they should have free choice of a physician. Improved medical care was also to go hand in hand with changed social conditions leading to a better life (Rosen, 1979). However, these proposals had little effect outside Virchow's small circle of colleagues.

The Germ Theory of Disease

Most members of the medical profession in the 1800s were primarily interested in improving the state of medical technology. They were not necessarily concerned with social reform. The success during this century of Louis Pasteur, Robert Koch, and others in bacteriological research that led to the conceptualization of the germ theory of disease, along with tremendous progress in the development of internal medicine, anesthesiology, pathology, immunology, and surgical techniques, convinced physicians to focus exclusively upon a clinical medicine grounded in exact scientific laboratory procedures. The practice of medicine in the twentieth century thus rested solidly upon the premise that every disease had a specific pathogenic cause whose treatment could best be accomplished by removing or controlling that cause within a biomedical framework. DuBos (1959) has pointed out that modern medicine's thinking has been dominated by the search for drugs as "magic bullets" that can be shot into the body to kill or control all health disorders. Because research in microbiology, biochemistry, and related fields has resulted in the discovery and production of a large variety of drugs and drug-based techniques for treating many diseases, this approach produced striking results.

Return to the "Whole Person"

As medicine moves into the twenty-first century, it is increasingly called upon to return to the health problems of the whole person, which extend well beyond singular causes of disease. Contemporary physicians are often required to deal with health disorders more aptly described as "problems in living," dysfunctions that involve multiple factors of causation, not all of them biological in nature. The evidence is now quite striking that the manner in which people respond to social, psychological, and cultural influences has much to do not only with whether they become sick, but also with the form, duration, and intensity of their symptoms and disabilities.

Thus it has become clear that modern medicine must develop insight into the behaviors characteristic of the people it treats.

To illustrate this point, consider that the major health disorders in urban-industrial countries are no longer a result of communicable diseases, but instead are the problems of chronic or long-term illnesses such as heart disease and cancer. Because chronic disorder can be influenced by many causes, health personnel should consider all aspects (social, psychological, and physiological) of a chronic condition.

Also, it is not uncommon for an individual suffering from a chronic disease to feel perfectly normal, even when irreversible damage to organs and tissues has already occurred. Because of the irremediable damage done to the body by a chronic disease, patients may be required to permanently change their style of living and modify their social relationships. So, as Anselm Strauss (1975) has pointed out, health practitioners should know how patients with chronic disorders:

1. manage medical crises
2. control their symptoms
3. carry out their prescribed regimens
4. adjust to changes in the course of the disorder
5. attempt to normalize their interaction with others
6. cope with the social isolation caused by reduced contact with others, and
7. seek the necessary money to pay for their treatment and possibly to support themselves and their dependents.

This is in addition to all else that physicians need to know about the behavior and life styles of individuals that influences whether or not they are likely to develop chronic disorders in the first place.

And as Strauss has also observed, many physicians and allied health personnel are not well trained in the behavioral sciences, nor do they know very much about the personal lives of their patients and their families. While they fully recognize that chronic disease is the most prevalent health problem in the United States, they continue to deal with it in the same way they formerly dealt with communicable diseases—by focusing on a particular category (heart, cancer, neurological disorder) of chronic illness rather than on chronic illness in general or on the patient. A probable explanation for the persistence of this type of approach may be the way in which physicians have been selected and trained. Kerr White (1972) explains that, in the past, medical schools selected students who were motivated primarily by curiosity about disease, instead of students motivated by humanistic concern for people. Although both types of physicians are needed, the emphasis on the former has tended to exclude the latter. Additionally, the experience of medical school itself appears to encourage medical students to take a detached view of their patients and become less idealistic (see Chapter Six). In a study of the manner in which medical students and physicians learn to cope with their personal emotions about death and dying, Robert Coombs and Pauline Powers (1975:258) found that physicians would intellectually dissect their patient into physical parts and concentrate upon treating only the pathological part. According to one of the more experienced physicians in their study, this was known as the "old scientific fragmentalization method," which allowed the doctor to deal only with the parts and not with the whole. Murray Wexler has aptly described this situation:

> In essence, this concept is characterized by a form of communication in which the patient is identified by the disease rather than by his human qualities. This attitude is characterized (perhaps caricatured) in a play about physicians, produced in the 1930's, in which one intern reminds his associate, "You'll have to check the gallbladder in 321."[2]

Objectivity in treating a disease may not necessarily be a bad thing. But some critics of medical education contend that medical schools are merely "trade" schools that train doctors to be little more than "technicians" or "mechanics" who work on the human body.

Medicine and Sociology

As Howard Rasmussen (1975) has made clear, medicine is now faced with two distinct alternatives. It can either redefine disease and restrict its treatment to specifically medical conditions, or it can accept a broad concept of disease (which includes problems in living) and change medical education programs to deal effectively with the wider spectrum of illness. This latter alternative forecasts a close association between medicine and the behavioral sciences of sociology, anthropology, and psychology, the beginnings of which are already in evidence. In 1969 a study originated within the American Sociological Association that reviewed behavioral science programs in nine major medical schools and found that such programs were well accepted.[3] Wexler characterized the findings of this study by noting that:

> The case studies are impressive documents. They describe in detail the enormous amount of effort that has been expended in trying to effect a major change in medical education and thinking. It would be necessary to have been a participant in medical education prior to 1960 to appreciate how drastically the scene has changed for the behavioral sciences. Anthropologists, psychologists, and sociologists are increasingly familiar figures in the lecture halls and seminar rooms, on ward walks, at grand rounds, on admissions committees, etc.[4]

As for sociologists, many hold joint teaching and research appointments between departments of sociology and health institutions, or are employed full-time in these institutions. Medical, nursing, pharmacy, and public health schools are all expanding the number of faculty positions for sociologists and adding courses in the behavioral sciences at a significant rate. The growing

---

[2] Murray Wexler, "The Behavioral Sciences in Medical Education," *American Psychologist*, 3 (April 1976), 276.
[3] The nine medical schools included in the study were the University of Connecticut, Duke University, Harvard University, the University of Kentucky, Michigan State University, the University of Missouri, the Pennsylvania State University Hershey Medical Center, Stanford University, and the University of Toronto. For the full report, see C. R. Fletcher et al., *A Study for Teaching Behavioral Sciences in Schools of Medicine* 3 vols. (Rockville, Md.: National Center for Health Services Research and Development, 1972).
[4] Wexler, "The Behavioral Sciences," p. 279.

interest of medicine in human behavior is also reflected in the much larger proportion of questions dealing with the behavioral sciences on national board examinations taken by medical students. In addition to courses in the behavioral sciences, sociologists lecture on medical sociology, social psychiatry, epidemiology, preventive medicine, community medicine, public health, and the social aspects of pharmacy. They also participate in studies of the utilization and evaluation of health services and the development of health policies on local, state, and national levels.

Some premedical students who major in sociology are now being admitted to medical schools (compared to practically none in the 1950s).[5] And one physician, George Reader, has argued that medical schools should require a background in sociology of all students who apply for admission on the grounds that sociological principles are basic to understanding how to be a better medical student and a better practicing physician. According to Reader:

> Interviewing patients can be made more of a science and less an art; obstacles to compliance with a therapeutic regime can be more easily recognized; quality of care can be measured more accurately; effects of health legislation can be made more predictable; and epidemiology gains new dimensions.[6]

This is not to say, however, that the growing acceptance of the behavioral sciences in medicine is proceeding without any serious problems. Not all medical educators and physicians agree about the importance of the behavioral sciences in the medical school curriculum, and many behavioral scientists have yet to identify those aspects of their subject matter best suited for solving practical medical problems. Nevertheless, the indication is that inclusion of the behavioral sciences in medical education is here and will continue for some time.

Sociology and Medicine

While the development of modern medicine emphasized the biological and neglected the behavioral sciences (with the exception of medically oriented psychiatry), the development of sociology, in turn, originally spurned the influence of biological elements on human social behavior. For that matter, a case can be made that modern sociology developed largely in opposition to biological theories that explained differences in human behavior on the basis of innate biological characteristics. One of the most significant factors in the thought of the French sociologist Emile Durkheim (1858–1917), whose theories have dominated a large portion of sociology's approach to human behavior, was his strong rejection of biology (see Nisbet, 1974). Neither in the gene pool of a particular race nor in the genetic composition of an individual did Durkheim find relevant evidence for

[5] Of the 160 persons with undergraduate majors in sociology who applied for admission to U.S. medical schools for the 1977–1978 year, 54, or 33.8 percent of the total were accepted. See *Medical School Admissions Requirements, 1980–81,* 30th ed. (Washington, D.C.: Association of American Medical Colleges, 1980).

[6] George G. Reader, "Should Medical Schools Require a Sociology Background?" *AAMC Education News,* 4 (December 1976): 3, 8.

sociology. Although recognizing that biological explanations of human behavior contribute to our understanding of human interaction, Durkheim
argued that they can never be *totally* sufficient explanations. Instead, the
basis for sound explanations of social behavior was to be found in the *social
processes of culture, environment, and human thought.* Thus social behavior must
be explained from the standpoint of such elements as norms, values, and
statuses which constitute the social basis of human group life. The persua-
siveness of Durkheim's argument and its support by other sociologists led to
the nearly total disregard of biology by social theorists. Only within the past
few years have the contributions of biology once again been given serious
sociological consideration; today the field of social biology represents a
promising but still highly underdeveloped area of study.

What prompted sociologists to organize medical sociology as an area of
sociological inquiry in its own right was neither medicine nor biology, but the
realization that medical practice represented a distinct segment of society
with its own unique social institutions, social processes, occupations, problems, and behavioral settings. The development of the sociology of medicine
was greatly influenced by the expansion of the National Institutes of Health
in the United States during the late 1940s, especially the establishment of the
National Institute of Mental Health, which provided the funding and
encouraged the interaction of researchers from both the social and the
medical sciences. According to August Hollingshead (1973), one of the early
participants, a major result of this interaction was the stimulus to both social
and medical scientists to formulate and implement joint projects. Thereafter, the growth of medical sociology proceeded at such a rate that since
1960 it has become the largest and one of the most active sections of the
American Sociological Association. The position of medical sociology was
further strengthened in 1966 when the *Journal of Health and Social Behavior*
became an official American Sociological Association publication.

The preceding discussion has briefly outlined the convergence of
medicine and sociology in contemporary American society. John McKinlay
(1971) has ventured to suggest that the time may come when the research
contributions of medical sociology will stand in the same relation to medicine
as do those of physiology, endocrinology, and biology as a body of knowledge
explaining human functioning in the medical sphere. It is still too early to
surmise whether or not McKinlay's prediction will prove true, because
medical sociology is a relatively new field and a considerable amount of
research still needs to be compiled and precisely formulated. However, the
work to date has been most impressive and promises even more exciting
contributions in the future. John Knowles (1979) is correct when he states
that medicine is a social science as well as a biological science and that it needs
the social sciences as never before.

PLAN OF THIS BOOK

The intent of this book is to provide an overview of the general field of
medical sociology from the standpoint of both the sociologist of medicine
and the sociologist in medicine. The material has been organized into four

major parts dealing with the following general topics: (1) Health and Society, (2) Health Practitioners, (3) Health Institutions, and (4) Health and Selected Social Problems.

Part I (Health and Society) is concerned with the relationship between social factors, illness, and the behavior of people who define themselves as being sick and in need of medical attention. Chapter Two (Social Epidemiology) discusses the role of the epidemiologist and the social variables of age, sex, race, and socioeconomic status on the overall health profile of people living in the United States. Broadly speaking, the epidemiologist's function is to explore the relationship between the environment and groups of people. Chapter Three (Mind, Body, and Society) is concerned primarily with the concept of stress and how social influences contribute to the development of stress-induced physical and mental disorders. Chapter Four examines the various theories and concepts that have been advanced to explain whether or not certain people will seek out a physician for assistance, utilize the other services of a health care delivery system, or treat their health problem without professional assistance. Chapter Five discusses Talcott Parsons' concept of the sick role, which has become a central theory in medical sociology. The sick role represents a temporary exemption from normal social functioning that is granted to certain individuals upon the condition that they seek professional care in order to get well. This theory has been a source of considerable controversy in medical sociology and this chapter will assess its validity.

Part II (Health Practitioners) looks at research findings in medical sociology pertaining to physicians, nurses, and other health personnel. Chapter Six deals with the physician's traditional role of professional dominance in the health occupations and the manner in which this dominant position is being challenged by laypersons who are changing their status from that of "patient" to that of health care "consumer"—with all that implies in terms of a different type of social relationship. Chapter Seven, on nurses and the other health practitioners, likewise examines the changing nature of occupational roles in medicine and the reverberations of these new concepts both within and outside the profession.

In Part III (Health Institutions), Chapter Eight explores the social development and structure of the hospital as a formal institution. This discussion includes an examination of the dual nature of its authority system and the effect of the organization of its services on the interaction between patients and staff. Chapter Nine considers health care delivery systems and social policy.

Part IV (Health and Selected Social Problems) examines selected social problems as they relate to health care. Chapter Ten explores changing concepts in mental health and social factors that have been found to be important indicators of mental disorders. Chapter Eleven discusses the social psychology of aging and the role of the aged in contemporary society. Chapter Twelve examines the fears and anxieties people express in regard to their own personal mortality and the manner in which they cope with the inevitability of their deaths. Evidence will also be discussed that suggests that the attitudes toward death and dying may be changing in American society.

SUMMARY

Throughout history human beings have been interested in and, in fact, deeply concerned with the effects of the social environment on the health of individuals and the groups to which they belong. Despite a promising beginning in ancient Greece, medicine developed in such a way that it ignored sociology. Much later, the formal beginnings of sociology dictated an opposition to biological and medical contributions. Yet sociology's interest in medicine as a unique system of human social behavior, and medicine's recognition that sociology can help health practitioners to better understand their patients and provide improved forms of health care, has begun to bring about a convergence of mutual interest between the two disciplines. More and more medical sociologists are being invited to join the staffs of medical institutions and to participate in medical research projects. Medical sociology courses and degrees are now more frequently offered by universities and colleges. The extensive growth of sociological literature in academic medicine is further evidence of the rising status of the medical sociologist. Although a considerable amount of work remains to be done, the medical sociologist at this time is in the enviable position of participating in, and influencing the development of, an exciting, significant, and relatively new field.

chapter 2

SOCIAL EPIDEMIOLOGY

Many sociologists working in the field of medicine are epidemiologists. Epidemiology is a discipline which has evolved relatively specialized methods for investigating health problems. Depending upon the particular health hazard being investigated, epidemiology draws upon the knowledge and techniques of several scientific fields. Besides sociologists, one will find physicians, public health workers, biologists, biochemists, entomologists, ornithologists, mammalogists, veterinarians, demographers, anthropologists, and perhaps even meteorologists (in studies of air pollution) involved in epidemiological work. In its strictest sense, epidemiology is the science of epidemics; however, present day epidemiologists have broadened their field to include not only epidemic diseases, but also all other forms of disease and bodily injury such as cancer, heart disease, alcoholism, drug addiction, suicide, and automobile accidents. The epidemiologist is, therefore, concerned with exploring human ecology as it relates to the health of human beings and their environment.

The primary focus of the epidemiologist is not on the individual, but on *the health problems of social aggregates or large groups of people.* The epidemiologist studies both the origin and the distribution of health problems in a population through the collection of data from many different sources. He or she then constructs a logical chain of inferences to explain the various factors in a society or segment of a society that cause a particular health problem to exist. Epidemiology is one of the most important investigative techniques in the study of health and disease.

The role of the epidemiologist can probably be best likened to that of a detective investigating the scene of a crime for clues. The epidemiologist usually begins by examining the sick person or persons and then extends the investigation to the setting where the patient(s) first became ill and is likely to become ill again. What the epidemiologist is looking for is the common denominator that links all the victims of a health problem together so that the cause of the problem can be identified and eliminated or controlled.

THE DEVELOPMENT OF SOCIAL EPIDEMIOLOGY

As a method of measuring diseases in human aggregates, epidemiology has been a relatively recent development. So long as human beings lived as nomads or in widely scattered and isolated communities, the danger from epidemics and infectious disease was relatively slight. However, once people began to crowd into primitive cities with unsanitary living conditions and an abundance of rats and lice, the probabilities favoring the development of communicable diseases greatly increased. The crowded conditions of urban living also insured that infectious diseases would spread more quickly and that disease-causing microorganisms would persist within the community for longer periods of time. In addition, the migration of peoples from one region of the world to another spread disease from geographic area to geographic area. Bubonic plague, for example, apparently reached Europe from China during the fourteenth century, cholera entered Great Britain by way of India in the seventeenth century, while Europeans brought smallpox to the Western Hemisphere during the exploration and settlement of the New World. History reveals numerous examples of explorers and travelers introducing the microorganisms of a dreaded disease to a community of unsuspecting people.

The bubonic plague that ravaged Europe between 1340 and 1750 marks one of the worst epidemic afflictions in all human history. It is estimated that one-quarter of the population of Europe died during its greatest prevalence (Paul, 1966). During one single month (September, 1665) in one city (London), approximately 30,000 people died from the plague. Describing conditions in the fourteenth century, historian Barbara Tuchman (1978:92) reports: "So lethal was the disease that cases were known of persons going to bed well and dying before they awoke, of doctors catching the illness at a bedside and dying before the patient." What made the disease especially frightening was that no one knew what caused it, how to prevent it, or how to cure it. Yet even though the pestilence affected the rich and poor alike, there was still a *social* difference in the death rates. The poor were much more likely to die from it than the rich. Tuchman says:

> Flight was the chief recourse of those who could afford it or arrange it. The rich fled to their country places like Boccaccio's young patricians of Florence, who settled in a pastoral palace "removed on every side from the roads" with "wells of cool water and vaults of rare wine." The urban poor died in their burrows, "and only the stench of their bodies informed their neighbors of their death." That the poor were more heavily afflicted than the rich was clearly remarked at the time, in the north as in the south. A Scottish chronicler, John of Fordum, stated flatly that the pest "attacked especially the meaner sort and common people—seldom the magnates." Simon de Covino of Montpellier made the same observation. He ascribed it to the misery and want and hard lives that

made the poor more susceptible, which was half the truth. Close contact and lack of sanitation was the unrecognized other half of it.[1]

The cause of the plague was thought by many to be God's wrath upon sinners; however, the realization eventually came that diseases could be transmitted from person to person or between animals and people. The origin of the plague turned out to be the flea of the black rat, but the pneumonic plague, the most deadly form of the bubonic plague, was transmitted from person to person. What actually ended the plague about 1750 was the appearance in cities of the aggressive brown rat. The brown rat tended to avoid humans, had fleas that were less effective carriers, and drove most of Europe's black rats out of urban areas. Another very important factor was the development of improved housing and sanitation.

One of the earliest epidemiological studies was conducted by Sir Percival Pott in England in 1775 (Graham, 1972). Pott observed that English chimney sweeps seemed to have a high incidence of cancer of the scrotum. He reasoned that the chimney sweep's occupation, which placed him in close and frequent contact with soot, might be the cause of cancer of the scrotum among those individuals who were susceptible to the disease. Pott suggested a relationship between a behavior (chimney sweeping) and a disease of a specific organ (cancer of the scrotum). He demonstrated that if behavior were changed by increased bathing, the incidence of the disease could be reduced. Pott's work showed that social activities can significantly affect susceptibility to a particular disease.

However, epidemiology as a form of systematic analysis did not develop until the nineteenth century. It was not until 1854 that the work of John Snow established the foundation of modern epidemiology. Snow was an English physician who plotted the geographic location of all reported cholera cases in London. He then went out into the neighborhoods of these victims and inquired into their day-to-day behavior. He wanted to know what they ate, what they drank, where they went, and the nature of all their activities. Eventually Snow began to suspect that cholera was transmitted by water, since the common factor in the daily lives of the victims was getting their water from the Broad Street pump. At that time, London obtained drinking water from several water companies, and a few of these companies apparently were providing water contaminated with cholera bacteria. By closing down the pump on Broad Street, Snow was able to stop the epidemic. He not only established a mode of investigation, but also demonstrated that research could lead to positive action.

At the time of Snow's research, the development of scientific medicine was well underway. The work of Pasteur and his immediate followers during the latter part of the nineteenth century revolutionized medical thought with the germ theory of disease, stipulating that bacteria were the source of infection in the human body. The findings of Snow, Pasteur, and others provided the epidemiologist with a framework of analysis. Recognition that

[1] Barbara W. Tuchman, *A Distant Mirror: The Calamitous 14th Century* (New York: Random House, 1978), p. 98.

germs were causal agents of disease served as a precursor to scientific determination that causal agents included: (1) biological agents, such as bacteria, viruses, or insects; (2) nutritional agents, such as fats and carbo-hydrates as producers of cholesterol; (3) chemical agents, such as dust, gases, or particles in the air; (4) physical agents, such as climate or vegetation, and (5) social agents, such as occupation, social class, or location of residence. What a person does, who a person is, and where a person lives can specify what health hazards are most likely to exist in that individual's life. The epidemiologist then identifies a particular host (person or group of persons or animals) most susceptible to these causal agents. The human host is also defined in terms of age, sex, lifestyle, and general physical condition. Next, the physical and social environment of the causal agent and the host is explored. The end result is intended to be an identification of *what* is causing a group of people to become sick or suffer injury.

When we use the term *social environment* in epidemiological research, we are referring to actual living conditions, such as poverty or crowding, and the norms, values, and attitudes that reflect a particular social and cultural context. Societies have socially prescribed patterns of living arrangements, as well as standards pertaining to the use of water, food and food handling, and household and personal hygiene. Therefore, the social environment provides information that can be used not only to identify causal agents and to trace the transmission process, but also to assist in ascertaining the most effective means of treatment and prevention within that particular environment.

Physical Distress: Manhattan, 1944

For example, in 1944 a well-known epidemiological study took place on Manhattan's skid row, an environment of poverty and alcoholism (Roueché, 1967). Known as the case of the "Eleven Blue Men," it involved eleven alcoholics who were admitted to a hospital with the skin of their extremities turning a blue color. At first the hospital physicians and local health authorities surmised that carbon monoxide poisoning had caused the skin condition, but the men lacked other symptoms of gas poisoning. By interviewing the patients, they discovered that each of the victims had eaten breakfast in the same cafe on the same day. It was also noted that all had eaten oatmeal for breakfast. A further discovery that the cook had used sodium nitrite, a mild poison, in the oatmeal instead of salt suggested food poisoning. Yet numerous people had eaten the poisoned oatmeal and only eleven had been affected, so an important question was left unanswered. The case was finally solved when an epidemiologist remembered that some-times alcoholics use salt instead of sugar on oatmeal because of a salt defi-ciency in their blood. The amount of sodium nitrite in the oatmeal had not been enough to poison anyone, but a busboy or someone who had the job of filling the salt shakers had made the same mistake the cook had, and put sodium nitrite in the shakers. It was this double dosage of sodium nitrite that produced the strong toxic effect. Knowledge concerning the behavior of alcoholics had provided the most significant clue in solving the case and providing the hospital doctors with the information they needed to help the men.

Mental Distress: Miami, 1974

Another example of epidemiological work took place in Miami, Florida, in 1974 (Roueché, 1978). A report came to the Dade County Department of Public Health that an elementary school was engulfed in a cloud of poison gas and several children were ill. Upon arriving at the school, the epidemiologist in charge of the case found total chaos. Ambulances, police cars, and fire engines—all with their lights flashing—were parked haphazardly around the school, as were dozens of cars and vans. Newspaper reporters and photographers and television news teams were swarming over the school. Even members of the city council were on hand. Only the children, who had been marched out of the building to the edge of the school grounds, appeared calm. According to a school secretary, the first victim, Sandy, an eleven-year-old girl, had felt sick during a practice session for the school chorus in the cafeteria. Sandy had walked to the clinic, but no one was on duty and she had collapsed unconscious on a couch. The secretary noticed her and tried to revive her. When Sandy failed to regain consciousness, the secretary had called the fire department's rescue squad who had put her on a stretcher and taken her to a hospital. Shortly thereafter, several other children became sick. Seven of these children were sent to the hospital and twenty-five others were sent home. Another forty children were treated at the school.

Entering the school, the epidemiologist noticed a strange odor. The sick children, who were being treated in the cafeteria, had a curious variety of symptoms. Two children were hyperventilating (breathing hard and fast), while others complained of headaches, chills, dizziness, abdominal pain, shortness of breath, and weakness. The source of the odor was discovered: it turned out to be a nontoxic adhesive used on a new carpet in the library, which had been put in some two weeks earlier. So the odor was not the cause, nor was anything wrong with the air-conditioning system. Bacterial infection was ruled out because the symptoms were missing and the interval between exposure (Sandy fainting) and the onset of the other illnesses was too short. Moreover, a telephone call to the physician treating the hospitalized children disclosed that these children appeared to be essentially normal—although not all the laboratory tests had been completed. The break in the case finally came when a member of the kitchen staff, an authoritative woman, called the epidemiologist over. She asked him to do something about all the confusion. She said there was absolutely nothing the matter with the children, that the whole situation was perfectly ridiculous, and that she wanted the children out of the cafeteria because she had to start getting ready for lunch. The epidemiologist had suspected that something was not quite right with the case all along. He had seen two children hyperventilating and knew that hyperventilation is a classic psychosomatic reaction to anxiety. Suddenly he realized the truth.

The truth was that the children were suffering from an epidemic of mass hysteria. The kitchen worker was correct in thinking that there was nothing fundamentally wrong with the children. She was incorrect, however, in thinking that the children's chills and nausea were solely imaginary. The symptoms were real, but brought on by hysteria. The entire episode had begun with Sandy feeling faint and leaving the cafeteria about 9:30 in the morning. The rescue squad arrived at ten o'clock and carried Sandy out of the clinic just as classes were changing and the children, including those who had been in the cafeteria with Sandy, entered the halls and saw Sandy on the stretcher. Somebody else complained of being sick and that triggered a wave of nausea. Then a doctor arrived, saw Sandy and the rescue squad and the other children, smelled the odor from the carpet, and said something about gas. This was a second trigger and more children felt sick.

Altogether, seventy-three children reported some symptoms of illness out of a total school enrollment of about 450. A study was done on the seven children who were hospitalized with Sandy. All knew Sandy and all were present when she left the rehearsal. Five were girls and two were boys. Among the girls, one tended to be sickly, one was well known as a hypochondriac, one typically hyperventilated when under stress, another felt sick on coming to school, and the remaining girl was a very close friend of Sandy. Of the two boys, one was always causing discipline problems and the other was highly excitable.

What about Sandy? She had actually been sick, most likely from a virus. Standing and singing for an hour in the cafeteria had been too much for her. She felt faint and subsequently passed out on the clinic couch. The social and psychological response to this event resulted in a collective sense of hysteria among some children and some of them felt sick because of it.

COMPLEX SOCIETIES

Not all health disorders in today's urban and industrialized societies lend themselves to such direct cause and effect relationships as the cases of the "Eleven Blue Men" and the mass hysteria in Miami. Many contemporary epidemiological problems are extremely complex, as the major health threat to contemporary society is from a variety of chronic and degenerative ills related to aging and the effects of man-made environments.

An illustration of the role of multicausality in modern social epidemiology is the Framingham, Massachusetts research project (Dawber et al., 1963). Begun during the 1950s, this study has shown in preliminary data that arteriosclerosis does not strike people at random as they age, but that highly susceptible individuals can be identified in advance. Some 5,000 persons were selected, mostly at random, to participate in the study. They were all between the ages of thirty and sixty and were free from any form of heart disease at the time of their initial examination. They were given relatively complete physical examinations every two years for a twenty-year period. The data clearly suggest that male sex, advancing age, high blood pressure, cigarette smoking, diabetes, and obesity constitute significant risk factors in whether or not a person develops heart disease.

Although heart disease joins cancer, stroke, accidents, and mental disorders as the leading causes of disability and death in advanced industrial societies, the underdeveloped nations of the world show different patterns of major health problems. In these societies, the traditional diseases of human history, influenced by poor sanitation and malnutrition, still prevail. Underdeveloped nations usually are characterized by a high birth rate and a high death rate, and a relatively young population because infectious diseases do not allow large numbers of people to live long enough to develop chronic disorders. A major distinction, therefore, in how diseases are distributed among population groups becomes apparent when the health profiles of industrialized societies are compared to those of underdeveloped nations. Although malnutrition may occur in the United States and heart disease may occur in rural India, these cases do not follow general societal patterns. Many epidemiologists insist that there is a regular sequence of health problems corresponding to each stage of a nation's change in social organization from a rural to an urban society and from an agricultural to an industrial producer. For example, Table 2–1 shows the leading causes of death in the United States in 1900 were influenza and pneumonia, and tuberculosis. In 1980 these disorders had been replaced by heart disease, cancer, cerebrovascular disease, and accidents as the major causes of death in an increasingly urban and industrialized society. Improvements in living conditions and medical technology had all but eliminated disorders such as tuberculosis, gastroenteritis, and diphtheria as major threats to life in 1980, but smoking, excessive consumption of calories and animal fats, stress reactions, inadequate physical activity, and other aspects of modern living had helped promote other health problems, such as heart disease and other cardiovascular disorders like cerebrovascular diseases and arteriosclerosis. Excessive alcohol intake had influenced the increase in deaths from accidents, diabetes, and cirrhosis of the liver.

The complexity of health disorders in modern nations has spurred the development of social epidemiology toward the concept that physical and psychological living systems are invariably linked together in a cause and effect relationship (Wilson, 1970). It appears that a psychological event, for

TABLE 2–1.   The Ten Leading Causes of Death in the United States, 1900 and 1980

1900	1980
Influenza and pneumonia	Heart disease
Tuberculosis	Cancer
Gastroenteritis	Cerebrovascular diseases
Heart disease	Accidents
Cerebral hemorrhage	Influenza and pneumonia
Chronic nephritis	Diabetes
Accidents	Cirrhosis of liver
Cancer	Arteriosclerosis
Diseases of early infancy	Suicide
Diphtheria	Diseases of early infancy

example, a thwarted need for love or affection, may not only affect an individual's personality but also have biological consequences due to excessive stress and tension within the body. Then, too, causes and effects are not necessarily contained within a particular living system, but may branch out into all areas of life in which an individual is involved. The loss of a limb can affect a person's concept of self and social relations with other people, and, conversely, remorse attributable to a social event may "cause" insomnia or the secretion of excessive hydrochloric acid within the stomach.

A study by Thomas Holmes (1962) and his associates in Seattle, Washington, serves to illustrate the interplay between mind, body, and disease in epidemiological research. Like John Snow's study of cholera in London, Holmes' investigation involved the distribution of a particular disease in a large urban area. Holmes discovered a high concentration of tuberculosis among men living alone in the center of Seattle. A study of those individuals who were hospitalized suggest that the onset of tuberculosis was closely associated with alcoholism, divorce, and/or the experience of relatively stressful life events, such as loss of a job or separation from a loved one. Another significant factor was social isolation. Not only was tuberculosis prevalent among skid row residents, but also among blacks who lived in otherwise all-white neighborhoods. This research suggested that the activation of tuberculosis was highly dependent upon a variety of circumstances. Susceptibility to the disease apparently increased when individuals were removed from their normal environments and were exposed to the stress of isolation and a possible accompanying change for the worse in self-concept.

THE LEGIONNAIRES' DISEASE

The most widely publicized and baffling epidemiological case in recent years was the mysterious Legionnaires' disease, which appeared without warning in Pennsylvania in July 1976. The common denominator in this episode was that all of the victims had either attended a state American Legion convention held at the Bellevue-Stratford Hotel in Philadelphia, or were delegates to a Eucharistic Congress of the Roman Catholic Church held at the same hotel a few days later, or for some reason had been in or near the hotel. Eventually some thirty-four persons were to die and 221 persons were hospitalized from the disease.

The American Legion Convention started out like most other such gatherings in the past: meetings, speeches, banquets, drinking, and making the rounds of nearby bars and night clubs. As the convention went on, some people began to feel ill, but most of those becoming sick did not experience the symptoms of headaches, muscle and chest pains, fever as high as 107, and pneumonia until after they returned to homes located throughout the state.

The first evidence of a possible epidemic came a week after the legionnaires had returned home. It came from a physician who suspected the possibility of an outbreak of typhoid. One of his patients had come to him complaining of fever and a loss of weight. Fearing cancer, the physician ordered laboratory tests, which suggested typhoid (many of the legionnaires had typhoid antibodies in their blood due to typhoid vaccinations). Upon hearing that he might have typhoid, the patient informed the physician that two other of his friends (also legionnaires who attended the convention) were in the same hospital (one of these men died a few hours later). Laboratory tests on these two men also produced results suggesting typhoid, and the physician notified a state public health center of his findings. Shortly thereafter, reports of persons showing similar symptoms were made from other communities in the state; some of these persons died.

As there was no information to link these people together, state health authorities had no idea that they were all legionnaires and had attended the state convention the week before. The realization that something terrible was happening occurred first to the legionnaires themselves when the news began to spread around the state about illnesses and untimely deaths among some of their fellows. One of the legionnaires became alarmed and began making telephone calls to various Legion posts to ascertain where else legionnaires were sick. By the Monday of the second week after the convention, enough information had been obtained that the Pennsylvania Department of Health issued a statewide alert on the mystery disease and its existence became prime news in the mass media. Teams of epidemiologists from the Federal Center for Disease Control in Atlanta, Georgia, and from the Pennsylvania Department of Health were rushed to various hospitals and towns where they interviewed the victims and their physicians, talked to family members, neighbors, and friends of the victims, and collected specimens for laboratory analysis. There was great relief when no new cases were reported, nor were there any secondary infections among persons having contact with the victims after they had returned home.

But there was no explanation of what had caused the disease. Several theories were advanced, but none of them provided the answer. Initially, it was thought that swine flu or some other type of influenza virus was the culprit. Laboratory tests showed, however, that it was not a virus; nor was it salmonella, a typhoid-like organism transmitted by food or water, or psittacosis, a respiratory disease carried by birds. Other diseases known to be transmitted by monkeys and hamsters were ruled out as was food poisoning (because it is seldom linked with pneumonia). Some people even suggested deliberate sabotage or germ warfare. At one point, epidemiologists focused on a fifty-foot water hose that connected the drinking water in the hotel with the cold water lines for air conditioning. A workman assigned to adjusting the air conditioners had come down with symptoms of the disease, and the possibility that chemically tainted water was responsible for spreading germs through the air was quickly investigated. This theory likewise failed, as did the possibility of nickel carbonyl gas poisoning, a substance used in the manufacture of plastics and synthetic rubber. The discovery of potentially fatal levels of nickel in tissue samples taken from some of the victims had suggested this lead.

When none of the theories was found to be adequate, the investigation was broadened to include further measures. Organs and other tissue specimens from the dead victims were subjected to extensive laboratory analysis and reanalysis. At the same time, questionnaires were administered to all persons known to have attended the convention who did not become ill. This was done in order to draw comparisons with those who were sick. The medical detectives sought to find the common link as they asked the legionnaires again and again what they ate, what they drank, where they went, what they did when they got there, what time they did it, and so forth.

For a time, it appeared that the answer might never be forthcoming. But finally in January 1977, about six months after the first reports of the disease, the cause was discovered. It took thousands of laboratory tests, several epidemiologists, and several dozen eggs to find out what happened. Two epidemiologists at the Federal Center for Disease Control, Dr. Charles Shepard and Joseph McDade, had quietly tested a theory that rickettsia, organisms of a class between viruses and bacteria, had been involved. The first tests were negative, but the researchers continued looking. Finally they tried injecting lung tissue from one of the victims into guinea pigs, and it produced a fever that suggested bacterial infection. Known bacteria were dismissed when they failed to react to the antibodies found in blood samples of the victims. Thus it appeared that the researchers were on to some type of new organism. The guinea pigs were again injected with the lung tissue material and again became sick. The spleens from the sick animals were next ground up and injected into the yolk sacs of fertilized chicken eggs. The egg embryos died. The bacteria found in the eggs were larger than rickettsia but smaller than known bacteria. Tests were repeated yet, unlike bacteria, the new organisms were extremely difficult to grow under artificial conditions. Eventually enough of the organisms were grown, and they were found to react against the antibodies from samples of the victims' blood. This meant that the new organism, which was named *legionellosis,* was the one that the victims' bodies were trying to fight off. Comparisons made with bacteria specimens stored at the Center for Disease Control revealed that the same or a highly similar organism had caused an outbreak of pneumonia at a psychiatric hospital in Washington, D.C. in 1965 and a respiratory disorder without pneumonia ("Pontiac fever") at a health department building in Pontiac, Michigan in 1968.

By 1980, at least seventeen occurrences of the disease had been documented in the United States and sporadic cases had been recorded in Great Britain, Canada, Australia, Switzerland, West Germany, the Netherlands, and Israel. As the capability for diagnosing Legionnaires' disease increases, it is expected that cases will be identified in other geographic areas as well (Cordes and Fraser, 1980). Among the most publicized outbreaks since the 1976 Philadelphia epidemic were those in Bloomington, Indiana (traced to water in the air-conditioning system at the University of Indiana's Memorial Union) in 1977–1978, in the garment district of Manhattan in New York City in 1978, and at the Wadsworth Veterans Administration Medical Center in Los Angeles from 1977 to 1980. Wadsworth had set up a special Legionnaires' disease laboratory, one of only a few in the United States, that ran tests on virtually every case of pneumonia that took place among patients in the hospital. It was discovered that an average of five cases a month had been occurring there. Yet despite the increase in new cases of Legionnaires' disease, the rates of all types of pneumonia did not increase at the hospital.

This meant that either Legionnaires' disease had been occurring there for many years but had gone unrecognized because no diagnostic test existed or that Legionnaires' disease is a new form of pneumonia replacing other forms that typically affected the types of patients usually seen at Wadsworth. The source of the contamination at Wadsworth was thought to be either in the air-conditioning system or the water supply.

Whether Legionnaires' disease is a new disease entity or has generally been active for some time without being detected is yet to be determined. The bacteria have been found in ponds, dust, soil, lakes, golf courses, mud, rivers, air-conditioning systems, and tap water in hospitals and office buildings in the United States and other countries where attempts have been made to locate it. Most outbreaks have been associated with buildings, such as hotels, hospitals, a golf course clubhouse, and a factory. The risk of contracting the disease seems to be more related to the amount of time spent in the area of presumed exposure than to any particular type of activity while there. The most prevalent period of time for Legionnaires' disease to occur is June through September, thus suggesting seasonality. Most cases occur in middle-aged or older adults, especially among people between the ages of fifty and sixty. Attack rates appear two to four times higher for men than for women, while cigarette smoking and alcohol consumption also seem to be risk factors. But many of the biological and social factors explaining how people catch the disease are still unknown. Nevertheless, as work continues, the Legionnaires' disease investigation already stands as one of the most challenging epidemiological problems of our time.

EPIDEMIOLOGICAL MEASURES

Several important analytic concepts assist the epidemiologist in describing the health problems of human groups. One of these concepts pertains to the definition of a *case*. A *case*, in epidemiological terms, refers to an instance of a disorder, illness, or injury involving a person. Another term is *risk*, defined simply as exposure to a health problem. Two other commonly employed concepts are those of *incidence* and *prevalence*. *Incidence* refers to the number of *new* cases of a specific health disorder occurring within a given population during a stated period of time. The incidence of German measles during a particular week would be the proportion of persons within a population who are reported as having developed the illness during the week in question. *Prevalence,* in contrast, would be the *total* number of cases of a health disorder that exist at any given time. Prevalence would include new cases as well as all previously existing cases. Prevalence rates are sometimes expressed as *point prevalence* (the number of cases at a certain point in time, usually a particular day or week), *period prevalence* (the total number of cases during a specified period of time, usually a month or year), or *lifetime prevalence* (the number of people who have had the health problem at least once during their lifetime). One way to distinguish between incidence and prevalence is to regard incidence as the rate at which cases appear, while prevalence is the rate at which all cases exist. To illustrate the difference between incidence and prevalence, consider that the incidence of influenza in a community might be low because no new cases had developed. Yet a measure of the disease's prevalence could be a larger figure because it would represent all persons who are currently sick from the illness.

Regardless of the size of the group under investigation, the epidemiologist is concerned with the computing of ratios. This is done to develop an accurate description of a particular health disorder in relation to a particular population. The epidemiologist accomplishes this task by collecting data from various sources such as face-to-face interviews or reports rendered by various health practitioners, institutions, and agencies. Once the relevant data are gathered, the epidemiologist computes a ratio which demonstrates the incidence and/or prevalence of the health problem. The ratio is always expressed as the total number of cases of a disease compared to the total number of people within a population:

$$\frac{\text{cases}}{\text{population}}$$

The simplest ratio computed by the epidemiologist is called the *crude rate,* which is the number of persons (cases) who have the characteristics being measured during a specific unit of time. Typical types of crude rates are birth rates and mortality rates. For example, the crude *mortality* (death) *rate* for a particular year is computed by using the number of deaths in that year as the numerator and the total number of residents in a specific population as the denominator. The results are then multiplied by either 1,000, 10,000, or 100,000 depending on whether the mortality rate being figured is for the number of deaths per 1,000, per 10,000, or per 100,000 people. The formula for computing the crude death rate in the United States for 1982 per 1,000 people would be as follows:

$$\frac{\text{Total deaths, all ages, 1982}}{\substack{\text{Estimated U.S. population} \\ \text{on June 30, 1982}}} \times 1,000 = 1982 \text{ death rate}$$

Crude death and birth rates, however, are usually too gross a measure to be meaningful for most sociological purposes. Sociologists are typically concerned with the effects of specific variables or social characteristics within a population such as age, sex, race, occupation, or any other measure of significant social differences. *Age-specific rates* are an example of rates used to show differences by age. Age-specific rates are computed in the same way as crude rates, except the numerator and the denominator are confined to a specific age group (a similar method can be used to determine sex-specific rates, race-specific rates, etc.). In order to calculate an age-specific rate, the procedure is to subdivide a population by age and then compare the number of cases in this subpopulation by the total number of persons within the subpopulation. If you wanted to compute the age-specific mortality rate for all infants for a particular year in the United States, for example, you would need to know how many infants there were in that year and the number of deaths that occurred in this age-specific group. The *infant mortality rate,* a measure of the deaths of all infants in a geographical area under the age of one year, is a very common age-specific rate in epidemiology. You would compute the 1982 U.S. infant mortality rate in the following manner:

$$\frac{\text{Total number of deaths in 1982 among persons aged less than one year}}{\text{Number of live births during 1982}} \times 1{,}000 = 1982 \text{ infant mortality rate}$$

The infant mortality rate has special significance for a society because it is traditionally used as an approximate measure of a society's sanitary and medical standards. For instance, the infant mortality rate in the United States in 1900 per 1,000 infants was 162.4; by 1940 this rate had been reduced to 47.0 as a result of improvement in health care, diet, and living conditions. After World War II further medical advances reduced infant mortality rates per 1,000 infants to 29.2 in 1950, 27.0 in 1960, 21.5 in 1969, 18.5 in 1972, and 14.1 in 1977. Infant mortality rates during the twentieth century have traditionally been lowest in technologically advanced societies such as Sweden, Japan, the Netherlands, Great Britain, the United States, Canada, and Australia. The highest rates have usually been in the underdeveloped countries of Asia, Africa, and South America.

Among the other major rates employed by social epidemiologists are *life expectancy rates,* the average number of years from birth to death that a person with particular social characteristics, e.g., according to age, sex, and race, can be expected to live. Life expectancy rates are expressed in two types of tables, the *generation* or *cohort life table* and the *current life table.* The *generation life table* presents life expectancy rates based upon the mortality experience of a particular cohort, such as all born in 1890, from moment of birth through consecutive ages in successive years. This table reflects the mortality experience of a cohort from birth until all members of the cohort have died.

The most frequently used life table is the *current life table,* which assumes that a hypothetical cohort is subject throughout its lifetime to the age-specific death rate prevailing for an actual population during a particular calendar year. Table 2–3 in this chapter is an example of a current life table reflecting the expectation of life statistics for males and females in the United States in 1977. Life tables are commonly used by insurance companies to determine premiums and other information regarding applicants for life insurance.

AGE, SEX, RACE, AND SOCIAL CLASS

The basic variables in social epidemiological research are age, sex, race, and social class or socioeconomic background. It has been found that each of these four variables represents differences among people that can be correlated with health and life expectancy.

Age

The most striking fact about age in the United States is the great increase in life expectancy. In 1900 the average number of years that an American could expect to live was 47.3; by 1977 this had increased to 73.2 years. The decline in mortality rates in this country has been influenced by two major factors: (1) the quantity and quality of available health services and (2) the rise in the American standard of living, which promoted significant improvements in living and work environments as well as in diet and recreational opportunities. The overall result has been that most Americans today die not from infectious diseases, but from biological decay and the effects of aging.

During the period between 1960 and 1977, the death rates have decreased for practically all age groups in the United States. Table 2–2 shows that the largest decreases have occurred for people eighty to eighty-four years of age and especially for those people over eighty-five. The slight (0.1) increase in death rates for fifteen- to twenty-four-year olds—who should be enjoying the most healthy period in their lives—is related to a rise in deaths from accidents, particularly automobile accidents. With the exception of accidents, most Americans appear to share a healthy childhood and young adulthood.

Also according to Table 2–2, the infant mortality rates for the years 1960 and 1977 show a decline which has been a consistent trend in the United States since 1900 when, as previously noted, the infant mortality rate

TABLE 2–2. Age Specific Mortality Rates per 1,000 Persons in the United States, 1960 and 1977

Ages	1960 Death Rate	1977 Death Rate	Change
Under 1 year	27.0	14.1	−12.9
1–4 years	1.1	0.7	−0.4
5–9 years	0.5	0.3	−0.2
10–14 years	0.4	0.3	−0.1
15–19 years	0.9	1.0	+0.1
20–24 years	1.2	1.3	+0.1
25–29 years	1.3	1.3	0.0
30–34 years	1.6	1.4	−0.2
35–39 years	2.3	1.9	−0.4
40–44 years	3.7	3.0	−0.7
45–49 years	5.9	4.8	−1.1
50–54 years	9.4	7.5	−1.9
55–59 years	13.8	11.3	−2.5
60–64 years	21.5	17.8	−3.7
65–69 years	31.4	24.8	−6.6
70–74 years	47.2	38.5	−8.7
75–79 years	72.0	60.7	−11.3
80–84 years	117.2	88.1	−29.1
85 years and over	198.6	147.2	−51.4

SOURCE: U.S. Department of Health, Education and Welfare, *Health United States, 1979* (Washington, D.C.: U.S. Government Printing Office, 1980).

was 162.4 deaths per 1,000 infants. These figures lend support to the assumption that if a person survives the first year of life in the United States, that person is likely to reach old age. From ages five to fifteen, the human body is at its highest stage of ability to resist disease and repair injury. The ability of the human body to maintain itself remains at a high level during the twenties, but then begins to decline slowly until the age of fifty when the aging process begins to accelerate.

As more and more Americans live to old age, aging has become a social problem in American society that manifests itself in the devalued social role of the aged, particularly with regard to older people's self-concept and feelings of uselessness and isolation. The stress of daily living, especially that associated with maintaining valued adult status, has a definite effect on the well-being of the elderly (Rosow, 1967, 1974). Studies of elderly subjects have demonstrated that the presence of an intimate and stable relationship with a close relative or friend is important in maintaining adjustment and psychological well-being (Lowenthal and Haven, 1968; Moriwaki, 1973). Yet this is a period of life when many people are alone.

Sociologists concerned with aging usually work in social gerontology, a subfield of gerontology that deals primarily with the nonphysical aspects of aging. These specialists study the ways in which the elderly adjust to their society and how society adapts to the elderly. As larger numbers of people live longer, new social and psychological questions relating to the aged must be answered. Chapter Eleven will consider the problems of aging in greater detail.

Sex

Sex differences in illness and death are highly significant in American society. The most striking generalization is that the life expectancy of the American female is much higher than that of the male. Male death rates exceed female death rates at all ages and for all causes except diabetes. The result is that, as of 1977, the average life expectancy in the United States of white females was 77.7 years compared to 70.0 years for white males. The same advantage also applies to the nonwhite female, who in 1977 had an average life expectancy of 73.1 years compared to 64.6 years for the nonwhite male.

While mortality rates for American females have not risen, the death rate for males, not counting military deaths in Vietnam, has increased since the 1960s. A rising mortality rate among young civilian males, for example, can be attributed to a greater proportion of violent deaths, again mostly from automobile accidents. In addition, for both white and nonwhite males, such health disorders as lung cancer, cirrhosis of the liver, and circulatory diseases caused death at progressively lower ages. The principal effect of rising male mortality rates in American society has been to increase the deficit in numbers of adult men. In 1910, because of increased immigration, there were approximately 106 men for every 100 women in the United States. By 1940, however, the ratio was even with about 100 men for every 100 women. From 1968 until the present, there have been about 95 men for

TABLE 2–3. Percent of Males and Females Surviving from Birth in the United
States, 1977

Percent Surviving from Birth	White Males	White Females	Non-White Males	Non-White Females
To age 1	98.6	98.9	97.6	98.0
To age 20	97.2	98.2	96.0	97.1
To age 65	70.7	83.8	55.8	72.7

SOURCE: U.S. National Center for Health Statistics, *Vital Statistics of the United States, 1977,*
Vol. II, Sec. 5, Life Tables (Washington, D.C.: U.S. Department of Health, Education and Welfare, 1980).

every 100 women, a ratio that represents the lowest point in a steady decline
since 1910.

Table 2–3 also demonstrates female superiority in life expectancy. In
1977, the U.S. National Center for Health Statistics projected that 98.9
percent of all females and 98.6 percent of all white males would survive to
age one from birth; by age sixty-five, however, only 70.7 percent of the white
males would be alive compared to 83.8 percent of the white females. The
lowest level of life expectancy belongs to the nonwhite male. Table 2–3
shows that 97.6 percent of the nonwhite males will survive from birth to age
one compared to 98.0 percent of the nonwhite females; by age sixty-five the
percent of surviving nonwhite males is 55.8 and the percent of surviving
nonwhite females is 72.7. Although the nonwhite female has a definite
advantage in longevity over the nonwhite male, her life expectancy is not
significantly higher than that of the white male. Thus despite the female
advantage, life expectancy in the United States is strongly affected by racial
background. For a long life in the United States it is best to be female and to
be white.

Men have a substantial health inferiority in terms of life expectancy
because of the combined result of two major effects: (1) biological and (2)
social-psychological. The male of the human species is at a biological disadvantage to the female. The fact that the male is weaker physiologically than
the female is demonstrated by higher mortality rates from the prenatal and
neonatal stages of life onward. Although the percentages may vary somewhat from year to year, the chances of dying during the prenatal stage are
approximately 12 percent greater among males than females and 130 percent greater during the neonatal (newborn) stage. Examples of neonatal
disorders common to male rather than female babies are such afflictions as
hyaline membrane disease (a respiratory disease) and pyloric stenosis (a
disorder of the pyloric muscle affecting the emptying of the stomach).
Neonatal males are also more prone to certain circulatory disorders of the
aorta and pulmonary artery and are subject to more severe bacterial infections. Females are less likely to get childhood leukemia and have a better
chance for survival when they do. As an organism, the male appears to be
more vulnerable than the female, even before being exposed to the differential social roles and stress situations of later life.

While the evidence is not conclusive, social and psychological influences are nonetheless presumed to play an important part in the determination of life expectancy. Accidents, for example, are a major cause of deaths among males of certain age groups but not among females, which strongly suggests a difference in sex roles. Men in general are expected to be more aggressive than women in both work and play. High accident rates among males may be attributed to the male's increased exposure to dangerous activities, especially those arising from high-risk occupations. The most dangerous job in the United States (according to the Metropolitan Life Insurance Company) is sponge diving, followed by (in order) motorcycle racing, trapeze and high-wire artists, structural steel workers, lumbermen, bank guards, munitions and explosive workers, anthracite coal miners, and state policemen. Being President of the United States is also hazardous. About one out of three U.S. Presidents has lived to enjoy his normal life expectancy.

Another factor contributing to excess male mortality rates may be occupational competition and the pressure associated with a job. The life style of the business executive or professional with his orientation toward "career" and his drive toward "success," marks of the upwardly mobile middle-class male in American society, is thought to contribute strongly to the development of stress among such men. Middle-aged professional males in the United States today are noted by life insurance companies as a high-risk group, particularly if they smoke, are overweight, and tend to overwork. It would thus seem that both the male sex role and the psychodynamics of male competitiveness are significancant factors affecting male longevity. Finally, it should be noted that cigarette smoking and alcohol abuse, behaviors associated with several potentially fatal diseases, remain more common among men than women. For example, the American Cancer Society reported in 1979 that smoking was responsible for 83% of the existing cases of lung cancer among men and about 43% of cases among women. Yet lung cancer among women was observed to be increasing. This trend was attributed to women smokers becoming older and their lungs beginning to reflect the damage. American women did not begin smoking in earnest until after World War II and their rates of lung cancer are now matching the earlier rise among males. Lung cancer ranked 8th among cancer deaths for women in 1961, but moved up to 2nd by 1979. Consequently, mortality rates for American women may change in the future as some women adopt behavior, namely smoking and drinking, that in the past was more characteristic of men.

While men have a higher rate of mortality, women appear to have a higher morbidity. That is, the female is sick more often; or at least the act of defining one's self as ill is more common among women. Data from the National Health Survey for 1957 through 1972 show that females report higher rates of acute illnesses, chronic illnesses, and disability due to acute illnesses than males of the same age (Verbrugge, 1976; Andersen and Anderson, 1979). These data indicated that males had higher rates of disability for chronic illnesses, but the excess rates were mostly for men working in physically demanding jobs where the risk of injury, impairment, and physical strain are greater than those routinely faced by women. More recent data from the 1977 National Ambulatory Survey showed that sixty percent of all visits to physicians' offices during that year were made by women and that women had significantly higher rates of surgery (120.2 operations per 1,000 women hospital patients versus 77.8 per 1,000 men hospital patients). In sum, women not only report more illness than men, they also exhibit greater use of health services. This pattern is consistent even when rates of utilization of maternity services are excluded from analysis.

Robert Wilson (1970) believes that there may be an inverse relationship between mortality and morbidity when sex differences are considered. Women may be sick more often, but live longer. Men may be sick less often, but die sooner. However, it is not actually known if females are ill more often than their male counterparts, even though the evidence points in this direction. Women may just be more sensitive to their bodily discomforts and more willing to report their symptoms to others. Nevertheless, as Lois Verbrugge (1976:401) explains, "whether the reasons for greater morbidity are mostly social and psychological, or mostly physical, the immediate social outcomes are the same." The outcome is that females report more illness and disability and, consequently, show a greater loss of productivity—whether their work is in the home or outside it. Employers cannot rely on females as readily as they can males to be at work or to feel like working while they are there. Females also spend more days at home in a sick role and thus tend to disrupt more family activities. And, since good health is generally considered to be a highly significant aspect of a good life, females are at a disadvantage compared to males. "Higher female morbidity, compared to males," states Verbrugge (1976:401), "means that females experience a less comfortable and satisfying life with regard to a cherished attribute. They simply do not feel as well as often as males."

While females are more fit biologically at birth, less often exposed to danger and highly stressful occupations, are more sensitive to their bodily states, and possibly enhance their life expectancy through increased use of medical services, the female advantage in longevity may be a mixed blessing. Women not only appear to feel physically ill more often than men, but many studies confirm that depression, manic-depressive psychoses, and anxiety are more prevalent among women (Cockerham, 1981). Female longevity has also resulted in a growing social problem, an increasing number of widows who are faced with important decisions about remarriage, employment, family life, and loneliness.

Race

One reflection of social inequality in the United States is the differences among the health profiles of racial groups. Nonwhite infants have traditionally had almost twice as high an infant mortality rate as white infants in American society. In 1960, for example, there were 43.2 infant deaths per 1,000 nonwhite infants compared to an infant mortality rate of 22.9 among whites. Although the spread in infant mortality rates has declined to a 7 percent margin as of 1977 (21.0 for nonwhites versus 14.0 for whites), the difference is still significant. The effect of social inequality upon infant mortality is most apparent when it is realized that racial differences in infant mortality rates are greatest during the postnatal period, when adverse environmental conditions have their greatest effect. Nonwhite infant mortality rates, on a par with those for white infants at birth, increase threefold during the first three to eight months of life. The association between *race and poverty* and between *poverty and high infant mortality* rates seems clearly established (Gortmaker, 1979; Brooks, 1980).

As previously indicated in our discussion of sex differences, the nonwhite male has the lowest life expectancy of any racial sex category. Table 2–4 shows that in 1977 the nonwhite male in the United States with a life expectancy of 64.6 years will generally live five and one-half years less than the white male (70.0 years) and approximately thirteen years less than the white female (77.7 years). The white female has a life expectancy 4.6 years greater than the nonwhite female.

The majority of people represented by health data on nonwhite Americans are black. The improvement in the social status of the black American has been related to a significant improvement in health status. However, as is evident from Table 2–4, advances in life expectancy have not been uniform for all segments of the U.S. population. A particular health problem for black Americans has been that of hypertension, or high blood pressure. While twenty-two million Americans suffer from hypertension, some five to six million of these are black. Thus, although blacks constitute approximately 10 percent of the American population, they have over 20 percent of the diagnosed hypertension. Between the ages of twenty-five and forty-four years, hypertension kills back males 15.5 times more frequently than it does white males. The ratio of black to white females dying from hypertension in the same age category is seventeen to one. Nearly 26 percent of all black females age seventeen and older have hypertension (National Center for Health Statistics, 1976b). The lowest proportion of the population with hypertension is white males (12.0 percent), while white females and

TABLE 2–4. Average Number of Years of Life Expectancy in the United States by Race and Sex, Since 1900

Life Expectancy at Birth by Year	White Males	White Females	Non-White Males	Non-White Females
1900	46.6	48.7	32.5	33.5
1950	66.5	72.2	59.1	62.9
1960	67.4	74.1	61.1	66.3
1970	68.0	75.6	61.3	69.4
1974	68.9	76.6	62.9	71.2
1977	70.0	77.7	64.6	73.1

SOURCE: U.S. National Center for Health Statistics, *Monthly Vital Statistics Report, Advance Report—Final Mortality Statistics, 1974*, Vol. 24, No. 11 (Washington, D.C.: U.S. Department of Health, Education and Welfare, February 3, 1976a) and *Vital Statistics of the United States, 1977*, Vol. II, Sec. 5, Life Tables (Washington, D.C.: U.S. Department of Health, Education, and Welfare, 1980).

and black males have about equal proportions (17.7 and 17.4 percent, respectively). The end result is that proportionately more black people (22.2 percent) than white (15.0 percent) are believed to have hypertension.

Various hypotheses have been suggested to explain racial differences in the incidence of hypertension:

1. The genetic hypothesis argues that blacks are genetically different from whites in ways that predispose them to hypertension.
2. The physical exertion hypothesis postulates that blacks are more likely than whites to be engaged in manual labor, and that greater physical exertion leads to higher mortality from hypertension.
3. The associated disorder hypothesis asserts that blacks are more prone to diseases such as pyelonephritis and syphilis that may result in secondary hypertension.
4. The psychological stress hypothesis theorizes that blacks are severely frustrated by racial discrimination and that this stress and the repressed aggression associated with it lead to a higher prevalence of hypertension.
5. The diet hypothesis emphasizes that blacks may have dietary patterns that increase their susceptibility to hypertension.
6. The medical care hypothesis argues that blacks receive poorer medical care than whites and that this results in greater morbidity and mortality from hypertensive disease, and perhaps a higher prevalence of secondary hypertension.

At the present time the exact causes of the higher rates of hypertension among blacks are not known. A 1970 analysis by Jan Howard and Barbara Holman of U.S. Public Health data strongly suggests that the disparity between blacks and whites cannot be explained solely on the basis of socio-economic factors. Instead they indicate that the genetic hypothesis and the psychological stress hypothesis seem to contribute most to an understanding of the phenomenon. They base their findings on the observation that even the highest status blacks have substantially higher mortality rates from hypertension than do lower status whites. However, the Howard and Holman study is not conclusive and it would be premature to favor either the genetic or the discrimination hypothesis at this time. The importance of their study is the relevance of an approach based on genetics or racial discrimination for future research.

Blacks and whites also differ in relation to health problems other than hypertension. Table 2–5 depicts some of these differences for the years between 1950 and 1977. Table 2–5 shows that the *age-adjusted* mortality rate for blacks was 1.39 times that of whites for deaths from the major cardiovascular diseases in 1950.[2] By 1977, the ratio had been reduced to 1.33. The same trend is evident for the two major components of the major cardiovascular diseases—diseases of the heart and cerebrovascular diseases. The

[2] Age-adjusted rates include a correction for differences in age distribution between the races which would otherwise possibly distort comparisons of overall mortality. In 1976–1977, approximately 35 percent of the black population was under seventeen years of age compared to 27 percent of the white population. About 41 percent of blacks were in the 17–44 age group compared to 40 percent of all whites, 17 percent of the blacks as opposed to 22 percent of the whites were 45–64 years of age, and 8 percent of the blacks and 11 percent of the whites were sixty-five years and over. The age-adjusted rates are what mortality levels would be if age distributions were identical for each racial group and provides a more accurate measure of

TABLE 2–5.   Black/White Mortality Ratios for Selected Causes of Death: United States, Selected Years 1950–1977

Cause of death	Year				
	1950	1960	1965	1970	1977
Major cardiovascular diseases	1.39	1.35	1.35	1.36	1.33
Diseases of the heart	1.27	1.19	1.20	1.23	1.24
Cerebrovascular diseases	1.81	1.89	1.96	1.85	1.75
Malignant neoplasms	1.04	1.15	1.17	1.23	1.31
Digestive organs and peritoneum	1.05	1.20	1.28	1.32	1.44
Respiratory system	0.80	1.06	1.07	1.20	1.32
Diabetes mellitus	1.24	1.72	1.86	2.05	2.21
Accidents	1.28	1.39	1.37	1.46	1.27
Suicide	0.36	0.42	0.47	0.49	0.54
Homicide	11.73	10.15	10.03	9.81	6.58

SOURCE: U.S. Department of Health, Education and Welfare, *Health United States, 1979* (Washington, D.C.: U.S. Government Printing Office, 1980).

ratio of the age-adjusted mortality rates for the black population in comparison to the corresponding white population declined between 1950 and 1977 from 1.27 to 1.24 for diseases of the heart and from 1.81 to 1.75 for cerebrovascular diseases. The persistently higher mortality rates for blacks for the major cardiovascular diseases are most likely related to the greater prevalence of hypertension among the black population. As for malignant neoplasms (cancer), Table 2–5 shows that the age-adjusted death rate for all cancers rose more rapidly for blacks than for whites between 1950 and 1977. The rate of increase was from 1.04 in 1950 to 1.31 in 1977. With an overall increase, it is not surprising that cancer of the digestive organs and the respiratory system also increased. The rise in mortality rates for blacks in cancer of the respiratory system from 0.80 in 1950 to 1.32 in 1977 is particularly striking. Differences in smoking patterns (while there is little difference between females, the proportion of black males who smoke is greater than white males) and increased exposure to carcinogenic hazards of urban-industrial living as a result of migration from rural areas may be the reason for this increase (HEW,1980).

Among the other selected causes of mortality shown in Table 2–5, diabetes has increased among blacks. In 1950, 1.24 times more blacks than whites died from diabetes compared to 2.21 times more blacks in 1977. This rise in mortality rates for diabetes for blacks in relation to whites, however, is somewhat inflated by a general decline for whites for deaths from the disease. The high point for mortality from diabetes for blacks was 2.25 in 1973 and the drop to 2.21 by 1977 may indicate that a decline for blacks is now occurring. The mortality rates for blacks for accidents rose to 1.46 times that of whites in 1970, but declined to 1.27 by 1977. The black rate for

---

racial differences by correcting for age differences. Age adjustment is computed by multiplying the specific rate for each age group in the total population. The rate is obtained by dividing the cumulative figures computed by the total population.

suicide has generally been significantly lower than that for whites, yet has risen from 0.36 in 1950 to 0.54 in 1977. Mortality rates for homicide show a marked decrease from 11.73 times that of whites in 1950 to 6.58 in 1977. What is indicated by mortality rates for the selected causes of death shown in Table 2–5 is that, with the exception of suicide, blacks remain at a significant disadvantage in comparison to whites. This disadvantage exists despite the overall increase in life expectancy for the black population in the United States.

Adverse differences in levels of a positive health profile are not limited to blacks, but also include Hispanic Americans and American Indians. Health data on Hispanic Americans are difficult to obtain because, until 1976, federal, state, and local agencies generally included Hispanic Americans with Anglos in the white category. The few existing studies on the health of Hispanic Americans suggest, however, that they have a higher infant mortality rate, a shorter life expectancy, and higher mortality rates from influenza, pneumonia, and tuberculosis than Anglo-Americans (Moustafa and Weiss, 1968). It should also be noted that Hispanic Americans appear to have lower mortality rates than Anglos from heart disease and cancer.

Joan Moore (1970) suggests that the high prevalence of tuberculosis and pneumonia and the relative absence of deaths from heart disease and cancer among Americans of Mexican descent are consequences of poverty. Heart disease and cancer usually strike the more affluent upper classes, while both tuberculosis and pneumonia are typical diseases of the poor segments of American society.

The same pattern is repeated for the American Indian as exists for the other U.S. minorities. In fact, American Indians may have the poorest health of all Americans, even though significant improvement in the overall level of health for American Indians was made during the 1970s. Indians have very high mortality rates for diabetes and tuberculosis. The incidence of tuberculosis among Indians is six times greater than that within the population as a whole. Indians also suffer more dysentery, strep throat, venereal disease, and hepatitis than other Americans. Other significant health problems of American Indians are alcoholism, dietary deficiency, cirrhosis of the liver, and gastrointestinal bleeding. In addition, chronic otitis media, a severe ear ailment that arises when simple ear infections are not treated, occurs among 10 percent of all Indian children.

Although the infant mortality rate for American Indians and native Alaskans declined dramatically from 82.1 per 1,000 live births in 1950 to 15.6 in 1977, this rate is still higher than that of whites. Death rates for Indians of all age groups for all causes are still higher than the death rates for other Americans. The leading cause of death for Indians in 1976 was accidents—139.6 deaths per 100,000 to 46.8 for the general population (HEW, 1979). This death rate is almost three times that of the rest of the country. Over 50 percent of all accidental deaths were from automobile accidents, especially for persons fifteen to thirty-four years of age. Indians do show low mortality rates for heart disease and cancer; as previously noted these health problems are generally related to high socioeconomic status.

They are also associated with old age and proportionately fewer Indians reach the higher age groups where these diseases are prevalent.

Two health problems commonly linked with American Indians are drinking and suicide. Although drinking appears to be a recognized evil in Indian communities (Dozier, 1966), it has generally remained the dominant mode of social activity for males (Waddell, 1973). A study of a tri-ethnic community in Colorado (Jessor et al., 1968) found that, in comparison to Anglos and Mexican-Americans, Indians not only drank more frequently and became drunk more often, but they also had more drinking-related problems. Indians were also more apt to drink to solve personal problems. Although not all studies agree that Indian drinking involves a high level of alcoholism, there is a consensus that Indians drink a lot and that they frequently get into trouble as a result (Levy and Kunitz, 1973; Cockerham, 1975). The overwhelming majority of crimes committed by Indians in the Southwest United States are committed under the influence of alcohol, and the proportion of Indians arrested for alcohol-related crimes in comparison to other ethnic groups is the highest in the nation (Stewart, 1964; FBI, 1979). Alcohol abuse undoubtedly contributes to the high rate of automobile and other accidents among Indians as well.

A strong case can not only be made for excessive drinking among American Indians as a group; existing data on suicide likewise support its general prevalence among Indians. For 1975, U.S. Public Health figures show that 26.0 Indians per 100,000 committed suicide compared to a rate of 12.6 suicides per 100,000 for all Americans. There are significant differences in Indian suicide by sex and age. Indian females in general and both Indian males and females over the age of forty-five show low rates of suicide. Yet Indian males between the ages of fifteen and forty-five show a suicide rate four times that of non-Indians. The problem of Indian suicides is, therefore, largely concentrated among young Indian males. The relatively high suicide rate of young Indian men is an indication of a very serious problem about the quality of life available to them.

Another possible threat to the health of the American Indian, one that has yet to be adequately researched, is drug abuse. Within some Indian tribal cultures there has existed a traditional use of drugs such as peyote and mescaline in religious rituals and folk medicine, but the general extent of Indian drug use remains relatively unknown at present. What little research does exist shows that, in comparison to all other ethnic groups, American Indian college students report a higher level of contact with drugs (Strimbu et al., 1973). This same pattern has also been found in a comparison of Indian and white high school students (Cockerham et al., 1976; Cockerham, 1977).

Indian health problems are further complicated by poor communication between Indians and white health professionals and by Indian mistrust of the white medical bureaucracy. A report on urban Indians living in a northern Arizona bordertown (Allen and Tollivier, 1974) discloses that Indians had difficulty in understanding white financial procedures and resented white attitudes of superiority. This latter complaint usually resulted from professionals' admonishing them about personal hygiene, quality of child care, and delay in seeking health care until an illness reached an emergency state. When Indians showed an inability to pay for services, they were often referred to reservation medical facilities, several miles away, that provided free services for Indians. Reservation authorities, on the other hand, were sometimes reluctant to provide health care to urban Indians who were not viewed as being their responsibility. As a result, urban Indians were left either seeking health services on the reservation or choosing to use only emergency care and free health clinics in town.

Besides the problems faced by urban Indians, reservation Indians are often subject to health care inferior to that of whites because of understaffing, underfunding, and poor facilities. A 1974 U.S. Senate study disclosed that only half of the fifty-one Indian Health Service Hospitals have been accredited as meeting minimum national standards by the Joint Commission on the Accreditation of Hospitals, and a mere sixteen were able to meet national fire and safety codes.

Therefore, despite the increase in life expectancy among American Indians, their overall health profile is far worse than that of whites or of the other U.S. minority groups, including blacks living in urban slums and Hispanic Americans in the Southwest.

Although some afflictions, such as hypertension and sickle cell anemia, appear to have a genetic basis, the great majority of health disorders among minority groups in American society are the result of environmental factors related to poverty. Alcoholism, drug addiction, suicide, lead poisoning, rat-bite fever, influenza, pneumonia, and tuberculosis are health disorders more common to the poor. Race becomes a significant health variable in the United States primarily *because* racial minorities typically occupy disadvantaged socioeconomic positions. A study by George Warheit et al. (1973) discloses, for example, that blacks, females, the aged, the poor, and those with the least formal education have the highest rates of symptoms of depression. However, when race, sex, age, and socioeconomic status were correlated, only sex and socioeconomic status were statistically significant. The major difference in depression scores between whites and blacks was accounted for by the socioeconomic variable, with most blacks occupying the lowest socioeconomic level.

Another example of the significant relationship between socioeconomic status and the quality of health of a racial minority group can be found by examining data that include Asian Americans. Asian Americans have the highest levels of income, education, and employment of any racial/ethnic minority group in the United States, often exceeding levels achieved by the white population (HEW, 1980). Consequently, it is not surprising that the lowest age-adjusted mortality rates in the United States are those of Japanese-Americans, with 3.3 deaths per 1,000 resident population in 1970.[3] Chinese-Americans had the next lowest rates with 4.9 deaths per 1,000. The highest age-adjusted mortality rates were those of blacks (10.4) and American Indians (8.2). Whites occupied an intermediate position with 6.8 deaths per 1,000. More recent data for 1977 pertaining to infant mortality rates again

[3]Separate mortality data for Hispanics are not available for 1970.

show Japanese- and Chinese-Americans with the lowest rates. According to Table 2–6, infant mortality in the United States has drastically declined since 1950. The most striking decline, as previously noted, has been that of American Indians from 82.1 deaths per 1,000 live births in 1950 to 15.6 in 1977. The decline for Japanese- and Chinese-Americans has been almost as great in terms of relative proportion, but these rates were much smaller to begin with and therefore not as dramatic. In 1977, Table 2–6 shows that blacks had the highest infant mortality rates (23.6 per 1,000), followed by American Indians (15.6), whites (12.3), Japanese-Americans (6.6), and Chinese-Americans (5.9).

Besides the low infant mortality rates of Japanese- and Chinese-Americans, with Chinese-Americans having the lowest rates of all, Table 2–6 also indicates some other patterns of interest. In 1950, American Indians had the highest infant mortality rates—almost twice as high as that of blacks. By 1977, Indian infant mortality rates had dropped so sharply that they were lower than the rates for blacks and only slightly more than the rates for whites. While infant mortality rates for blacks had declined by nearly one-half (43.9 versus 23.6) between 1950 and 1977, the black rate was nearly 100 percent higher than that of whites (23.6 versus 12.3) in 1977. Hence, the gap between black and white infant mortality rates actually increased from 1950 to 1977 even though the rates for both races declined significantly (in 1950, the black-white gap was 43.9 versus 26.8—a difference of 64 percent).

Although infant mortality rates are only one indicator of health in a society, they are nevertheless an important measure of the quality of life available to a people. Such rates, along with the other data discussed in this section, point toward the fact that, with the exception of Asian Americans, racial/ethnic minority groups in the United States have a lower life expectancy and poorer level of health than the white population. However, poor health for nonwhites in general may largely be accounted for by their being lower class rather than nonwhite.

TABLE 2–6.   Infant Mortality Rates by Race, United States, Selected Years, 1950–1977

| Mortality Rate and Year | Race | | | | |
	Black	American Indian	Chinese-American	Japanese-American	White
Infant mortality rate[1]	Number of deaths per 1,000 live births				
1950	43.9	82.1	19.3	19.1	26.8
1960	44.3	49.3	14.7	15.3	22.9
1970[2]	32.6	22.0	8.4	10.6	17.8
1977[2]	23.6	15.6	5.9	6.6	12.3

[1] Infant mortality rate is the number of deaths for infants under one year of age per live births.
[2] Excludes deaths of nonresidents of the United States.
SOURCE: U.S. Department of Health, Education and Welfare, *Health United States, 1979* (Washington, D.C.: U.S. Government Printing Office, 1980).

Social Class

The uneven distribution of health among racial groups in American society repeats itself when the distribution of health among socioeconomic groups or social classes is considered. On nearly every measure, membership in lower social classes carries health penalties similar to those of nonwhites. To be poor is by definition to have less of the things (including health care) produced by society.

Before the 1930s, the medically indigent patient was dependent largely on the charity of medical institutions and private physicians. Many times this charity was erratic. In addition, many of the urban clinics providing treatment for the poor were established and maintained as teaching facilities for medical and nursing students. Hence, treatment was sometimes oriented more toward educational needs than toward patient needs. Since the 1930s, however, there has been a considerable increase in the number and types of facilities as well as an improvement in the quality of medical care available to the poor, yet many problems remain.

A long-standing impediment to the sound application and control of medical care for the poor has been inadequate coordination and unnecessary duplication of many services. Anselm Strauss (1970) points out that medical systems in the United States have not met the needs of the poor because they have never been designed to do so. The manner in which the poor live and perceive their social environment has not been considered in the organization and norms of American medical care. Strauss believes that the parochial nature of modern medical organizations is at fault because the poor lack experience in organizational life and middle-class norms. For example, Strauss discusses the breakdown in communication between middle-class health professionals and the poor by noting that many health professionals assume that the poor (like themselves) have regular meals, lead regular lives, try to support families, keep healthy, and plan for the future. To prescribe the same type of treatment for all diseases for all people does not take into account the fact that people live their lives differently. Strauss (1970:16) illustrates this point by asking, "What does 'take with each meal' mean to a family that eats irregularly, seldom together, and usually less than three times a day?"

A review of relevant research discloses that a number of studies substantiate the relationship between poverty and lack of access to *quality* medical care in the United States (see Elam, 1969; Kosa et al., 1969; Hurley, 1971; Mechanic, 1972; Dutton, 1978; Gortmaker, 1979). Despite evidence of more frequent visits to physicians made possible by greater health insurance coverage through Medicaid and Medicare, lower-class people are still treated within the framework of welfare medicine and still live on a day-to-day basis within the environment of poverty. It appears also that professional health practitioners are likely to "prefer" upper-class patients or at least to provide more personalized care for the upper-class sick (Miller, 1973). Strauss (1970:11–12) summarizes the position of the poor in American medicine by stating, "The poor definitely get second-rate medical care. This is self-evident to anyone who has worked either with them or in public medical facilities."

An interesting study by Aaron Antonovsky (1972) on life expectancy and social class further reinforces the importance of the socioeconomic differential by suggesting that, on every measure, social class position influences one's opportunity for longevity. Antonovsky conducted a statistical investigation of approximately thirty studies of mortality rates in the United States and Europe. Other than rates for coronary heart disease, which is prevalent among achieving and affluent males, Antonovsky found that the upper socioeconomic classes were favored in all dimensions of life expectancy.[4] "The inescapable conclusion," stated Antonovsky (1972:28),"is that class influences one's chances of staying alive." The only major contradiction found by Antonovsky involved a Dutch study (DeWolff and Meerdink, 1954); however, the population in this study demonstrated few social class differences and, as a whole, had one of the lowest death rates ever recorded. This research by the Dutch scientists suggests the important hypothesis that as differences between social classes decline, overall mortality rates of a population may similarly decline.

Since many health disorders appear related to poverty, it is a logical assumption that if poverty were not a factor retarding the availability of quality medical care, the incidence and prevalence of illness in the lower social classes would be reduced. Following World War II, socialized medicine was introduced in Great Britain to provide the lower classes with the same medical care available to the upper classes. It should be noted, however, that poverty and social class differences remained—only health care was supposedly equalized. Results have shown that the equalization of health care alone has not reduced the disparity in health between social classes. Mortality rates remained higher for the lower classes. According to Marvin Susser and William Watson (1971), Britain's experiment failed to reduce health disparities precisely because living conditions and life style could not be equalized; the physical environment of poverty and poor nutrition continued to adversely affect lower-class health.

As has already been indicated, types of health disorders seem to vary by social class. Heart disease is more prevalent among the upper classes and tuberculosis and influenza frequent the lower classes. There is also evidence that, in the case of cancer, location of the disease in the body may have a social class relationship. Saxon Graham (1972), for instance, reports on several studies that suggest lower-class females are more likely than upper-class females to develop cancer of the cervix because of an earlier and higher frequency of sexual intercourse and multiple pregnancies. In turn, breast cancer has been found to be more prevalent among upper-class women who have nursed fewer children than their lower-class counterparts.

The most important relationship, however, between social class and health is not how social class influences the location of cancer in the body. Rather, it is the manner in which social class impacts upon the opportunities

---

[4]Fuchs (1974) reminds us of an opposite conclusion. He says that high income can harm health as well if it is reflected in a rich diet, heavy smoking, lack of exercise, automobile accidents, and other expressions of "high" living. All things considered, however, the greatest disadvantage in life expectancy for most people seems to be low income when considered in terms that are strictly socioeconomic.

a person has for a generally healthy life. Crowded living conditions, poor diet, inferior housing, low levels of income and education, and enhanced exposure to violence, alcoholism and problem drinking, and drug abuse—all combine to decrease the life chances of the poor.

SUMMARY

This chapter has been concerned with social epidemiology and the basic sociological variables of age, sex, race, and social class as indicators of health differences. The social epidemiologist is like a detective, investigating the scene of a crime in which the criminal is a disease or some other form of health menace. The epidemiologist is primarily concerned not with individuals, but with the health profiles of social aggregates or large populations of people. Important tools of the epidemiologist are the ratios used to compute descriptions of mortality, incidence, and prevalence. These rates can be either crude rates or standardized rates reflecting age-specific data, sex-specific data, and so on.

The section on age disclosed that as more and more persons live to older ages in American society, some very serious problems emerge concerning the social role of the elderly. As for sex differences, in general females have a very definite advantage over males with regard to life expectancy. This advantage involves both biological and social-psychological factors. White Americans also have a definite advantage in health over nonwhite Americans. Other than race, however, the most significant socioeconomic variable affecting nonwhites is that they are likely to be poor, and poverty, as far as medical care is concerned, may be equated with second-rate treatment. Socialized medicine in Great Britain failed to reduce health differentials between the social classes because social class differences themselves were not reduced. Thus, the environment of poverty continued to influence a higher prevalence of disease among the British lower classes.

chapter 3

THE INTERACTION OF MIND, BODY, AND SOCIETY

Social influences upon the onset and the subsequent course of a particular disease are not limited to such variables as age, sex, race, social class, and the conditions of poverty as they relate to life style, habits, and customs. It is also important to recognize that interaction between the human mind and body represents a critical factor in regard to health. Although the evidence is not conclusive, a considerable amount of literature in both medicine and the social sciences maintains that psychological responses to social events can cause stress (see, for example, Levine and Scotch, 1970; McGrath, 1970; Moss, 1973; House, 1974). Accordingly, stress can be defined as an emotional-psychophysiological state of an organism that occurs in a situational context, involving stimuli which serve as cues to elicit fear or anxiety responses (Janis, 1958).

Usually stress is thought to occur when individuals are faced with a situation where their usual modes of behavior are not adequate and the consequences of not adapting to the situation are perceived as serious (McGrath, 1970). In general, it appears that there are four possible types of reactions to stress: (1) the normal, where anxiety is followed by an effective defensive reaction; (2) the neurotic, where anxiety is so great that the defense is rendered ineffective; (3) the psychotic, where anxiety is misperceived or possibly ignored; and (4) the pyschophysiological, where defense fails and anxiety results in changes in body tissues (Kaplan, 1975). The majority of the studies on stress indicate that most, if not all, stress is socially induced as a result of interaction between people (Moss, 1973). A review of selected sociological theories developed by Emile Durkheim, Charles Cooley, William I. Thomas, and Erving Goffman will serve to demonstrate how social processes, from the standpoint of both the wider society and the individual, can produce social conditions considered stressful by the individuals involved.

Durkheim: Functionalism

Emile Durkheim (1858–1917), who formulated the functionalist approach in sociology, was primarily interested in the characteristics of groups and social structures. He was most concerned with those social processes and constraints that integrate individuals into the larger social community. He believed that when a society was strongly integrated, it held individuals firmly under its control (Durkheim, 1950, 1956). Individuals were integrated into a society as a result of their acceptance of community values reinforced through social interaction with others believing in this same value system. Especially important were participation in events celebrating a society's traditions and also involvement in work activities.

As members of society, individuals were constrained in their behavior by laws and customs. These constraints were "social facts," which Durkheim (1950:13) defined as "every way of acting, fixed or not, capable of exercising on the individual an external constraint." Robert Nisbet (1966) has suggested that the import of Durkheim's analysis is to give society an existence outside of and above the individual. Social control is, therefore, real and external to the individual.

Among Durkheim's works, the most pertinent to an understanding of the social determinants of stress is his 1897 study, *Suicide* (1951). In explaining the differential rates of suicide among various religious and occupational groupings, Durkheim suggested that suicide was not entirely a matter of free choice by individuals. He believed that suicide was a social fact explainable in terms of social causes. Durkheim distinguished between three major types of suicide, each dependent upon the relationship of the individual to society. These three types were (1) egoistic suicide, in which people become detached from society and, suddenly on their own, are overwhelmed by the resulting stress; (2) anomic suicide, in which people suffer a sudden dislocation of normative systems where their norms and values are no longer relevant, so that controls of society no longer restrain them from taking their lives; and (3) altruistic suicide, in which people feel themselves so strongly integrated into a demanding society that their only escape seems to be suicide.

Durkheim's typology of suicide suggests how a society might induce enough stress among people to cause them to take their lives. Egoistic suicide is a result of stress brought about by the separation of a strongly integrated individual from his or her group. Durkheim uses the example of the military officer who is suddenly retired and left without the group ties which typically regulated his behavior. Egoistic suicide is based upon the overstimulation of a person's intelligence by the realization that he or she has been deprived of collective activity and meaning. Anomic suicide is characterized by an overstimulation of emotion and a corresponding freedom from society's restraints. It is a result of sudden change that includes the breakdown of values and norms by which a person has lived his or her life. Sudden wealth or sudden poverty, for example, could disrupt the usual normative patterns and induce a state of anomie or normlessness. In this situation a chronic lack of regulation results in a state of restlessness, unbounded ambition, or perhaps crisis, in which norms no longer bind him or her to society.

Whereas egoistic and anomic forms of suicide are both due to "society's insufficient presence in individuals" (Durkheim, 1951:256), altruistic suicide represents the strong presence of a social system encouraging suicide among certain groups. Suicide in the altruistic form could be characterized as the avoidance of stress by people who prefer to conform to a society's normative system rather than risk the stress of opposing it. Examples of altruistic suicide are the practice of hara-kiri in Japan, where certain social failures on the part of an individual are expected to be properly redressed by his or her suicide, or the traditional Hindu custom of the widow's committing ritual suicide at her husband's funeral.

Although altruistic suicide is relatively rare in Western society, stories commonly appear in daily newspapers of people killing themselves for reasons that could be considered egoistic or anomic. Yet the significance of Durkheim's orientation toward social processes for the understanding of the stress phenomenon extends well beyond the issue of suicide, since this is only one of many possible ways a person might find to cope with social and psychological problems. What is particularly insightful is Durkheim's notion of the capability of the larger society to create stressful situations where people are forced to respond to conditions not of their own choosing.

For example, in a 1976 Federal Government report, M. Harvey Brenner linked increased incidence of heart disease, stroke, kidney failure, mental illness, and even infant mortality to rising unemployment. Brenner's thesis is that there are few areas of our lives not intimately affected by the state of the economy. He argues that economic recession increases the amount of stress on an individual by comparing economic cycles with health statistics for approximately seventy years prior to the publication of his work. Brenner found that heart attacks increase during periods of recession. Usually the first wave of deaths follows the recession by three years, with a second wave occurring five to seven years after the recession. The lag was thought to be due to the length of time it takes heart disease to cause death. Waves of kidney failure deaths generally lagged two years behind a recession, while death from strokes took about two to four years to follow an economic downturn. Infant mortality rates were particularly striking during periods of recession according to Brenner. Mothers suffering from the stresses of the recession tended to have higher blood pressure and be less healthy themselves, thereby giving birth to a child whose chances for survival had likewise been weakened.

What causes stress during an economic recession was the intensified struggle for the basic necessities of life (food, clothing, shelter, health care, and education for children) and a possible loss of self-satisfaction and social status associated with unemployment while trying to survive on savings, welfare, and unemployment insurance. These stresses were often found to be enhanced by a rise in drinking and smoking at the same time. What is happening, suggests Brenner, is that social stress from economic conditions increases exposure to the major risk factors known to accompany many health disorders.

In an earlier work, Brenner (1973) focused on the relationship between the economy and mental health. He examined rates of employment and mental hospital admissions in New York over a period of 127 years from 1841 to 1968. He believed that regardless of the number and combination of factors that predispose certain individuals toward becoming mentally ill, the question that needed to be answered was why mental disorder appears *when* it does. Brenner found that rates of mental hospitalization increased during economic downturns and decreased during upturns, thereby suggesting that economic factors may precipitate mental disorder.

Brenner provided two explanations for his findings. He preferred a "provocation" hypothesis that stress resulting from being dislocated from one's usual lifestyle or prevented from improving it during a downward shift in the economy caused vulnerable people to reach the point at which they required hospitalization in a mental institution. Another explanation is also possible and is described by Brenner as an "uncovering" hypothesis. This alternate view suggests that economic downturns do not promote mental disorder but simply "uncover" those people already mentally ill by stripping them of their existing economic resources. These people who are mentally "borderline" may be able to support themselves during periods of economic affluence, only to become the first to lose their jobs when times are bad. In fact, in a declining economic cycle, mental hospitals may be an attractive source of food and shelter for these marginal individuals.

Although Brenner prefers the hypothesis that economic downturns "provoke" mental disorder, his data also support the finding that such downturns "uncover" mentally disordered people. Additional research is needed to determine whether "provocation" or "uncovering" is actually at work; to a significant degree both hypotheses may be relevant. The import of Brenner's work is that it shows that downward trends in economic activity may stress certain people to the point that they require mental hospitalization, particularly those with the fewest financial resources.

Another study of the effect of economic change on the psychological well-being of individuals is that by Ralph Catalano and C. David Dooley (1977) conducted in Kansas City, Missouri. This study examined the relationship between depressed moods and stressful life events as correlated with rises in inflation and rates of unemployment. Catalano and Dooley found that unemployment was significantly related to depression and stress, but that inflation was related to neither. Thus, unemployment appeared to be an especially strong predictor of depressed mood and stressful life events. The study did not test Brenner's "uncovering" hypothesis and explored his "provocation" hypothesis only partially; yet the data tended to support the "provocation" explanation that economic change put enough stress on certain people to cause mental problems. In contrast to Brenner's study, economic upturns as well as downturns produced stress.

Even though the research of Brenner and of Catalano and Dooley demonstrates how large-scale societal processes, specifically those of economic change, can be correlated with adverse physical and mental health, the relationship is not that simple. It is very difficult to substantiate a precise cause-and-effect relationship between a major social event like an economic depression and the health problems of a particular individual because of the wide range of variables that may intervene in the individual's situation and modify the effect. Possible intervening variables could be those of personality, social support, genetics, social class, socialization, and so forth. For instance, research on the effects of social support (that is, feelings of being loved, accepted, cared for, and needed by others) on persons subjected to unemployment (Gore, 1978), stressful life events (Lin et al., 1979), and occupational stress (LaRocco et al., 1980) shows that social support can act as a buffer against stress. Those persons with the strongest level of social support had fewer health problems than did those with little or no support.

The advantage of macro-level forms of analysis like functionalism, however, is that this approach shows how social and economic circumstances beyond the direct influence or control of the average person can create stressful circumstances that force people to respond to them. For some people, the stressful circumstances may promote ill health.

Cooley, Thomas, and Goffman: Symbolic Interaction

While Durkheim emphasized the influence of the larger society upon the individual, Cooley, Thomas, and Goffman reflect the symbolic interactionist approach to human behavior, which views human group life from the perspective of the individual. This approach sees the individual as a creative, thinking organism who is able to choose his or her behavior instead of reacting more or less mechanically to the influence of social processes. It assumes that all behavior is self-directed on the basis of symbolic meanings which are shared, communicated, and manipulated by interacting human beings in social situations. Of special relevance to a sociological understanding of stress is Charles H. Cooley's (1864–1929) theory of the "Looking-Glass Self." Cooley (1964) maintained that our self-concepts are the result of social interaction in which we see ourselves reflected in the meanings other people attach to us as social objects. Cooley compares the reflection of our self in others to our reflections in a looking glass:

> Each to each a looking glass
> Reflects the other that doth pass.

Cooley's looking-glass self concept has three basic components: (1) we see ourselves in our imagination as we think we appear to the other person; (2) we see in our imagination the other person's judgment of our appearance; and (3) as a result of what we see in our imagination about how we are viewed by the other person, we experience some sort of self-feeling, such as pride or humiliation. The contribution of this theory to an understanding of stress is that an individual's perception of himself or herself as a social object is related to the reaction of other people. Quite obviously stress could result from the failure of the observer to reflect a self-image consistent with that of the subject. Thus, stress can be seen as having a very definite social and personal component based on perception of a social event.

The work of William I. Thomas (1863–1947) is also relevant for its understanding of crisis as residing in the individual's "definition of the situation" (Volkart, 1951). Thomas stated that so long as definitions of a social situation remain relatively constant, behavior will generally be orderly. However, when rival definitions appear and habitual behavior becomes disrupted, social disorganization and personal demoralization may be anticipated. The ability of an individual to cope with a crisis situation will be strongly related to socialization experiences that have taught the person how to cope with new events in general.

Consequently, Thomas makes two particularly important contributions concerning stress. First, he notes that the same crisis will not produce the *same effect uniformly in all people,* and second, he explains that adjustment and control of a crisis situation result from an individual's ability to compare a present situation with similar ones in the past and to revise judgment and action upon the basis of past experience. The outcome of a particular situation depends, therefore, upon an individual's definition of a situation and upon how that individual comes to terms with that situation. As David Mechanic (1978:293) states, "Thomas' concept of crisis is important because it emphasizes that crises lie not in situations, but rather in the interaction between a situation and a person's capacities to meet it." Saxon Graham and Leo Reeder (1972:91) add that in Thomas' notion of adaptation ". . . the individual's repertoire of coping behavior is a crucial element in understanding the ways in which people come to terms with a given stressful situation."

Erving Goffman, a contemporary figure in American sociology, is noted for the dramaturgical or "life as theatre" approach. The symbolic interactionist orientation is obvious in Goffman's (1959) belief that in order for social interaction to be viable, people need information about the other participants in a joint act. Such information is communicated through (1) a person's appearance, (2) a person's experience with other similar individuals, (3) the social setting, and (4) most important, the information a person communicates about himself or herself through words and actions. This fourth category of information is decisive because it is subject to control by the individual and represents the impression the person is trying to project —which others may come to accept. This information is significant because it helps to define a situation by enabling others to know in advance what a person expects of them and what they may expect of him or her. Goffman calls this process "impression management."

Goffman says people live in worlds of social encounters in which they act out a line of behavior, a pattern of verbal and nonverbal acts by which individuals express their view of a situation and their evaluation of the participants, particularly themselves. The positive social value individuals claim for themselves by the line that others assume they have taken during a particular encounter is termed a "face." This face is an image of self projected to other people who may share that face. One's face is one's most personal possession and is the center of security and pleasure, but Goffman is quick to point out that a person's face is only on loan to him or her from society and can be withdrawn if the person conducts himself or herself in a manner others deem as being unworthy. A person may be in the "wrong face" when information about that person's social worth cannot be integrated into his or her line of behavior or a person may be "out of face" when he or she participates in an encounter without the line of behavior of the type that participants in that particular situation would be expected to take.

Goffman further explains that the maintenance of face is a condition of interaction, not its objective. This is so because one's face is a constant factor taken for granted in interaction. When people engage in "face-work," they are taking action to make their activities consistent with the face they are projecting. This is important because every member of a social group is expected to have some knowledge of face-work and some experience in its use, such as the exercise of social skills like tact. Goffman sees almost all acts involving other people as being influenced by considerations of face; for example, a person is given a chance to quit a job rather than be fired. A person must be aware of the interpretations that others have placed upon his or her behavior and the interpretations that he or she should place upon their behavior. Therefore, Goffman's view of the self is that it has two distinct roles in social interaction: first, the self as an image of a person formed from the flow of events in an encounter; and second, the self as a kind of player in a ritual game who copes judgmentally with a situation.

Goffman's principal contribution to our understanding of stress arises from his claim that the self is a sacred object. The self is more important than anything else to us because it is always with us and represents who we are. For someone to challenge the integrity of that self as a social object is an embarrassing situation. Each self is special, and in social relationships that very special self we have tried to nourish and protect for a lifetime is put on display. Goffman has said that role-specific behavior is based not upon the functional requirements of a particular role, but upon the *appearance* of having discharged a role's requirements. Thus, stress could be induced when people perceive their chosen face or performance in a given situation to be inconsistent with the concept of self they try to maintain for themselves and others in that situation. Otherwise, people might not be so willing to take such great care that they act out lines of behavior considered appropriate to their situation.

STRESS

The theories of Durkheim, Cooley, Thomas, and Goffman demonstrate a relationship between social interaction and stress, but they do not explain the effect of stress upon the human body. Embarrassment and psychological discomfort can be socially painful, yet the effects of stress can transcend the social situation and cause physiological damage as well. Hence, a physiological perspective of stress must be considered.

Walter Cannon (1932) believed that the real measure of health is not the absence of disease, but the ability of the human organism to function effectively within a given environment. This belief was based upon the observation that the human body undergoes continuous adaptation to its environment in response to weather, microorganisms, chemical irritants and pollutants, and the psychological pressures of daily life. Cannon called this process of physiological adaptation *homeostasis,* which is derived from the Greek and means "staying the same." Homeostasis refers to the maintenance of a relatively constant condition; for example, when the body becomes cold, heat is produced; when the body is threatened by bacteria, antibodies are produced to fight the germs; and when the body is threatened by an attack from another human being, the body prepares itself either to fight or to run.

As an organism the human body is thus prepared to meet both internal and external threats to survival, whether these threats are real or symbolic. A person may react with fear to an actual object or to a symbol of that object—for example a bear versus a bear's footprint. In the second case, the fear is not of the footprint, but of the bear that the footprint represents. Symbolic threats in contemporary urban societies could include types of stimuli such as heavy traffic, loud noises, or competition at work, all of which can produce emotional stress related more to a social situation than to a specific person or object.

Whether or not the stressful situation actually induces physiological change depends upon an individual's perception of the stress stimulus and the meaning that the stimulus holds for him or her. A person's reaction, for instance, may not correspond to the actual reality of the dangers that the stimulus represents; that is, a person may overreact or underreact. Thus there is considerable agreement that an individual's subjective interpretation of a social situation is the trigger that produces physiological responses (Moss, 1973). Situations themselves cannot always be assumed beforehand to produce physiological changes.

Physiological Responses to Stress

Cannon (1932) formulated the concept of the "fight or flight" pattern of physiological change to illustrate how the body copes with stress resulting from a social situation. When a person experiences fear or anxiety, the body undergoes physiological changes that prepare it for vigorous effort and the effect of possible injury. Physiological changes in the body as a result of stress situations primarily involve the autonomic and neuroendocrine systems. The autonomic nervous system controls heart rate, blood pressure, and gastrointestinal functions—processes that occur automatically and are not under the voluntary control of the central nervous system. The autonomic nervous system is delicately balanced between relaxation and stimulation and is activated primarily through the hypothalamus, which is located in the central ventral portion of the brain. It is composed of two major divisions, the parasympathetic and the sympathetic systems. The parasympathetic system is dominant when there is no emergency and regulates the vegetative processes of the body such as the storing of sugar in the liver, the constriction of the pupil of the eye in response to intense light, and the decreasing of heart rate. When there is an emergency, the sympathetic system governs the body's autonomic functions and increases heart rate so that blood flows swiftly to the organs and muscles that are needed in defense. It also inhibits bowel movements and dilates the pupil of the eye in order to improve sight.

Besides the autonomic nervous system, the endocrine glands perform an important role in the body's physiological reaction to stress. The neuro-endocrine system consists of the adrenal and pituitary glands, the parathy-roids, the islets of Langerhans, and the gonads. They secrete hormones directly into the blood stream because they lack ducts to carry their hor-mones to particular glands. The two glands that are the most responsive to stress situations are the adrenal and pituitary glands. The adrenal gland secretes two hormones, epinephrine and norepinephrine, under stimula-tion from the hypothalamus. Epinephrine accelerates the heart rate and helps to distribute blood to the heart, lungs, central nervous system, and limbs; also it makes the blood coagulate more readily so that as little blood as possible will be lost in case of injury. Norepinephrine raises blood pressure and joins with epinephrine to mobilize fatty acids in the blood stream for use as energy. The function of the pituitary gland is, upon stimulation by the hypothalamus, to secrete hormones that, in turn, stimulate other endocrine glands to secrete their hormones.

At first, most medical scientists believed that only the adrenal gland was involved in stress reaction; however, in 1936 Hans Selye demonstrated the existence of a pituitary-adrenal cortical axis as having a profound effect upon body metabolism. Selye (1956) developed a theory known as the *general adaptation syndrome*. He believed that after an initial alarm reaction, a second stage of resistance to prolonged stress was accomplished primarily through increased activity of the anterior pituitary and adrenal cortex. If stress continued and pituitary and adrenal defenses were consumed, Selye indicated that a person would enter a third stage of exhaustion. He described this third stage as a kind of premature aging due to wear and tear on the body. However, it now seems that the entire endocrine system, not just the pituitary and adrenal glands, are involved in some manner in stress reaction. Under acute stimulus, hormone secretions by the endocrine glands increase; under calming influences, secretions decrease.

Most threats in modern society are symbolic, not physical, and they do not usually require a physical response. Today the human organism faces emotional threats with the same physical system used to fight enemies. Yet modern society disapproves of such physical responses as fighting. Socially, the human organism is often left with no course of action, perhaps not even verbal insults. This inability to respond externally leaves the body physiolog-ically mobilized for action which never comes, a readiness that can result in damage to the body.

A number of studies have shown that the human organism's inability to manage the social, psychological, and emotional aspects of life—to respond suitably to a social situation—can lead to the development of cardiovascular complications and hypertension, peptic ulcers, muscular pain, compulsive vomiting, asthma, migraine headaches, and other health problems (see, for example, McNeil, 1970; Moss, 1973; House, 1974). Some research suggests that even the onset of cancer is related to changes and disappointments in social relationships (LeShan, 1966).

James House and his associates (1979), for example, found that perceived stress on the job was consistently related to self-reports of angina, ulcers, and anxiety problems, and to medical assessments of high blood pressure and other coronary disease risk factors. Moreover, the data, collected from over 1,800 blue-collar workers at a large rubber, plastics, and chemical manufacturing plant in the Northeast United States, indicated that perceived stress was also positively associated with self-reports of respiratory and dermatological symptoms—but only among certain workers exposed to potentially noxious physical and chemical irritants. House et al., raise the possibility that stress poses an additional threat to these blue-collar workers by rendering them more susceptible to the effects of noxious environmental agents on their skin and lungs.

Further evidence reflecting the effect of stress upon the body is the growing accumulation of data supporting a link between a certain type of behavior (Type A) and coronary heart disease. Type A behavior is characterized as that of excessive drive, intense ambition and aggressiveness, and involvement in competitive activities and a demanding work schedule. It is thought to be most common among middle- and upper-class males with a strong desire for overachievement, money, status, and personal recognition. Type B behavior, in contrast, is the relative absence of such psychological traits and situational pressures. According to a series of longtitudinal studies, men with Type A behavior, as compared with those who primarily show Type B behavior, have been found to have a significantly higher risk of heart disease (Jenkins, 1971; Cohen et al., 1979). People with a tendency toward Type A behavior may be more likely to select stressful occupations or to perceive stress in the jobs they choose. The end result is the same, however. The Type A person suffers greater emotional strain through his or her work role in the attempt to be highly successful and, in doing so, enhances the probability of having a heart attack.

PSYCHOPHYSIOLOGICAL MEDICINE

The belief that mind and body interact has led to the development of psychophysiological medicine. This branch of medicine rests on the premise that discomforting social situations produce stress, which plays a role in causing or contributing to the occurrences of a physiological disorder or illness. However, the reader is reminded that while the concept of stress-related illness and disease is generally accepted, the literature on stress remains characterized by disagreement and uncertainty.

A major problem is that stress is a subjective phenomenon and difficult to measure except for a few external physiological indicators such as galvanic skin response (GSR), electroencephalograph (EEG), and electromyograph (EMG); and internal indicators such as changes in the secretion and excretion of hormone levels in the blood and urine. Yet the external physiological indicators do not always represent reliable measures of internal bodily states; and while internal indicators of hormone levels may provide more exact measures of rapid change within the body, they are difficult to generalize to other individuals in the same circumstances. Gordon Moss

(1973) notes that the wide range of individual physiological responses to a social situation cannot be adequately explained without considering an individual's *subjective* understanding of the situation. Nevertheless, psychophysiological medicine represents a definite attempt by medicine to cope with the interplay of mind and body. Three of the major psychophysiological approaches to the mind–body problem are outlined below.

The Psychoanalytic Perspective

The development of a psychoanalytic approach to psychophysiological medicine is due primarily to the work of Franz Alexander and his colleagues at the Chicago Psychoanalytic Institute during the 1930s. Alexander relied heavily upon Sigmund Freud's studies of hysteria conversion. As a result of his work with hypnosis, Freud observed that hysterical symptoms disappeared under hypnosis in patients who had repressed their emotions. Freud believed that hysterical symptoms in his patients were converted into symbolic expression in disturbed bodily functions. An intense emotion would disappear from consciousness and reappear with a physiological effect, such as paralysis of a limb. Freud called this process the hysterical conversion symptom because emotional tension was converted into an organic effect, since it was unable to find other symbolic expression.

Several clinical studies have supported Freud's explanation for hysteria, although it should be noted that such studies have been able to account only for pathogenic symptoms occurring in muscles under voluntary control (Alexander and Selesnick, 1966). Other research has suggested that much more than simple repression is needed to explain the full effect of hysteria (Shapiro, 1965). Yet the significant insight for future research was that mind and body do interact.

While Freud and many of his associates continued to concern themselves with questions regarding conflict within the structure of the personality and the nature of the id, the ego, and the superego, Alexander explored his theory that personality conflicts were not problems of structure, but instead represented emotional tensions. Alexander was particularly concerned with the tendency of the human personality to punish itself as a primary component of neurotic symptoms (Wyss, 1973). Failure to achieve gratification during childhood was thought to weaken the capacity of the individual to tolerate anxiety and depression during adulthood, and to predispose the individual to ego regression and conversion to physiological disorders during stress situations. Alexander believed that *specific* psychological conflicts within the personality could be the basis for explaining *specific* physiological manifestations. For example, diarrhea was thought to be caused by an oral-dependent longing to give, while ulcers were supposed to be related to oral-receptive longings derived from an excessive need to accomplish.

Disagreement among psychoanalysts about the correlation between specific personality and organic disorders resulted in a further clarification of the psychoanalytic position on psychophysiological medicine. Roy Grinker (1953) has revised the contemporary basic assumptions of the psychoanalytic approach by explaining that stress can manifest itself in a number of linked open systems. Stress that occurs in one system may be transferred to other systems, so that several systems are involved in the human's adaptation to stress. Grinker maintains that five basic systems are involved in handling stress: (1) the enzymatic system, which includes the endocrine system, (2) the organic system, (3) the nervous system, (4) the psychological system, and (5) the sociocultural system. When anxiety becomes too intense within one system, other systems intervene to absorb the effects. These other systems do not become involved until the anxiety is too much for one particular system.

Despite the fact that the psychoanalytic perspective has been very influential in psychiatry, its approach suffers some serious limitations. For one thing, there is at present no reliable correlation between specific psychological problems and predisposition to a particular illness (Ludwig et al., 1969). Also important is the criticism that psychoanalytic theory is too abstract, poorly specified, and usually not dependent upon controlled scientific research (Moss, 1973; Mechanic, 1978); additionally, it views people as unusually weak and ineffectual against the biological and social forces that act upon them.

The Attitude Specificity Perspective

The theory of attitude specificity is the result of the work of David Graham and his colleagues (1962) on the question of whether or not certain personalities are associated with particular diseases, as Alexander tried to demonstrate. On the basis of patient interviews, Graham concluded that hypertension could be correlated with a feeling of being always prepared to meet all threats, and hives could be correlated with a feeling of being mistreated. Graham obtained some interesting results through hypnotic sugggestion. He induced attitudes in patients during hypnosis that resulted in symptoms of hypertension and hives. For example, in order to produce hypertension, patients were told the following while in a hypnotic state:

> We're going to do something to you; you have to be ready, on guard, prepared for whatever it is. It might be a burn, an electric shock, a needle stick. It's going to come; you just have to sit there and wait and try to be ready for whatever it is. You feel that you may be attacked and hurt at any instant; it may be painful, it may be dangerous. You feel that you are in danger. You're threatened every instant, you have to watch out.[1]

Patients receiving this message usually showed signs of high blood pressure after hypnosis. The symptoms were mild and did not persist, but appeared nevertheless. This research is not conclusive, but does suggest the possibility of a relationship between certain attitudes and a specific physiological response.

---

[1] David J. Graham, J. D. Kabler, and Francis K. Graham, "Physiological responses to the suggestion of attitudes specific for hives and hypertension," *Psychosomatic Medicine*, 24 (1962), 160–61.

The Life Situation Perspective

The life situation approach to psychophysiological disease is based on the work of Harold Wolff (Wolf and Goodell, 1968), whose theories are drawn largely from laboratory and clinical observations, such as his classical study of "Tom's" stomach and its reaction to stress. The study of "Tom's" stomach was based upon a patient known as "Tom" whose stomach protruded through his abdomen, providing his physicians with a "window" into his stomach. It was observed that the lining of the stomach responded to emotional disturbances by stomach secretions of hydrochloric acid. When Tom was depressed or withdrawn from other people, the opposite effect occurred and his stomach was pale, bloodless, and generally empty of digestive secretions. This research clearly suggested a strong relationship between the functioning of the stomach and emotional states. Often Tom's stomach revealed emotional conflict before Tom's behavior did.

Wolff believed that stress resulted from interaction between the external environment and the human organism, with the major variable being the past experience of the organism. Both physically and socially threatening life situations called forth reactions in the human organism whose ability to maintain homeostasis was based upon the capacity to withstand these threats. Wolff felt that all the organic systems could be involved in a response to threats, and he insisted that a person's attitudes determined the extent of a physiological response. Stress, therefore, was derived largely from an individual's perception of the social situation and that individual's perception was based on several factors, particularly past experience, but also attitudes, cultural pressures, psychological needs, early conditioning influences, and genetic background.

Wolff's work is generally considered to be reasonably sound and he has made an important contribution by noting that many organic systems can be influenced by a social situation to the point that susceptibility to disease is enhanced and organs themselves are perhaps damaged through hyperactivity. Mechanic (1978) notes that the principal advantage of Wolff's approach is that it is relatively simple to understand and that his research procedures are closely related to his theory. However, Wolff's theory, while useful, has not been substantiated.

In fact, definite conclusions concerning the specific mind-body relationships in psychophysiological medicine generally must await further research and clarification. The best that psychophysiological medicine offers us at the present time are a few guidelines for the direction of future research.

SOCIAL FACTORS AND STRESS

There is a considerable amount of empirical research in medical sociology dealing with stress and stress-related topics. Selected findings from the work of Schwab and Pritchard (1950), Mechanic (1968), and Moss (1973) will be reviewed here. Also relevant research on group influences and changes in life events will be considered. The intent of this section is to show how contemporary sociologists are helping to improve our understanding of stress.

Stress Situations

Robert Schwab and John Pritchard (1950) classified types of situations they believe may lead to physiological disorders and chronic disease. Their classification system was based not only upon the type of situation, but also the duration of the influence of the situation and the degree of stress induced by that situation.

Stress situations were typed as either (1) short stress situations, in which mild stress occurred whose effects lasted from seconds to hours; (2) moderate stress situations, in which the effects lasted from days to weeks; and (3) severe stress situations, in which the effects lasted from weeks to months and even years. Examples of a short stress situation are annoying insects, public appearances before large audiences, and doors slamming. In other words, these are the so-called minor burdens and annoyances of everyday life which probably do not produce the onset of stress-related disease. Moderate stress situations are characterized by overwork, temporary absence of loved ones, gastric upsets, or minor psychological setbacks during social interaction. Severe stress situations would be death of loved ones, severe financial reverses, perpetuation of intolerable social situations, illness, or perhaps prolonged absence from loved ones. The moderate and particularly the severe stress situation would be capable of producing a serious physiological response.

Specific types of stress formulated by Schwab and Pritchard were those of (1) trauma, such as fear in armed combat; (2) infection from disease; (3) financial reverses and the feeling of frustration; (4) death of a loved one; (5) fear of an unknown situation such as recovery from surgery; (6) fright; (7) chronic worry; (8) fatigue from overwork; (9) fatigue from extensive travel; (10) rejection and the feeling of isolation; (11) disappointment; and (12) conflict.

Schwab and Pritchard believe that the common element in their typology of stress situations, other than duration, is that of the disruption of social relationships, either threatened or actual. Other research agrees that the greatest source of potential stress is the disruption or threat of disruption of an individual's social ties to another person or persons (Dodge and Martin, 1970).

Stress Adaptation

Mechanic (1962b, 1978) attempts to explain the social determinants of stress from the standpoint of the social structure of the community rather than from the personal experiences of the individual alone. He draws on the work of William I. Thomas (Volkart, 1951), who pointed out that the meaning of a crisis lies not in the situation, but rather in the interaction between the situation and the person's ability to rise above it. The outcome or effect of a crisis depends on how well a person comes to terms with the situation. Stress, therefore, refers to difficulties experienced by the individual as a result of perceived challenges.

Mechanic believes that in social situations people have different skills and abilities in coping with problems; not everyone has an equal degree of control in managing emotional defenses nor the same motivation and personal involvement in a situation. In analyzing any particular situation, an observer must consider not only whether an individual is prepared to meet a threat, but also whether or not he or she is motivated to meet it.

Extending his concept of stress from the individual to societal components, Mechanic states that a person's ability to cope with problems is influenced by a society's preparatory institutions, such as schools and the family, two organizations designed to develop skills and competencies in dealing with society's needs. A person's emotional control and ability to defend are also related to society's incentive systems—that is, society's rewards (or punishments) for those who did (or did not) control their behavior in accordance with societal norms. As for a person's involvement or motivation in a situation, Mechanic explains that society's evaluative institutions provide norms of approval or disapproval for following particular courses of action.

Hence, the extent of physiological damage or change within an individual depends on (1) the stimulus situation, which includes the importance of the situation to the individual and the extent of his or her motivation; (2) an individual's capacity to deal with the stimulus situation, such as the influence of genetic factors, personal skills, innate abilities, and past experiences; (3) the individual's preparation by society to meet problems; and (4) the influence of society's approved modes of behavior. Mechanic (1962b:8) emphasizes the contribution of society toward an individual's adaptation to stress by stating ". . . that whether or not a person experiences stress will depend on the means, largely learned, that he has available to deal with his life situation."

Mechanic's model represents an important contribution toward our understanding of stress by showing the importance of adaptation and explaining how that adaptation is based on an individual's perception of life situations combined with his or her degree of preparation by society to cope with stressful circumstances. Mechanic thus identifies adaptability as the key variable in whether or not a person will eventually suffer organic damage. The major criticism of Mechanic's work, however, is that he fails to deal adequately with the relationship between social processes and specific physiological responses (Moss, 1973). This leaves his theory too general to be of specific utility, but it provides considerable insight into the social factors involved in coping with stress.

Biosocial Resonation

Moss (1973) has conceptualized a model of stress which he calls *biosocial resonation*. The significance of this model lies in its sophisticated attempt to link sociology with body physiology. Moss (1973:241) defines biosocial resonation as "the continuing reciprocal influences of physiological and social behavior in social interaction." He sees human beings as living in a social world composed of communication networks. These networks are groups or configurations of interacting people who transmit social information. This information includes conceptions of the environment and the norms and values that specify preferred patterns of social interaction. As long as the information of a communication network is perceived by the individual as being both accurate and effective, that person is likely to personally identify with the network.

Moss believes that conformance to the norms of the communication network and participation within that network will reduce a person's opportunity to come into contact with members of other networks and their information, which might be of an incongruous nature. Information incongruity can have the effect of causing an individual to question his or her own information. Consequently, there is a mismatch between neural representations of information and current perceptions. However, in modern society it is difficult, if not impossible, not to come into contact with incompatible networks and incongruous information. If the information from an incompatible network is judged acceptable, then a change is likely to take place in the perception of the individual and possibly among other persons in the same communication network.

Stress and physiological change are likely to occur when a person experiences information incongruities. After thoroughly reviewing the literature on stress research, Moss determined that information processing leads to changes in the central nervous system, the autonomic nervous system, and the neuroendocrine system, all of which can alter the susceptibility to disease among "tuned" people. "Tuning" is a term used by Moss to describe a disruption in a person's autonomic functioning. Some people have more of a tendency to be tuned than others because of genetic inheritance or life experiences. Moss states:

> Perception of information incongruities that are highly salient and/or remain unresolved can produce pronounced, repeated, and/or prolonged general physiological responses that may establish tuning. Tuned individuals' general susceptibility is greater than that of balanced individuals because more general physiological responses are more easily elicited and likely to be more pronounced and prolonged for tuned individuals than for balanced individuals.[2]

Moss believes that a communication network can take steps to reduce stress reactions among the network's membership through the processes of social immunity, social cure, and social therapy. *Social immunity* is the ability of a communication network to prevent members from encountering information incongruities by providing correct information, or through the isolation of its members. *Social cure* is the ability of a communication network to satisfy a member's concern about the encountered information incongruities, while *social therapy* refers to the activities and information of a network in relieving a member's symptoms accompanying encounters with information incongruities. A communication network's social immunity, social cure, and social therapy are most effective when a member strongly identifies with the network. When these processes are inadequate, information incongruities

---

[2]Gordon E. Moss, *Illness, Immunity, and Social Interaction* (New York: Wiley, 1973), p. 245.

are likely to remain unresolved and increase the probability of a prolonged physiological response, which will in turn increase an individual's susceptibility to disease.

To date, Moss's theory of biosocial resonation has not been empirically tested. In the absence of research applications of his model, the primary weakness of Moss's theory lies in its failure to account adequately for a lack of consensus within the information network itself. Even though Moss recognizes that conflict within a network is possible, he seems to assume that a network will generally be cohesive, and he does not adequately explain what happens when it is not. Moss is also somewhat vague as to the effects of information incongruities between several networks within which an individual may participate and the problems that may arise when a particular network's information is incongruous with the wider society, as in the case of a deviant subgroup.

The merit of Moss's theory, however, lies in its important emphasis upon the advantages of group membership in providing social support for the individual. Subjective feelings of belonging, being accepted, and being needed have consistently shown themselves to be crucial in the development of feelings of well-being and the relieving of symptoms of tension. The vagueness of a few facets of Moss's theory should not detract from its overall potential utility. Theoretically, Moss's model represents a most extensive and concise synthesis of sociological and biological processes incorporated in the stress experience.

Stress and the Social Group

An individual's perception of an event may be influenced by his or her intelligence, past experience, socialization, and awareness of stimuli, but the influence of group membership is also important. Moss has indicated that the significance of a group or comunication network in influencing physiological responses lies in its providing corrective information to counteract incongruities and in isolating members from opposing information perspectives. There is often a tendency among members of small groups to develop a consensus about how social events should be perceived; this process minimizes individual differences, reduces uncertainty, and maintains group conformity (Hare, 1976). Conformity to group-approved attitudes and definitions has long been hypothesized in sociology and social psychology as reducing anxiety by ensuring acceptance from persons and groups important to the individual (Presthus, 1978). Much of human behavior is seen as the result of an individual's search for relief from anxiety by conforming to authority and group norms.

Life Changes

Another important factor in the production of stress is the occurrence of significant changes in a person's life experiences. Research in this area has generally focused on the reactions of people both to extreme situations, like wars and natural disasters, and to ordinary life events. This research is reviewed in the next two sections.

Extreme Situations.   Extreme situations like natural disasters would appear to be a likely source of stress because of the great anxiety people usually attach to being caught in such circumstances. But a common misconception about disasters is that people flee in panic from the site of a potential disaster area. In reality, it is usually difficult to get people to evacuate their homes, even when the possibility of damage or destruction is imminent (Tierney and Baisden, 1979). Some people are even attracted to potential disasters and take risks to see a tidal wave, tornado, or hurricane. Trying to view a disaster and being a victim of one, however, are two entirely different matters. Past research has shown that such extreme situations as earthquakes and tornados can induce stress (Barbara Dohrenwend, 1973). Mass media reports commonly show or describe people in large-scale disasters as experiencing intense feelings of grief, loss, anguish, and despair. When tornado victims in rural Arkansas were interviewed shortly after a severe twister had touched down in their community, the great majority (about 90 percent) reported some form of acute emotional reaction (Fritz and Marks, 1954).

Thus, there is sound reason for understanding the social and psychological consequences of disasters, especially from the standpoint of developing and implementing programs to assist disaster victims. Still, only in the last twenty-five years or so have behavioral responses to disasters been treated to systematic study. What data have been obtained, according to a review by Kathleen Tierney and Barbara Baisden (1979:35) for the National Institute of Mental Health, indicate that most researchers tend to agree that "very few people become grossly psychotic in the face of major disasters and the incapacitating psychological reactions are unusual phenomena in catastrophes."

This is not to say that disaster victims generally escape all psychological trauma—quite the contrary. There is almost unanimous agreement that disasters do promote acute psychological stress, emotional difficulties, and anxiety related to coping with grief, property damage, financial loss, and adverse living conditions. Tierney and Baisden (1979:36) state that "while few researchers would claim that disasters create severe and chronic mental illness on a wide scale, victim populations *do* seem to undergo considerable stress and strain and *do* experience varying degrees of concern, worry, depression, and anxiety, together with numerous problems in living and adjustment in postdisaster." Groups of people with special needs in the aftermath of disasters are usually children and the elderly. Older people, in particular, find it difficult to adjust to life after a disaster. Low-income groups also present special problems in that often they are left without any material resources and become especially dependent on aid.

A pattern that emerges in studies of natural disasters and psychopathology is that the disaster experience, though severe, is usually short in duration, and the effects on mental health likewise tend to be short-term and self-limiting. The question thus arises about the possible effects of stress in extreme situations lasting long periods of time, such as the experiences of people exposed to the brutalities of Nazi concentration camps and the horrors of war. There is evidence that many concentration camp survivors have suffered persistent emotional problems and are particularly prone to physical illness and early death (Eitinger, 1964, 1973). However, as Aaron Antonovsky (1979) notes, other concentration camp survivors have adjusted quite well to the effects of having been subjected to a most terrible experience and are now living lives that are essentially normal. Antonovsky states:

> More than a few women among the concentration camp survivors were well adapted, no matter how adaptation was measured. Despite having lived through the most inconceivably inhuman experience, followed by Displaced Persons camps, illegal immigration to Palestine, internment in Cyprus by the British, the Israeli War of Independence, a lengthy period of economic austerity, the Sinai War of 1956, and the Six Day War of 1967 (to mention only the highlights), some women were reasonably healthy and happy, had raised families, worked, had friends, and were involved in community activities.[3]

When considering what differentiates people who are generally vulnerable to stress-related health problems, not just concentration camp survivors, from those who are not so vulnerable, Antonovsky argues that a strong sense of coherence is the key factor. Coherence, in his view, is a personal orientation that allows an individual to view the world with feelings of confidence, faith in the predictability of events, and a notion that things will most likely work out reasonably well. One achieves this sense of coherence as a result of life experiences in which one meets challenges, participates in shaping outcomes (usually satisfactory), and copes with varying degrees of stimuli. Hence, the person has the resources to cope with unexpected situations if they arise. On the other hand, people whose life is so routine and completely predictable that their sense of coherence as defined above is weakened will find it difficult to handle unpleasant surprises and events. They are likely to be more susceptible to stress-induced health dysfunctions as they are overwhelmed by events. What Antonovsky appears to be saying is that people who have the capability to come to terms with their situation rather than to be overcome by it are those who are most likely to emerge in a healthy condition.

A similar conclusion can be made about soldiers fighting in combat. Environmental stresses faced by combat infantrymen are among the hardest faced by anyone. These stresses include the overt threat of death or injury, the sight and sounds of dying men, battle noise, fatigue, loss of sleep, deprivation of family relationships, exposure to rain, mud, insects, heat or cold, and so forth—all occasioned by deliberate exposure to the most extreme forms of violence intentionally directed at the soldier by the opposing side. Charles Moskos (1970) has compared combat with the Hobbesian analogy of primitive life: both can be nasty, brutish, and short. Yet somehow men generally come to terms with the circumstances, since most combat soldiers do not become psychiatric casualties. Two factors may be largely responsible. First is the existence of external group demands for discipline and efficiency under fire. Observing helicopter ambulance crews and Green Berets in Vietnam, Peter Bourne (1970), a psychiatrist, found these soldiers to be

[3]Aaron Antonovsky, *Health, Stress, and Coping* (San Francisco: Jossey-Bass, 1979), p. 7.

subjected to strong group pressures to be technically proficient regardless of friendship ties. This finding was particularly true of the Green Berets, who urged their detachment leaders to prove themselves in combat in order to be worthy of their role. Although at times this social pressure added to the stress of the leaders, when the entire group faced an enemy threat there was unusual group cohesion and considerable conformity in the manner in which the threat was perceived and handled.

Second, Bourne suggests that there is a further psychological mobilization of an internal discipline in which the individual soldier employs a sense of personal invulnerability, the use of action to reduce tension, and a lack of personal introspection to perceive his environment in such a way that personal threat is reduced. Whether Bourne's findings are representative of other types of combat soldiers is subject to question, since helicopter ambulance crews and Green Berets are highly self-selected volunteers for hazardous duty. Nevertheless, Bourne's study supports the conclusion of others (Rado, 1949; Cockerham, 1978) that one of the most efficient techniques that allows soldiers generally to adjust to battle is to interpret combat not as a continued threat of personal injury or death but as a sequence of demands to be responded to by precise military performances. In failing to find significant physiological change (excretion of adrenal cortical steroids) occurring among most soldiers during life-threatening situations, Bourne suggests that the men allowed their behavior under stress to be modified by social and psychological influences that significantly affected physiological responses to objective threats from the environment.

What is obvious from this discussion of the effects of stress resulting from exposure to extreme situations is that such situations are relatively rare for most people and whatever stresses are generated among those persons subject to them usually is temporary and disappears after a while. Many people are not emotionally affected at all, even though the circumstances are exceedingly stressful. Consequently, as Bruce Dohrenwend (1975:384) points out, if stressful situations play a major role in causing mental disturbances, the relevant events must be more ordinary and frequent experiences in the lives of most people, such as marriage, birth of a first child, death of a loved one, loss of a job, and so on. Though such events are not extraordinary in a large population, they are extraordinary in the lives of the individuals who experience them.

Life Events.   Life events research does not focus on one particular life event (for example, exposure to combat) and claim that it is more stressful than another life event (for example, unemployment). Rather, it is generally based on the assumption that the *accumulation* of several events in a person's life eventually builds up to a stressful impact (Dohrenwend and Dohrenwend, 1974; Bruce Dohrenwend, 1975). However, what types of events, in what combinations, over what periods of time, and under what circumstances promote stress-induced health problems is not at all clear at the present time.

An important area of contention in life events research, for example, is the issue of whether any type of change in one's life, either pleasant or unpleasant, produces significant stress, or whether stress is largely a result of unpleasant events only. Considerable evidence supports the idea that any type of environmental change requiring the individual to adapt can produce a specific stress response (Selye, 1956). Barbara Dohrenwend (1973), for one, has concluded from her research on heads of families in the Washington Heights area of New York City that stressfulness is best conceived of as emanating from life change itself rather than from just the undesirability of certain life events. S. Leonard Syme (1975) has reported on studies in North Dakota and California where it was found that rates of coronary heart disease were twice as high among men who had experienced several lifetime job changes and geographic moves as compared to men with no such changes. The findings were not attributable to differences in diet, smoking habits, obesity, blood pressure, physical activity, age, or familial longevity, but to changes in the situations in which people lived.

In addition, research by Peggy Thoits and Michael Hannan (1979) on the impact of an income-maintenance experiment on a large sample of low-income adults living in Seattle and Denver found that a change in income raised the psychological distress levels of the experimental subjects. In this case, the change was increased income in the form of financial grants. Yet the increased or stabilized income caused more distress even though it supposedly facilitated the subjects' ability to cope with problems. Here change per se was stressful, even though the change (increased income) was one most people would regard as positive.

Other research clearly comes down on the side of unpleasant events as being the most important. Lloyd Rogler and August Hollingshead (1965) compared a matched set of twenty "well" families with twenty "sick" families (defined as having either the husband or wife or both diagnosed as schizophrenic) of lower-class status in Puerto Rico. Based upon recall of life events by the subjects and others in the community, the study found no significant differences in the family lives of the normals and schizophrenics during childhood and adolescence. Members of both groups were exposed to the same conditions of poverty, family instability, and lower-class socialization. There was also a lack of difference in their respective adult lives, with the notable exception that for those persons who became schizophrenic, there was a recent and discernible period—*prior to the appearance of overt symptomatology*—during which they were engulfed by a series of insoluble and mutually reinforcing problems. Schizophrenia thus seemed to originate from being placed in an intolerable dilemma brought on by adverse life events largely stemming from intense family and sexual conflicts related to unemployment and restricted life opportunities.

Robert Lauer (1974) tested a "future shock" hypothesis on college students in a midwestern university regarding whether the rate or speed of change and the type of change, either positive or negative, were the most important variables in stress produced by change. Though stress was directly related to the perceived rate of change, his findings indicated that the effect of rapid change can be moderated by whether or not the change was perceived to be desirable. Rapid change and undesirability were the most stressful conditions. Still other research involving heads of households in New Haven, Connecticut by Catherine Ross and John Mirowsky II (1979) found that the undesirability of events predicts symptomatology better than change alone does. Employing multivariate analysis and controlling for undesirability, Ross and Mirowsky observed that the effects of desirable events, ambiguous events, change per se, and the number of events experienced were not significant. They conclude that undesirability is *the* characteristic of life events most associated with increased symptoms of mental disorder. Moreover, research by George Brown and Tirril Harris (1978) on depression among women in London, England found that long-term depression results from negative circumstances, not positive ones. And finally, the research reported earlier in this chapter by Brenner (1973) and Catalano and Dooley (1977) illustrates the adverse effect of economic downturn on mental health as a type of unpleasant life event.

Besides the type of change and the speed with which it occurs, the extent to which change affects a person's life may also be important. Libby Ruch (1977) investigated this and suggests that life change actually has three dimensions: (1) the degree of change evoked, (2) the undesirability of change, and (3) the aspect of one's life that is affected (for example, personal, occupational). But Ruch found that the degree of change is more significant than either desirability or the area of life affected. That is, the greater the change, the more likely stress will result. In subsequent research, Ruch (Ruch et al., 1980) found that women with changes in their lives prior to being raped had significantly more problems adjusting in the aftermath of the assault than rape victims with little or no changes in their lives before the attack. Although too much change may indeed be stressful, too little change in a person's life also may induce stress (Wildman and Johnson, 1977). It is not at all clear, however, that too much or too little change is a determining factor in stress-related health problems. Thomas Rundall (1978), for instance, has found that patients with higher levels of life change prior to surgery did not have appreciably more difficulty or sickness when recovering than patients lacking changes in their lives. In sum, the research pertaining to life events is contradictory and in need of clarification.

Life events research also entails serious problems of accurately measuring the presumed relationships between stress and particular life experiences. The most influential instrument at present is the Social Readjustment Scale developed by Thomas Holmes and Robert Rahe (1967). This scale is based on the assumption that change, no matter how good or how bad, demands a certain degree of adjustment on the part of an individual: the greater the adjustment, the greater the stress. Holmes and Rahe have carried their analysis one step further and have suggested that changes in life events occur in a cumulative pattern that can eventually build to a stressful impact. Thus, the type of change does not matter so much; the extent to which change disrupts normal patterns of life is important.

The Holmes and Rahe Social Readjustment Rating Scale, an adaptation of which is shown in Table 3–1, lists certain life events that are associated with varying amounts of disruption in the life of an average person. It was constructed by having hundreds of people of different social backgrounds rank the relative amount of adjustment accompanying a particular life experience. Death of a spouse is ranked highest, with a relative stress value of 100; marriage ranks seventh with a value of 50, retirement tenth with a

TABLE 3-1.   Life Events and Weighted Values

Life Event	Value	Life Event	Value
Death of spouse	100	Son or daughter leaving home	29
Divorce	73	Trouble with in-laws	29
Marital separation	65	Outstanding personal	
Jail term	63	achievement	28
Death of close family member	63	Wife beginning or stopping	
Personal injury or illness	53	work	26
Marriage	50	Beginning or ending school	26
Fired at work	47	Revision of habits	24
Marital reconciliation	45	Trouble with boss	23
Retirement	45	Change in work hours	20
Change in health of family	44	Change in residence	20
Pregnancy	40	Change in schools	20
Sex difficulties	39	Change in recreation	19
Gain of new family member	39	Change in social activity	18
Change in financial state	38	Change in sleeping habits	16
Death of close friend	37	Change in number of family	
Change of work	36	get-togethers	15
Change in number of		Change in eating habits	15
arguments with spouse	35	Vacation	13
Foreclosure of mortgage	30	Minor violations of law	11
Change of responsibility			
at work	29		

SOURCE: Adapted from T. H. Holmes and R. H. Rahe, "The Social Readjustment Rating Scale," *Journal of Psychosomatic Research,* 11 (August 1967), Table 3-1, 213. Reprinted with permission from the authors and Pergamon Press Ltd.

value of 45, taking a vacation is ranked forty-first with a value of 13, and so forth. Holmes and Rahe call each stress value a "life change" unit. They suggest that as the total value of life change units mounts, the probability of having a serious illness also increases, particularly if a person accumulates too many life change units in too short a time. If an individual accumulates 200 or more life change units within the period of a year, Holmes and Rahe believe such a person will risk a serious disorder.

Although used extensively and found to measure stress and life events about as well or better than other scales (Dohrenwend et al., 1978; Ross and Mirowsky, 1979), the Holmes and Rahe Social Readjustment Rating Scale nevertheless contains some serious flaws that need to be overcome in future research if the scale is going to be continued as a major research tool. Some studies have found that the scale does not adequately account for differences in the relative importance of various life events among ethnic and cultural subgroups (Rosenberg and Dohrenwend, 1975; Hough et al., 1976; Askenasy et al., 1977). In other words, the Holmes and Rahe scale measures the quantity of change rather than the qualitative meaning of the event (Ruch, 1977). Other research suggests that some life events, such as divorce, can be regarded as a *consequence* of stress instead of a *cause*. For example, events such as "change in sleeping habits," "change in number of arguments with spouse," "sex difficulties," and "fired at work" may be products of stress rather than causes (Holmes and Masuda, 1974). This situation confounds the relationships being measured.

Another problem is that the scale does not account for intervening variables, such as social support, that might modify the effects of stress for many individuals. While interpersonal influence can be stressful in itself because of discrepancies, conflicting expectations, excessive demands to achieve or maintain a certain level of performance, or simply because of the volume of influence originating from several sources (Mettlin and Woelfel, 1974), there is little doubt that supportive interpersonal influences can help reduce stressful feelings (Gore, 1978; Liem and Liem, 1978; Lin et al., 1979; LaRocco et al., 1980). In fact, the lack of affective support may be the most important stress-inducing factor for some people (Brown et al., 1972).

Obviously, life events research is in need of more extensive development. The relationship between stress and life events as a precipitating factor in causing or contributing to the onset of physical and mental disorders is a highly complex phenomenon and not easily amenable to a simple cause-and-effect explanation. Though some researchers have suggested that life events may not make a meaningful contribution to health problems (Gersten et al., 1977), there appears to be a general recognition in the behavioral sciences that subjective stress is important. The research reported in this section attests to that. In addition, some of the strongest support comes from genetics, which has accumulated strong evidence of a genetic role in mental disorder but looks to social factors as instrumental in explaining the mechanisms that trigger genetic predispositions and help shape the existing variability (Weiner, 1975). Hence, the issue seems to be not so much whether social factors like life events are important, but in what specific ways they are important.

However, in a review of the relevant literature, Bruce and Barbara Dohrenwend (1975) indicate that clarification of the methodological problems traditionally involved in life events research is forthcoming. More attention is being given to the problems involved in defining relevant life events, obtaining accurate samples from representative populations, and improving measurement techniques. Investigation is now underway, according to Barbara Dohrenwend (1975), of intrinsic differences between types of events and cultural differences between people who interpret those events. Also under study are different styles of coping with both expected and unexpected events and the extent to which life events are experienced as within or outside an individual's control. This type of research suggests that the life change approach to the study of stress will become increasingly significant in the near future.

SUMMARY

The study of the relationship between social factors and stress-related diseases has advanced significantly in the past fifteen years, but the precise nature of this relationship is not yet fully understood. It is clear from existing studies, however, that the experience of stress is a subjective response on the part of an individual as a result of exposure to certain social experiences.

Before an assessment can be made of the effect of stress upon an individual, it will be necessary to know: (1) the nature of the threat itself; (2) the objective social environment within which the threat appears; (3) the psychological style and personality of the individual involved; (4) the subjective definition of the threat by the individual; (5) the social influences acting upon the individual, particularly the psychological supports offered by group membership; and (6) the duration of the threat. Obviously stress research represents a very complex investigative effort. But the potential contribution of such research to both the social and medical sciences is great. As House (1974) has pointed out, stress research offers opportunities to learn more about a phenomenon which has implications not only for understanding disease processes, but also for understanding a wide range of human behavior, such as suicide, delinquency, social movements, family violence, child abuse, mental health, and many other important social problems.

chapter **4**

THE PROCESS
OF SEEKING
MEDICAL CARE

Just as certain people perceive specific social conditions to be stressful and others do not, so too will some people recognize particular physical symptoms such as pain, a high fever, or nausea, and seek out a physician for treatment; others with similar symptoms may attempt self-medication or dismiss the symptoms as not needing attention. These differences in deciding whether or not to seek medical care have been and are continuing to be the subject of extensive investigation in medical sociology. Although the exact processes involved in making the decision to obtain medical care are not fully identified or understood at present, enough data have been collected in recent years to support a relationship between individual interpretation of deviation in physical functioning and social and psychological factors.

For those individuals and groups concerned with the planning, organization, and implementation of health care delivery systems, the question of what social influences encourage or discourage a person from seeking medical treatment is of great significance. An understanding of the help-seeking process in medicine can have a tremendous impact upon the structuring of health services for maximum utilization by people living in a community, both in terms of providing better medical care and making that care more accessible to the people who need it.

Medical sociologists and other behavioral scientists also want to find out how help-seeking behavior for medical care relates to the wider range of behaviors in which people attempt to obtain services generally. This type of research is essential to understanding what makes social life possible. The focus of this chapter, however, will be upon reviewing the social processes influencing the decisions of individuals to use professional medical services. First, relevant sociodemographic variables will be examined. These, however, explain only that variations in health services utilization exist, rather than *why* they exist. Thus our second topic will be selected social-psychological models of medical help-seeking. Only when certain conditions are satisfied in a person's mind can we expect him or her to go to the doctor.

SOCIODEMOGRAPHIC VARIABLES

A significant portion of past research in medical sociology has concerned itself with the effect of sociodemographic variables on the utilization of health care services. The reader should keep in mind that help-seeking behavior often involves interaction between several variables acting in combination to influence specific outcomes in specific social situations. Nonetheless, attempts to isolate some sociodemographic variables have resulted in studies of such factors as age, sex, ethnicity, and socioeconomic status, explaining how they relate to the behavior of people seeking medical care.

Age and Sex

The findings for age and sex have been fairly consistent: use of health services is greater for females than for males and is greatest for the elderly. As indicated in Chapter Two on social epidemiology, it is clear from existing data that females report a higher morbidity and, even after correcting for maternity, have a higher rate of hospital admissions (Andersen and Anderson, 1979). If extent of knowledge about the symptoms of an illness is considered, it also appears that women generally know more about health matters than men (Feldman, 1966; Nathanson, 1977). In addition, the proportion of females in a household appears to be strongly related to the number of physician visits for that household. It has been shown, for instance, that the larger the proportion of females in a particular household, the greater the demand or requirement for physicians (Wan and Soifer, 1974).

Perhaps it is obvious to say that people over sixty-five years of age are in poorer health and are hospitalized more often than other age groups (Susser and Watson, 1971; Andersen and Anderson, 1979). But the general literature on health care utilization, including fairly recent studies in Rhode Island (Monteiro, 1973a; Kronenfeld, 1978), Los Angeles County (Galvin and Fan, 1975), and in five New York and Pennsylvania counties (Wan and Soifer, 1974), substantiates the supposition that elderly people are more likely to visit a physician. In Los Angeles County, Michael Galvin and Margaret Fan (1975) found public insurance and disability were directly related to the frequency of physician visits. Thus since older people were more likely both to be physically disabled and to have public insurance (Medicare or Medicaid) coverage, they tended to visit a doctor fairly often.

One of the clearest indicators of the public's contact with the medical profession is the portion of the population who visit physicians. Table 4–1 shows the number of physician visits per person in the United States by sex and age for 1975. Except for birth through age fourteen, females exhibited a lifelong pattern of visiting doctors more often than males. Table 4–1 indi-

TABLE 4–1.   Number of Physician Visits per Person per Year in the United States by Sex and Age, 1975

Age in Years	Males	Females
Under 5	7.3	6.4
5–14	3.6	3.2
15–24	3.3	5.5
25–34	3.7	6.7
35–44	3.4	6.1
45–54	4.2	6.5
55–64	5.3	6.4
65–74	6.3	6.8
75 and over	6.5	6.7
All ages:	4.3	5.7

SOURCE: National Center for Health Statistics, *Physician Visits, Volume and Interval Since Last Visit, United States—1975*, Series 10, No. 128 (Washington, D.C.: Department of Health, Education and Welfare, 1979).

cates three peaks in the visitation pattern for females. Initially, there are high rates during childhood, followed by a decline until a second rise during the childbearing years. After thirty-five, there is once again a decline, but physician visits by females steadily increase after age forty-five. For males, there are high rates of visits during childhood, followed by comparatively low rates of physician services until a gradual increase begins at age forty-five. For the entire period under review, females saw a physician 5.7 times a year compared to 4.3 visits for males.

Ethnicity

Several studies in medical sociology have attempted to relate a person's utilization of health care services to his or her cultural background. One of the most systematic studies has been Edward A. Suchman's (1965a) study of the extent of the belief in and acceptance of modern medicine among several ethnic groups in New York City. Suchman sought to relate individual medical orientations and behaviors to specific types of social relationships and their corresponding group structures. He believed the interplay of group relationships with an individual's personal orientation toward medicine affected his or her health-seeking behavior.

To measure the influence of group structure, scales were developed to assess three levels of group involvement: the community level (the tendency of people to interact with other people of their own ethnic background), the social group level (the degree to which individuals belonged to limited friendship groups of long duration), and the family level (the dominance of family ties in an individual's life according to submissiveness to family authority and tradition). Group structures were further classified as either cosmopolitan or parochial. To measure individual medical orientations, three scales were also designed to assess the cognitive (knowledge of disease), the affective (skepticism of the ability of health professionals to treat disease), and the behavioral (dependency in illness and need for help) aspects of dealing with sickness and medical care. A person's individual attitudes were regarded as either scientific or popular.

Suchman felt that individual medical orientations and group structures were related in that members of cosmopolitan groups would hold scientific attitudes and parochial group members would hold popular and nonscientific beliefs. Although a serious question exists concerning the validity of combining different levels of group structure and aspects of individual medical beliefs into two gross, summary classifications of cosmopolitan-parochial and scientific-popular (see Reeder and Berkanovic, 1973)—and not all of Suchman's hypotheses were supported by his data—there was substantial confirmation.

Members of parochial groups did appear to subscribe to popular beliefs about medicine instead of scientific views. Persons in a parochial group were also found to have close and exclusive relationships with family, friends, and members of their ethnic group, and to display limited knowledge of disease, skepticism of medical care, and high dependency in illness. They were more likely than the cosmopolitan group to delay in seeking medical care and more likely to rely upon a "lay-referral system" in coping with their symptoms of illness. A lay-referral system consists of nonprofessionals—family members, friends, neighbors, etc.—who assist an individual in interpreting his or her symptoms and in recommending a course of action. The concept of the lay-referral system originated with Eliot Freidson (1960), who described the process of seeking medical help as involving a group of potential consultants, beginning in the nuclear family and extending outward to more select, authoritative laypersons, until the "professional" practitioner is reached. Freidson suggests that when cultural definitions of illness contradict professional definitions, the referral process will often not lead to the professional practitioner. The highest degree of resistance to using medical services in a lay-referral structure is found in lower-class neighborhoods characterized by a strong ethnic identification and extended family relationships. As Darwin Sawyer (1980) indicates, the decision to seek out a physician is based not just on professional standards of appropriate illness behavior but also on lay norms, and the two may be in conflict.

By contrast, the cosmopolitan group in Suchman's study demonstrated low ethnic exclusivity, less limited friendship systems, and fewer authoritarian family relationships. Additionally, they were more likely than the parochial group to know something about disease, to trust health professionals, and to be less dependent on others while sick.

Studies of racial/ethnic minorities in the United States, such as blacks and Mexican-Americans, seem to support Suchman's theory. The next two sections will discuss some of this research.

Blacks. Ralph Hines (1972) claims that preventive medicine is largely a white middle-class concept which provides a patient with an elaborate structure of routine prenatal and postnatal care, pediatric services, dental care, immunizations, and screening for the presence of disease. Even today it may be exceptional for some blacks to seek contact with health professionals without first turning to pseudo- and paramedical healers among friends and relatives or to consult with druggists and practical nurses. Only after a series of successive failures at treatment Hines believes, do these blacks turn to official health agencies for help. Hines blames the failure to use preventive health facilities on a lack of value orientation regarding such services. It can probably be attributed to a lack of financial resources as well. For those blacks living at a subsistence level, the only option seems to be welfare medicine, which by its very nature is often bureaucratic and impersonal. Thus being black—and especially being poor —appears to militate against the use of certain health services.

The tendency of some low-income black people to seek the services of lay practitioners rather than physicians is illustrated in the work of Loudell Snow (1978), who studied black folk healers in Chicago. Black folk healers and their patients, according to Snow, subscribe to a belief system that— unlike modern medicine—does not differentiate between science and religion. All life events, including illness, are viewed in relation to the total environment as either natural or unnatural, good or evil. Being healthy is an instance of good fortune like having a good job, a faithful spouse, and so forth. Being sick is an example of misfortune like unemployment and marital strife. Thus, life is *generally* good or bad and the cure for *one* problem, says Snow, might cure *all* problems.

Additionally, Snow notes that folk diagnosis of a health problem emphasizes the *cause* of the problem, not the symptoms. Having a body rash might initially be seen as stemming from a lack of cleanliness, but come to be defined as the result of black magic. In this belief system, what is important is not the rash, but what or who brought on the rash. Snow gives the following example:

> Even when a direct cause-and-effect relationship is known which is equivalent to the professional view this may be supported by religious or magical overtones. The sister of one of my informants died of bacterial meningitis, an etiology clearly understood by the family. But why did the organism invade her system at all? In their view to punish the father for "drinking and running around with women."[1]

Another prominent belief is that all illnesses can be cured, if not by medicine, then by magic. This belief is supported by the idea that illnesses are either natural or unnatural. Natural illnesses are those maladies caused by abusing the natural environment (staying out too late, eating too much, failing to wear warm clothing) or brought on as a punishment by God for sin or for not living up to the Lord's expectations. Thus, in the case of divine punishment, the afflicted person must make contact with God either directly or indirectly through an intermediary such as a faith healer. "Prayer and repentence," reports Snow (1978:73),"not penicillin, cure sin."

[1]Loudell F. Snow, "Sorcerers, Saints, and Charlatans: Black Folk Healers in Urban America," *Culture, Medicine, and Psychiatry* 2 (1978):71.

Unnatural illnesses are outside of "God's plan" and beyond self-treatment or treatment prescribed by friends and relatives. And, if the mind is affected, unnatural illnesses are thought to be beyond the capabilities of physicians, who are usually associated just with the treatment of natural illnesses that have obvious physical symptoms. The cause of an unnatural illness can be worry or stress, but often the etiology is ascribed to evil influences or acts of sorcery. When black magic is suspected it is necessary to find a healer with unusual magic or religious powers who can successfully intervene for the victim.

Snow observed that the term "healer" in Chicago's black community included a bewildering array of persons performing different healing roles. The variety of healers is reflected in the number of names used to describe them, such as healer, root doctor or root worker, reader advisor, spiritualist, or conjure man or woman. If voodoo is practiced, a male healer may be called *houngan* or *papaloi*, a female healer would be a *mambo* or *maraloi*. Few of them refer to themselves as "doctor," since healing is only part of their services. Instead, their given name is likely to be prefaced by a kinship, religious, or political title, such as Sister, Brother, Mother, Reverend, Bishop, Prophet, Evangelist, Madam. These healers will depend on word of mouth for patient referrals or they may advertise by newspaper or leaflet. They will claim to have received their ability to heal as a result of: (1) learning (which confers little status since almost anyone can be expected to learn); (2) during an altered state of consciousness, such as a profound religious experience or a divine "call" to healing; or (3) ability conferred at birth. Snow states (1978:79), "they will probably have in common only the assertion that the abilities are a gift from God."

Many healers do not require direct personal contact with the recipient of services, but will conduct business over the telephone or by mail. If the individual's complaint involves sorcery, the use of some substance, such as oils, potions, or perfumes, will be required purchases; if witchcraft is at work, a thought, prayer, or verbal spell is necessary. In the case of witchcraft, it might be necessary to purchase candles to assist the healer in effecting a solution. For example, when Snow complained in a letter to "Sister Marina" that she had problems sleeping and eating, was losing weight, and did not seem to enjoy life any more, Sister Marina replied in writing:

> I am so sorry I took so long to write but I had to take your letter into my church to see if what I suspected about your case was true. I had suspected an unnatural problem and I was right. But writing everything to you that I have learned would have to fill 10 pages of paper and maybe you still would not fully understand so I am asking you to phone me so that I can explain to you better the history of your case and let you know what will be needed to help you. I have lit a special candle for you and my spirits have told me since you have written to me you have felt slightly better. But if you want to be helped call me.[2]

Snow wrote back asking if Sister Marina could help her by mail and she

---

[2] Snow, "Sorcerers, Saints, and Charlatans," p. 99.

received a warning by return mail that if she did not hurry it might be too late to save her. Sister Marina wrote:

> In order for me to take your case I must burn 9 candles for you to find out just what it is I must do to get rid of this UNNATURAL PROBLEM and remove this EVIL! And each candle cost $10.00 each it would come up to $90.00 to help and if you do not either bring it to Chicago or send it within a week and 1/2 which would be about 11 days I cannot except your case because you might get too bad off and then no one will be able to help if you decide to come to see me please call me a day ahead of time and let me know.[3]

How effective black folk healers like Sister Marina are in treating their clients is not known. Some of these healers are likely to be frauds. Yet the advantage they offer to their clients is that they are readily available, results are usually quick and sometimes guaranteed, and they claim to be able to solve any problem. Their abilities are supposed to be derived from divine authority and, if they fail, they can attribute the failure to the will of God. In essence, what black folk healers appear to accomplish is to reduce the anxieties of their clients, and they are most effective in dealing with health problems that have some emotional basis. What is particularly significant in the reduction of anxiety, and what distinguishes their practice, is the recognition that health problems are an integral part of such other problems of daily life as lack of money, a strayed spouse, loss of a job, or envious relatives or neighbors. Consequently, black folk healers treat the whole person, not just a single symptom, which is often the case with a physician. Moreover, physicians tend to charge significantly higher prices for their services, are not as readily available in low-income areas, and may be unable to show quick results because of the patient's delay in seeking treatment or the severity of the disorder, or both.

While the Snow study dealt with low-income blacks living in an urban area, other data on similar blacks living in a rural setting point toward the same kind of pattern. Julian Roebuck and Robert Quan (1976) compared the health practices of fifty black and fifty white lower-class households in a small town in Mississippi. Although the white households tended to have a somewhat higher average income, practically all of the households received supplemental income from public assistance and welfare programs. Overall educational levels for both black and white households was between the fifth and sixth grades, and those household members who were employed held jobs that were either semiskilled or unskilled. There were important differences, however, when it came to seeking treatment for health problems. More white (68 percent) than black (48 percent) households sought health care only from physicians. More black (42 percent) than white (24 percent) households obtained care from a combination of practitioners—physicians, marginal healers, and illegal healers. Somewhat more whites (8 percent) than blacks (4 percent) went to marginal healers (defined as chiropractors, osteopaths, pharmacists, podiatrists, nurse-midwives). As for illegal healers

---

[3] Snow, "Sorcerers, Saints, and Charlatans," p. 99.

(defined as folk practitioners, spiritualists, sorcerers), 6 percent of the black households used this source only compared to none of the white households.

In general, Roebuck and Quan found that lower-class blacks usually waited longer than lower-class whites before seeking the services of a healer when sick. Blacks were less oriented toward Western scientific medicine than whites and believed more in the effectiveness of illegal healers (who were sometimes used along with physicians). One black respondent, for example, stated: "The doctor thought I had a stroke because I couldn't move, but the hoodoo man said someone had placed stumbling blocks in front of me and he chased it away" (Roebuck and Quan, 1976:157). Another black respondent said: "I saw Sister Cherokee [spiritualist] and she rubbed some olive oil on the back of my neck and told me I was suffering from high blood—exactly what the doctor told me!" (Roebuck and Quan, 1976:157). Many of the blacks not only believed in the effectiveness of the illegal healers but had a corresponding lack of faith in physicians as well. None of the whites used the illegal healers in any capacity, nor expressed confidence in their methods.

Other research conducted by Snow (1977) among lower-class blacks in a community in the Southwest United States shows health practices similar to those found by Snow in Chicago and Roebuck and Quan in Mississippi. Sick people are typically channeled through a lay-referral system of family and neighbors to a source of medical treatment, which in many cases will not be a physician. Sometimes physicians are consulted only as a last resort. When visits to physicians' offices by ambulatory (walk-in) patients are considered, National Center for Health Statistics (1979a) data for 1975 and 1976 show that 7.8 percent of the total office visits by patients of *all* races were made by blacks.[4] This represented an average annual visit rate of 1.9 office visits per year for each black person in the United States, considerably below the rate of 2.8 office visits per person per year estimated for the entire United States population for this period. Table 4–2 shows office visits per year for black patients by sex and age as compared to patients for all other races for 1975–1976. In each sex and age category, black rates for visitations to physicians' offices is lower than rates for all other patients.

While blacks appear to seek health care in physicians' offices less frequently in comparison to the total population, black patients tend to use other sources of ambulatory services with relatively greater frequency. The National Center for Health Statistics (1979a), for example, estimates that blacks visit hospital outpatient clinics and emergency rooms at rates two to three times greater than whites. Data from the 1974 Health Interview Survey, shown in Table 4–3, help illustrate this trend. According to this national survey, 60.1 percent of all whites used a private doctor's office or clinic as their major source of care. The category of "all other," which consists largely of blacks, shows a considerably smaller proportion of 45.3 percent

[4]Ambulatory patients are people who present themselves for personal health services, but who are not bedridden nor patients in health care institutions. An office is a place that a physician uses for ambulatory practice and does not include hospital outpatient clinics, emergency rooms, etc.

TABLE 4–2. Number of Office Visits per Year for Black Patients and Patients of All Races, by Sex and Age: United States, 1975–1976

Sex and Age	Black Patients	All Patients
TOTAL	1.9	2.8
Sex		
Female	2.2	3.3
Male	1.4	2.5
Age		
Under 15 years	1.0	2.0
15–24 years	1.5	2.2
25–44 years	2.5	2.7
45–64 years	2.8	3.4
65 years and over	2.7	4.3

SOURCE: National Center for Health Statistics, *Advance Data—Office Visits by Black Patients, National Ambulatory Medical Care Survey: United States, 1975–76*, No. 50 (Washington, D.C.: U.S. Department of Health, Education and Welfare, July 23, 1979).

reporting private doctor's office or clinic as major source of care. Higher percentages of whites used group practices (17.3 percent versus 12.2 percent) and received medical advice from physicians over the telephone (17.4 percent versus 6.7 percent). Conversely, higher percentages of "all others" used hospital outpatient clinics (16.4 percent versus 7.8 percent) and emergency rooms (16.4 percent versus 13.8 percent), and public health clinics (5.4 percent versus 2.2 percent).

Except for the larger percentage of females (64.1 percent) than males (51.9 percent) using private doctor's office or clinic, the percentages shown in Table 4–3 for sources of care by age, geographic region, and place of residence do not show striking differences. Major sources of care by income, however, fall into a pattern similar to that shown by race. A greater percentage of those persons reporting higher incomes use the private doctor's office or clinic, group practice, or telephone. Whites had likewise preferred these same sources of health care. People with low incomes made more use of hospital outpatient clinics, hospital emergency rooms, public health clinics, and neighborhood health clinics. Since many racial/ethnic minority groups tend to have low incomes, it is not a coincidence that utilization patterns by race and income are similar.

Patterns of help-seeking behavior for medical care by blacks in American society are not influenced as much by race or ethnicity as they are by conditions of poverty and the limitations of low income. For most purposes, visits to private doctors' offices and clinics are not covered by health insurance in the United States and the cost must usually be borne by the patient. Efforts by blacks to use public medical facilities and, in some cases, folk healers, can

TABLE 4–3. Number and Percent of Persons Utilizing Specific Sources or Places of Outpatient Medical Care During Year Prior to Interview, by Selected Characteristics: United States, 1974

Characteristic	Number of Persons in Thousands	Source or Place of Care									
		Private Doctor's Office or Clinic	Group Practice	Telephone	Hospital Outpatient Clinic	Hospital Emergency Room	Company or Industry Clinic	Public Health Clinic	Neighborhood Health Center	Home	Other
		Percent of persons utilizing any services									
All persons[1]	207,334	58.2	16.6	16.1	8.9	14.1	3.1	2.6	1.0	1.5	2.5
Sex											
Male	100,024	51.9	14.6	12.2	8.4	15.1	4.7	2.2	0.8	1.2	2.8
Female	107,309	64.1	18.4	19.7	9.4	13.2	1.6	2.9	1.1	1.8	2.2
Age											
Under 17 years	62,953	55.6	19.8	23.0	8.3	16.2	0.2	3.7	1.4	1.3	2.1
17–44 years	80,778	58.9	15.1	14.5	9.6	15.4	5.5	2.8	1.0	1.0	3.4
45–64 years	42,862	58.0	15.3	11.0	9.1	10.7	4.0	1.3	0.4	1.4	1.9
65 years and over	20,740	63.9	15.3	11.6	7.5	9.5	0.4	1.0	0.5	4.6	1.1
Color											
White	180,725	60.1	17.3	17.4	7.8	13.8	3.1	2.2	0.7	1.6	2.4
All other	26,608	45.3	12.2	6.7	16.4	16.4	3.2	5.4	2.8	1.2	2.7
Family Income											
Less than $5,000	32,316	54.6	13.0	10.4	13.1	15.9	1.7	5.0	2.2	2.0	2.7
$5,000–$9,999	47,398	56.2	14.8	14.4	10.0	15.6	3.0	3.3	1.1	1.4	2.2
$10,000–$14,999	51,666	59.1	17.7	17.9	7.7	14.3	3.4	2.1	0.8	1.1	2.2
$15,000 or more	63,265	62.5	19.7	19.6	7.2	12.5	3.9	1.4	0.4	1.7	2.9
Geographic Region											
Northeast	49,196	61.4	10.8	16.1	9.4	15.9	3.6	1.7	0.9	2.7	3.2
North Central	55,543	57.7	18.7	17.8	8.5	13.8	3.6	2.1	0.9	1.2	2.4
South	65,232	60.8	16.9	14.6	8.5	13.8	2.6	3.4	1.1	1.1	1.9
West	37,363	55.2	22.1	16.0	9.6	12.7	2.5	2.9	0.9	1.2	2.4
Place of Residence											
SMSA	142,954	58.6	16.6	17.4	9.8	14.8	3.7	2.5	1.1	1.7	2.7
Central city	62,520	54.9	15.4	15.3	12.5	15.3	3.9	3.4	1.7	1.9	2.7
Outside central city	80,435	61.4	17.5	19.1	7.7	14.4	3.5	1.8	0.6	1.5	2.6
Outside SMSA	64,379	57.5	16.7	13.0	6.9	12.6	1.7	2.8	0.7	1.2	2.0
Nonfarm	56,856	58.0	16.3	13.5	7.1	13.0	1.8	2.8	0.7	1.3	2.2
Farm	7,523	53.9	19.8	9.7	5.4	9.6	0.8*	2.1	0.6*	0.5*	0.9*

[1] Includes persons with unknown income.

SOURCE: National Center for Health Statistics, Advance Data—Access to Ambulatory Health Care: United States, 1974, No. 17 (Washington, D.C.: U.S. Department of Health, Education and Welfare, February 23, 1978).

be seen as attempts to cope with health problems within the context of one's resources and social environment. Even though black Americans have made significant progress in obtaining equal opportunity in employment and education, largely as a result of the civil rights movement of the 1960s, the disparity between blacks and whites in regard to social and economic benefits still exists for many black people. This continued socioeconomic disadvantage translates into continued health disadvantages.

Mexican-Americans. Many Mexican-Americans are also prone to use the services of nonprofessionals in health care matters. Taher Moustafa and Gertrud Weiss (1968) state that low-income Mexican-Americans often consult physicians only late in their illness and in general demonstrate a lack of confidence in professional health personnel. Instead they tend to favor the use of "folk" medicine, which involves treatment by friends, relatives, or neighbors who employ patent medicine and home cures for ailments.

Mexican-American folk healers are known as *curanderos*. Like black folk healers, curanderos blend religion and folk medicine into a single therapeutic approach. They likewise classify illnesses primarily on the basis of *what* causes the disorder rather than the symptoms and they do not separate the natural from the supernatural when it comes to diagnosis and treatment. Most of their patients are lower class. Unlike black folk healers, curanderos do not charge for their services or they charge very little. They may ask for a small donation (perhaps a dollar or two) for expenses or they may accept a small gift such as vegetables or a chicken.

Curanderos also appear to use religion to a much greater extent than black folk healers. Ari Kiev (1968) points out that religion, based upon a Spanish Catholic tradition, is central to the curandero, who believes life is ordained by the divinity and good health and happiness can only be achieved by those who keep God's commandments. A patient who suffers, therefore, is seen as helping God's plan for the universe since it is believed that God allows men to suffer in order to learn. The example of Christ suffering on the cross is often used to illustrate that suffering and illness can be a worthwhile experience. Thus, the curandero views helping the patient accept suffering as a major task. In this context, suffering is explained as being part of the patient's burden for the world's sin and ignorance and a necessary role in God's plan for the universe. The more religious the curandero appears to be and the more convincing he or she is in influencing others to accept the will of God, the more highly regarded the curandero is as a healer. One effect the curandero uses to help accomplish this task is to establish a work setting that supports his or her image. Kiev describes it like this:

> Each curandero works in his own unique setting, depending usually upon his degree of affluence. The basic atmosphere created is invariably the same. In general, the curandero sees patients in part of his home set aside for treatment. These rooms, even in poor slums, are distinctive because of the great number of religious objects contained in them. The presence of numerous pictures and statues of the Virgin Mary and Jesus, of various sized crosses and religious candles, which are often arranged around an altar in a corner of the room,

creates an atmosphere of religious solemnity which makes one forget the poverty of the slum or the humble shack of the curandero. Indeed, in such treatment rooms one feels as if in a church, and cannot help but view the curandero with awe and respect.

> The therapeutic effect of this "temple in the home" cannot be minimized. The quiet calm can invoke a feeling of security and protectiveness in the frightened and anxious. . . . perhaps most important is the authority the curandero derives through his relationship to the setting. It makes him the object of respect and awe and puts him in command of much of the power that derives from the patient's response to the setting and the symbolism. By relying upon religious symbols and objects that have great meaning for the patients, he can immediately establish himself as a man of wisdom and authority, which undoubtedly increases the patient's willingness to cooperate and his expectations of relief.[5]

Besides prayer and religious counseling, the curandero employs a variety of folk drugs and herbs to produce a cure (rattlesnake oil, mineral water, garlic, sweet basil, wild pitplant, licorice, camphor). To a very large extent this approach is based on sixteenth-century Spanish medicine, derived largely from Greek and Arabic sources, and influenced by beliefs of the Mayans and Aztecs. Prevalent in this view is the Hippocratic notion of bodily equilibrium. Hippocrates, the famous physician of ancient Greece, believed that good health resulted from the equilibrium within the body of four humors of blood, phlegm, black bile, and yellow bile. Important, too, was the harmony of the body with living habits and the environment. As long as the four humors were in balance, the body was healthy. If an imbalance occurred, however, and more of one type of humor than another was present, a person was sick. Because the body is perceived as being a mix of cold and hot conditions, curanderos use "hot" foods and medicines to treat "cold" conditions (drowsiness, chills) and "cold" foods and medicines to treat "hot" conditions (fever, hypersexuality).

The most dreaded form of disorder, either physical or mental, is that caused by witchcraft. Witches, or *brujas,* are evil persons who supposedly have made pacts with the devil and use supernatural powers in the form of curses, magic, herbs, or ghosts to harm other people. According to William Madsen (1973), who studied Mexican-Americans living in south Texas, even though belief in witchcraft is more strongly denounced than other folk theories of disease by the churches and in newspapers and schools, conservative lower-class Mexican-Americans showed an almost universal acceptance of the existence of witchcraft. Hence, curanderos were needed to provide "good" power to offset "evil" influences.

Kiev (1968) points out that curanderismo persists in the American Southwest because it works in many cases. The advantage the curandero brings to the treatment setting is that he or she works in a subculture supportive of beliefs in the effectiveness of the curandero's methods. Especially important is the anxiety-reducing approach of the curandero, carried out within the context of family and friends, that defines the treatment as

[5]Ari Kiev, *Curanderismo* (New York: Free Press, 1968), pp. 129–30.

therapeutic and positive according to the norms and values of the Mexican-American community. While Anglos may view illness as impersonal and unemotional in origin, caused by germs, lower-class Mexican-Americans may see illness as related to one's interpersonal relationships, community life, and religion.

In San Jose, California, Margaret Clark (1959) observed that physicians or nurses who denied the existence of the "evil eye" or other syndromes of "folk" medicine were regarded as either "liars" or "fools." Madsen (1973) found in south Texas that even when Mexican-American patients consulted a physician, they would terminate the relationship unless the response to treatment was rapid. Yet when modern medicine produced a cure, Madsen observed that credit for that cure was often attributed to folk treatments which preceded, accompanied, or followed scientific treatment. Hospitalization, except in time of crisis, was also avoided like a plague. "To be separated from the family," Madsen (1973:95) states, "and isolated in an Anglo world is well-nigh intolerable for the conservative Mexican-American. Next to prison, the hospital is most dreaded as a place of isolation in an impersonal and enigmatic world."

However, a study in Nebraska (Welch et al., 1973) suggests that some Mexican-Americans are not exceptionally different from Anglos in their attitudes toward health care. This study found that Mexican-Americans have family doctors, go regularly to the dentist, and freely utilize other official health services. Madsen, too, mentions a greater frequency of physician visits among Mexican-Americans, particularly for the treatment of children. In south Texas, reliance upon modern medicine was most likely among the upper classes and those with the highest level of education. The assimilation of Anglo norms and values by Mexican-Americans apparently includes a tendency toward increased physician contact. Yet, folk medicine is still a viable form of help-seeking behavior for lower-income Mexican-Americans. The few existing large-scale social surveys of the help-seeking behavior of Mexican-Americans in regard to professional medical services still point toward relatively low rates of utilization, perhaps the lowest rates of any racial/ethnic minority group in the United States. At least this is the trend suggested by studies conducted in Los Angeles (Berkanovic and Reeder, 1973; Galvin and Fan, 1975) and Alameda (Roberts and Lee, 1980) Counties in California and the 1977 Health Interview Survey consisting of data collected on a nationwide basis (HEW, 1980). Mexican-Americans appear to have somewhat lower rates than Anglos and blacks for visits to physicians and substantially lower rates for physical examinations and eye examinations. Mexican-Americans have higher rates for visits to dentists than blacks, but these rates are markedly lower than those for Anglos. Lower utilization rates for Mexican-Americans seem to be largely a function of socioeconomic status (lower income and education) rather than ethnicity (Roberts and Lee, 1980).

Social Networks.   What is suggested by Suchman's (1965a) study and studies of low-income blacks and Mexican-Americans is that, under certain conditions, close and ethnically exclusive social relationships tend to channel help-seeking behavior, at least initially, toward the group rather than professional health care delivery systems. Yet Reed Geertsen et al., (1975) replicated Suchman's study in Salt Lake City and found an opposite trend. They observed that the Mormon community, with its strong value on good health and education, and its emphasis upon family authority and tradition, demonstrated that group closeness and exclusivity can increase, rather than decrease, the likelihood of an individual responding to professional health resources. They concluded that people who belong to close and exclusive groups, especially tradition- and authority-oriented families are (1) more likely to respond to a health problem by seeking medical care if it is consistent with their cultural beliefs and practices, or are (2) less likely to seek medical care if their cultural beliefs support skepticism and distrust of professional medicine.

Geertsen et al., focused on the family rather than the ethnic group as the critical social unit in determining help-seeking behavior; the family is the person's first significant social group and usually the primary source of societal values. Thus knowledge of disease and family authority appear as the key intervening variables in a person's medical orientation, as knowledge assists in recognition of symptoms, while family authority impels the sick person into the professional health care system. Alternatively, low knowledge about disease and/or weak family authority could act as inhibiting factors in obtaining professional treatment.

In Boston, Jeffrey Salloway (1973) observed similar processes in the help-seeking behavior of the gypsy community. Gypsies, according to Salloway, are among the poor, uneducated, and ethnically distinct of American society whom most studies have found to exhibit the lowest rates of health care utilization. Salloway's study demonstrated, to the contrary, that gypsies were rather sophisticated when it came to obtaining treatment in Boston's complex, urban medical system. Although nonliterate or semi-literate, gypsies operated an extensive communication network in their community through which they informed each other on a regular basis who was sick, where they were being treated, who was treating them, and how pleased or displeased the patient, family, and other interested parties were with the treatment. Visits of gypsies to health practitioners or a visit by a practitioner to the gypsies was invariably a public affair. Information about the problem and its treatment were shared and became part of a general fund of community knowledge.

Salloway points out the existence of an extensive accumulation of data among family and friends concerning past diagnoses, the treating agency, the prescription, and the prognosis for specific disorders. Gypsies were also very much aware of the differences in the quality of care available at local hospitals and out-patient clinics, including the specialities they offered, and the identity of care providers receptive to their needs. They were thus able to utilize available health care services more extensively than many disadvantaged minority groups because of an unusual intragroup network of communication.

What is suggested here is not that ethnicity per se is important, but that ethnicity represents a social experience that influences how a particular person perceives his or her health situation. Individuals are born into a family of significant others—significant because they provide the child with a specific social identity. This identity includes not only an appraisal of physical and intellectual characteristics, but knowledge concerning the social history of a particular family and group with all that means in terms of social status, perspective, and cultural background. As the child becomes older and takes as his or her own the values and opinions of the immediate family or group, or those of the wider society as presented through the mediating perspective of the family, the child is considered to be properly socialized in that he or she behaves in accordance with group-approved views.

Admittedly, children can either accept or reject the social perspective put forth by their family as representative of their own social reality; yet the choices offered to them in the process of their socialization are set by adults who determine what information is provided and in what form it is presented. Thus, although children may not be entirely passive in the socialization experience, what is important, as Peter Berger and Thomas Luckmann (1967) explain, is that they have no choice in the selection of their significant others so that identification with them is quasi-automatic. This further means that children's internalization of their family's interpretation of social reality is quasi-inevitable. While this initial social world presented to children by their significant others may be weakened by later social relationships, it can nevertheless be a lasting influence on them.

Therefore, it is not surprising that a person's family or social group often guides the perceptual process or signals the perspective from which the total society is viewed. For this reason, medical sociologists like John McKinlay (1972) and Salloway (1973) have emphasized the social network as a determining factor in help-seeking behavior. A social network refers to the social relationships a person has during day-to-day interaction which serve as the normal avenue for the exchange of opinion, information, and affection. Typically, the social network is composed of family, relatives, and friends that comprise the individual's immediate social world, although the concept of a social network can be expanded to include increasingly larger units of society.

In the case of health care utilization, the role of the social network and its specific values, opinions, attitudes, and cultural background act to suggest, advise, or coerce an individual into taking or not taking particular courses of action regarding health care. Conformity with the social network's recommendations could reduce a person's anxiety by ensuring the approval of significant others. McKinlay (1973) found, for example, that people with close-knit and interlocking social networks tended to display greater conformity with these reference groups than those with loose-knit, differentiated social networks.

To return to our discussion of ethnicity, patterns of help-seeking behavior among lower-class ethnic groups appear to be strongly influenced by both the conditions of poverty and the existence of tightly knit social networks. Another variable that confounds the effect of ethnicity is socioeconomic status. August Hollingshead and Frederick Redlich's (1958) influential study of social stratification and mental illness clearly points out that the higher a person's socioeconomic position, the less ethnic the person appears to be. In other words, middle-class blacks, Mexican-Americans, Asian Americans, etc., tend to take on white or Anglo middle-class norms and values as part of their participation in middle-class society. Included in this process of socialization, and the obtainment of status through the sharing of common norms, values, and lifestyle, is the adoption of middle-class perspectives toward health care utilization. Socioeconomic status, as measured by income and education, seems to be a much stronger predictor of health services utilization than ethnicity. Ethnicity as a predictor of help-seeking behavior is thus apparently limited to its role in providing a cultural context for decision making within social networks.

Socioeconomic Status

Another major approach to the study of help-seeking behavior has been its correlation with socioeconomic status. Until recently, it was generally believed that lower-class persons tended to underutilize health services because of the financial cost and/or a subculture of poverty that failed to emphasize the importance of good health. The seminal study in this regard was Earl Koos's *The Health of Regionville* (1954). Koos conducted his study in a small community in New York where he found it possible to rank the local residents into three distinct socioeconomic classes. Class I consisted of the most successful people in town in terms of financial assets. Class II represented middle-class wage earners who were the majority of citizens, while Class III represented the least skilled workers and poorest members of the community.

The relationship between socioeconomic status and the seeking of medical care by Regionville's people is shown in Table 4–4, which summarizes the responses by socioeconomic class to indicate whether each of a selected list of easily recognized symptoms were considered to be significant enough to be brought to the attention of a doctor.

Table 4–4 shows that Class I respondents demonstrated a much higher level of recognition of the importance of symptoms than either Class II or Class III. Only two of the symptoms, loss of appetite and backache, were reported by less than three-fourths of Class I as needing medical attention. Otherwise, almost all Class I respondents were prepared to go to a physician if a symptom appeared. For only one symptom, persistent coughing, did Class I respondents not have the highest percentage and this difference was negligible.

Class III respondents, on the other hand, showed a marked indifference to most symptoms. Seventy-five percent of the lower-class respondents considered ten of the seventeen symptoms not serious enough to warrant medical attention. Only three symptoms (excessive vaginal bleeding and blood in stool and urine) achieved a response of 50 percent or more, and all of these were associated with unexplained bleeding.

Thus, in Regionville at the time of Koos's study in the early 1950s, symptoms did not necessarily lead to seeking medical treatment, especially among the lower class. In addition, Class III persons were also inhibited

TABLE 4–4.   Percent of Respondents in Each Social Class Recognizing Selected Symptoms as Requiring Treatment

Symptom	Class I (N = 51)	Class II (N = 335)	Class III (N = 128)
Loss of appetite	57	50	20
Persistent backache	53	44	19
Continued coughing	77	78	23
Persistent joint and muscle pains	80	47	19
Blood in stool	98	89	60
Blood in urine	100	93	69
Excessive vaginal bleeding	92	83	54
Swelling of ankles	77	76	23
Loss of weight	80	51	21
Bleeding gums	79	51	20
Chronic fatigue	80	53	19
Shortness of breath	77	55	21
Persistent headaches	80	56	22
Fainting spells	80	51	33
Pain in chest	80	51	31
Lump in breast	94	71	44
Lump in abdomen	92	65	34

NOTE: Percentages have been rounded to the nearest whole number.
SOURCE: From Earl. L. Koos, *The Health of Regionville* (New York: Columbia University Press, 1954), p. 32. Reprinted with permission of Columbia University Press.

from seeking treatment because of cost, fear, and relative need as related to age and the role of the sick person. The very young, the elderly, and breadwinners were most likely to receive medical attention among the poor. Another important factor in help-seeking behavior for Class III persons was group expectations about symptoms, further suggesting the importance of the social network. Backache, for example, was a symptom the poor commonly defined as not being a serious ailment. For the poor, having a backache was nothing unusual.

For a time, Koos's study helped establish the premise that lower-class persons are less likely than others to recognize various symptoms as requiring medical treatment and that these beliefs contribute to differences in the actual use of services. This premise was supported by the conclusions of surveys by the National Center for Health Statistics in 1960 and 1965, which found that higher-income persons were utilizing the physician to a much greater extent than lower-income persons.

In 1968, however, the National Center found a changing pattern of physician utilization. It was now the middle-income group, consisting of those persons earning between $3,000 to $9,999 a year, who had become the underutilizers. Highest rates of physician visits were either persons with the lowest (under $3,000) level of income or the highest level (over $10,000). The higher rate for the low-income group was largely due to Medicaid and Medicare health insurance programs. Medicaid, administered at the state level, provides coverage intended to help pay the cost of health care for the poor. Medicare, a federal program, provides coverage for the elderly, who are overrepresented in the low-income group.

Since 1968 several studies (Bellin and Geiger, 1972; Bice et al., 1972; Monteiro, 1973a; Sparer and Okada, 1974; Benham and Benham, 1975; Galvin and Fan, 1975; Andersen and Anderson, 1979) have confirmed that it can no longer be assumed that low-income persons underutilize physician services. Between 1963 and 1970, as the effects of Medicaid and Medicare became realized, the use of physician services by low-income persons increased to the point that the significance of the relationship between income and utilization was greatly diminished (Benham and Benham, 1975). In fact, by 1970, it could be demonstrated that the poor had the higher rates of physician use than any other income group. For example, according to data collected by Ronald Andersen and Odin Anderson (1979) for selected years between 1928 and 1974, the low-income group had the lowest rates (2.2 visits per person per year) of physician utilization from 1928 to 1931. The middle-income group ranked in the middle (2.5 visits) and the high-income group had the highest number of (4.3) visits. This pattern remained until 1970, when the low-income group emerged with the highest rates (5.2 visits), followed by the high-income group (4.9 visits) and the middle-income group (4.4 visits).

Table 4–5 shows the number of physician visits per person per year in the United States for 1975. These rates, based upon National Center for Health Statistics (1979b) data, show physician visits by income, race, and education. The lowest-income group (less than $5,000 annually) has the highest rate at 6.0 physician visits per person per year. The next income group ($5,000 to $9,999 annually) shows 5.2 visits and the highest-income group ($10,000 or more annually) has the lowest rate of 4.9 visits. Hence, the traditional association of higher income with greater physician use is not supported. Since the 1950s, rates of physician visits by the higher income group have remained about the same (approximately five visits per person

TABLE 4–5. Number of Physician Visits per Person per Year by Family Income, Race, and Education of Head of Family: United States, 1975

Characteristic	Mean Number of Physician Visits per Person per Year
Family Income	
Less than $5,000	6.0
$5,000–$9,999	5.2
$10,000 or more	4.9
Race	
White	5.1
Black	4.7
Education of Head of Family	
Less than 5 years	4.8
5–8 years	4.9
9–11 years	4.9
12 years	4.9
13 years or more	5.5

SOURCE: National Center for Health Statistics, *Physician Visits, Volume and Interval Since Last Visit, United States—1975*, Series 10, No. 128 (Washington, D.C.: U.S. Department of Health, Education and Welfare, April 1979).

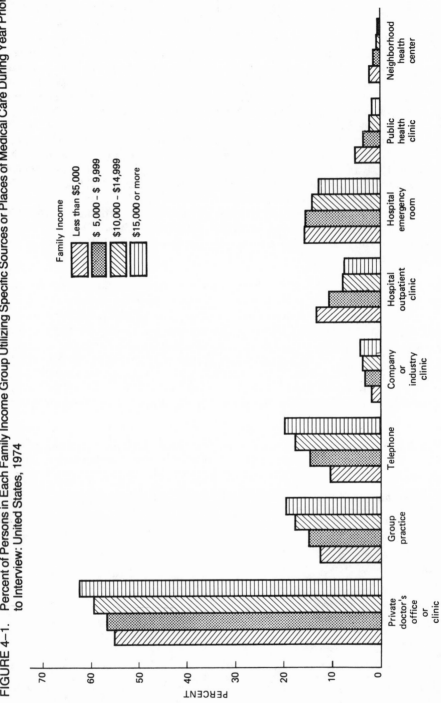

FIGURE 4–1.   Percent of Persons in Each Family Income Group Utilizing Specific Sources or Places of Medical Care During Year Prior to Interview: United States, 1974

Family Income

Less than $5,000
$ 5,000 – $ 9,999
$10,000 – $14,999
$15,000 or more

SOURCE: National Center for Health Statistics, *Advance Data—Access to Ambulatory Health Care: United States, 1974*, No. 17 (Washington, D.C.: U.S. Department of Health, Education and Welfare, February 23, 1978).

per year), while the rates for the other two income groups have increased to the point that they now make the most physician visits.

As for race and education, Table 4–5 shows that whites have more visits (5.1 per year) to physicians than blacks (4.7 per year). Heads of families with the highest level of education (thirteen years or more) also see doctors more often (5.5 visits) than heads of families with less education. The lowest rates of physician visits by education (4.8 visits) are for family heads with the lowest level of education (less than five years). The other groups ranked by education show the same rate of 4.9 visits. While it might be assumed that blacks and people with the least education would have shown significant advances in rates of utilization because many of them are likely to have low incomes and possibly be eligible for Medicaid benefits, such is not the case. Among low-income persons, apparently whites and the relatively better educated are utilizing physicians more than others in this category.

Even though the poor are visiting doctors in greater numbers, this does not mean that they use the same sources of medical treatment in proportions equal to that of higher-income groups. Figure 4–1 depicts the sources of medical care used by family income groups in the United States in 1974. Figure 4–1 is a graphic representation of the data shown in Table 4–3 on family income and source of ambulatory care. Differences between income groups in regard to where they seek care are obvious and consistent. People in families with higher incomes were more likely than those with lower incomes to have received medical services in private doctors' offices and clinics, group practices, or over the telephone. The higher-income groups were slightly more likely to contact company or industrial clinics. However, the reverse situation was true for other sources of care. Figure 4–1 shows that people in families with lower incomes were more likely to contact hospital outpatient clinics, emergency rooms, public health clinics, and neighborhood health centers. Although families of all income groups are seen to use each source shown in Figure 4–1, a clear pattern emerges of a dual health care system—a "private" system with a greater proportion of the higher income groups and a "public" system with a preponderance of lower income groups. In the public system, the patient is likely to receive less quality medical care, spend longer amounts of time in waiting rooms, not have a personal physician, cope with more bureaucratic agencies, and return after treatment to a living situation that is less conducive to good health.

Furthermore, when actual *need* for health services is taken into account, low-income persons appear to use fewer services than high-income persons (Aday and Andersen, 1975; Kravits and Schneider, 1975; Dutton, 1978). Diane Dutton (1978) points out that statistics showing increased use of health services by the poor can be misleading. She argues that the poor have higher rates of disability due to illness and that the poor also tend to be more likely to seek symptomatic care.[6] The nonpoor, in turn, are more likely to

[6]Dutton additionally states that utilization rates for children, which are hidden in overall rates, show almost twice as many physician visits for high-income children than their low-income counterparts. She bases this argument on 1971 National Center for Health Statistics data, but 1975 data show no significant differences in such rates for children. In 1975, the rate for low-income children was even slightly higher than that of high-income children (4.7 visits per year versus 4.6 visits).

seek preventive care, which is aimed at keeping healthy people well, instead of waiting to seek help when symptoms appear. Thus, the poor appear to have more sickness and, despite the significant increase in use of services, still do not obtain as much health care as they actually need. Using data collected in Washington, D.C. during 1970–1971, Dutton tested three different explanations concerning why the poor would show lower use rates in relation to actual need than the nonpoor: (1) financial coverage, (2) the culture of poverty, and (3) the systems barrier.

The financial coverage explanation consists of the claim that the poor cannot afford to purchase the services they need—the cost is high, income is low, and insurance programs are inadequate. Dutton found this explanation to be weak. Public health insurance, notably Medicaid, had stimulated use of services by the poor to a much greater extent than private health insurance had done for the nonpoor. Unlike many private insurance plans, Medicaid paid for most physician services and thereby promoted physician utilization. Conversely, private insurance, with the exception of prepaid plans, had less impact on seeking physician services.

The culture of poverty explanation is derived from the premise that attitudes and norms characteristic of poor people tend to retard use of services. For example, the poor may view society and professional medical practices as less than positive as a result of their life experiences. The poor may also be more willing to ignore illness or not define it as such because they must continue to function to meet the demands of survival. Dutton found the culture of poverty explanation to have some validity when combined with measures of income. As income decreased, belief in preventive checkups and professional health orientation also decreased, while degree of social alienation increased. "Of course," says Dutton (1978:359), "these differences may not reflect cultural variation so much as realistic adaptation to economic circumstances; preventive care may well be less important than paying the rent, and purchasing a thermometer may be viewed as an unaffordable luxury." Nevertheless, Dutton argues that attitudes related to the culture of poverty do play an important role in explaining differences in the use of health services between income groups, particularly the use of preventive care.

In Dutton's view, the strongest explanation for low use of services by the poor in relation to need was the systems barrier explanation. This explanation focused on organizational barriers inherent in the more "public" system of health care typically used by the poor, such as hospital out-patient clinics and emergency rooms. This type of barrier pertains not just to the difficulty in locating and traveling to a particular source of care, but also includes the general atmosphere of the treatment setting, which in itself may be impersonal and alienating. For example, as Anselm Strauss comments:

> The very massiveness of modern medical organization is itself a hindrance to health care for the poor. Large buildings and departments, specialization, division of labor, complexity, and bureaucracy lead to an impersonality and an overpowering and often grim atmosphere of hugeness. The poor, with their meager experience in organizational life, their insecurity in the middle class world, and their dependence on personal contacts, are especially vulnerable to this impersonalization.

Hospitals and clinics are organized for "getting work done" from the staff point of view; only infrequently are they set up to minimize the patient's confusion. He fends for himself and sometimes may even get lost when sent "just down the corridor." Patients are often sent for diagnostic tests from one service to another with no explanations, with inadequate directions, with brusque tones. This may make them exceedingly anxious and affect their symptoms and diagnosis. After sitting for hours in waiting rooms, they become angry to find themselves passed over for latecomers—but nobody explains about emergencies or priorities. They complain they cannot find doctors they really like or trust.

. . . To the poor, professional procedures may seem senseless or even dangerous—especially when not explained—and professional manners impersonal or brutal, even when professionals are genuinely anxious to help.[7]

Dutton (1978, 1979) found from her research that low-income patients in "public health care systems confronted a lack of preventive examinations (physicians had little time for counseling patients or providing preventive care), high charges for services, long waiting times, and relatively poor patient–physician relationships. Dutton's (1978:361–362) position was that this situation posed a highly significant barrier that discouraged low-income patients "from seeking care, *above and beyond* the deterrent effects of inadequate financial coverage and negative attitudes toward professional health care." Low utilization was therefore seen as a normal response to an unpleasant experience.

The majority of people in the Dutton study were black. Subsequent research by Thomas Rundall and John Wheeler (1979) on the effect of income on use of preventive care involved a sample of respondents living in Washtenaw County, Michigan who were mostly white. Dutton's findings were confirmed. There was no support for the financial coverage explanation. There was some support for the culture of poverty explanation in that the poor perceived themselves as relatively less susceptible to illness (they could tolerate unhealthy conditions) and therefore were less likely to seek preventive services. However, there was strong support for the systems barrier explanation. People with relatively high incomes were more likely to have a regular source of care and those individuals with a regular source of care were more likely to use preventive services.

Having a regular source of care has increasingly been identified as an important variable in help-seeking behavior (see also Aday and Andersen, 1975; Andersen and Aday, 1978; Kronenfeld, 1978). Ronald Andersen and LuAnn Aday (1978), for instance, have suggested that a variable having great impact on physician use is the presence of a particular physician who is the person's regular source of care. This situation implies that the patient is relatively comfortable with the relationship and has some trust in the physician's skills at diagnosis and treatment. Low-income people receiving medical care in the public sector are less likely to have a personal physician and must be treated by whatever physician happens to be on duty in a hospital or clinic. If they have to maneuver between several clinics and public assistance agencies to obtain either treatment or authorization for treatment, low-

[7] Anselm L. Strauss, "Medical Ghettos," *Where Medicine Fails* (Chicago: Aldine, 1970), pp. 14, 15.

income people will be subject to even more fragmented and ill-coordinated patterns of health care.

What is necessary to improve this situation, according to Rundall and Wheeler (1979), is increased health education for low-income people and changes in the organization of health care that will provide regular sources of treatment that will respect the dignity of the patient. Simply expanding public health insurance programs does not seem to be a sufficient measure for increasing health services utilization by the poor in relation to their need for services.

Discussion

There are, of course, other variables related to help-seeking behavior —for example, education, marital status, and the time, energy, effort, and distance required to see a doctor. Generally, education has been found to be related to socioeconomic status in that well-educated persons, usually in the upper income group, tend to have more knowledge of disease and more sensitivity to symptoms. This may be changing, however, as the poor have shown evidence of a relatively high degree of sophistication with respect to those symptoms that should be brought to the attention of a physician (Bellin and Geiger, 1972). Findings regarding marital status vary, but generally it seems that the influence of a spouse encourages a married person to maintain a state of good health. Often single persons, widows, and widowers show lower rates of physician visits than married persons. The effects of time, energy, effort, and distance have also been found as significant barriers to physician utilization, but these factors may likewise be changing due to the greater availability of health services in some low-income areas to treat patients covered by Medicaid and Medicare.

These trends have prompted some medical sociologists to suggest that perhaps sociodemographic variables are no longer as important in determining health care utilization as they were once thought to be (Bice et al., 1972; Anderson and Barktus, 1973). Also, age has been found to lack significance in explaining the relationship between income and physician visits (Monteiro, 1973a). The sex variable may be significant only because women report more illnesses than do men. The masculine role probably dictates a "business as usual" attitude even though a man may feel sick. The influence of ethnicity on health care utilization is largely due to the shared framework within which ethnic groups view the provision of health services. Because of the widespread influence of the mass media and the availability of increased upward social mobility, middle-class norms and values may become more important influences on health care utilization, regardless of ethnicity.

Nonetheless, sociodemographic variables should not be ignored as explanations for seeking medical care. American society has not become so homogenized that sociodemographic differences between people have totally disappeared, nor are they likely to in the foreseeable future. Andersen and his associates (Aday and Andersen, 1975; Andersen et al., 1975), for example, have developed a multivariate behavioral model of health services use.

This model consists of predisposing, enabling, and need components which describe a person's decision to use health services. The predisposing component consists of sociodemographic variables and attitudes and beliefs about health care. The enabling component refers to factors such as family income, health insurance coverage, availability of services, and access to a regular source of care. The predisposing and enabling components establish the conditions within which a person is or is not likely to seek health services when stimulated by need (symptoms, disability, or diagnosis). This model has been used in several studies and shown modest success in describing variance in health services utilization on the basis of such variables as age, sex, education of head of household, and having a regular source of care (Andersen et al., 1975; Andersen and Aday, 1978; Mechanic, 1978). A particular problem with this model, however, is that it is descriptive and lacks a theoretical foundation. Such models offer insight into *what* is going on by describing the process taking place, but do not explain *why* the process is occurring. Knowledge about sociodemographic variables and health services utilization is important information, yet what is also needed is the development of social psychological models that underlie the perceptual processes guiding the seeking of health care.

SOCIAL-PSYCHOLOGICAL MODELS OF HEALTH CARE UTILIZATION

The major social-psychological models of help-seeking behavior discussed in this chapter refer to the concepts of health behavior and illness behavior. Health behavior is the activity undertaken by a person who believes himself or herself to be healthy for the purpose of preventing disease, while illness behavior is the activity undertaken by a person who feels ill for the purpose of defining that illness and seeking relief from it (Kasl and Cobb, 1966).

Health Behavior and the Health Belief Model

One of the most influential social-psychological approaches designed to account for the ways in which healthy people seek to avoid illness is the Health Belief Model of Irwin Rosenstock (1966) and his colleagues (Becker, 1974). The Health Belief Model is derived to a great extent from the theories of Kurt Lewin and other psychologists who believe that people exist in a life space composed of regions with both positive and negative valences (values). An illness would be a negative valence and would have the effect of pushing a person away from that region, unless doing so would cause the person to enter a region of even greater negative valence (e.g., risking disease might be less negative than failing at an important task). While people are pushed away from regions with negative valences, they are attracted toward regions of positive valences. Thus, a person's behavior might be viewed as the result of seeking regions which offer the most attractive values.

Within this framework, human behavior is seen as being dependent upon two primary variables: (1) the value placed by a person upon a particular outcome and (2) the person's belief that a given action will result in that outcome. Accordingly, the Health Belief Model, shown in Figure 4–2, sug-

FIGURE 4–2.   The Health Belief Model

INDIVIDUAL
PERCEPTIONS

MODIFYING
FACTORS

LIKELIHOOD
OF ACTION

Demographic variables (age, sex, race, ethnicity, etc.)
Sociopsychological variables (personality, social class, peer and reference group pressure, etc.)
Structural Variables (knowledge about the disease, prior contact with the disease, etc.)

Perceived benefits of preventive action
minus
Perceived barriers to preventive action

Perceived Susceptibility to Disease "X"

Perceived Seriousness (Severity) of Disease "X"

Perceived Threat of Disease "X"

Likelihood of Taking Recommended Preventive Health Action

Cues to Action
Mass media campaigns
Advice from others
Reminder postcard from physician or dentist
Illness of family member or friend
Newspaper or magazine article

SOURCE: Marshall H. Becker (ed.), *The Health Belief Model and Personal Health Behavior* (San Francisco: Society for Public Health Education, Inc., 1974), p. 334. Reprinted with permission of Marshall H. Becker.

gests that preventive action taken by an individual to avoid disease "X" is due to that particular individual's perception that he or she is personally susceptible and that the occurrence of the disease would have at least some severe personal implications.

Although not directly indicated in Figure 4–2, the assumption in this model is that by taking a particular action, susceptibility would be reduced, or if the disease occurred, severity would be reduced. The perception of the threat posed by disease "X," however, is affected by modifying factors. As shown in Figure 4–2, these factors are demographic, sociopsychological, and structural variables which can influence both perception and the corresponding cues necessary to instigate action. Action cues are required, says Rosenstock, because while an individual may perceive that a given action will be effective in reducing the threat of disease, that action may not be taken if it is further defined as too expensive, too unpleasant or painful, too inconvenient, or perhaps too traumatic.

So despite recognition that action is necessary and the presence of energy to take that action, a person may still not be sufficiently motivated to do something. Thus, the likelihood of action also involves a weighing of the perceived benefits to action contrasted to the perceived barriers. Therefore, Rosenstock believed that a stimulus in the form of an action cue was required to "trigger" the appropriate behavior. Such a stimulus could be either internal (perception of bodily states) or external (interpersonal interaction, mass media communication, or personal knowledge of someone affected by the health problem).

The Health Belief Model has been employed successfully in several studies of (preventive) health behavior, such as the taking of penicillin prophylaxis for heart disease (Heinzelman, 1962), vaccination against Asian influenza (Leventhal et al., 1960), the seeking of dental care (Kegeles, 1963; Gochman, 1971, and dietary compliance among obese children (Becker et al., 1977). Help-seeking behavior was observed in each of these studies to be based upon the value of the perceived outcome (avoidance of personal vulnerability) and the expectation that preventive action would result in that outcome. For example, the Gochman (1971) study found that if children are motivated to have good health in general, their perception of vulnerability to tooth disease and the benefits of visiting the dentist will result in their intentions to seek future dental care. Conversely, those children with low health motivation are not as likely to have the future intention of seeing a dentist. In the Becker et al. (1977) study, 182 pairs of mothers and their obese children were divided into three groups while the children participated in a weight reduction program. The groups consisted of (1) a high fear group (shown alarming material about the potentially unfavorable consequences of being fat in later life), (2) a low fear group (shown similar but less threatening information), and (3) a control group (shown no additional information). Children in the control group did not lose weight. Children in the low fear group lost some weight initially, but also tended to put some of it back on. The high fear group lost the most weight and did not put any of it back on. The intervention of a fear-arousal cue in the high fear group had a marked effect on the mothers' notions of the perceived susceptibility, seriousness, and benefits of compliance for their children.

Unfortunately, the usefulness of the Health Belief Model is limited in that it has been applied mostly to preventive situations in which the behavior studied is voluntary. Obviously, however, many people who seek health services are motivated to take action only by the appearance of clear and definite symptoms. Therefore, it remains to be seen whether an improvement in health and the avoidance of future disease are strong enough motivating factors for healthy people to use health care delivery systems.

Nevertheless, the Health Belief Model has demonstrated considerable utility in the study of health behavior and may yet be modified to account for illness behavior as well (see Kirscht, 1974; Becker, 1979). The merit of the model is that even when an individual recognizes personal susceptibility, he or she may not take action *unless* the individual also perceives that being ill will result in serious difficulty. Thus, the individual's subjective assessment of the health situation becomes the critical variable in the utilization of health services. In fact, a person's subjective assessment may be more important than an objective medical diagnosis. Several studies show no (sometimes even a negative) correlation between medical estimates of health and patient compliance (see, for example, Becker and Maiman, 1975). David Mechanic (1972) has noted that the difficulty in preventive medicine is that common sense approaches do not necessarily match clinical approaches, and common sense often determines whether or not health services are sought. Furthermore, once a patient subjectively feels well, physicians may be faced with the additional problem of encouraging the patient to continue to follow medical advice.

Illness Behavior

In contrast to health behavior, illness behavior pertains to people who perceive themselves as being sick. Mechanic and Volkart (1961:52) describe illness behavior as "the way in which symptoms are perceived, evaluated and acted upon by a person who recognizes some pain, discomfort or other signs of organic malfunction."

Several studies have suggested that laypersons generally define illness in terms of the ability or nonability to carry out activities. Dorrian Apple (1960), for instance, noted that laypersons' judgments about whether or not a person is sick were based upon two criteria: (1) the recency or novelty of the experience, behavior, or attribute, and (2) the degree to which the experience interferes with normal activities. Barbara Baumann (1961) found that laypersons distinguish between health states according to three major factors: (1) feelings of well-being, (2) an absence of symptoms, and (3) a state of being able to perform those activities that a person in good health should be able to do. Conversely, to be sick would mean feeling bad, the presence of symptoms, and not being able to engage in usual activities. Andrew Twaddle (1969) also identified three signs people perceived as illness: (1) changes in feeling states, the most important being the occurrence of pain and weakness; (2) incapacity for normal role performance; and (3) other symptoms or changes in the biological state of the organism regarded as important because of their presumed implications for future activities.

Thus, what laypersons recognize as illness is in part deviance from a standard of normality established by common sense and everyday experience. Especially important is the capacity to act out one's social roles in a normal fashion. However, other factors are also important. Mechanic and Volkart (1961) have suggested that a given illness manifests specific characteristics with regard to symptom recognition and the extent of danger. Illness recognition is determined by how common the occurrence of the illness is in a given population and how familiar people are with its symptoms. Illness danger refers to the relative predictability of the outcome of the illness and the amount of threat or loss that is likely to result. When a particular symptom is easily recognizable and relatively devoid of danger, it is likely to be defined as a routine illness. When a symptom occurs infrequently, making identification more difficult, and is combined with an increasing perception of danger, there is likely to be a greater sense of concern.

Yet, as Mechanic (1978) has noted, recognition of a symptom, while certainly a necessary condition to motivate help-seeking behavior, is not in itself sufficient for a definition of illness. Some illnesses, such as appendicitis, may have obvious symptoms, while other illnesses, such as the early stages of cancer, may have little visibility. Also there are cases of persons who, despite symptoms, delay seeking health care. Cancer patients have been known to avoid cancer screening procedures because of their anxiety about learning the truth and being forced to confront what it means to have cancer (Becker and Maiman, 1975). Therefore, the characteristics of illness recognition and illness danger can be significant influences on the manner in which people perceive a disease.

We can see an example of this in the experience of British sociologist Ann Holohan (1977), who visited a physician to receive treatment for what she thought would be diagnosed as an infection in her breast resulting from an injury a few months previously. She recognized she had a health problem but saw no particular danger from it. The physician discovered a lump in her breast and asked her to report to a hospital for a biopsy. The effect of this request was "shattering" because she had not even considered the possibility that she might have cancer. The discovery of the lump had come as a complete surprise and knowledge of its existence left her reeling with dismay. She suddenly had difficulty hearing her physician as he quoted the odds for and against the possibility of the tumor being malignant. She reports:

> His voice seemed to be coming from a distance, and I could only pick up stray words. Physically he appeared to become smaller and smaller, his voice fainter and fainter, while a jumble of thoughts about my family and survival pressed in on me. Inwardly I protested "it cannot be me." Yet I found myself writing automatically in my diary "hospital admission" and the date. It was sandwiched between the social commitments of a normal weekend—meeting friends, attending a concert, and I knew I would not be there.
>
> I got up, struggled to preserve normality (this seemed enormously important) and was astonished to hear myself asking mundane questions about admission procedures for tomorrow. He opened the door and still in a state of utter turmoil, I walked into the street. It seemed incredible that nothing had changed—the sun was still shining, the road sweeper gathering the leaves. I sat in my car, and with the conventional constraints removed, immense waves of panic engulfed me. I drove blindly home and recall very little of the actual journey. I felt this alien, pathological change was inexorable, gone was the reassuring external cause of my symptoms. Yet clearly I was no "sicker" than before my consultation. All that had changed was the possibility of a medical label for my symptom.[8]

Upon her return home, Holohan did some housework as a form of denial. She reasoned that if she could still perform household chores she could not be seriously ll. She considered not going to the hospital for the

<hr>

[8]Ann Holohan, "Diagnosis: The End of Transition," in A. Davis and G. Horobin (eds.), *Medical Encounters: The Experience of Illness and Treatment* (New York: St. Martin's Press, 1977), pp. 87–88.

biopsy, but she was unsure about what might happen if she declined to go. The thought of even touching the lump in her breast was repulsive to her. Her course was set. Illness recognition and danger were too strong to ignore. She felt she had to have the biopsy because the situation could be very serious. She entered the hospital and the results of the biopsy indicated that she did not have a malignant tumor. While leaving the hospital, however, another woman who was being discharged for the same reason remarked to her: "I wonder what would have happened if it had been the other way. It's like asking what's on the other side" (Holohan, 1977:96).

Mechanic (1978:268–269) has formulated a general theory of help-seeking since his initial work with Volkart in the early 1960s. He suggests that whether or not a person will seek medical care is based on ten determinants: (1) visibility and recognition of symptoms; (2) the extent to which the symptoms are perceived as dangerous; (3) the extent to which symptoms disrupt family, work, and other social activities; (4) the frequency and persistence of symptoms; (5) amount of tolerance for the symptoms; (6) available information, knowledge, and cultural assumptions; (7) basic needs that lead to denial; (8) other needs competing with illness responses; (9) competing interpretations that can be given to the symptoms once they are recognized; and (10) availability of treatment resources, physical proximity, and psychological and financial costs of taking action. In addition to describing these ten determinants of help-seeking behavior, Mechanic explains that they operate at two distinct levels: other-defined and self-defined. The other-defined level is, of course, the process by which other people attempt to define an individual's symptoms as illness and call those symptoms to the attention of that person. Self-defined is where the individual defines his or her own symptoms. The ten determinants and two levels of definition supposedly interact to influence a person to seek or not seek help for a health problem.

The central theme that forms a backdrop for Mechanic's general theory of help-seeking is that illness behavior is a culturally and socially learned response. A person responds to symptoms according to his or her definition of the situation. This definition may be influenced by the definitions of others, but is largely shaped by learning, socialization, and past experience as mediated by a person's social and cultural background. Although Mechanic's theory provides a plausible explanation of the decision-making process leading up to contacting a physician, it does not explain what happens after the initial contact is made (Wolinsky, 1980). Nor does the theory detail the manner in which the determinants and levels of definition interact with one another. It also does not account for health behavior in which healthy persons seek a physician for preventive care. Finally, Mechanic's theory has not been tested to date in any systematic fashion to determine its validity. As a general theory of help-seeking behavior, Mechanic's theory has its shortcomings. As a theory of perceptual considerations relevant to an initial decision by a person to visit a physician for health care, Mechanic's work helps to explain the context of the decision-making process.

One approach that provides insight into the entire sequence of events involved in seeing a physician beyond the initial visit is Suchman's (1965b)

FIGURE 4–3. Suchman's Stages of Illness Experience

	I Symptom Experience	II Assumption of the Sick Role	III Medical Care Contact	IV Dependent-Patient Role	V Recovery and Rehabilitation
Decision	Something is wrong	Relinquish normal roles	Seek professional advice	Accept professional treatment	Relinquish sick role
Behaviors	Application of folk medicine, self-medication	Request provisional validation for sick role from members of lay referral system—continue lay remedies	Seek authoritative legitimation for sick role—negotiate treatment procedures	Undergo treatment procedures for illness—follow regimen	Resume normal roles
Outcomes	Denial (flight into health) → Delay → Acceptance	Denial → Acceptance	Denial → Shopping → Confirmation	Rejection → Secondary gain → Acceptance	Refusal (chronic sick role) → Malingerer → Acceptance

SOURCE: Rodney M. Coe, *Sociology of Medicine* (New York: McGraw-Hill, Inc., 1970, 1978), p. 108. Reprinted with permission of McGraw-Hill, Inc.

description of the stages of illness experience. According to Suchman, when individuals perceive themselves becoming sick they can pass through as many as five different response stages, depending upon their interpretation of their particular illness experience. These stages, shown in Figure 4–3, are (1) the symptom experience, (2) the assumption of the sick role, (3) medical care contact, (4) the dependent-patient role, and (5) recovery and rehabilitation.

The illness experience begins with the symptom stage, in which the individual is confronted with a decision about whether or not "something is wrong." The decison of the person involved may be to deny the symptoms as not needing attention, to delay making a decision until the symptoms are more obvious, or to accept the symptoms as evidence of a health disorder. The person may also attempt to treat himself or herself through the application of folk medicine or self-medication.

If the decision is made to accept the symptom experience as indicative of an illness, the person is likely to enter Suchman's second stage of the sick role. Here the person is allowed to relinquish normal social obligations provided permission is obtained from the person's lay-referral system. The lay-referral system can grant the individual provisional permission to assume the sick role. "Official" permission to adopt the sick role, however, can come only from the physician, who acts as society's agent as the authority on illness. Thus, while lay remedies may continue, the individual is again faced with a decision to deny the illness and abandon the illness experience or accept the provisional sick role and perhaps seek medical treatment.

If professional assistance is sought, the person enters the third stage of medical care contact. At this stage, the person attempts to obtain legitimation of his or her sick role status and to negotiate the treatment procedure. The illness experience may be confirmed or denied by the physician. If there is a disagreement between physician and patient, the patient may go "shopping" for another physician's diagnosis which might prove more acceptable.

If both patient and physician agree that treatment is necessary, the person passes into the dependent-patient stage. Here the person undergoes the prescribed treatment, but still has the option either to terminate or to continue the treatment. Sometimes patients settle for the "secondary gain" of enjoying the privileges accorded to a sick person, such as taking time off from work, and do not seriously try to get well. Or both patient and physician may cooperate to allow the patient to enter the fifth and final stage of recovery and rehabilitation. In this stage the patient is expected to relinquish the sick role and resume normal social roles. This may not happen, as in the case of a chronic illness or when the patient chooses to malinger in an illness experience even though technically well.

Although an illness experience may not involve all of the stages described by Suchman and can be terminated at any particular stage through denial, the significance of Suchman's model is that each stage requires the sick person to take different kinds of decisions and actions. In evaluating the experience of illness, the sick person must interpret not only his or her symptoms, but also what is necessary in terms of available resources, alternative behaviors, and the probability of success. Suchman's model is similar in its approach to the positions advocated by Rosenstock (1966), Mechanic and Volkart (1961), and Mechanic (1978), who likewise agree that individual perception is the key variable in assessing modes of coping with problems of health and illness. Rosenstock's Health Belief Model stressed the perception of personal susceptibility and the benefits of taking preventive action, whereas Mechanic and Volkart emphasized perception from the standpoint of illness recognition and illness danger and Mechanic, some years later, focused on illness behavior as a learned response.

SUMMARY AND CONCLUSION

This chapter has reviewed the major theories and findings of medical sociology concerning the process of seeking medical care and the utilization of health care services. While there is no single theory or approach that has earned general consensus, the existing literature reveals the two most important variables in health care utilization to be the perceived severity of symptoms and the ability to pay for the rendering of services.

Social-psychological models of help-seeking behavior have emphasized the importance of self-perception as it relates to a person's understanding of a particular symptom. Especially important is whether or not the person perceives himself or herself as able to perform normal social roles. Studies concentrating on ethnicity as a factor have pointed to the role of the social network in influencing the perceptual process according to the network's own sociocultural orientation. Social networks have been shown to be either barriers to the seeking of professional treatment, as in the case of blacks (Hines, 1972) and Mexican-Americans (Clark, 1959; Madsen, 1973), or as important forces channeling the sick into professional health care delivery systems, as in the case of gypsies (Salloway, 1973) and Mormons (Geertsen et al., 1975). Although some patients, notably cancer patients, may delay seeing a doctor because they are fearful about having their perceptions confirmed (Becker and Maiman, 1975), the generalization can be made that the more symptoms are perceived as representing a serious illness, the more likely it is that a person will seek professional services.

The ability to pay for health services has traditionally accounted for significant socioeconomic differences in health care utilization. Today it appears that public health insurance and social welfare monies have enabled the poor to visit physicians as frequently as the upper-income groups. However, whether increased physician visitation has resulted in a corresponding rise in the quality of health care provided the poor remains to be determined. Then, too, the poor still reside in an environment of poverty that perpetuates their increased risk to health hazards. Among those persons without public health insurance—those covered by private health insurance plans that still leave considerable cost for the individual consumer, or those without any health insurance—the ability to pay remains an important obstacle to help-seeking behavior.

This chapter also discussed the sociodemographic variables of age and sex, which were found to be consistent predictors of seeking medical care.

Elderly persons and females generally report more illness than younger persons and males, so it is not surprising that they tend to consult physicians more readily. Although some researchers have suggested that the significance of sociodemographic variables has been reduced to the point where they are no longer of major importance in analyzing help-seeking behavior, sociodemographic differences in health care utilization still exist and probably will continue to do so for some time to come.

Two other aspects of help-seeking behavior require further study: (1) the analysis of the organizational characteristics of health care services themselves, and (2) the relationship of seeking health care to other forms of help-seeking behavior. As McKinlay (1972) has noted, the social organization of services is another factor highly related to help-seeking behavior. Several studies on organizational structure and processes point to the tendency of bureaucracies to develop particular orientations toward their clients. These may result from the structure of rules and regulations or from differing social values, norms, beliefs, and lifestyles between the providers and the consumers; in any case, many of these orientations have been shown to limit services and perhaps neglect those clients in greatest need.

The organizational nature of health care institutions will be considered more fully in Chapter Nine, but it is important to note at this point that the full impact of bureaucratic processes on help-seeking behavior has not yet been documented. This is despite the fact that medical sociologists have condemned the structure of welfare medicine for its impersonal nature (Strauss, 1970) and have warned that cultural antagonism between health care providers and consumers may increase the psychological cost to the consumer of using the services (Berkanovic and Reeder, 1974; Dutton, 1978).

Further research is also needed in the area of relating action to seek medical care to help-seeking behavior in general. It appears that the initial step in help-seeking behavior is the individual's perception that something is either lacking or amiss. The next step is to decide whether a particular problem should be handled medically by visiting a physician or in some other way—by visiting a bartender, a friend or relative, a minister, or a lawyer. In other words, how does the decision to utilize health care services fit into the wider range of help-seeking behaviors for different types of problems? In the case of health care, there should be a belief that a cure can be obtained and that the cost in terms of time, money, effort, and energy is worth the total expenditure. Do people go to their bartenders, lawyers, or ministers for the same reasons? Furthermore, why do some people go to a physician with problems that could be handled as well or better by a bartender, lawyer, or minister? There is a great deal we do not know about what motivates someone to seek help in general or a certain type of help in particular.

chapter 5

THE SICK ROLE

Each society's definition of illness becomes institutionalized within its cultural patterns, so that one measure of social development is a culture's conception of illness. In primitive societies illness was defined as an autonomous force or "being," such as an evil spirit, which attacked people and settled within their bodies in order to cause them pain or death. During the Middle Ages illness came to be defined as a punishment for sins, and care of the sick was regarded as religious charity. Today illness is defined as a state or condition of suffering as the result of a disease or sickness. This definition is based upon the modern scientific view that an illness is an abnormal biological affliction or mental disorder with a cause, a characteristic train of symptoms, and a method of treatment.

ILLNESS AS DEVIANCE

The medical view of illness is that of deviance from a biological norm of health and feelings of well-being. This view involves the presence of a pathogenic mechanism within the body that can be objectively documented. The diagnosis of a disease, for example, results from a correlation of observable symptoms with knowledge about the physiological functioning of the human being. Ideally, a person is defined as ill when his or her symptoms, complaints, or the results of a physical examination and/or laboratory tests indicate an abnormality. The traditional identifying criteria for disease are: (1) the patient's experience of subjective feelings of sickness; (2) the finding by the physician that the patient has a disordered function of the body; and (3) the patient's symptoms conforming to a recognizable clinical pattern. The clinical pattern is a representation of a model or theory of disease held by the diagnostician. In diagnosis, logic is the basic tool.

The physician's function in the treatment of illness involves, first, arriving at a diagnosis and, second, applying remedial action to the health disorder in such a way as to return the human organism to as normal a state as possible. The evaluation of illness by the physician contains the medical definition of what is good, desirable, and normal as opposed to what is bad, undesirable, and abnormal. This evaluation is interpreted within the context of existing medical knowledge and the physician's experience. On this basis the medical profession formulates medical rules defining biological deviance and seeks to enforce them by virtue of its authority to treat those persons defined as sick.

In medical sociology, illness may be viewed as a deviant social state brought about by disruption of normal behavior through disease (a biological state). Sociologists generally prefer describing illness as a social rather than a biological event because the condition of suffering denoted by illness is a subjective experience that usually results in individuals' modifying their behavior. Therefore, while a disease represents a medical entity that can be defined in terms of biological, physiological, and psychological functioning, an illness can be regarded as a social entity definable in terms of social functioning (Suchman, 1965a).

The sociological view of illness as deviance was initially formulated by Talcott Parsons (1951) in his concept of the sick role—characteristic behaviors a sick person adopts in accordance with the normative demands of the situation. Parsons saw being sick as a disturbance in the "normal" condition of the human being, both biologically *and* socially. Previously, the sociological study of health and illness had relied upon the medical perspective; efforts were in fact limited to correlating social factors with biological factors based on references provided solely by the health practitioner. This medically oriented approach emphasized the physiological reality of the human organism, but neglected the sociological reality that a person is sick when he or she *acts* sick.

The basis for describing illness as a form of deviant behavior lies in the sociological definition of deviance as any act or behavior that violates the social norms within a given social system. Thus deviant behavior is not simply a variation from a statistical average. The statistical view of deviance, as Howard Becker (1973) has explained, is far too limited because it would define left-handed, red-headed people as deviant only because they would vary from the majority of people, who are right-handed brunettes.

Instead, a pronouncement of deviant behavior involves making a *social judgment* about what is right and proper behavior according to a social norm. Norms reflect expectations of appropriate behavior shared by people in specific social settings, or they may be more general expectations of behavior common to a wide variety of social situations. Conformity to prevailing norms is generally rewarded by group acceptance and approval of behavior; deviation from a norm, however, can lead to disapproval of behavior, punishment, or other forms of social sanctions being applied against the offender. Many norms allow for variation of behavior within a permissible range, but deviant behavior typically violates the range of permissible behavior and elicits a response from other people intended to control that behavior. Most theories of deviant behavior in sociology are concerned with behavior common in crime, delinquency, mental disorders, alcoholism, and drug addiction. These forms of behavior typically *offend* someone.

It is important to note that not all forms of deviant behavior produce undesirable consequences for a society. Deviance from the usual norms in such fields as art, music, theatre, literature, and the dance often provides very positive rewards both for the creative deviant and the society. However, illness as deviance is typically regarded as an undesirable circumstance for both the sick person and for society. For the sick person, an illness obviously can mean discomfort and either permanent or temporary disruption of normal biological and social functioning, including death. Illness also entails the risk of economic hardship for the sick person's family. For society, illness can mean a reduction in the ability of a social group or organization to carry out its usual tasks and perform its normal social functions.

While sociologists have suggested that the explanation for illness as a social event can be found outside of biology and medicine by including illness within the general category of deviant behavior, this approach has been relatively recent. The early causal theories of deviance in sociology were essentially biological models that defined the source of deviance as something inherent in certain individuals. Undesirable behavior was thought to be caused by the genetic inheritance of criminal traits or perhaps a capricious genetic combination. The biological view of deviance has been generally rejected by contemporary sociologists as concentrating exclusively on the physiology of the individual and completely overlooking the implications of social norms and social judgments about an individual's behavior.

In turn, these social judgments are influenced by various aspects of social change. For example, in our past agrarian society, illness occurred largely in small-group contexts such as the family. It was a common occurrence and the roles of being sick or attending sick people were part of a role-set that included expectable variations in behavior as well as "normal" behavior. The routine nature of illness and its occurrence in primary groups (as well as the relatively limited scope of treatment techniques) tended to draw illness into the area of expectable, nondeviant behavior. However, far-reaching changes have occurred in industrialized society: the decline of family cohesiveness, changing theories in the treatment of disease, and the evolution of complex medical techniques that often require hospitalization. These developments have tended to draw disease out of the area of the expectable into a highly specialized, institutionalized, somewhat mysterious context. Similarly, our attitudes toward sick people have increasingly tended to alienate them, transferring them to the care of specialists who operate outside the context of the familiar and over whom ordinary people have few powers of control. This transfer itself, coupled with our submission to hospital routines and medical "wonders," creates a specialized set of circumstances that lead to a definition of illness as deviance. The physically sick, like the insane and criminals, represent a social category of people removed from the mainstream of society if their illness is judged severe enough. Of course, the insane and criminals are much more stigmatized by society than the physically sick, but the point is that the pattern of treatment (removal from society and treatment by specialists) allows the person who is physically sick to be similar—though not identical—with the insane who go to asylums or criminals who go to prisons. Since the methods for dealing with ill persons and criminals or the insane are in certain respects similar, we can see a basis for defining illness as deviance.

THE FUNCTIONALIST APPROACH TO DEVIANCE

While sociologists reject biological models of deviance, present-day functionalism, stressing societal process, systems, equilibrium, and interrelationships, represents a modern version of a homeostatic theory of deviance. This model is not organic or physiological. It does not find the causes of deviant behavior in individual needs, drives, instincts, genetic combinations, or any other purely individual patterns. It does find the source of deviant behavior in the relationships between individuals and social systems. This approach is based on the view that society is held together in a cohesive range of equilibrium by harmonious patterns of shared norms and values. What makes social life possible is the *expectation* that people will behave in accordance with the norms and values common to their particular social system. This process is "functional" because it results in social harmony and counterbalances "dysfunctional" processes, like crime and mental illness, that disrupt the social order. The tendency of a society toward self-maintenance through equilibrium is very similar to the biological concept of homeostasis in which the human body attempts to regulate physiological (internal) conditions within a relatively constant range in order to maintain bodily functioning. A person may suffer from warts, indigestion, a broken leg, or perhaps even from a nonmalignant cancer and still be *generally healthy*. Likewise, a social system is viewed in the functionalist perspective as maintaining social functioning by regulating its various parts within a relatively constant range. A social system may have problems with crime and delinquency but be "healthy" because of its overall capacity to function efficiently.

Because functionalist theorists perceive social systems as composed of various closely interconnected parts, they argue that changes, decisions, and definitions made in one part of the system inevitably affect, to some degree, all other parts of the system. Thus, a person's position within the social system subjects him or her to events and stresses originating in remote areas of the system. Behavior that is adaptive from one's own perspective and peculiar circumstances may be regarded as deviant by society at large. The individual then has the choice of continuing the adaptive behavior and being defined as deviant or trying to change that behavior even though the person sees it as necessary for his or her own survival. Many people, not surprisingly, continue the disapproved behavior and are therefore pressured by society into being deviant. Such people run the risk of confrontation with those authorities, such as psychiatrists, the police, and the courts, charged with controlling or eliminating dysfunctional social processes. Deviance in a social system is thus reduced through the application of social sanctions against the offender. These sanctions include the use of jails, prisons, and mental hospitals to remove the deviant from society to ensure social order and cohesion.

According to functionalist theory, illness is dysfunctional because it also threatens to interfere with the stability of the social system. The medical profession functions to offset the dysfunctional aspects of illness by both curing and preventing disease and by establishing technology by which handicapped persons can assist in self-maintenance and in maintenance of the social system. This analytical approach is the basis for Parsons' theory of the sick role, a central concept in medical sociology today.

THE SICK ROLE

Talcott Parsons' (1951) concept of the sick role represents the most consistent approach to explaining the behavior characteristic of sick people in Western society. It is based upon the assumption that being sick is not a deliberate and knowing choice of the sick person, though illness may occur as a result of motivated exposure to infection or injury. Thus, while the criminal is thought to violate social norms because he or she "wants to," the sick person is considered deviant only because he or she "cannot help it." Parsons warns, however, that some people may be attracted to the sick role in order to have their lapse of normal responsibilities approved. Generally society accounts for the distinction between deviant roles by punishing the criminal and providing therapeutic care for the sick. Both processes function to reduce deviancy and change conditions that interfere with conformity to social norms. Both processes also require the intervention of social agencies, law enforcement or medicine, in order to control deviant behavior. Being sick, Parsons argues, is not just experiencing the physical condition of a sick state; rather it constitutes a social role becaue it involves behavior based on institutional expectations and reinforced by the norms of society corresponding to these expectations.

A major expectation concerning the sick is that they are unable to take care of themselves. It thus becomes necessary for the sick to seek medical advice and cooperate with medical experts. This behavior is predicated upon the assumption made by Parsons that being sick is an undesirable state and the sick person wants to get well.

Parsons insists that illness is dysfunctional because it represents a mode of response to social pressure that permits the evasion of social responsibilities. A person may desire to retain the sick role more or less permanently because of what Parsons calls a "secondary gain," which is the exemption from normal obligations and the gaining of other privileges commonly accorded to the sick. Hence, medical practice becomes a mechanism by which a social system seeks to control the illnesses of its deviant sick by returning them to as normal a state of functioning as possible.

The specific aspects of Parsons' concept of the sick role can be described in four basic categories:

1. *The sick person is exempt from "normal" social roles.* An individual's illness is grounds for his or her exemption from normal role performance and social responsibilities. This exemption, however, is relative to the nature and severity of the illness. The more severe the illness, the greater the exemption. Exemption requires legitimation by the physician as the

authority on what constitutes sickness. Legitimation serves the social function of protecting society against malingering.

2. *The sick person is not responsible for his or her condition.* An individual's illness is usually thought to be beyond his or her own control. A morbid condition of the body needs to be changed and some curative process apart from personal will power or motivation is needed to get well.

3. *The sick person should try to get well.* The first two aspects of the sick role are conditional on the third aspect, which is recognition by the sick person that being sick is undesirable. Exemption from normal responsibilities is temporary and conditional upon the desire to regain normal health. Thus, the sick person has an obligation to get well.

4. *The sick person should seek technically competent help and cooperate with the physician.* The obligation to get well involves a further obligation on the part of the sick person to seek technically competent help, usually from a physician. The sick person is also expected to cooperate with the physician in the process of trying to get well.

The Patient–Physician Role Relationship

Parsons' concept of the sick role is a useful sociological approach to illness because it views the patient–physician relationship within a framework of social roles, attitudes, and activities that both parties bring to the situation. The patient–physician role, like all other roles, involves a basic mutuality; that is, each participant in the social situation is expected to be familiar with both his or her own and others' expectations of behavior and the probable sequence of social acts to be followed. *The sick role evokes a set of patterned expectations that define the norms and values appropriate to being sick, both for the individual and for others who interact with the person.* Neither party can define his or her role independently of the role partner. The full meaning of "acting like a physician" depends on the patient's conception of what a physician is in terms of the social role. The physician's role is, as Parsons tells us, to return the sick person to his or her normal state of functioning.

The role of the patient likewise depends on the conception the physician holds of the patient's role. According to Parsons, the patient is expected to recognize that being sick is unpleasant and that he or she has an obligation to get well by seeking the physician's help. The patient–physician role relationship is therefore not a spontaneous form of social interaction. It is a well-defined encounter consisting of two or more persons whose object is the health of a single individual. It is also a situation that is too important to be left to undefined forms of behavior; for this reason, patients and physicians tend to act in a stable and predictable manner.

The patient–physician relationship is intended by society to be therapeutic in nature. The patient has a need for technical services from the physician, and the physician is the technical expert who is qualified and defined by society as prepared to help the patient. The goal of the patient–physician encounter is thus to promote some significant change for the better in the health of the patient.

Although the patient–physician relationship involves mutuality in the form of behavioral expectations, the status and power of the parties are not equal. The role of the physician is based upon an imbalance of power and technical expertise favorable exclusively to the physician. This imbalance is necessary because the physician needs leverage in his or her relationship with the patient in order to promote positive changes in the patient's health. Accomplishment of this goal sometimes requires procedures that can be painful or discomforting to the patient, yet the patient must accept and follow the treatment plan if the physician is to be effective. The physician exercises leverage through three basic techniques: (1) professional prestige, (2) situational authority, and (3) situational dependency of the patient. A physician's professional prestige rests upon technical qualifications and certification by society as a healer. The physician's situational power, on the other hand, refers to the physician's having what the patient wants and needs. By contrast, the patient is dependent because he or she lacks the expertise required to treat the health disorder.

The role of the physician is also enhanced by a certain mystique reflecting faith in the power to heal. This aspect of the physician role results from the dependence of the patient on the physician for life and death decisions. Since the physician has the responsibility to "do everything possible" and because the survival of the patient may be at issue, the patient may be likely to regard the physician with a strong emotional attachment in the hope or belief that the physician has a "gift" or natural skill in the healing arts. Since medical practice is sometimes characterized by uncertainty, a physician's presumed talent can be a very important dimension in the patient–physician relationship. Exact proof of the existence of many minor ailments and most chronic diseases is either not possible, or attempts to establish such proof may not be justifiable because of the hazards to the patient involved in the investigation. Despite the great advancement of the science of medicine during the twentieth century, the physician must still sometimes act on the basis of a hunch.

An interesting analog to the patient–physician relationship is the child–parent relationship. For some people an illness can foster a childlike state of dependency. However, while the role of the child is an immature role, the role of the patient represents a "disturbed" maturity (Wilson, 1970). Both the child and the sick person lack the capacity to perform the usual functions of the adult in everyday life, and both are dependent on a stronger and more adequate person to take care of them. Also the physician can be like a parent figure in that he or she provides support and controls rewards significant to the dependent party. The primary reward for the child would be approval, while the primary reward for the sick person would be to get well. Yet the physician and the parent are unlike in the magnitude of their involvement with the dependent party and the depth of their emotional feelings. Obviously, the states of childhood and patienthood are not totally similar, yet the similarity is a striking one because the extremely sick person who is helpless, technically incompetent in treating his or her disorder, and perhaps emotionally disturbed over his or her condition of illness can be very dependent and fully capable of acting in childlike ways.

The Sick Role and Illness Behavior Among Physicians

According to Eliot Freidson (1970a:206), physicians create the social possibilities for acting sick because they are society's authority on what "illness really is." They decide who is sick and what should be done about it.

In essence, physicians are "gatekeepers" to most professional health resources since these resources (such as prescription drugs and hospitals) cannot be used without their permission. Thus, Friedson argues that the behavior of the physician and others in the health field constitutes the embodiment of certain dominant values in society. These dominant values were described by Parsons (1951, 1979) and include the idea that health is positive and should be sought after. Stipulated in his concept of the sick role is that the sick person is expected to cooperate with the physician and *work* to achieve his or her own recovery and return to normal functioning. Therefore, if sick laypersons are expected to work toward achieving a healthy state, it would appear that physicians, as "gatekeepers" to that state, would be expected to do likewise from the point of view of society.

Moreover, Freidson suggests that physicians tend to have a bias toward finding illness in their patients. Most of their activities, claims Freidson (1970a:255), "are permeated by the tendency to see illness everywhere and to see the environment as being more dangerous to health than does the layman." He cites the *medical decision rule* as the guiding principle behind everyday medical practice. The medical decision rule, described by Thomas Scheff (1966), is the notion that since the work of the physician is for the good of the patient, physicians tend to feel that it is better to impute illness to their patients than to deny it and risk overlooking or missing it. Although this approach most likely promotes tendencies toward "overprescribing" (Castle et al., 1977) and "unnecessary surgery" (Nickerson et al., 1976), these consequences should not be too surprising. Patients desire and demand services, while physicians are trained to actively intervene in their health problems. Consequently, Freidson states:

> While the physician's job is to make decisions, including the decision not to do anything, the fact seems to be that the everyday practitioner feels impelled to do something, if only to satisfy patients who urge him to do something when they are in distress.[1]

Such an expectation by patients, regardless of whether it is necessary from the standpoint of actual physical need, portrays the physician as being somewhat compelled by existing norms to go along with the patient's demands. Furthermore, another of the basic propositions of Parsons' concept of the sick role is that a temporary exemption from normal social functioning is to be granted the sick upon condition that they seek professional treatment. This "duty to seek help" reflects the normative expectation in Western society that equates the role of being sick with the role of the physician as previously discussed. However, what do physicians do when they themselves feel sick? If physicians treat their own ailments in a medical mode requiring some degree of physician skills, they are implying that their patients should do likewise and are reinforcing patient expectations.

[1] Eliot Freidson, *Profession of Medicine* (New York: Dodd, Mead, 1970), p. 258. Richard Tessler et al., (1976) reminds us that the role of the physician is quite broad and that physicians must be attentive not only to a patient's complaints but also to whatever factors caused the patient to come to a doctor at a particular point in time. Distress may not be only physical in nature; instead, purely social-psychological needs can trigger physician use as well.

The author and his colleagues (Cockerham et al., 1980) investigated this situation among a sample of 375 physicians in east central Illinois. The physicians were presented with a list of fourteen minor symptoms, described in medical terms, that are frequently experienced by many people and that would usually be expected to disappear if left untreated. The symptoms consisted of such ailments as stuffy nose, sore throat, diarrhea with slight fever, muscle ache, back pain, heartburn, stiff neck, recurrent headache, mild insomnia, and so forth. Three responses ("ordered diagnostic studies on myself," "sought care from other physician," and "treated myself with prescription drugs") were labeled physician-dependent actions because they required involvement with a physician. Other responses ("did nothing," "took a drink," "interrupted my daily routine," "treated myself with over-the-counter drugs," etc.,) could all be done without a physician. The intent of the study was to find out if the physicians might ignore their own symptoms (recognizing their self-limiting nature), treat their symptoms in a manner similar to any layperson who did not go to a physician, or treat them with an action requiring access to, or in this case, being a physician.

It was found that three of the minor ailments (sore throat, diarrhea with slight fever, and recurrent low back pain) elicited a high frequency of physician-dependent action and four ailments (stuffy nose, loose stools, muscle ache, and stiff neck) elicited a moderate frequency. The most likely form of physician-dependent action was taking prescription drugs, although some physicians consulted other physicians or ordered diagnostic studies on themselves. Older physicians were more likely to take a physician-dependent action than younger physicians, which is not inconsistent with usual medical advice, as even minor health problems tend to linger with age. No difference appeared among the physicians according to type of medical specialty. Family practitioners and pediatricians tended to treat their ailments in the same mode as psychiatrists and surgeons. This uniformity of response suggests agreement among the physicians over a basic medical perspective that most likely results from general medical training, socialization, and experience.

Both the primary form of the physician-dependent responses (prescription drugs) and the uniformity by specialty demonstrate a general adherence to the medical model, which holds that disease, or whatever physicians define as disease, should be treated in a biomedical framework emphasizing physiologic and biochemical techniques. Even for some minor ailments, scientific knowledge of disease appears to encourage physician-dependent action, thereby indicating that normative expectations to seek a medical solution are pervasive in American society and that physicians do, indeed, reinforce this expectation with their own behavior. Thus, both physicians and laypersons may tend to act on the assumption that some action is better than no action even though no action may be necessary or, perhaps for reasons of risk and cost, be preferable. These findings suggest that both physicians and the public may act in a similar ritualistic manner when it comes to dealing with their own physical discomforts and that the norm to seek professional care, as outlined by Parsons, is quite strong.

Medicine as an Institution of Social Control

Besides Parsons' analytical insight into the ramifications of the patient-physician relationship, implicit in his concept of the sick role is the idea that medicine is (and should be) an institution for the social control of deviant behavior. Some medical sociologists (Twaddle, 1969; Freidson, 1970a) have expressed concern that medicine is indeed an institution for the control of deviance and is taking responsibility for an ever greater proportion of behaviors defined as deviant. In other words, acts that might have been defined as sin or crime and controlled by the church or the law are increasingly regarded as illnesses to be controlled through medical care. Thomas Szasz explains this trend as follows:

> Starting with such things as syphilis, tuberculosis, typhoid fever, and carcinomas and fractures we have created the class, "illness." At first, this class was composed of only a few items all of which shared the common feature of reference to a state of disordered structure or function of the human body as a physical–chemical machine. As time went on additional items were added to this class. They were not added, however, because they were newly discovered bodily disorders. The physician's attention has been deflected from this criterion and has become focused instead on disability and suffering as new criteria for selection. Thus, at first slowly, such things as hysteria, hypochondriasis, obsessive-compulsive neurosis and depression were added to the category of illness. Then with increasing zeal, physicians and especially psychiatrists began to call "illness" . . . anything and everything in which they could detect any sign of malfunctioning, based on no matter what the norm. Hence, agoraphobia is illness because one should not be afraid of open spaces. Homosexuality is an illness because heterosexuality is the social norm. Divorce is illness because it signals failure of marriage.[2]

If Szasz's view is correct, there appears to be a long-term trend toward making illness and deviance not only synonymous, but also toward treating deviance exclusively in a medical mode. Eliot Freidson (1970a) has argued that medicine has established a jurisdiction far wider than justified by its demonstrable capacity to "cure." Nonetheless, the medical profession has been highly successful in gaining authority to define deviant behavior as illness—behavior properly handled only by the physician. Andrew Twaddle (1973:756) points out that "today there are few, if any, problems of human behavior that some group does not think of as medical problems." Therefore, to the extent that the control of human behavior is the basis of social organization and to the extent that the control of deviant behavior is becoming the function of the medical profession, Parsons' concept of the sick role helps us understand contemporary mechanisms of social stability.

Research Applications of the Sick Role

Parsons' concept of the sick role, as Freidson (1970a:228) has explained, represents "a penetrating and apt analysis of sickness from a distinctly sociological point of view." This comment is particularly appropriate when it is recognized that the sick role has stimulated a considerable body of research

[2]Thomas S. Szasz, *The Myth of Mental Illness* (New York: Harper & Row, 1974), pp. 44–45.

in medical sociology. To mention only a few such studies, Paul Chalfant and Richard Kurtz (1971) utilized Parsons' sick role concept in explaining social workers' denial of the sick role to alcoholics. Social workers in this study felt that drinking was motivated behavior and that alcoholics could avoid their disorder if they desired to do so. Hence, the alcoholic was not entitled to exemption from normal responsibilities.

Howard Waitzkin (1971) hypothesized that adoption of the sick role: (1) in the family can lead to the prevention of disruptive strains in family relationships; (2) in mental hospitals can reduce conflict between patients and staff; (3) in totalitarian countries can permit limited deviant behavior that satisfies frustrations capable of threatening the stability of the regime; (4) in penal institutions can allow a prisoner to deviate temporarily within a carefully controlled environment; (5) in the armed forces allows an individual the only authorized escape route from his or her normal duty; and (6) can allow some individuals to escape military service altogether through certification as being physically unsuitable.

Another application of the sick role is found in Stephen Cole and Robert LeJeune's (1972) study of welfare mothers. Cole and LeJeune observed that among welfare mothers in New York City the general norm was to accept the dominant cultural view that being on welfare is a result of personal failure. Welfare mothers who had given up hope of getting off welfare were prone to adopt the sick role in order to legitimize their self-defined failure. This study concluded that the sick role may provide a "substitute" status by way of exemption from normal role responsibilities for persons who lack other socially approved statuses. What is implied here is that certain people may seek out the sick role in society so they can legitimize their failure to perform adequately.

A similar finding was noted in a more recent study by Arnold Arluke and his associates (1979) of 1,000 patients discharged from two large New York City hospitals. Arluke et al. found that low-income and elderly patients are most likely to agree that a person has the right not to be held responsible for his or her illness. For some elderly people, it was believed that the sick role provided a sense of legitimacy for an otherwise dependent state. Consequently, these elderly people were most unwilling to give up the role. Younger people and people who lived alone were most likely to agree that a person has the duty to try to get well.

CRITICISM OF THE SICK ROLE

Although Parsons' concept of the sick role has demonstrated research utility as a framework for explaining illness-related behavior and has become a basic concept in medical sociology, the model has some serious defects which have led a few sociologists to suggest that it should be abandoned entirely (see Kosa and Robertson, 1969; Berkanovic, 1972). Gerald Gordon (1966) has pointed out that, although widely accepted, Parsons' sick role concept is not based upon systematic observation and has not been empirically validated. Gordon states that the sick role concept has been accepted primarily because of its prima facie reasonableness and logical construction.

Parsons' sick role theory can be criticized because of (1) behavioral variation; (2) types of illnesses; (3) the patient–physician relationship; and (4) the sick role's middle-class orientation.

Behavioral Variation

Much of the criticism of the sick role theory has been directed toward its lack of uniformity among various persons and social groups. David Mechanic (1962a), for example, has suggested that age, sex, and the importance of social roles and learned responses to symptoms vary among individuals. In a 1964 study of illness behavior among children, he found important sex and age differences in attitudes toward illness. Boys appeared to have more stoical attitudes toward illness than girls, and older children appeared to have more stoical attitudes than younger children.

In a random sample of people living in New York City, Gordon (1966) found at least two distinct and unrelated statuses and complementary role expectations associated with being sick. When a prognosis was believed to be serious and uncertain, expectations of behavior generally conformed to Parsons' description of the sick role; however, when a prognosis was known and not serious, the notion of an "impaired role" emerged from Gordon's data, which required normal role responsibilities and rejected role exemptions despite sickness.

Twaddle (1969) reported at least seven configurations of the sick role, with Parsons' model being only one, in a study of Rhode Island married couples in late middle age. The exact configuration of the alternative sick roles discovered by Twaddle depended in part on cultural values and whether or not a person defined himself or herself as "sick." Not only were there differing personal definitions of "being sick," but also not all of the respondents stated they expected to get well and not all of them cooperated with the physician. Twaddle found that the sick role, as defined by Parsons, was much more applicable to Jews than to either Protestants or Italian Catholics. Jews were more likely to see themselves as being sick, as expecting to get well, and as cooperating with the physician. Protestants were the most resistant to seeing a physician, and Italian Catholics were generally the least cooperative with the physician. There were also other important ethno-cultural differences in the Twaddle study. Protestants, for example, were much more likely to regard functional incapacity (usually an inability to work) as the first sign of illness, while Italian Catholics were more likely to emphasize changes in feeling states such as pain. Jews, however, tended to emphasize fear of eventual outcomes rather than feeling states or functional incapacities.

A well-known study by Mark Zborowski (1952) demonstrated important group differences pertaining to pain. While pain is clearly a biological phenomenon, Zborowski observed that responses to pain are not always biological but vary among ethno-cultural groups. Zborowski's sample consisted of eighty-seven male patients and sixteen healthy males in New York City who were primarily of Jewish, Italian, and "Old American" ethnic backgrounds. The so-called "Old Americans" were defined as white, native-born, and usually Protestant patients whose family had lived at least two generations in the United States; they also did not identify with any particular foreign nationality. All of the patients suffered from neurological ailments, such as herniated discs or spinal lesions, which represented disorders where the pain involved would vary only within fairly narrow limits.

Although the level of pain was thought to be generally similar, Zborowski found significant variation in the responses to pain. Jews and Italians tended to be more sensitive to pain and more prone to exaggerate the experience of pain than Old Americans. While Jews and Italians were similar in responding to pain in the hospital, the two ethnic groups differed in the home setting. At home the Italian was masculine and authoritative, but in the hospital he was emotional. The Jewish patient was emotional in both settings. Zborowski observed that Jewish patients also used their suffering as a device for manipulating the behavior of others. But once satisfied that adequate care was being provided, the Jewish patient tended to become more restrained in his response.

In contrast, the Old American patients tried to conform to the medical image of the ideal patient. They cooperated with hospital personnel and avoided being a nuisance as much as possible. The Old American patients also avoided expressing pain in public, and when examined by the physician they tended to assume the role of a detached observer by becoming unemotional and attempting to provide an efficient description of their internal state to aid in a correct diagnosis. If their pain was too much for them to control, they would withdraw to their rooms and express their pain privately.

The attitudes toward pain also varied. Zborowski reported that Italians were more concerned with the discomfort of the pain itself and were relatively satisfied and happy when immediate relief was provided. The Italian patient also tended to display a confident attitude toward the physician. The Jewish patient, however, was not particularly confident about his physician, and he seemed to be more concerned about the significance of his pain for his general state of health rather than about any specific and immediate discomfort. While Italian patients sought pain killers, Jewish patients were reluctant to take drugs because they were apprehensive about the habit-forming characteristics of the drugs. The Old Americans, like the Jews, were also primarily concerned about what pain signified for their general state of health, but unlike the Jews, they were optimistic about the power of medicine and its ability to provide a cure. Hence, they displayed great confidence in the decisions made by the physicians.

In an effort to explain these ethno-cultural differences, Zborowski believed that Jewish and Italian mothers demonstrated overprotective and overemotional attitudes about their sons' health and that this socialization experience fostered the development of anxieties regarding pain among the Jewish and Italian patients. Zborowski also noted that Jewish and Italian parents had tended to prevent physical injury to their sons by prohibiting them from playing rough games and sports. On the other hand, Old American parents had socialized their sons to expect to get hurt in sports and to fight back. Old American boys were taught "not to be sissies," "not to cry," and "to take pain like a man." If such a child were actually injured, he was expected not to get emotional but to seek proper treatment immediately.

Research by John Campbell (1978) involving a sample of 264 children and their mothers in Washington, D.C. supports Zborowski's findings in regard to the responses of the "Old Americans." Although Campbell did not focus on the role of ethnicity, his data showed that those children who were older and whose parents were of higher socioeconomic background tended to take "a stiff-upper-lip" or "business-as-usual" approach to illness. "This Spartan orientation," says Campbell (1978:46), "bears more than a passing resemblance to the responses to pain that Zborowski described as typifying his 'Old American' subjects—responses that tended to be approved by members of the medical profession—who themselves, perhaps not coincidently, would be assigned to higher SES [Socioeconomic Status] levels." According to Campbell, parents *do* make a difference when it comes to socializing their children to handle their emotions and reject the sick role.

As for other studies of ethnic variation, Irving Zola's (1966) comparison of American patients of Irish, Italian, and Anglo-Saxon descent at two hospitals in Boston also supported Zborowski's findings. In general, the Italians tended to dramatize their symptoms, while Zola found that the Irish would often deny their symptoms and the Anglo-Saxons would speak of their health problems in a detached and neutral manner lacking in anxiety. Zola concluded that there were indeed distinct differences between cultural groups and the way in which they communicated complaints about their health.

Besides ethnic variation, there may be other ways in which people interpret the sick role. A study of Rhode Island heart patients (Monteiro, 1973b) found differing expectations of behavior between patients and laypersons. Heart patients believed that laypersons exempted them from normal role responsibilities following a heart attack. Laypersons, however, reported an opposite expectation and said that heart patients should not be exempt from normal responsibilities. Instead laypersons believed that heart patients should resume their normal activities after a heart attack while being careful to "not overdo it." Other research has shown that, among heart patients having surgery, women tend to adopt the sick role more frequently than men and to be less ready to resume their work roles after surgery (Brown and Rawlinson, 1977). Thus, there may be differences by sex in regard to acceptance of the sick role as well.

A study by Louise Blackwell (1967) on healthy and well-educated adults between the ages of twenty-five and forty-four suggested that upper- and upper-middle-class people expect to cope with physical and psychiatric health disorders by themselves before seeking professional help. The study shows that these persons may have strong feelings of responsibility for coping with their own health conditions, depending on the manifestation of the illness and the explicitness of the pathology.

Emil Berkanovic (1972) came to a similar conclusion in his research on sick role conceptions among Los Angeles city employees. Although his sample cannot claim to be representative of city employees generally, his findings do suggest that some people feel they are able to define appropriate illness behavior under certain circumstances. These people do not reject medical theories of illness, but simply feel competent to decide what is the correct behavior for the sick person, provided the symptoms are recognized and the outcome of the illness is known. Berkanovic points out that often the physician is consulted only as a last resort and only after all other sources of health information fail to provide an adequate explanation.

What is indicated by all of these studies is that Parsons' concept of the sick role does not account for all of the considerable variations in the way people view sickness and define appropriate sick role behavior for themselves and others.

Type of Illness

The second major category of criticism regarding Parsons' concept of the sick role is that it seems to apply only to acute illnesses, which by their nature are temporary, usually recognizable by laypersons, and readily overcome with a physician's help. Yet chronic illnesses, such as cancer and heart disease, are by definition not temporary, and often the patient cannot be expected to get well as Parsons' model suggests, no matter how willing the patient may be to cooperate with the physician. Therefore, temporary exemptions from normal role responsibilities for the chronic patient are both inappropriate and perhaps impossible.

Research on patients with chronic disorders (Kassebaum and Baumann, 1965) has shown that they perceive the sick role differently from patients with acute illnesses. Chronic patients were faced with the impossibility of resuming normal roles and the necessity of adjusting their activities to a permanent health disorder. However, in a reconsideraton of the sick role, Parsons (1975) argued that even if the goal of a complete recovery is impractical, many chronic diseases can be "managed" so that the patient is able to maintain a relatively normal pattern of physiological and social functioning. While diabetes, for example, cannot be cured in the sense that pneumonia can, Parsons insists that a chronic disease like diabetes should not be placed in a totally different category from that of "curable" illnesses if the patient can be returned to a normal range of functioning. True, this explanation may allow the sick role concept to account for some chronic disorders; still it cannot be applied to a wide range of illness situations such as the bedridden patient or the terminally ill patient.

Problems also arise in applying the sick role to the mentally ill, in that while the sick role stipulates a person should seek professional care, people who go to psychiatrists for help may be stigmatized for doing just that (Segall, 1976). People who admit to a history of mental illness often have problems finding jobs, and a considerable body of research literature describes the difficulties former mental patients have in coping with rejection from other people. In addition, many mental hospital patients refuse to accept the idea that they are mentally ill and most patients, rather than voluntarily seeking help, are admitted to mental institutions involuntarily (Cockerham, 1981).

Patient–Physician Role Relationship

A third major area of criticism of Parsons' sick role model is that it is based upon a traditonal one-to-one interaction between a patient and a physician. This form of interaction is common because the usual setting is the physician's office, where Parsons' version of the sick role is conceptualized. It is the setting where the physician has maximum control. Yet quite different patterns of interaction may emerge in the hospital, where perhaps a team of physicians and other members of the hospital staff are involved. In the hospital the physician is one of several physicians and is subject to organizational constraints and policies. If the patient is at home, the patient–physician relationship may also again vary because the patient and his or her family can much more clearly influence the interaction.

In addition, the pattern of relationships outlined in Parsons' sick role is modified if the client is a target of preventive techniques rather than strictly therapeutic measures. A considerable portion of contemporary medical practice is concerned not with restoring a single patient to his or her normal social functioning, but with maintaining and improving public health. The patient–physician relationship is different when the target is a group of individuals, particularly if the health problem is not a disabling illness but a behavioral problem such as smoking cigarettes, or an environmental problem such as water or air pollution. In this situation the physician or health agent must usually be persuasive rather than authoritative, since he or she lacks the leverage to control the client group. The physician must convince the group that certain actions, such as physical examinations or x-ray examinations for tuberculosis, are good for them. In defense of Parsons' sick role, however, it should be noted that the behavior needing to be changed in such cases is often "normal" rather than "sick."

Middle-Class Orientation

Finally, it should be noted that Parsons' sick role model is a middle-class pattern of behavior. It emphasizes the merits of individual responsibility and the deliberate striving toward good health and a return to normality. It is oriented to the middle-class assumption that rational problem solving is the only viable behavior in the face of difficulty and that effort will result in positive gain. It fails to take into account what it is like to live in an environment of poverty where success is the exception to the rule.

Also, many people in the lower socioeconomic classes may tend to deny the sick role, not only because they may not have the opportunity to enjoy typically middle-class secondary gains, but also because the functional incapacity of the poor person may render him or her less likely to be able to earn a living or survive in conditions of poverty (Kassebaum and Baumann, 1965; Kosa et al., 1969). Therefore, people living in a poverty environment might work, regardless of how sick they might be, so long as they feel able to perform some of their work activities.

Parsons' Sick Role: Conclusion

Despite the considerable criticism of Parsons' sick role concept in recent sociological literature, the reader should note that this model represents a significant contribution to medical sociology. Parsons insists that illness is a form of deviance and that as such it is necessary for a society to return the sick to their normal social functioning. Thus, Parsons views medicine as a mechanism by which a society attempts to control deviance and maintain social stability. In light of the trend toward classifying more and more social problems as medical problems, Parsons' explanation of the function of medicine has broad implications for the future treatment of deviants in our society.

While recognizing that some criticisms of Parsons' theory are valid, we should note that at least some of this criticism is based upon a misunderstanding of Parsons. Apparently some critics incorrectly assume that Parsons viewed the sick role as a fixed, mechanical kind of "cage" that would produce similarities of behavior among sick people regardless of variant cultural backgrounds and different personal learning experiences. Instead what Parsons has given us is an "ideal type" of the sick role. By definition, ideal types do not exist in reality. They are abstractions, erected by emphasizing selected aspects of behavior typical in certain contexts, and they serve as bases for comparing and differentiating concrete behaviors occurring in similar situations in different sociocultural circumstances.

Therefore, it can be concluded that Parsons' model is a useful and viable framework of sociological analysis within certain contexts. Although the theory is an insufficient explanation of all illness behavior, it does describe many general similarities and should not be abandoned. In fact, writing in a later article, Parsons (1975) admitted that he did not believe it was ever his intention to make his concept cover the whole range of phenomena associated with the sick role. Two possibilities exist: (1) using the model as an "ideal type" with which various forms of illness behavior can be contrasted or (2) expanding the concept to account for conditions generally common to most illness situations.

LABELING THEORY

By failing to account for the behavioral variations within the sick role, the functionalist approach to illness has neglected the various aspects of acting sick. Chapter Four, on the process of seeking medical care, pointed out that two people having much the same symptoms may behave quite differently. One person may become concerned and seek medical treatment, while another person may ignore the symptoms completely. Z. Lipowski (1970) has noted that individual strategies in coping with illness vary from passive cooperation to positive action to get well and from fear at being diagnosed as ill to actual pleasure in anticipation of secondary gains. Several writers, Freidson (1970a) in particular, have taken the position that illness as deviant behavior is relative and must be seen as such; this is the perspective of labeling theory.

Labeling theory is based on the concept that what is regarded as deviant behavior by one person or social group may not be so regarded by other persons or social groups. Howard Becker (1973), one of the leading proponents of labeling theory, illustrates the concept in his study of marijuana users. His analysis reveals a discrepancy in American society between those people who insist that smoking marijuana is harmful and that use of the drug should be illegal, and those who support a norm favoring marijuana smoking and who believe that use of the drug should be legalized. While the wider society views marijuana smoking as deviant, groups of marijuana smokers view their behavior as socially acceptable within their own particular group.

Becker's position is that deviance is therefore created by social groups who make rules or norms. Infractions of these rules or norms constitute deviant behavior. Accordingly, deviance is not a quality of the act a person commits, but instead is a consequence of the definition applied to that act by other people. The critical variable in understanding deviance is the social audience, because the audience determines what is and what is not deviant behavior.

The applicability of labeling theory as a vehicle for explaining illness behavior is that while sickness may be a biological state existing independently of human knowledge, illness is a social state created and formed by human perception. Thus, as Freidson (1970a) has pointed out, when a veterinarian diagnoses a cow's condition as an illness, the diagnosis itself does not change the cow's behavior. But when a physician diagnoses a human's condition as illness, the diagnosis can and often does change the sick person's behavior. Thus, illness is seen by labeling theorists as a condition created by human beings in accordance with their understanding of the situation.

For example, among the Kuba people of Sumatra, skin diseases and injuries to the skin are quite common because of a difficult jungle environment (Sigerist, 1960). A person suffering from a skin disease would not be considered to be sick among the Kuba because the condition, while unhealthy, is not considered abnormal. In parts of Africa, such afflictions as hookworms may not be considered abnormal because of their prevalence. Margaret Clark (1959) points out that among the Mexican-Americans in her study conducted in the southwestern United States, such disorders as diarrhea and coughing were so common they were considered "normal," though not necessarily good. Examples such as these have led to the realization that an essentially unhealthy state may not always be equated with illness when the people involved are able to function effectively and the presence of the disorder does not affect the normal rhythm of daily life. Therefore, judgments concerning what is illness and what is deviant behavior are relative and cannot be separated from the social situations in which people live.

Labeling Theory and Illness Behavior

Labeling theory has so far failed to develop a theory of illness behavior comparable to Parsons' model. The closest equivalent deriving from the symbolic interactionist view (labeling theory) is that of Eliot Freidson (1970a). Freidson indicates that the key to distinguishing among sick roles is the notion of legitimacy. As shown in Table 5–1, he maintains that in illness states, there are three types of legitimacy: (1) *conditional legitimacy,* where the deviants are temporarily exempted from normal obligations and gain some extra privileges on the proviso that they seek help in order to rid themselves

TABLE 5–1.   Freidson's Types of Deviance for Which the Individual Is Not Held
Responsible, by Imputed Legitimacy and Seriousness

Imputed Seriousness	Illegitimate (Stigmatized)	Conditionally Legitimate	Unconditionally Legitimate
Minor Deviation	Cell 1. "Stammer" Partial suspension of some ordinary obligations; few or no new privileges; adoption of a few new obligations.	Cell 2. "A Cold" Temporary suspension of few ordinary obligations; temporary enhancement of ordinary privileges. Obligation to get well.	Cell 3. "Pockmarks" No special change in obligations or privileges.
Serious Deviation	Cell 4. "Epilepsy" Suspension of some ordinary obligations; adoption of new obligations; few or no new privileges.	Cell 5. "Pneumonia" Temporary release from ordinary obligations; addition to ordinary privileges. Obligation to cooperate and seek help treatment.	Cell 6. "Cancer" Permanent suspension of many ordinary obligations; marked addition to privileges.

SOURCE: From Eliot Freidson, *The Profession of Medicine*, p. 239. Copyright © 1970 by Harper & Row, Publishers, Inc. Reprinted by permission of the publishers. (Formerly published by Dodd, Mead.)

of their deviance; (2) *unconditional legitimacy,* where the deviants are exempted permanently from normal obligations and are granted additional privileges in view of the hopeless nature of their deviance; and (3) *illegitimacy,* where the deviants are exempted from some normal obligations by virtue of their deviance, for which they are technically not responsible, but gain few if any privileges and take on new, handicapping obligations.

Although the health professional would argue that there is no such thing as an illegitimate illness, Freidson suggests that there are illegitimate ways of acting sick. Applying the distinction of "minor" and "serious" deviations to this typology of legitimacy, Freidson constructs an illustrative framework for his theory (see Table 5–1). Cells 1 and 4 demonstrate the condition of illegitimacy in its minor (a stammer) and serious (epilepsy) modes. In these illness states, an individual may be exempted from normal obligations but gains few if any privileges—and takes on an additional handicap, stigma. Cells 2 and 5 suggest the situation of conditional legitimacy where a cold (minor) and pneumonia (serious) represent conditions that temporarily exempt the individual from normal obligations and grant him or her privileges on the grounds that he or she seek help. With a cold, a few obligations are suspended, but with pneumonia there is release from all ordinary obligations. Cell 5 would thus be the only illness state corresponding to Parsons' sick role. Cells 3 and 6 represent situations of unconditional legitimacy; the minor variation in Cell 3 (pockmarks) gains no special privileges or obligations. Cell 6, chronic illness in the form of cancer (serious), also represents a permanent condition, but here the deviant gains permanent exemptions from normal obligations because of the terminal nature of his or her deviance.

Freidson's classification of six distinct varieties of deviance as illness implies different consequences for both the individual and for his or her society. The management of the deviant and his or her treatment by other people depends on the label or definition applied to the deviant's health disorder by the social audience. Freidson's model accounts for the problematic aspects of illness relative to social situations. A person with a skin disease in the Kuba tribe or a person with hookworms in Africa could be classified in Cell 3 as unconditionally legitimate, because the afflicted person would gain no special privileges or changes in obligations since the disorder would be common to most people who functioned normally in their society.

Freidson's concept, however, is strictly theoretical and has not been extensively tested. Whether it can account for variations in illness behavior is therefore still a matter of speculation. While Freidson's model is useful in categorizing illness behavior according to prevailing American middle-class norms, it fails to explain differences in the way people define themselves as being sick and in need of professional medical care. The merit of Freidson's model, on the other hand, is that it does go beyond Parsons' concept of the sick role by describing different types of illness and by pointing out that illness is a socially created label.

Criticism of Labeling Theory

The inadequacy of labeling theory as an explanation of illness behavior lies in its restricted approach to the nature of illness. Labeling theorists choose one (perhaps obvious) element of a complex interactive pattern and stress the unique importance of that element to the neglect of other factors involved. Few would deny that groups create deviance when they establish norms. Admittedly, the reaction of an "audience" to variant types of behavior influences the individual's self-concept and also influences society's counter-behavior. Yet, from a scientific viewpoint, behavior does not become deviant because it is so labeled by an audience but rather on account of its observable consequences. Audiences may label the drinking of cyanide in a variety of interesting ways, but the hard and observable fact is that drinking cyanide results in the death of the drinker, regardless of how it is labeled. Thus it might be argued that the relative deviance of, say, smoking marijuana occurs because there is no scientifically verifiable knowledge of the consequences of smoking marijuana. The same statement may be made with respect to other deviances such as homosexuality.

Certainly all of this is *not* to deny the importance of labeling as an influence on behavior. Studies directed toward an analysis of the influence of labeling in specific situations can guide our thoughts from a vague and general approach to the subject toward an organized framework. But there is the danger that interest in, and enthusiasm for, the labeling approach may turn it into dogma rather than hypothesis, a result obviously to be avoided.

The central assertion of labeling theory is that acts termed deviant are so defined only with reference to the character of the reaction to them by the social audience. Thus, the essential feature of a deviant act is external both to the act itself and to the actor. As Jack Gibbs (1971) has pointed out, if deviant acts and actors share common characteristics other than societal reaction, these common characteristics have yet to be defined or explained. Nor does labeling theory explain why certain people commit deviant acts and others in the same circumstances do not. All this seems to pose the question of whether or not societal reaction alone is sufficient to explain deviant behavior; the answer seems to be that it is not. In a later reconsideration, Becker (1973:179) agreed that labeling theory "cannot possibly be considered as the sole explanation of what alleged deviants actually do."

Labeling Theory: Conclusion

When compared to Parsons' concept of the sick role, labeling theory does address itself to the specific variations in illness behavior that seem to be present among differing socioeconomic and ethno-cultural groups in American society. It also provides a framework of analysis for illness behavior according to the definition and perception of particular social groups, and allows the social scientist to account for differences between social settings and types of illnesses as well. Over and against these advantages, labeling theory suffers from vagueness in its conceptualization; it also remains to be seen whether the concept of illness as deviance can be explained to rival the Parsonian concept. While Freidson's model has potential, it has not attracted the attention accorded to Parsons' sick role. But most important, there is serious doubt whether societal reactions in and of themselves are sufficient to explain the generalities of behavior occurring among the sick.

ILLNESS AS SOCIAL DEVIANCE?

This chapter has discussed the various approaches to illness as deviance. The question remains whether this perspective of illness is useful or adequate for sociological studies. The conceptualization of illness as deviant behavior does make illness a sociologically relevant variable; but it also restricts the analysis of illness to the framework of a social event. This is in accord with the major intention of the illness-as-deviance perspective in sociology: to focus exclusively on the social properties of illness and thus to exclude biological properties definable only by the physician. Yet by dwelling exclusively on the social properties of illness, the deviance perspective severely limits its capacity to deal with questions of disease etiology and the biological aspects of illness as a condition of suffering, both of which are necessary for a thorough conceptualization of illness behavior.

It can also be argued that while deviance is behavior contrary to the normative expectations of society, sickness itself does not counteract social norms (Pflanz and Rohde, 1970). The members of any society are expected to become ill now and then during their lives. Accordingly, if illness is deviance and since deviance is regarded as a violation of expectations of behavior, it would be necessary to assume that society expects people not to become ill, just as it expects them not to commit a crime or become a homosexual or drug addict.

The illness-as-deviance approach may, therefore, not be particularly suitable in understanding and defining the behavior of the sick. Instead it may be more appropriate for sociologists to integrate their perspective with the medical definition of illness and disease to provide a more comprehensive explanation of illness behavior. As Freidson (1970a:206) has indicated, by being the authority on what "illness really is," medicine does indeed create the social possibilities for acting sick and medicine's perspectives should be considered. However, many contemporary sociologists remain content with the illness-as-deviance approach to illness. Yet the inadequacies of both Parsons' concept of the sick role and of labeling theory clearly suggest that a new and more comprehensive concept of illness behavior is needed. This problem remains an important area of future concern for medical sociologists.

SUMMARY AND CONCLUSION

This chapter has dealt with theories that attempt to explain the relationship between illness and society. Not surprisingly, no single, comprehensive theory has been either devised or received general acceptance. Medical sociology therefore takes its place with the other branches of sociology in exhibiting a number of interesting hypotheses, all of which must be tested with regard to method and aim of research, validity of conclusions, and tendency to reality-obscuring enthusiasm. Is all of this evidence of conflict in sociology itself? It could be, and has been called so, but the present author prefers to view it as positive evidence that the discipline is alive and struggling to arrive at some consensus about certain aspects of human group life.

Parsons' concept of the sick role included the following postulates: (1) an individual's illness is grounds for exemption from normal responsibilities and obligations; (2) an individual's illness is not his or her fault and he or she needs help in order to get well; (3) the sick person has an obligation to get well because being sick is undesirable; and (4) the obligation to get well subsumes the more specific obligation of the sick person to seek technically competent help. Parsons also demonstrated the utility of medicine as an institution of social control by virtue of its mission of treating the deviant sick.

Although Parsons' concept of the sick role has provided a useful framework for understanding illness behavior, it has not been generally sufficient because of its failure (1) to explain the variation within illness behavior; (2) to apply to chronic illness; (3) to account for the variety of settings and situations affecting the patient–physician relationship; and (4) to explain the behavior of lower-class patients. Nonetheless, if we realize the limitations of Parsons' sick role theory, we can continue to apply it to behavior as an ideal-type model. Whatever knowledge we gain from such use must be supplemented by other approaches, including those discussed in this chapter. Human behavior is still variable beyond our present understanding and no alternative can be completely disregarded. Labeling theory, for instance, provides a useful approach for dealing with the problematic aspects of illness behavior. However, a definitive sick role concept using labeling theory has yet to be developed. We also suggested that perhaps the illness-as-deviance approach is too limiting a perspective, since it fails adequately to incorporate biological notions of illness into its theoretical structure. A synthesis of biological and social factors might be achieved in an adaptation theory of illness, but such a theory still awaits meaningful formulation.

Note that there are points of agreement among all of the theories discussed. Admittedly, these are general viewpoints that require specific analysis and validation, but they do represent typically sociological approaches. Among them are:

1. *The idea that both health and illness are more than individual matters.* They depend on such social factors as the state of medical knowledge, cultural evaluation of behavior, awareness of relationships among different kinds of behavior, and the relative reward/punishment conditions accompanying the fact of being sick. Thus health and illness are no longer purely biological phenomena but sociological events as well.

2. *The viewpoint that what a society does about illness depends on many sociocultural factors, by no means all of them logically based or scientifically validated.* Some of them—for example, the declining cohesiveness of the family and the increasing variability of family relationships—influence what we do about illness but they do not develop in connection with the fact of illness. They develop as a result of pressures from a changing economic system, shifts in population size and composition, and changes in religious and ethical outlooks, among other things; yet they affect society's behavior toward illness and the ill. We cannot understand this changed behavior itself if we relate it only to illness; we must see it as part of a much broader series of social developments.

3. *Recognition that since social systems can function only through people, the health or illness of all members of society should be a matter of group concern.* Present methods of health delivery may be defective from a moral or ethical viewpoint because many segments of our population do not have access to medical procedures that are commonly available to other segments. One reason for this situation is that "underprivileged" segments of the population are perceived (very probably wrongly perceived) as being less important for the survival of the system than are the "privileged" segments. This then becomes a social problem and not a medical problem. Whether individuals are diagnosed as ill or not, how they consider the fact of their illness, the behavior of other people toward them as ill persons, all depend not on their individual characteristics, but on their position in the social system.

4. *The realization that group behavior results from the interaction of people within a specific context and that individual behavior in most of its expressions reflects group behavior.* Since our own society is a complex one, consisting of many different groups in which widely different behaviors are viewed as appropriate, we

should expect (and we actually find) widely different attitudes to illness and many variant behaviors toward illness. Yet despite individual variations in behavior resulting from the confrontation by unique individuals of a multiplicity of situations, similarities of behavior among people are more common than differences within a given context.

PART II

HEALTH PRACTITIONERS

chapter **6**

THE PHYSICIAN IN
A CHANGING SOCIETY

There are about 380,000 medical doctors actively practicing medicine in the United States (HEW, 1980).[1] They constitute less than 10 percent of the total workforce, yet the entire health care industry in the United States is subordinate to their professional authority, regardless of whether the task is patient care, research, or administration. Physicians not only control the conditions of their own work, but also the work of most of the other members of the health profession as well. Consequently, the status and prestige accorded to the physician by the general public is recognition of the physician's monopoly of one of society's most essential functions: the definition and treatment of health disorders.

    The Kingsley Davis and Wilbert Moore (1945) theory of social stratification partially explains the physician's status in American society. Davis and Moore suggest that differential rewards and prestige are necessary as a means of ensuring that essential tasks are accomplished. All societies, therefore, need some method of allocating members into important positions so they will be motivated to perform the duties these positions require. In complex societies, these positions usually require skilled personnel. Thus, arrangements must be made to ensure that not only motivated people but also skilled people are available to fill these important positions, and the Davis-Moore argument is that it is necessary to make such positions attractive so that people will want to compete for them. Rewards are related to the social importance of a particular position and the relative availability of

[1]According to official U.S. government figures, there were 380,000 M.D.s in active practice in the United States in 1978; approximately 60 percent of these physicians provided office-based patient care. For every 100,000 Americans, it was estimated there were about 171 physicians. See National Center for Health Statistics, *Health Resources Statistics* (Washington, D.C.: U.S. Department of Health, Education and Welfare, 1980).

qualified persons. Thus the greatest rewards are associated with those roles that (1) have the greatest importance for society and (2) require the greatest training or talent. Accordingly, the status, prestige, and financial reward of the physician in American society is a result of society's need to place able persons in the critically important position of providing medical care.

THE PROFESSIONALIZATION OF THE PHYSICIAN

However, the social importance of the medical function and the limited number of people with the training and talent to perform as physicians are not the only criteria explaining the professional dominance of the physician group. A particularly important factor is the organization of the medical profession itself. William Goode (1957, 1960) has noted that two basic characteristics are sociologically relevant in explaining professionalism: prolonged training in a body of specialized, abstract knowledge and an orientation toward providing a service.

Moreover, once a professional group becomes established, Goode indicates that it begins further to consolidate its power by formalizing social relationships that govern the interaction of the professionals with their clients, their colleagues, and with official agencies outside the profession. Recognition on the part of both clients, outside agencies, and the wider society of the profession's claim to competence, as well as the profession's ability to control its own membership, is necessary if professional decisions are not to be reviewed by outside authorities. Once this situation (public acceptance of claims to competence and the profession's control of its membership) occurs, Goode believes that additional features of the profession can be established. Goode (1960:903) described these features as follows:

1. The profession determines its own standards of education and training.
2. The student professional goes through a more stringent socialization experience than the learner in other occupations.
3. Professional practice is often legally recognized by some form of licensure.
4. Licensing and admission boards are manned by members of the profession.
5. Most legislation concerned with the profession is shaped by that profession.
6. The occupation gains income, power, and prestige ranking, and can demand high-caliber students.
7. The practitioner is relatively free of lay evaluation and control.
8. The norms of practice enforced by the profession are more stringent than legal controls.
9. Members are more strongly identified and affiliated with the profession than are members of other occupations with theirs.
10. The profession is more likely to be a terminal occupation. Members do not care to leave it, and a higher proportion assert that if they had it to do over again, they would again choose that type of work.

What Goode has accomplished, for our purposes, is the development of guidelines for analyzing the development of the medical profession in American society. While physicians in the United States have traditionally shared a basic service orientation, the second requirement, that of lengthy training in a specialized and abstract body of knowledge, was initially lacking. Most American medical practitioners in the period before the American Revolution were ship's surgeons, apothecaries, or clergy who had obtained a familiarity with medical knowledge in Europe (Major, 1954; Stevens, 1971; Coe, 1978). Few practitioners had been educated in either a university setting or a medical school. Anyone who wanted to practice medicine could do so and could claim the title of "doctor," which in Europe was reserved exclusively for persons educated at a university. The most distinguished early American physicians were those trained at the University of Edinburgh, Great Britain's foremost medical school in that era. From this small group of British-trained physicians came the impetus for establishment of the first American medical school in 1765 at the College of Philadelphia. This medical school, which later became part of the University of Pennsylvania, was subsequently joined in the years prior to 1800 by the organization of other medical schools at King's College (Columbia), Harvard, and Dartmouth.

After 1800, American medical schools virtually mushroomed, as school after school was established. But the quality of medical education in the United States remained low and physicians themselves had little prestige as late as 1850. Not only did the doctors of the day offer little hope in curing disease, but sometimes their methods were either unpleasant or fatal. Often patients were bled, which tended to weaken their condition, or they were administered purgatives, which caused them to vomit. By the middle of the nineteenth century, states E. Richard Brown (1979:62–63), "cholera victims were given an even chance of being done in by the disease or by the doctor."

The best medical training at this time was in Europe, especially in France and Germany where medical research was flourishing. In France, Louis Pasteur's germ theory of disease, advanced during the mid-1800s, revolutionized medicine and provided the foundation for the discovery, classification, and treatment of numerous diseases. By the last quarter of the century, however, Germany assumed the leading role in the scientific development of medicine. Medical scientists in Germany like Rudolf Virchow, who unveiled a general concept of disease based on cellular pathology (1858), and Robert Koch, whose work in bacteriology led to the discovery of the bacillus for anthrax (1876), tuberculosis (1882), and cholera (1883), became important figures in medicine. Their work, and the work of their colleagues, stimulated the growth of clinics, university-affiliated laboratories, and high standards of admission for medical training in Germany and Austria. Beginning in 1870, large numbers of American students flocked to the famous clinics and laboratories of German and Austrian universities. First Vienna and then Berlin became *the* centers of medical knowledge. It is estimated that between 1870 and 1914 approximately 15,000 American doctors received at least part of their training in German-speaking universities (Stevens, 1971). Most of these doctors returned to the United States to set up lucrative private practices by introducing into their work the latest scientific techniques, which, as Brown (1979:73) explains, "at least *seemed* effective in reducing suffering and ameliorating the symptoms of disease." Brown describes the situation as follows:

Physicians who had the money to take an extra year's study in Europe were able to build more prestigious practices than the ordinary American-trained doctor. Usually they would take themselves out of direct competition with the majority of physicians by specializing in gynecology, surgery, opthalmology, or one of the other new branches of medicine. They quickly formed a new elite in the profession with reputations that brought the middle and wealthy classes to their doors.[2]

Other European-trained physicians returned to develop medical laboratories and pursue the scientific investigation of disease. Henry Bowditch, for example, founded the first experimental physiology laboratory in the United States at Harvard University in 1871, while William Welch, who discovered staphylococcus in 1892, began the first pathology laboratory in America at Bellevue Hospital medical school in New York City in 1878. By 1900, the entire medical school faculties of Harvard, Johns Hopkins, Yale, and Michigan had been trained in Germany.

In the meantime, medical science continued to record impressive technical achievements. During the 1800s these achievements included René Laennec's (1816) invention of the stethoscope; the work of Crawford Long (1842), Robert Liston (1846), and William Morton (1846) on ether as an anesthetic; Claude Bernard's (1849) discovery of glycogen and the development of a theory of hormonal secretions providing the basis for endocrinology; Joseph Lister's (1866) use of antiseptic procedures in surgery; William Welch's (1892) discovery of staphylococcus; Wilhelm Roentgen's (1895) development of the x-ray; and Ronald Ross' (1895) research on the cause of malaria. Thus, by the beginning of the twentieth century, American medical doctors were clearly able to claim the two core characteristics of a profession as outlined by Goode—a service orientation and a body of specialized knowledge.

Moreover, at the beginning of the twentieth century medical research in the United States began to surpass that of Europe. American medicine had been influenced by the British until 1820, the French until the American Civil War, and then the Germans. By 1895, however, the Americans were ready to forge ahead thanks to the vast sums of money poured into medical research by private American philanthropic foundations, such as those funded by the Carnegie and Rockefeller families. According to Brown, physicians in America strongly supported the rise of scientific medicine because it gave them greater effectiveness in a rapidly industrialized society and provided them with higher status, prestige, and income. Wealthy industrialists supported scientific medicine because it appeared to be a good investment in maintaining the moral, social, and economic order of corporate capitalism. Nevertheless, the result was, to quote Rosemary Stevens (1971:135), that "under the impact of new knowledge, the rapid improvement of medical schools, and the proliferation of hospitals and clinics which

[2]E. Richard Brown, *Rockefeller Medicine Men: Medicine and Capitalism in America* (Berkeley: University of California Press, 1979), p. 73.

in turn generated new information, medicine was becoming vastly more efficient."

The American Medical Association

Another important step was necessary before American physicians could take advantage of their evolving professional status—the organization of physicians into a professionally identifiable group. With the founding of the American Medical Association in Philadelphia in 1847 physicians could mark the beginning of a new era in medicine (see American Medical Association, 1951; Burrow, 1963; Coe, 1970; Fishbein, 1947; Freidson, 1970a; Hyde and Wolff, 1954; Stevens, 1971). Weak and ineffectual in the beginning, the American Medical Association gradually extended its authority to become the single greatest influence on the organization and practice of medicine in the United States.

Two internal organizational measures were highly significant in this process. First, in 1883 the *Journal of the American Medical Association* appeared. This journal not only disseminated the latest medical knowledge and contributed to the prestige of the association, but also developed an awareness among the members of the AMA of their primary allegiance to the medical profession. Second, in 1902 an important reorganization took place when the AMA was divided into component societies on the local level (district or county medical societies), constituent societies (state or territorial medical associations), a national House of Delegates, a Board of Trustees, and national officers.

As a result of this change, the basic unit of the AMA had become the local society. Most important, it had the authority to set its own qualifications for membership. In theory, all "reputable and ethical" licensed physicians were eligible to join the local society, but final approval of membership was dependent upon the local society's arbitrary discretion. The power of the local society was further enhanced because AMA organizational structure permits no formal right to a hearing or right to appeal the local society's decisions. Thus threats of denial of membership or of expulsion from the local society represent powerful sanctions, since there is no alternative medical association and AMA membership can be critically important to a physician's career. Often such membership influences patient referrals, consultations, specialty ratings, and other professional and social contacts important to a highly successful medical practice.

In 1975 the AMA had a membership of 180,000 physicians. This figure represents less than 60 percent of all active and inactive doctors of medicine. Nonmembers include those who have retired, who have not satisfied local residence requirements, who have violated the AMA code of ethics, and who are employed by the government, the armed forces, research agencies, or universities and thus believe they do not need the benefits of membership. Other physicians may not belong because for some reason they are unacceptable to the local society, because they themselves disapprove of the AMA's policies or because such membership is not important to them. Often foreign doctors are excluded and sometimes racial/ethnic minorities, especially black physicians in the South, have been denied membership. Although the AMA has tried to discourage this practice, it has not always been successful because of the authority of the local societies to determine membership qualifications. James Burrow (1963), in his political history of the AMA, has pointed out that local societies have the power to enforce conformity at their level, but the national organization is relatively weak in implementing national policies.

Despite the strength of local societies, there is little dispute within the AMA concerning its national objectives. As Eliot Freidson (1970a) and others have pointed out, the actual exercise of power in the American Medical Association is concentrated in the hands of a relatively limited number of physicians. Many members have either not been interested in the association's internal politics or have been too busy with their own medical practices to devote time to professional problems. The vast majority has usually been content to let the AMA represent the medical profession with Congress and other governmental agencies. The association in turn keeps its membership informed about significant medical and health legislation on both state and national levels.

Additionally, there is no forum for effective dissent within the AMA because public debates are disapproved in order to project an image of a united profession in the association's interaction with outside agencies. Dissenting issues within the AMA must first win major support at the local level or they are not considered further. And the *Journal of the American Medical Association* seldom publishes views other than official policy. Opposition groups within the AMA are further prevented from gaining power because of the indirect system of elections for national officers. Only the House of Delegates, which consists of representatives from each state, elects people to the top offices and to the Board of Trustees, which exercises day-to-day control over the association. Many influential appointments to AMA councils and committees are made directly by the Board of Trustees and are not voted upon by either the general membership or the House of Delegates.

In an examination of the American Medical Association by David Hyde and Payson Wolff in the *Yale Law Journal* (1954), the overall power base of the AMA was described as resulting from three primary sources: (1) power over the medical profession, (2) a strong economic position, and (3) the social status of the physician. The power of the AMA over the medical profession was described as the power of *consent, monopoly,* and *coercion.* Hyde and Wolff speculated that the AMA did have the consent of a majority of physicians to represent organized medicine. This consent was derived from an awareness among medical doctors that a formal organization was needed to enforce professional integrity, to advance professional interests, and to resist lay attempts to control medical matters. Monopoly resulted from the AMA's position as the only nationally recognized professional association available to the physician. The AMA's power of coercion was due to its authority to ostracize offending physicians and also to the incorporation of AMA guidelines into state medical practice laws and licensing procedures.

One of the most significant guiding principles of the AMA has been its view of the physician as an independent practitioner largely free of public control who engages in private medical practice on a fee-for-service basis.

Since the 1920s a considerable portion of the AMA's energies have gone toward maintaining this situation, particularly in regard to the issue of national health insurance, which the AMA believes will inhibit the ability of the medical profession to provide quality medical care because it is likely to reduce the physician's freedom to control both the conditions of practice and the setting of fees. A more extensive discussion of the complex national health insurance controversy will be presented in Chapter Nine, but at this point it is important to note that the major public image of the American Medical Association has become that of a protective trade association seeking to ensure that challenges to the physician's position as an individual entrepreneur of health services is not hindered. With a slight majority of American physicians (over 50 percent) represented in its membership, the AMA has been able to claim that it speaks for organized medicine. However, this claim may be misleading as there is evidence that the AMA's membership is declining in numbers (AMA membership included 219,000 dues-paying physicians in 1973 compared to 180,000 in 1975 and 175,000 in 1980) and that it does not represent the opinions and attitudes of a growing minority of physicians.

In two studies of Yale University School of Medicine students and graduates, Lee Goldman (1974a, 1974b) observed that support for reform legislation in health insurance went well beyond the AMA's compromise efforts. The strongest predictor of medical attitudes was political ideology. Physicians who identified themselves as politically conservative were more likely than liberals to be members of the AMA and to oppose national health insurance. But only 50 percent of the Yale sample either belonged to the AMA or planned to apply for membership.

While Yale physicians may not be typical of all other physicians, Goldman's studies do imply that perhaps a substantial portion of American physicians may not be represented by the views of the American Medical Association. Consequently, there may be considerably more variation in the medical and political attitudes of medical doctors in the United States than has been previously assumed. If this is the case, then the reputation of the AMA as a powerful lobby in Washington, D.C., may, to some extent, be spurious, despite conflicting evidence (see Burrow, 1963). David Mechanic (1972:28) seems to find for a weaker AMA when he explains that the idea of any particular political group's being able to dominate health policy is not consistent with the history of recent social legislation in health care. Although the AMA opposed both Medicare and the Regional Medical Program, these programs became law.

However, the evidence does not go so far as to conclude that the AMA no longer yields significant influence in health legislation. In fact, as Mechanic has also pointed out, even legislation that passed Congress over the objections of the AMA has taken those objections into account and attempted to protect the interests of the medical profession as much as possible. With its organization, influence, and financing, the AMA will likely remain a very important factor in future legislative battles in the health sector and will continue to be instrumental in shaping the overall direction of the medical profession. As Stevens (1971:532) has surmised in her excellent analysis of the medical profession, the primary future role of the AMA seems likely to be that of a negotiating body with government and a governmental agent (by way of providing professional standards and discipline), rather than a protective trade association or the spokesman for medical education and health workforce development. The AMA still has a critical role in policy development and administration of any national programs dealing with health care.

The Control of Medical Education

The professionalization of medicine would not have been possible without control over the standards for medical education. At the beginning of the nineteenth century, the United States had seen the emergence of a vast number of proprietary medical schools. These schools, in the absence of any educational controls, were designed to offer medical degrees as part of a profit-making venture. It is estimated that about 400 proprietary medical schools existed during the 1800s; generally they had low standards of instruction, poor facilities, and admitted any student who could pay the required tuition. Since proprietary schools competed with other schools of this type and with schools affiliated with universities, they attempted to make their programs as attractive as possible. One school, for example, gave free trips to Europe upon graduation to any students who paid fees regularly and in cash for three years (Stevens, 1971). Anyone who had the financial resources could obtain a medical degree and practice medicine, especially in the developing American West.

In 1904 the AMA established the Council on Medical Education to originate suggestions for the improvement of education and to become the association's agency for implementing educational change. The Council eventually became an important regulating agency that operated both to establish high standards in medical schools and to strengthen the AMA's influence in medical education. The subsequent success of this effort was stimulated by one of the most important events in the history of medical education: the Flexner Report.

Sponsored by the Carnegie Foundation for the Advancement of Teaching, Abraham Flexner visited every medical school in the country and issued his famous report in 1910. Hoping to obtain funds from the prestigious Carnegie Foundation, most medical schools were anxious to discuss their problems and shortcomings while extending their full cooperation to Flexner in assessing their particular situation. The Flexner Report came out as a devastating indictment of the lack of quality medical education in the United States. Only three medical schools—Harvard, Western Reserve, and Johns Hopkins—were given full approval; many other schools were characterized by Flexner as "plague spots," "utterly wretched," "out-and-out commercial enterprises," "wholly inadequate," and so forth (Stevens 1971:67).

Flexner strongly recommended that medical schools consist of a full-time faculty and that both laboratory and hospital facilities be made available to medical students. He also urged that standards concerning the admission of students to medical schools be established and that the qualifications of medical school faculty be raised significantly. He likewise believed that medical education should be conducted by universities on a graduate level and that teaching and research functions be integrated within the institution offering the instruction. The example of a model medical school was Johns Hopkins University, with its medical education system containing a medical school, a nursing school, and a university hospital. Johns Hopkins required the bachelor's degree or its equivalent for admission as well as specific premedical college-level courses.

Although widespread protests arose from the affected schools, the Flexner Report induced considerable improvement in medical education. The better schools improved their programs and the lesser schools eventually closed because of the bad publicity, financial adversity, and failure to meet the requirements of state licensing boards. Many states refused to certify the graduates of inferior medical schools, and money from various foundations was usually channeled only into those schools with good reputations. Since the sole source of medical school ratings continued to be the AMA's Council on Medical Education, the medical profession was able to retain an effective monopoly over educational regulation.

In summary, by the mid-1920s, the medical profession had consolidated its professional position to the point that it clearly had become a model of professionalism. According to Goode's analysis of the characteristics of a profession, the medical profession had not only met the basic criteria of being a service occupation supported by prolonged training in a specialized knowledge, but furthermore, it had determined its own standards of education and training, had successfully demanded high-caliber students, had staffed its own licensing and admission boards, had shaped legislation in its own interests, had developed stringent professional sanctions, had become a terminal occupation, and was free of formal lay evaluation and control. Although threatened by social legislation regarding reforms in health care, physicians constitute, and will in all probability remain, the dominant professional group in the rendering of medical service in the United States.

THE SOCIALIZATION OF THE PHYSICIAN

To understand the perspectives of physicians as a professional group, it is important also to consider the manner in which physicians are selected and trained as medical professionals. In the 1980s, nearly 15,000 students will be selected annually out of some 45,000 applicants to begin training at 119 medical schools in the United States. Some 80 percent of these first-year students will be male; the remaining 20 percent represents a significant increase for females. In the 1960s only about 9 percent of all first-year medical students were female. There has also been an increase in the percentage of racial minority students, especially blacks. Since 1969, the percentage of racial minorities in first-year classes has risen from 3 to 7 percent. Despite these changes, the majority of medical students in the United States remain white and male.

Typically, first-year medical students will be between the ages of twenty-one and twenty-three and will have at least a bachelor's degree with a 3.4 (on a 4.0 scale) premedical grade point average. Most likely the undergraduate college major will be in biology, chemistry, zoology, premedical, or psychology. Because these students are motivated and committed to a well-defined, terminal career goal, they have a high probability of successfully completing medical school once accepted; about 95 percent of all entering medical students currently attain the M.D. degree.

Several studies on the social origins of American medical students clearly show that most are from upper- and upper-middle-class families. Although there are signs that increasing numbers of lower-middle- and lower-class students are entering medical school, most medical students are homogeneous in terms of social class affiliation. For instance, Howard Becker et al. (1961), in a major study of students at the University of Kansas Medical School in the late 1950s, found that lower-class medical students, by virtue of their undergraduate education and commitment to becoming successful physicians, had clearly assimilated middle-class norms and values.

Family influence seems to be an important variable in encouraging and reinforcing the ambitions of the future recruit to the medical profession. Having a parent or close relative who is a physician also seems to be a distinct advantage. Natalie Rogoff (1957) observed in a study of medical students at the University of Pennsylvania that the more frequent the contact with a physician, the easier it was to form the idea of becoming a physician. Of those students with a physician father, 74 percent had made a decision to go to medical school before the age of fourteen. For medical students with either a distant relative as a physician or no family relationship to a physician, the percentage indicating a career decision under the age of fourteen was 52 percent and 40 percent respectively. In the Becker et al. study, a random sample of medical students disclosed that 48 percent of the sample had parents or other relatives who practiced medicine and another 23 percent were friendly with their family physician or knew other physicians as friends. Altogether, 71 percent of the total sample had some contact with members of the medical profession prior to making their decision about becoming a medical doctor. Samuel Bloom (1973) found that while medical students at the State University of New York Downstate Medical Center tended to make a career decision for medicine relatively late, those students having sustained contact with a physician through immediate or close family relationships likewise tended to consider medicine as a career earlier than other students. These findings support Oswald Hall's (1948) contention that the decision to study medicine is largely social in character, that is, it originates in a social group that is able to generate and nurture the medical ambition.

The reason given by most medical students for choosing a career in medicine has been generally that of wanting "to help people." At Tulane University Medical School, Leonard Reissman and Ralph Platou (1960) found that a majority of both junior and senior medical students could be described as "humanitarians," rather than "scientists" or "professionals." A major characteristic of the "humanitarian" student was a strong orientation toward working with patients and enjoying interpersonal relations. Becker et al. likewise found that first-year medical students had idealistic long-range perspectives about why they selected medicine as a career. These perspectives were summarized as follows (Becker et al., 1961:72):

1. Medicine is the best of all professions.
2. When we begin to practice, we want to help people, have enjoyable, satisfying work while upholding medical ideals. We want to earn enough money to lead comfortable lives, but this is not our primary concern.

Some medical students no doubt enter medical school in order to make money or for the prestige of the M.D. degree, or both. According to John Columbotos (1969), physicians from a lower-class social origin were more likely than upper-class doctors to emphasize success values as reasons for going into medicine. But once in medical practice, social class background became less significant. Those physicians who were initially success-oriented became less so after commencing their practices, while the reverse occurred with those who were less success-oriented. Columbotos suggested this trend was most likely due to socialization by colleagues. Success-oriented physicians were probably encouraged to be less obvious about their ambitions, and the less success-oriented were most likely encouraged to strive for the level of status indicative of their professional group. Becker et al. noted that most entering medical students *assumed* they would be well-paid. Hence, making money was apparently secondary to helping patients. Many resented the notion that they were solely out to make money.

Once the medical student begins training, he or she is expected to acquire a foundation of knowledge in the basic medical sciences and the techniques employed in the actual practice of medicine. Included in this process is the internalization of ethical and moral principles that are essential if the physician is to be trusted by patients, colleagues, and the community and is to maintain professional autonomy. Most courses of study range from thirty-two to forty-five months, and the educational experience is usually divided into basic medical science studies and clinical studies. Basic medical science studies consist of courses in anatomy, biochemistry, physiology, pathology, pharmacology, microbiology, physical diagnosis, clinical laboratory procedures, and often behavioral science. The clinical programs consist of learning to use basic medical science to solve clinical problems by working with patients under the supervision of the faculty. The students also rotate through clerkships in various medical services, such as medicine, surgery, pediatrics, obstetrics-gynecology, psychiatry, and other specialties.

Much of the sociological research concerning medical education has focused on the consequences of that experience other than mastery of medical knowledge. Renée Fox (1957) found that medical students at Cornell Medical School acquired basically two traits as a result of their medical training: ability to be emotionally detached from the patient and to tolerate uncertainty. Fox, whose work was part of an extensive study of student physicians (see Merton et al., 1957), noted that the medical student experienced three types of uncertainty. First, there was uncertainty resulting from an awareness of not being able to learn everything about medicine. Second, there was the realization that limitations existed in current medical knowledge and techniques. The first two uncertainties led to a third type of uncertainty in which medical students had problems distinguishing between personal ignorance and the limits of available knowledge. However, Fox observed that as the student acquired medical knowledge and gained experience, along with a sense of personal adequacy in medicine, he or she learned to cope with the uncertainty and to assess conflicting evidence objectively in arriving at a diagnosis. This process was assisted by the realization that other medical students were coping with the same problems and that the faculty also experienced uncertainty in their everyday work.

At the University of Kansas Medical School, Becker et al. (1961) determined that the students developed a strong appreciation of clinical experience (actually working with patients rather than reading about disease and studying it in the laboratory) and that they acquired a sense of responsibility about patients. They also learned to view disease and death as medical problems rather than as emotional issues. The focal point of their passage through medical school was to graduate; since they could not learn everything they needed to know to practice medicine, they directed their efforts toward finding the most economical ways of learning. Generally, they tried to guess what the faculty wanted them to know, and then they studied this material for the examinations. Even so, they found that they put in an eight-hour day of classes and laboratories. They also studied four to five hours on week nights and continued studying on the weekends.

One aspect of medical training that appears even in more recent studies of medical students in California (Coombs, 1978), Canada (Haas and Shaffir, 1977; Shapiro, 1978), and Israel (Adler and Shuval, 1978) is the finding that the experience tends to promote impersonal attitudes toward patients. Robert Coombs, for example, found that in a California medical school the faculty gave little real guidance in how to manage patients except to serve as role models for emotional control and a businesslike demeanor. In Canada, Jack Haas and William Schaffir found the students to be initially dismayed by how the teaching faculty and other hospital staff members treated patients. One student reported:

> What I do remember about Phase II that really got me when I did go to a cancer clinic at the Fensteran and I saw the way they were just herding in ladies that had hysterectomies and cancer, and just the way the doctors would walk right in and wouldn't even introduce us as students, and just open them up and just look and say a lot of heavy jargon. And the ladies would be saying, "How is it?", "Am I better, or worse?" And they say in this phony reassuring tone, "Yes, you're fine," and take you into the hallway and say how bad the person was.

> They hardly talked to the patient at all. Like this was a big check up after waiting three months or six months and then the doctor whips in for two minutes to take a quick look and then they're gone. We would get in there and he'd hold the speculum and we'd all take a look and we would just herd right out again into another room and have a look and herd out again. I thought the dehumanization was awful.[3]

In trying to cope with the situation, the students began to rationalize that the large number of patients seen by the physicians precluded them from doing anything more than attending to the patient's medical condition.

---

[3]Jack Haas and William Shaffir, "The Professionalization of Medical Students: Developing Competence and A Cloak of Competence," *Symbolic Interaction*, 1 (1977), 82.

There were just too many patients and not enough time to deal with psycho-social problems. In fact, in their own work, the students found themselves depersonalizing patients so they could concentrate on learning what was medically important. A student described the situation this way:

> I think you realize that there is a structural problem, and there are a lot of demands made on you and you are forced to act in certain ways just to accomplish your work. But right now in the training phase, I find if the clinical preceptor takes me around to listen to six patients with heart murmurs and I only have five minutes with each patient, I don't get concerned that I'm not getting it on with the patient, because I'm trying to learn about heart murmurs.[4]

Earlier, the Becker et al. study had attempted to assess the general impact of such attitudes by exploring the charge that medical students become cynical as a result of their medical education. In reply, Becker and his colleagues noted that medical students did appear to enter medical school openly idealistic, but once in medical school, their idealism was replaced with a concern for getting through. Becker observed that medical students may in fact become cynical while in school, but he also pointed out that attitudes are often situational. Thus when graduation approached, idealism seemed to return as the students could set aside the immediate problem of completing their program of study. What had happened was that medical students had been isolated in an institutional setting and forced to adjust to the demands of that setting. But once the medical student was ready to return to the mainstream of society, the student again became concerned about service to humanity. In an earlier article, Becker and Blanche Greer (1958) had argued that cynicism on the part of medical students represented growth toward a more realistic perspective. What appeared as a harmful change of attitude was actually part of a functional learning process fitted to the physician's role of maintaining an objective perspective of health and disease. The more recent Coombs (1978) study likewise found that medical students' cynicism did not develop into a generalized personality trait. The students in this study learned to balance emotional attitudes with sensitivity toward patients.[5]

---

[4]Haas and Shaffir, "The Professionalization of Medical Students," p. 71.
[5]Some physicians do not need to spend a lot of time with patients. Consider, for example, the report of William Nolen (1970:191–192), who was undergoing training as a resident in surgery at a hospital on Long Island, New York:

> Steele was no slouch as a diagnostician. He was one of those surgeons who have a sixth sense about symptoms and could learn more about a patient in five minutes than most doctors do in an hour. I took him to see one of our rare service cases, an eight-year-old boy admitted for possible appendicitis. Steele spent two minutes with him and we stepped back into the corridor.
> "Did you notice the way he kept his right knee bent? Did you see that he wasn't moving his abdomen at all when he breathed? Did you get a look at how dry his tongue was? That kid's got peritonitis. Put him on [surgery] schedule."
> "But his white count is only nine thousand and his temperature is normal," I objected.
> "Nolen, let me tell you something," Steele said. "Try looking at the patient instead of the chart. The chart isn't sick."
> The boy had a ruptured appendix with peritonitis.

In summary, the Fox and Becker et al. studies demonstrate that the experience of a medical education provides not only basic knowledge and techniques concerning the diagnosis and treatment of health disorders, but also inculcates the norms and values of the medical profession. Fox points out that medical students develop a tolerance for uncertainty and a detached concern for patients, while Becker et al., found that medical students developed an appreciation of clinical experience and medical responsibility for patients. A later study of Harvard interns (Miller, 1970) corroborated *clinical perspective* and *medical responsibility* as the enduring perspectives acquired by interns.

There were, however, some differences between the Fox and Becker et al. studies. The most notable difference concerned Fox's impression that medical students were socialized into the physician role by anticipating their future behavior patterns as physicians during their student years. In contrast, Becker et al. did not find that medical students were socialized into a physician role. Kansas medical students were too busy trying to excel academically, and the faculty did not allow them to assume professional attitudes. Moreover, they had very low status in an apparently inflexible hierarchy. A major criticism of this finding is that even though Becker and his associates did not observe socialization taking place, that does not mean that the medical students did not recognize the dimensions of the physician role and did not incorporate these dimensions into their perspective for use at a future time.

Other research (Huntington, 1957; Lief, 1971) has clearly supported the thesis that the medical student goes through a process of anticipation, which is aided by increasing responsibility and competence during the clinical years of medical school. Thus, student self-image was gradually replaced by a professional self-image as "doctor" the nearer the medical student approached graduation. Mary Huntington (1957) discovered that medical students felt least like "doctors" around their fellow students or the medical school faculty, but their professional image was enhanced by their interaction with patients who attributed physician status to them.

However, in a later article Fox (1974) speculated that medical students in the 1970s were different from their 1950s counterparts. Although contemporary medical students are still likely to be white middle-class males, they are probably "late-deciders" for a career in medicine, with their decision coming during the second half of their undergraduate studies. The new medical student may be unsure as to whether he or she wants to be a physician even at the beginning of the medical school program. These new students are seen by Fox as staunchly egalitarian in their concept of the physician, the physician–patient relationship, and relationships with non-physician members of the health care team. In other words, they disapprove of the "physician as God" image and feel they are concerned about patients as people, not just as diseased specimens. they likewise hope to improve society by improving health care, especially for the poor.

There are data that support Fox's description of the "new" medical student. Daniel Funkenstein (1971), for example, in a study of consecutive classes at Harvard Medical School between the late 1950s and early 1970s classes at Harvard Medical School between the late 1950s and early 1970s found that members of the later classes tended to show a stronger desire to be socially responsible and to believe that quality medical care had to be provided to all segments of society without regard for finances. At Yale University, Goldman (1974b) noted that medical students demonstrated more liberal attitudes toward political and medical issues than did older doctors. Another study by Goldman and Ebbert (1973) found, in addition, that Yale medical school graduates did not become more politically conservative as they became older. If these findings can be generalized beyond Yale students, the implications of Goldman's work are that the medical profession may receive a new generation of doctors with medically liberal views that may tend to persist over time. What is further indicated is that an increasing supply of new physicians receptive to the reorganization of health care delivery may influence the development of some profound changes in the American system of medical practice in the future.

But for some physicians the possibility remains that medical training has focused their attention more on technical procedures than on dealing with patients as people. As Donald Light (1979) points out, in emphasizing clinical judgments and techniques physicians run the danger of becoming insensitive to complexities in diagnosis, treatment, and relations with patients. The result can be errors and malpractice suits. Light (1979:320) explains: "Their emphasis on techniques can make them oblivious to the needs of clients as *clients* define them; yet it is clients' trust that professionals will solve their complex problems which provides the foundation of professional power." Zeev Ben-Sira (1980), for instance, has found in Israel that, especially for lower-class patients, some emotional support by the physician will not only reduce the patient's uncertainty about the type and outcome of treatment, but will also have a significant impact on the patient's evaluation of treatment.

THE POWER STRUCTURE OF AMERICAN MEDICINE

Before considering the possible sociological consequences of increased liberalism among members of the latest generation of medical doctors, it is important to examine the power structure of the medical profession in order to identify the factors with which any movement toward change will have to contend. One of the early influential studies concerning the power structure of the medical profession was done by Oswald Hall (1946, 1948) in an eastern American city. Subsequent to the ambition to be a doctor and the successful completion of medical school, Hall identified three additional stages in the career of a physician: (1) gaining admittance to various medical societies; (2) developing, retaining, and improving a clientele; and (3) developing a set of informal relationships with colleagues that facilitate the accomplishment of the other objectives.

The Hospital

A most significant factor in a successful urban medical career, according to Hall, was affiliation with a prestigious hospital, because the more important hospital positions were usually associated with the more finan-cially rewarding medical practices. Therefore, gaining an appointment at a prestigious hospital represented a crucial point in the career development of the urban physican.

Of particular significance was the initial appointment because, as Hall (1948:330) explains, "the internship that a doctor has served is a distinctive badge; it is one of the most enduring criteria in the evaluation of his status." In a study of the Harvard Medical Unit at Boston City Hospital, Stephen Miller (1970) found that the "best" internship was not necessarily determined by the quality of teaching, the type of patient, or the range of responsibility interns were allowed to assume, though these factors were important. The "best" referred to the reputation of the program and its location.

Most medical specialists, scientists, and teachers, according to Miller, are trained in Chicago, New York, or Boston. So the reputation of an internship in the medical education and research institutions of these cities would serve as credentials to assist the candidate's entry into the academic medical circles of any particular urban center. For those physicians wishing to become general practitioners, the optimal setting for an internship would be in communities where they hoped to build a medical practice. Even at the local level, the initial hospital appointment was important in that it facilitated the formation of friendships and professional relationships that could help to enhance a career. Usually the location of an internship will determine the system of medical institutions and the group of physicians the intern will be associated with in the future.

For example, Miller observed that the Harvard program of graduate medical training was much more than a way to meet licensing requirements; it was a means by which an academic appointment at a "name" medical school could be secured. As one of the Harvard interns explained to Miller:

> I'm going into academic medicine, and I wanted the internship which was the best or very good; I think of the word "prestige," a great deal of prestige in being part of this group. It just has a very good reputation, you know. It will look good on paper.[6]

All interns, however, do not receive their first choice for an internship since there are usually many more applicants than positions in the programs with the best reputations. Hall found that the likelihood of gaining an appointment depended much less on superior technical competence than on the future intern's acceptability to the institution of choice. It was not the individual traits that were important, but whether those traits could be assimilated by the institution itself. The department head of a large Catholic hospital told Hall that:

> One of our most important problems here is picking interns. the main qualifi-cation as far as I can see is "personality." Now that is an intangible sort of thing.

[6]Stephen J. Miller, *Prescription for Leadership: Training for the Medical Elite* (Chicago: Aldine, 1970), p. 81.

It means partly to mix well, to be humble to older doctors to the correct degree, and to be able to assume the proper degree of superiority toward the patient. Since all medical schools are now Grade A, there is no point in holding competitive examinations. So the main problem confronting the selection committee is that of getting interns who will fit well into the pattern of the hospital.[7]

A similar pattern of attitudes toward applicants was apparent in the Miller study in Boston. One of the senior resident physicians in the study informed Miller that:

> . . . interviews here do not carry a great deal of weight, and people are accepted or rejected mostly in terms of where they stood in their medical school class and the kind of recommendations they get. But I suppose, in general, what we look for in the interview is some assurance that the fellow is reasonably mature and sensible. The people coming here obviously are all intelligent. We look for what their interests in the future might be. I think, by and large, people coming here are interested in academic careers, and somebody who is interested in general practice in Rudolph Junction, probably, this isn't the internship for him.[8]

Many of the interns in the Harvard Medical Unit at Boston City Hospital were graduates of "name" medical schools. About 50 percent had graduated from Harvard and another 30 percent were from schools like Cornell, Yale, and Johns Hopkins. The remaining 20 percent were from less well-known medical schools. Thus, it was possible for the graduate of a "lesser" school to begin an internship with the Harvard group in order to acquire the background for an academic appointment at higher level medical institutions. As Miller explained, there were not enough "name" medical school graduates for all the internships available; then, too, the Harvard Medical Unit limited the number of Harvard graduates it would accept in order to avoid the "inbreeding" of its faculty.

Yet the process of selection for the Harvard Medical Unit was not entirely democratic. Since many graduates of the program had gone on to the faculties of other medical schools, a large number of schools featured alumni of the Unit, in effect a "colony" of physicians with the same medical background. Their letters of recommendation as former students, graduates, and people known to the Harvard Medical Unit greatly assisted the acceptability of applicants. Miller noted that all of the interns from lesser known schools in his study of the Harvard Medical Unit program were graduates of medical schools where Harvard alumni constituted a colony. Miller (1970:70) stated: "Most learned about the program from, discussed it with, and were advised to choose it by Harvard Medical Unit alumni." So not only were initial appointments important for the future careers of the interns, but also the gaining of these appointments was influenced to a certain degree by having recommendations from the "right" people. Hall found a similar trend in his study of the medical career.

[7]Oswald Hall, "The Stages of a Medical Career," *American Journal of Sociology*, 53 (March 1948), 330.
[8]Miller, *Prescription for Leadership*, pp.59–60.

Another consideration in understanding the importance of the hospital is that within the hospital, physicians are arranged in a hierarchy of status—intern, resident, staff member, and associate staff member. Each level represents progress in a medical career and indicates the status and privileges of the doctors involved. There are differences in status not only within hospitals, but also between hospitals. Hall noted in his study that the major hospitals were organized according to social class and ethnic differentials. The leading physicians in the community were characterized by Hall as upper-class Yankees who attended expensive universities as undergraduates and the better known medical schools, especially Harvard. Then they held internships at the dominant Yankee hospital. These Yankee physicians entered the practice of medicine in their community from the vantage point of being associated with the "best" hospital.

In contrast, Hall found that Italian M.D.s found it difficult to gain a position at Yankee hospitals. Instead they sought an alternate route of career advancement in Catholic hospitals, which could both provide a good career and protect the Italian physician from Yankee competition. The point made by Hall was that the successful practice of medicine involved participation in a hospital system which in turn provided the physician with integration into the other medical institutions in the community. The marginal men in medical practice, according to Hall, were those who had abandoned the shelter of a hospital affiliation and had gone out on their own in the wider competitive field of medicine. This same pattern appeared in the Miller study. One of the Harvard Medical Unit interns, who was a native of Boston and wanted to practice medicine there, made it quite clear that being without "connections at the Harvard hospitals" was like being in "exile" (Miller, 1970:80).

The Clientele

The next stage described by Hall is that of acquiring a clientele and retaining and improving it. Hall likened this process to that of a commercial enterprise in that the physician needed to play the role of a promoter. In other words, the physician was required to interact with patients so as to secure their approval of the services provided. Freidson (1960) has pointed out that the lay referral system not only channels the patient to certain doctors, but also helps the patient to make a decision about returning to a particular doctor. Freidson notes that the first visit to a doctor is often tentative, especially in a community large enough to support more than one doctor. Freidson (1960:378) states: "Whether the physician's prescription will be followed or not, and whether the patient will come back, seems to rest at least partly on his retrospective assessment of the professional consultation." Thus, the patient not only passes through the lay referral system on the way to the physician, but also on the way back by discussing the doctor's behavior, diagnosis, and prescription with family and friends. In a given community, certain doctors are often chosen more frequently than others merely because they are fashionable or popular. Most physicians become aware of lay expectations and learn to deal with them if they expect patients to return.

Furthermore, Hall observed that success in medicine involves improving the practice by attracting the desired type of patient and discouraging those patients who do not fit into the physician's conception of his or her practice. It may also be true that more affluent patients desire to be treated with others of their kind; so a physician who treats both the rich and the poor in the same setting and under the same circumstances would run the risk of offending the rich. Michael Miller (1973) has observed that upper-class patients will change physicians sooner than lower-class patients.

Although the evidence is not conclusive, existing studies generally suggest that physicians tend to favor upper- and middle-class patients. Besides being perceived as more likely to pay their bills, upper- and middle-class patients also reflect values, norms, and attitudes similar to those of the physician. Raymond Duff and August Hollingshead (1968), for example, found that physicians tended to be more attentive to upper-class patients by "overidentifying" with them. Conversely, J. A. Roth has described the manner in which he believes the poor are regarded by many physicians:

> They are considered the least desirable patients. The doctor has probably dealt with "their kind" during his years as a student and resident in outpatient and emergency clinics, and he has concluded that they are often dirty and smelly, follow poor health practices, fail to observe directions or meet appointments, and live in a situation which makes it impossible to establish appropriate health regimes.[9]

This type of statement seems to imply that lower-class patients receive inferior medical care not only because of differences in health service availability, accessibility, comprehensiveness, and so forth, but also because physicians themselves may be biased toward treating more affluent patients. Some studies (Anderson and Sheatsley, 1967) support this statement, but others do not (see Knowles, 1963), and the issue remains unresolved at the present time. Hall found that the more successful physicians required a certain amount of "charity" work in order to demonstrate a "serious" intent to practice medicine. Yet apparently few physicians desire to work full-time in poverty programs (Fredericks et al., 1974).

The best medical practice in Hall's study was the specialized practice because Hall believed the specialist was accorded superior status by others in the medical profession.[10] Other observers (Stevens, 1971; Mechanic, 1972) have also pointed toward the trend in specialization, which has resulted in the decline in number of general practitioners and the domination of the medical profession by specialty groups. A specialized practice, however, is dependent on having a group of colleagues who refer patients to the specialist. Generally, referring physicians are reciprocated by fee-sharing or by the referral of patients back to the general practitioner. A specialized practice also requires access to hospital facilities, and hospital connections in themselves facilitate the development of referral relationships between physicians.

---

[9]J. A. Roth, "The Treatment of the Sick," in *Poverty and Health*, J. Kosa, A. Antonovsky, and I. Zola, eds. (Cambridge, Mass.: Harvard University Press, 1969), p. 227.

[10]The tremendous growth in the number of medical specialists has reduced the number of general practitioners and has made it more difficult to obtain primary care in the United States. This issue will be discussed in Chapter Nine, Health Care Delivery and Social Policy.

In a study of internists (specialists in internal medicine) in private practice in Chicago, Stephen Shortell (1973) found that they tended to refer their patients to other specialists on the hospital staff where they held a primary appointment. The influence of the hospital appointment was such that it provided both formal and informal channels of communication about who was available in the various specialties and what relative advantages they had to offer. Furthermore, the ability to follow up on a patient after care had been turned over to another specialist or specialists depended on the internist's being on the same hospital staff.

Shortell's study traced the informal organization of medical practice by extensively examining the referral process. He found that patterns of referrals were related to the professional status of the physicians and operated according to the relative rewards and costs perceived by physicians at different levels of the status hierarchy. High status internists, for example, tended to refer their patients to other high status colleagues, while lower status internists also more often referred their patients to higher status physicians than to their peers. Higher status physicians thus tended to be the major recipients of referrals. High status physicians primarily choose each other as referral partners because the exchange helps validate their own personal status and maintains the status structure of their own group as well. Lower status physicians, however, tend to refer patients outside their group because of the prestige rewards of dealing with higher status physicians and because of a potential loss of clientele to fellow low status competitors. The reasoning was that low status physicians were much more likely to be concerned about building their medical practice and thereby might tend to retain patients sent to them. High status physicians, on the other hand, would already have a successful practice and would not be so desirous of acquiring more patients on a regular basis.

The "Inner Fraternity"

Hall's study pointed toward the existence of an "inner fraternity" in medicine that operated to recruit new members, to allocate these new members to positions in the various medical institutions, and to help them secure patients through referrals. Hall believed that the urban power structure of the medical profession consisted of four major groups of physicians. The first group was the "inner core," which Hall described as the specialists who have control of the major hospital positions. Immediately outside this inner core were the new recruits at various stages of their careers who were intended to inherit positions in the inner core at some time in the future. Next were the general practitioners who were linked to the inner core by the referral system. Besides these three groups were the marginal physicians, those who would remain on the fringes of the system because the inner core had its own methods of selecting recruits. According to Hall, the key to understanding the power structure of the medical profession was found in the system of control exercised by the inner core. The inner core displayed three major characteristics that enabled it to control the medical profession. First, it was a highly cohesive group of specialists with relatively identical educations and socioeconomic backgrounds, technical interdependence, and daily working relationships. Second, the social bonds between different specialists allowed these powerful physicians to integrate the various specialties into a cohesive body. And third, the inner core was able to organize the medical market by controlling the process in which patients were referred from one physician to another.

What Hall's analysis has provided in terms of understanding the power structure of the medical profession is the realization that a doctor's career takes place in a system of formal and informal relationships with colleagues. Formal relationships develop as a result of a physician's position within the prevailing medical institutions in a particular community. The control of the dominant posts within these institutions, especially hospital appointments, is the critical variable that distinguishes influential from noninfluential doctors. Informal relationships also develop over time as physicians interact with one another frequently and arrive at definitions of the quality of each other's work and personal characteristics. Thus, claims to position, status, and power become recognized and are perpetuated within the profession, and mechanisms for recruitment into the inner core become established in both formal and informal ways.

Hall's study took place during the 1940s. Whether or not the conditions he described at that time still hold true today is largely a matter of conjecture because recent studies of the power structure of the medical profession have been lacking. However, what data do exist seem to substantiate the major points made by Hall. Donald Freeborn and Benjamin Darsky's 1974 study of a medical community in a medium-sized Canadian city involved a sample of physicians who practiced medicine as private, fee-for-service practitioners similar to the majority of American physicians. They also found that a definite power structure existed along the lines described by Hall—with one important exception. As in the Hall study, influence and power among physicians were related to control by a small group of the major medical institutional resources in the community. Influence and power were exercised in both a formal and informal fashion, but emanated from the same people. Generally, the top influentials were older physicians who had been able to gain control over the positions of power in the hospitals and medical association. But in contrast to the Hall study, the top influentials were not necessarily specialists (many were general practitioners) and they were not a closed "inner core." Instead a network of common friendships prevailed at all levels of influence; the most influential physicians were those who had gained their position of power as a result of long years of service to the community and the medical society. Over time they had developed extensive personal relationships which allowed them to achieve and maintain key positions in the major medical institutions.

In the United States, Robert Marshall and his associates (1978) investigated the career outcomes in a national sample of physicians who graduated from medical school in 1960. They found that medical careers were structured along a status hierarchy which operated as an informal system of mobility beginning in medical school. Some of the physicians were encouraged by sponsors (influential physicians) to enter elite career paths and join them in an elite status. Other students, to use Elliott Krause's (1971) term, were "cooled out" to follow the paths of least status.

The most significant variable to emerge from this discussion of the power structure of the American medical profession is that of institutional position. The medical profession is based upon a variety of institutions— hospitals, clinics, medical schools, the AMA, and so forth. The policies and practices of these institutions are determined by those individuals who occupy decision-making positions within them. Power and influence among physicians (as in any other group) derive from being in a position to direct or at least share in a decision-making process that formulates significant professional policies.

An obvious but important factor is that the most important institutional positions are held by physicians who have pursued their career within the mainstream of the medical profession; they have achieved the best educational experiences and hospital appointments, as well as AMA membership, or vice versa. Most likely these individuals are specialists who occupy an institutional position such as administrator, faculty member, or researcher. If this is the case, and in all probability it is, what is further implied is that changes in the organization of medical practice in the United States would most likely not originate within the medical profession itself. This logical inference seems to derogate existing studies (Goldman and Ebbert, 1973; Goldman, 1974a, 1974b) which suggest liberal, change-oriented tendencies among the latest generation of medical doctors. Yet positions of power within the medical profession continue to be held by physicians who have succeeded in the present conservative system, a system that is oriented toward maintaining the private, fee-for-service, independent practitioner model. Perhaps the medical profession may eventually promote change if new physicians maintain their liberal tendencies until they reach positions of influence, but at this time it appears more probable that changes in the organization of medical care in the United States will have to occur as a result of pressure outside the system. The most likely source for this pressure is dissatisfied groups of health care consumers working to institute legislation limiting the control of physicians over medical practice.

THE PHYSICIAN AND SOCIAL CHANGE

Current public dissatisfaction with the delivery of health care in the United States results from two major issues: (1) lack of quality health care for all Americans, and (2) rising financial costs of health care. Both of these issues are related to the fact that most health care in the United States is organized around the economic concept of profit for health providers and health institutions within a free enterprise system. Accordingly, some argue that the present system should be changed because the profit motive discriminates against the poor, encourages the unnecessary duplication of many services, and introduces a dehumanizing connotation to the provision of a service intended to relieve human suffering. Others argue that the profit motive leads to greater efficiency in providing services, increased incentive for research and development, and more responsiveness to the patient. As previously noted, Chapter Nine will explore the financial issues involved in health care delivery, but it should be recognized that the issue of profit is an integral part of the structure of organized medicine in this country as is the medical professional's lack of flexibility in confronting social issues.

Part of organized medicine's lack of social responsiveness may be attributed to medicine's development as a profession. Howard Rasmussen (1975) has pointed out that professionalism in American medicine has resulted in at least three undesirable consequences. First, it has fostered the development of a view of disease largely confined to specific organs or physiological systems, but which fails to consider a more holistic view of patients as people. This conflicts directly with a major societal demand that contemporary practice come to terms with a wide spectrum of disorders related more to problems of living than to specific chemical and physical abnormalities of the body. Second, professionalism has led to the development of a highly rigid stratification system in medical practice which has promoted an increasingly large gap between physicians and nonphysician medical personnel. And for certain functions the nonphysician health worker may have a more important service to provide the patient than the physician. Third, professionalism has resulted in the separation of professional training so that a common educational base is lacking between physicians and paramedicals that might allow a health care team to work more effectively as a cohesive group. Overall, the physician has emerged in the role of a "super-physician" in a "super-hospital" where ultimate responsibility for the patient belongs to this deified being, who, as an individual, may not have the time, interest, training, or ability to cope with the entire range of modern patient care. Thus, while the health care needs of American society are those of the late twentieth century, organized medicine has continued to pursue a pattern of professional behavior based upon the image of medical practice at the turn of the century when the physician worked as an independent, fee-for-service, private general practitioner.

Social Control of Medical Practice

The social control of medical practice has traditionally presented special problems for American society. It has been argued that since physicians themselves have established the medical standards enforced by governmental regulating agencies and since laypersons are generally unable to judge technical performance, the two most common forms of social control in an industrial society—bureaucratic supervision and judgment by the recipient of services—are lacking (see Rueschmeyer, 1972). However, the argument continues that the problem of controlling organized medicine is solved by the medical profession's emphasis on the strong self-control of the individual physician, an ethical stance reinforced by both the formal and informal sanctions of a community of colleagues. Society is thus justified in granting the physician professional autonomy because he or she is a member of a self-controlled collectivity providing a vital function for society's general good. This argument contains three serious defects.

First of all, it is important to note that laypersons do judge technical performance regardless of whether they are competent to do so. Freidson's

(1960) discussion of the lay-referral system made it quite clear that lay avenues of influence and authority exist independently of the physician and operate to guide the patient either toward or away from the services of a particular physician. This activity may not only determine the physician's success in attracting patients but also affect the physician's mode of medical practice. As Freidson (1960:379) has stated, "in being *relatively* free, the medical profession should not be mistaken for being *absolutely* free from control by patients." The choices of clients act as a form of social control over professionals and can militate against the survival of a group as a profession or the career success of particular professionals (Goode, 1957:198).

Several studies show that patients do terminate their relationships with physicians and actively shop around for other doctors who are more able to meet their expectations (Ben-Sira, 1976, 1980; Hays-Bautista, 1976; Larson and Rootman, 1976; Kasteler et al., 1976). Besides lack of confidence in a physician's technical competence, other factors commonly identified as influencing patients to change doctors are the unwillingness of doctors to spend time talking to them, the high cost of services, the possible inconvenience of a particular doctor's office location and hours, and unfavorable assessments of the doctor's personality.

A second major defect in the argument legitimizing the medical profession's autonomy has to do with physicians' efforts at peer regulation. In a study of a medical group practice, Freidson (1975) found indeed that rules and standards existed to define the limits of acceptable performance by physicians associated with the group. However, norms governing colleague relations, essentially *rules of etiquette*, restricted the evaluation of work and discouraged the expression of criticism. Etiquette was a more important norm than accountability, and it undermined attempts at critical evaluation and control by overlooking fault in order to maintain group harmony. Confrontation with a colleague was considered distasteful even in private and was unthinkable in public. In this medical practice setting, the norms of etiquette had not only seriously limited the exercise of professional control, but had also reduced the scope of procedures colleagues were willing to review.

Marcia Millman (1977a, 1977b) noted a similar situation in her study of three private, university-affiliated hospitals. Many doctors in this study were willing to criticize their colleagues for errors in small group discussions and behind the other's back. But they were strongly reluctant to criticize another doctor's mistakes at any official meeting because of what Millman termed "a fear of reprisal" and "a recognition of common interests."

Millman's examination of medical mortality and morbidity conferences, in which patient deaths were reviewed as a regular hospital procedure, was particularly illustrative of the collective rationalization of mistakes. The atmosphere of these conferences was likened to such social events as weddings or funerals, in which the participants were expected to show tact and restraint in order to remain on friendly terms. Restricted to members of the hospital's medical staff, the conferences were intended to be educational, not punitive. Only certain cases (conspicuous was the absence of cases involving patient deaths by gross medical mismanagement) were picked for review because, as one hospital chief of medicine stated, "it's got to be a cordial affair." Millman described the meetings as follows:

> At Lakeside Hospital, the chief of medicine stands on the stage and presides as a master of ceremonies. As one member of the staff after another testifies about how he or she was led to the same mistaken diagnosis, the responsibility for the mistake is implicitly spread around. As in a good detective story, the case is reconstructed to show that there was evidence for suspecting an outcome different from the one that turned out to be the true circumstance. Responsibility for the error is also neutralized by making much of the unusual or misleading features of the case, or by showing how the patient was to blame because of uncooperative or neurotic behavior. Furthermore, by reviewing the case in fine detail, the physicians restore their images as careful, methodical practitioners, and thereby neutralize the sloppiness and carelessness that are made obvious by mistakes.[11]

Millman contended that a "gentlemen's agreement" existed among the hospital physicians to overlook each other's mistakes. According to Charles Bosk (1979), in a study of physicians in a surgical training program at a major university medical center, there was a general recognition that honest errors exist and all physicians make them. Technical errors, if they were made in "good faith," were less serious than moral errors. A moral error was making the mistake of being unreliable, uncooperative, lacking in responsibility to patients, and failing to acknowledge subordination to superiors on the staff. Technical errors, on the other hand, could be forgiven and often had the result of motivating the offending physician to work harder, spend more time with patients, doublecheck procedures, and learn from the mistake. By admitting mistakes and trying to make up for them, the physician remained a good colleague. Moral errors, conversely, resulted in unfavorable letters of recommendation for those seeking jobs and social isolation from other physicians in the hospital.

Whether or not the lack of physician peer control described by Freidson and Millman and the rather weak control studied by Bosk is typical of most medical practice settings is not known. However, if the so-called malpractice crisis in American medicine during the mid-1970s can be regarded as any kind of valid indicator, it would appear that incompetence in medicine, or at least a greater public awareness of medical malpractice, is not entirely uncommon. David Makofsky (1977) has estimated that approximately 5 percent of all practicing physicians are unfit for practice because of ignorance of modern medicine, drug addiction, or mental illness. He claims that 30,000 Americans die annually from faulty drug prescriptions and ten times that number suffer dangerous side effects. Unnecessary and poorly performed surgery is also regarded as a serious problem. To cite an extreme case, in 1973 a superior court in California awarded two million dollars to a patient for damages resulting from an unnecessary back fusion operation performed by a drug-addicted orthopedic surgeon. The surgeon admitted to the court that he had performed unnecessary surgery on at least thirty-eight other persons because he needed the money.

[11]Marcia Millman, "Masking Doctors' Errors." *Human Behavior,* 6 (1977), 17.

In rebuttal it can be argued that physicians can be the victims of malpractice suits that have no merit in fact. Yet malpractice suits have risen dramatically in recent years (from a few hundred a year in the 1950s to about 10,000 a year in the 1970s), and so have the rates physicians pay for malpractice insurance. Some major malpractice insurance companies have refused to continue insuring doctors because of high losses resulting from malpractice settlements. In a vicious circle, physicians have charged increasingly higher prices for their services to cover the higher rates charged by those companies still writing malpractice policies. It has been found that some physicians and hospitals even pass on *more* than 100 percent of the costs of their malpractice insurance to patients (Greenwald and Mueller, 1978). Many physicians are also practicing "defensive medicine," which is the ordering of unnecessary laboratory tests and procedures to make sure that they cannot be accused of carelessness, neglect, or incompetence. This practice likewise increases the cost to the patient of obtaining medical care.

In some states, emergency legislation has been passed to provide state-backed malpractice insurance coverage designed to protect both doctors and hospitals. But there are also powerful interest groups, including some physicians and lawyers specializing in personal injury lawsuits, who oppose significant change in the present system and are in a position to influence legislation (Rottenberg, 1978). At present, no single solution exists in any state, and the malpractice crisis remains one of the most significant issues affecting the doctor–patient relationship.

In addition to the malpractice crisis, another symptom of ineffective control of the medical practice is the high cost to the government of Medicare and Medicaid due to physician corruption. In 1975 and 1976, investigations of fraud in Medicare and Medicaid services in New York City disclosed that over 300 million dollars a year had been paid to doctors for false claims (Makofsky, 1977). Some physicians were arrested and sentenced to prison for misrepresenting care they supposedly gave Medicare and Medicaid patients.

This discussion is not intended to convey the impression that physicians are generally untrustworthy. Instances of corruption and fraud appear to be rare. In fact, Freidson (1975) argues that it can be assumed that physicians are usually dedicated to their patients. State medical societies do cooperate with state licensing agencies to remove the medical licenses of demonstrably incompetent physicians, thus preventing them from legally practicing medicine. Furthermore, Professional Standards Review Organizations were established in 1970 in conjunction with Medicaid and Medicare to review and evaluate the medical care given to patients eligible to use these services. PSROs are composed of licensed physicians and osteopaths who determine if the services rendered are medically necessary, meet professional standards of quality, and are provided as efficiently and effectively as possible (see Shindell et al., 1976). Although some latitude in the interpretation of standards is likely in any diagnostic category, Freidson (1975:251) points out that a consensus of opinion will at least exclude "the blatant, gross, or obvious deviations from common knowledge and practice."

Nevertheless, medical standards and practices continue to be regulated by the practitioners themselves. Thus it is generally difficult to find a physician who will be openly critical of another physician or who will publicly testify against a colleague. Mistakes and errors in medical practice, either through neglect or ignorance, can sometimes be defended as "a difference of opinion." Millman (1977a) suggests that possibly all doctors have at some time made a terrible mistake in their careers and realize that they may do so again. Therefore, in matters of peer regulation, they tend to follow the Golden Rule: "Do unto others as you would have them do unto you."

The third major defect in the professional autonomy argument arises from the fact that the autonomy granted the medical profession is granted *conditionally*, on the assumption that it will resolve significant issues in favor of the public interest. However, traditional AMA resistance to innovations in medical care that might threaten the fee-for-service pattern has been cited as an example of greater professional concern with matters of self-interest than with public welfare (Stevens, 1971). It therefore seems warranted for society to restrict the autonomy of the medical profession, and this claim has provided the basis for the present challenge to organized medicine launched by consumer groups working to enact legislative change.

Changing Relationships

Leo G. Reeder (1972) has formulated the clearest case to date that shows the changing relationship between physicians and their patients. He identifies three significant trends in contemporary society. One is the *shift in medicine away from the treatment of acute diseases toward preventive health services* intended to offset the effects of chronic disorders. Since the control of acute diseases has largely been accomplished, it is no longer the most important task for modern medical practice. Reeder explains:

> In a system dominated by curative or emergency care there is a "seller's market." The customer is suspect; client-professional relationships tend to be characterized by the traditional mode of interaction so well described in the literature. On the other hand, when prevention of illness is emphasized, the client has to be persuaded that he has a need for medical services such as periodic check-ups. The person has to be encouraged to come into the physician's office for medical care. Under these circumstances, there are elements of a "buyer's market"; in such situations there is more of a tendency for the "customer to be right."[12]

The other two features of societal change noted by Reeder are the *growing sophistication of the general public with bureaucracy* and the *development of consumerism*. Reeder claims that the increased development of large-scale bureaucratic industrial systems has ensured a similarity of experiences and attitudes in contemporary society and this has tended to "level" or make more familiar the bureaucratic aspects of modern medicine. Also significant is the development of consumerism. Reeder states that during the 1960s, the concept of the person as a "consumer" rather than a patient became established; doctors were regarded as "health providers," so a new relationship of

[12]Leo G. Reeder, "The Patient-Client as a Consumer: Some Observations on the Changing Professional-Client Relationship," *Journal of Health and Social Behavior*, 13 (December 1972), 407.

provider–consumer emerged in direct opposition to the old relationship of physician–patient with its emphasis upon patient dependency. The new concept places the consumer on a more equal basis with the physician in the health care interaction. It also provides the philosophy behind the increased consumer involvement in health legislation and other matters as consumer interest groups.

In an age of "consumerism," the social role of the physician and the overall physician–patient relationship can hardly escape modification. In general, this modification will take the form of physician and patient inter-acting on a more equal footing in terms of power dependency, reciprocity of expectations, and responsibility for outcome. There is already evidence, in such inherently uncertain areas of medical practice as genetic counseling, that the physician–patient relationship as a provider–consumer encounter has become more prevalent in health care interaction (see Sorenson, 1974).

Other indications of change in the physician–patient relationship, however, can be added to those mentioned by Reeder. These indicators are: (1) health-protective behavior, (2) the women's health movement, and (3) the wholistic health movement.

Health-Protective Behavior. Health-protective behavior, as de-scribed by Daniel Harris and Sharon Guten (1979:18), is "any behavior performed by a person, regardless of his or her perceived or actual health status, in order to protect, promote, or maintain his or her health, whether or not such behavior is objectively effective toward that end." Health-protec-tive behavior is clearly related to the concept of consumerism in health care. In both consumerism and health-protective behavior, the person is an active and rational participant in decision making about health as a commodity. The difference is that in consumerism people are making choices about health care services provided by medical professionals, while in health-protective behavior they are making choices about health by protecting it themselves. In other words, they are *producers* of health rather than just *consumers* of health care services. An obvious example of health-protective behavior in American society is the decrease in the smoking of cigarettes. Between 1970 and 1980, the percentage of males who smoked declined from 52 percent to 37 percent and the percentage of female smokers dropped from 32 percent to 28 percent. Other examples pertain to the increased public awareness of and participation in personal physical fitness programs—especially jogging, hiking, and tennis. Harris and Guten found, for instance, in a study of 842 adults in a random sample of households in Cleveland, Ohio, that practically everyone performed some regular, routine behaviors for protecting his or her health. The most common activity was that of practicing good nutrition and eating sensibly. Other activities were rest and relaxation, physical exercise, personal hygiene, regular medical checkups, and so forth.

This result is consistent with the findings of a survey conducted in Alameda County, California among a sample of nearly 7,000 adults who were interviewed in 1965 and again in 1974 in regard to personal health practices. Seven good health practices were identified in this study:

(1) sleeping seven to eight hours a night; (2) eating breakfast almost every day; (3) seldom if ever eating snacks; (4) controlling one's weight; (5) exercising; (6) limiting alcohol consumption to fewer than five drinks at one sitting; and (7) never having smoked cigarettes. People reporting six or seven of these health practices were shown to have better health status and live longer than people reporting fewer than four of them.

People who take such health-protective measures, in all probability, would approach their dealings with a physician in a consumer mode rather than just being an unquestioning, passive recipient of services.

Women's Health Movement. The women's health movement represents an attempt by women to combat sexist discrimination in medicine. As part of this movement, feminist health organizations have evolved which advocate natural childbirth, midwifery, home deliveries of babies, self-help, and recognition of the rights and intelligence of patients (Davidson and Gordon, 1979). A particular focus has been on the manner in which some male physicians treat women patients and health workers as inferior because of their sex. Reviews of both past and present medical literature have found images of women patients that depict them as being naturally frail, sickly, incompetent, submissive, and in need of physician consultation fairly regularly. In examining the relationship between male physicians and female patients in the early twentieth century, Barbara Ehrenreich and Deirdre English noted:

> The doctors' view of women as innately sick did not, of course, *make* them sick, or delicate, or idle. But it did provide a powerful rationale against allowing women to act in any other way. Medical arguments were used to explain why women should be barred from medical school (they would faint in anatomy lectures), from higher education altogether, and from voting. . . . Medical arguments seemed to take the malice out of sexual oppression: when you prevented a woman from doing anything active or interesting, you were only doing this for her own good.[13]

Other research supports this theme. For example, in a review of gynecology textbooks over a 125-year period, Diana Scully and Pauline Bart (1979) found that very little had changed over the years in regard to stereotypes of women patients. There were consistent statements that attributed inferior sexuality and natural submissiveness to women, as well as relegating them to primary roles of reproduction and homemaking. One textbook, published in the early 1970s, cautioned gynecologists to inform their patients to be sure and follow the lead of their husbands in sexual relations but not to become completely passive since some overt advances are attractive and provocative. No one likes to "take a tone-deaf individual to a concert," was one reminder the gynecologists were told to give the women who came to see them for advice about their role in the sex act (Scully and Bart, 1979:222). Another gynecology textbook published in the 1970s made it clear that a

[13] Barbara Ehrenreich and Deirdre English, "The 'Sick' Women of the Upper Classes," in *The Cultural Crisis of Modern Medicine*, J. Ehrenreich, ed. (New York: Monthly Review Press, 1979), pp. 127–128.

woman's "power and purpose" was to preserve the family as a happy place. And in line with this goal it was natural and normal for a woman to submit willingly to her husband's advances to accommodate his sex drive.

The image of women was also found to be less than satisfactory in pediatric textbooks. Mary Howell (1979) observed that one text portrayed pediatricians as the champions for children, even over and against their mothers. "Mothers are variously blamed," says Howell (1979:204), "when their children become ill: for bothering the doctor too often, for not having brought the child in early enough, for being unduly alarmed, for not having recognized signs and symptoms of 'real' illness." In essence, when it came to doing the right thing for their children in obtaining medical care, mothers were unreliable and unable to make accurate judgments.

There is evidence, however, that adverse attitudes and stereotypes about women are beginning to be modified among members of the medical profession. Visible changes are occurring in the approaches of some physicians and hospitals toward treating women (Davidson and Gordon, 1979). A particularly significant source of change is found in the increasing numbers of women physicians. The first American woman to graduate from medical school was Elizabeth Blackwell in 1849. Yet not until 1970 did women account for at least 10 percent of all first-year medical students. In the 1980s women probably will constitute 25 percent of the entering classes. Women are also entering areas of medicine that were typically reserved for men in the past. American Medical Association statistics show that in 1977, for instance, 430 women entered residency programs in general surgery—a specialty that has been exclusively male. In 1972, the top specialty choices of women beginning their resident training were pediatrics, psychiatry, and pathology. In 1977, the top choice was internal medicine, followed by family practice and general surgery. Thus, women physicians are not only entering different specialties than before, but they are also entering specialties where they deal with a wider range of patients. Consequently, we have the beginnings of a new trend in medicine which may not only affect the physician–patient relationship (in terms of improved communication and willingness to relate to patients as people) but may also have an impact on the general image of women held by the medical profession.

Wholistic Health.   Wholistic health refers to church-based family practice involving an interdisciplinary team of physicians, nurses, religious counselors, and volunteer laypersons who work together to treat all aspects of a person's health needs. According to the Society of Wholistic Medicine:

> Wholistic health care is based on the metaphysical affirmation of body, mind, and spirit integrated in a whole, independent of and greater than the sum of its parts. In practice, wholistic care means actively searching with people all dimensions of their lives (physical, emotional, intellectual, spiritual, interpersonal) for causes and symptoms of disease, then creatively exploring these same aspects for treatment strategies to restore or maintain health.[14]

[14] Nancy Loving Tubesing, *Whole Person Health Care: Philosophical Assumptions* (Hinsdale, Ill.: Society for Wholistic Medicine, 1977), p. 1.

The notion of wholistic health centers was first formulated by Granger Westberg, a minister, who set up the first clinic at a Lutheran church in Springfield, Ohio in 1970. His experience as a hospital chaplain convinced Westberg that chaplains often entered into relationships with patients too late in the illness experience. He believed religious assistance to patients would be more valuable if clergy could work with both patients and doctors at the very start of any health problem. After presenting his ideas, he was encouraged to start a model clinic in 1967 by the American Medical Association's Committee on Medicine and Religion. The clinic was slow in attracting patients, but eventually proved successful. Careful to work closely with members of the medical profession, Westberg was able to obtain financial support to establish other wholistic centers in northern Illinois, and interest in the concept has spread beyond the Midwest.

At present, wholistic health centers emphasize health screening and education programs; care in the early stages of illness; coordination of care involving physicians, ministers, and referrals to medical specialists; attention to life stress factors; and facilitating the idea of "people-helping-people" (Tubesing et al., 1977). The physician–patient relationship is modified not only by the team approach to patient care, but also by the requirement that the patient participate and possibly even take the lead in his or her own health care (Weeks and DeVries, 1978). While some physicians regard the wholistic approach as "unscientific" and "a fad," the movement appears to be gaining momentum (Yahn, 1979).

SUMMARY

This chapter has examined the role of the physician in a changing society. From an initial service orientation and through the development of a body of specialized knowledge, the physician has been able to organize a professional group and control medical education in such a way as to dominate the entire health care industry in the United States. Yet there are increasing signs, such as the appearance of liberal tendencies among some members of the latest generation of medical doctors and the emergence of consumer interest groups in health affairs, that suggest that the professional dominance of the physician may be modified. Most likely the typical power dependency role of the physician–patient relationship will be transformed into more of a provider–consumer relationship in the future. This will mean, however, a basic change in the approach of traditional medicine toward health care delivery in modern social systems.

chapter 7

NURSES AND OTHER HEALTH PRACTITIONERS

Although the dominant form of social interaction in the health care relationship has traditionally been that of the one-to-one encounter between the physician and the patient, the technical complexity and range of contemporary medical care have evolved well beyond this exclusive two person social system. Modern medical treatment has come to involve a great variety of health personnel who specialize in treatment, laboratory procedures, therapy, rehabilitation, and administration. Over four million people in the United States are currently employed in nonphysician tasks related to health care.

Yet, as Robert Wilson (1970) has pointed out, many of the occupational roles that are synonymous with the practice of modern medicine have tended to be modelled on the ideal image of the physician, with its high standards of education, ethics, technical achievement, and independence of action. Wilson (1970:34) states: "In a sense, each variety of health worker gauges his status and professional selfhood in terms of how closely he approaches the doctor on a scale of privilege and responsibility." But the problem inherent in this imitative relationship is that while it may encourage physicianlike aspirations and standards among paramedicals, it represents, as Wilson notes, an unrealistic and often frustrating situation. Almost all of these workers will never achieve professional equality with the physician within the existing framework of medical practice.

Other than physicians and a few consulting professions such as clinical psychology, most occupations performing tasks of patient care can be classified as paramedical because they are organized around the work of the physician and are usually under the physician's direct control. Eliot Freidson (1970a:49) claims that these paramedical occupations—nurse, pharmacist, laboratory technician, physical therapist—reflect four characteristic features that account for their subordinate position in the practice of medicine. First of all, Freidson notes that the technical knowledge employed by paramedical occupations tends to be discovered, developed, and approved by physicians. Second, paramedical workers usually assist physicians in their work rather than replace the basic skills of diagnosis and treatment. Third, paramedical workers are subordinate to the physician because their work largely occurs at the "request of" the physician; the "doctor's orders" provide them with their work requirements. And fourth, among the various occupational roles in the health field, the American public ascribes considerably less prestige to nonphysician workers than to physicians.

A related point concerning this prestige differential is that the social backgrounds of those persons recruited into paramedical work are generally lower than those of physicians. While physicians usually come from upper- and upper-middle-class social origins, people in paramedical occupations frequently have lower-middle, working-class, and lower-class backgrounds. Also, women and members of racial/ethnic minority groups are found in a greater proportion among paramedical personnel than among medical doctors. However, if all the characteristics of the paramedical occupations, as outlined by Freidson, were reduced to the single most important distinction between these health care workers and physicians, that distinction would be the physician's ultimate control over their work, which effectively blocks their claims of professional autonomy.

One negative aspect of this situation is that physicians sometimes do not enjoy a good reputation with their coworkers (Bates, 1970). It has been pointed out that the physician is the "last of the autocrats" (Melick, 1959). He or she tends to regard other health personnel as working for him or her rather than working for the patient, while relegating them to a "nonprofessional limbo" in which they are seen essentially as "servants rather than as associates or colleagues" (McGraw, 1966).

Just as the physician–patient relationship appears to be moving toward less dependency and increased equality for the patient, signs of a similar trend have begun to appear in the physician–registered nurse relationship. The time may come, as Wilson (1970) suggests, when patients will be treated by a medical team in which the physician is no longer an all-powerful figure, but collaborates with other health workers as first among equals. An examination of the physician–nurse relationship may therefore assist social scientists to determine more accurately the nature of the future role relationships among health personnel. The final section of this chapter will discuss other health practitioners, namely osteopaths, chiropractors, quacks, folk healers, and faith healers.

NURSING: PAST AND PRESENT

The licensed registered nurse ranks second in status only to the physician in the social organization of health providers in the United States. Many nurses consider themselves to be full-fledged professionals despite their lack of formal autonomy over their work role. Nursing represents the largest single group of health workers in the United States, with an estimated 1,112,000 people employed as licensed registered nurses in 1978; another 402,000 people were estimated to be employed as licensed practical nurses (HEW,

1980). About 75 percent of all licensed registered and practical nurses in the United States work in hospitals and nursing homes, while the remainder are employed in doctors' offices, public health agencies, schools, industrial plants, programs of nursing education, or as private duty nurses.

Registered nurses are responsible for the nature and quality of all nursing care patients receive, as well as for following the instructions of physicians regarding patients. In addition, they supervise practical nurses and other health personnel involved in providing patient care. The primary task of licensed practical nurses is the bedside care of patients; they may also assist in the supervision of auxiliary nursing workers such as nurse's aides, orderlies, and attendants. These auxiliary nursing personnel, who numbered about 1,037,000 in the United States as of 1978, assist registered and practical nurses by performing less skilled medical care tasks and by providing many services designed for the overall personal comfort and welfare of patients.

Whereas the licensed registered and practical nurses and nurse's aides are generally women, orderlies and attendants are usually men employed to care for male patients and perform whatever heavy duties are required in nursing care. Nursing tasks obviously occur in a system of social relationships that are highly stratified by sex. The registered nurse, who has the most advanced training and professional qualifications of any of the nursing workers, is generally a female who is matched occupationally with a physician, whose role is dominant and who is usually a male. The registered nurse, in turn, supervises lesser trained females (practical nurses and nurse's aides) and lesser trained males (orderlies and attendants). Thus emerges the traditional stereotype of the physician as father figure and the nurse as mother figure. "This perception," according to Hans Mauksch (1972:217), "creates a woman who serves sacrificially, who supports and protects a dominant male, and who identifies her successes as a nurse with her successes as a woman."

The Early Development of Nursing as an Occupation

While males have been known historically to perform nursing tasks, the social role of the nurse has been profoundly affected by its identification with traditionally feminine functions (Davis, 1966, 1972; Strauss, 1966, 1971; Olesen and Whittaker, 1968; Freidson, 1970a, 1970b; Mauksch, 1972; Schulman, 1972;). For instance, Mauksch (1972:208) has pointed out that in many European languages the very word *sister* not only refers to nuns but also generically identifies the nurse. In the English language, the word "nurse" carries with it a connotation of the mother's relationship to her child. Accordingly, the initial image of the nurse in Western society was that of a "mother-surrogate," in which nursing was equated with the mothering function (Schulman, 1972).

Following the rise of Christianity in the Western world, the practice of nursing as a formal occupation was significantly influenced by the presence of large numbers of nuns who performed nursing services under the auspices of the Roman Catholic Church. Prior to the late nineteenth century, hospitals were generally defined as places for the poor and lower social classes, often little more than "flophouses"; anyone who could afford it was usually cared for at home. Nursing activities in hospitals were thus viewed as acts of charity because they were usually carried out under difficult and unpleasant circumstances, as nurses served the personal needs of patients who were usually dirty and illiterate as well as diseased. Nursing under these conditions was regarded by the Church as a means by which those persons providing the services could attain spiritual salvation by helping those less fortunate. Hence the original concept of nursing was not as a formal occupation with its own body of knowledge and specialized training procedure; rather its primary focus as religious activity was in spiritual considerations. Nuns were not under the authority of doctors and they could refuse any orders they did not believe appropriate for themselves or their patients. Nuns were also reported to have refused to treat certain categories of patients such as unwed mothers or persons with venereal disease (Freidson, 1970a).

Besides nuns, there were secular nurses working in public hospitals. But these women were characterized as "women off the streets" or "of bad character," who were considered as little or no better than the low class of patients for whom they provided their services. Well into the nineteenth century, nursing could be described as an activity for women who lacked specialized training in medical care, a supportive work role that was not officially incorporated into the formal structure of medical services. Moreover, nursing was not an occupation held in high regard by the general public.

Florence Nightingale

The role of nursing in Western society was changed in the middle of the nineteenth century through the insight and effort of Florence Nightingale. Nightingale, an English Protestant from a respectable middle-class family, believed that God had called her to the service of Christianity as a result of a vision she had experienced in 1837. There was some confusion, however, on Nightingale's part as to exactly what service she was expected to render. Being a Protestant, she could not choose to become a Catholic nun. She solved her dilemma by deciding to become a nurse. Over the strong objections of her family and after a delay of several years, she was finally able to secure training as a nurse from a Protestant minister in Germany.

Returning to England in 1853, Nightingale established a hospital for "Sick Gentlewomen in Distressed Circumstances" and staffed it with trained nurses from good families. She insisted that nursing was intended to become an honorable and respected occupation and she sought to achieve this through a formal training program with recruits from upper- and middle-class social backgrounds. Good intentions notwithstanding, Nightingale's hospital was not entirely successful because of the role conflict between the duties of the nurse and the prevailing standards of proper behavior for "ladies." Some of her nurses, for example, were reluctant to view nudity or to be present at physical examinations (Freidson, 1970a).

However, in 1854 the Crimean War afforded Nightingale a much better opportunity to establish nursing as a formal occupation. She organized a contingent of nurses and, assisted by money raised by public subscription, she and her group sailed for the Crimea, where Great Britain, France,

Sardinia, and Turkey were involved in war with Russia. Once there, Nightingale offered to the British military authorities the nursing services of her women for the sick and wounded troops.

At first the military refused to employ her nurses and she retaliated by refusing to allow any of the nurses to provide patient care on their own initiative. Instead the nurses worked only when their assistance was specifically requested by physicians. Eventually such requests were forthcoming and Nightingale's nurses received considerable publicity in the British press as "angels of mercy." In fact, Nightingale's nurses had captured the imagination of the British public and when Nightingale returned to England after the war she found herself hailed as a heroine. Capitalizing upon her fame and popularity, she instigated a successful fund-raising effort that brought in enough money to organize a nursing school at St. Thomas Hospital in London. Other schools were also established and within a few years the "Nightingale system" became the model for nursing education.

Nightingale's approach to nursing training emphasized a code of behavior that idealized nurses as being responsible, clean, self-sacrificing, courageous, cool-headed, hard-working, obedient to the physician, and possessing the tender qualities of the mother; this idealized portrayal of nurses saw them as nothing less than "disciplined angels" (Strauss, 1966). In reality, Nightingale had incorporated the best attributes of the mother and the housekeeper into her ideal nurse. This image did little to establish the view of nurses as having the qualities of leadership and independence necessary for true professional status. Although Nightingale had been able to establish nursing as a distinct and honorable occupation, her philosophy perpetuated the traditional social role of the nurse as a female supervised and controlled by a male physician. Perhaps in her time there was no other way to gain access to an official position within the male-dominated field of medicine, but the overall effect of subordination to the physician's orders weakened nursing's efforts in its struggle to achieve professionalization.

Nursing Education

Florence Nightingale's ideas formed the basis for establishing the first accredited schools of nursing in the United States. These schools, founded in 1873, were located at Bellevue Hospital in New York City, the Connecticut Training School in New Haven, and the Boston Training School. Although they were intended to be separately administerd, the new nursing schools were affiliated with hospitals that provided financial support and required, in turn, that the students furnish much of the nursing services on the hospital wards. During the late nineteenth and early twentieth centuries, the number of hospitals and hospital nursing schools grew rapidly. At the same time, increasing numbers of women entered the labor market due to immigration from abroad or migration from rural to urban areas. Nursing was an attractive occupation for many of these women because it afforded an opportunity for a woman to make a living and to also have a respectable position in the community.

But as Anselm Strauss (1966) and others have pointed out, many of the students in these early nursing schools did not receive the training that the

Nightingale system required. Since only a few trained nurses were available and money was often in short supply, many hospital administrators and physicians, perhaps also unaware of Nightingale's techniques for training nurses, used nursing students as inexpensive and exploitable sources of hospital labor. As a result, much of the effort of nursing educators during the first decades of the twentieth century was directed at securing less hospital service and more education for nursing students in hospital schools. They also sought a university-based nursing school, with the first one being formed at the University of Minnesota in 1909.

While nursing educators were able to improve the standards of education for their students, they failed to obtain centralized control over educational programs. Unlike medical schools, which follow a prescribed and generally similar program of education leading to the M.D., nursing has been characterized by a curious assortment of different types of educational experiences—all of which can qualify the student as a registered nurse. For example, there are currently three types of programs available for R.N.s: (1) two-year associate degree programs usually located in junior or community colleges; (2) hospital-based diploma schools requiring two and one-half to three years of study; (3) four-year and five year university baccalaureate programs.

The most prestigious of the nursing education programs is the baccalaureate program, which is intended to provide training not only in nursing skills and theory, but also to provide the background for becoming a nursing educator or leader. But, as Mauksch (1972:211) makes clear, the graduates of any nursing program—despite the differences in time, money, effort and, supposedly, intellect demanded by their programs—are virtually identical in terms of the basic skills required for their jobs.

The major source of nurses in the United States has traditionally been the hospital-based diploma school. College-based programs, with their combination of occupational training and liberal arts education, have become increasingly popular with nursing students in the last few years, although diploma schools provide more day-to-day experience with patients. As Table 7–1 shows, in 1961 diploma schools accounted for over 80 percent of all nursing graduates, but by 1970 this percentage had declined to 52.3 percent and the period between 1970 and 1977 witnessed a further rapid decline to 25.6 percent. Although the percentage of graduates from baccalaureate programs increased over the period covered by Table 7–1, the primary beneficiary of declining numbers of diploma graduates had been the associate degree programs. With only 3 percent of the total number of nursing graduates in 1961, associate degree programs had grown to produce 45.2 percent of the total by 1977.

The associate degree programs are relatively inexpensive, require only two years of training, and yet place their graduates on the same career track as graduates of diploma and baccalaureate degree schools. Originally conceived as a middle-range level of nursing education somewhere between the training required to perform simple or assisting nursing tasks and that required for complex tasks, the work role of the associate degree graduate has expanded into supervisory and management functions. Some controversy has arisen over this trend since it requires associate degree nurses to

TABLE 7–1.   Schools of Nursing (R.N.) by Types of School and Percent of Graduates (1961, 1965, 1970, 1977)

Type of School	1961 (N = 30,267)	1965 (N = 34,686)	1970 (N = 43,639)	1977 (N = 77,633)
Diploma	83.6	77.3	52.3	25.6
Associate Degree	3.0	7.2	26.8	45.2
Bachelor's Degree	13.4	15.5	20.9	29.2
TOTALS	100.0%	100.0%	100.0%	100.0%

SOURCE: National Center for Health Statistics, *Health Resources Statistics* (Washington, D.C.: U.S. Department of Health, Education and Welfare, 1978).

function beyond their intended level of training, but the trend continues because of the expectations of nursing service administrators about the capabilities of AD graduates (Miller, 1974). Although problems regarding the work role persist, AD programs have become the largest single source of nurses in the United States.

Despite the remarkable growth of the associate degree programs and the growing acceptance of their graduates in nursing, their appearance has presented a special problem in terms of nursing's claims of professional status since the AD programs are essentially vocational rather than professional. A strategy to avoid this situation was to designate associate degree nurses as "technical" nurses and baccalaureate degree nurses as "professional" nurses, while advocating that all nurses be graduates of college programs at some time in the future. Although this became the official position of the American Nurses' Association in 1965, it was not accepted by the majority of its membership, who had graduated from diploma schools. These nurses replied that it would be a hardship for them to quit work and return to college and they pointed out that a liberal arts education did not help a nurse perform better nursing procedures (Olesen and Whittaker, 1968). The end result was that among R.N.s the baccalaureate nurses are regarded as the *most* "professional"—leaders of organized nursing—yet associate degree and diploma nurses still consider themselves to be "professionals."

A related problem that also affects nursing's claims to professionalism is the open recruitment of nurses (Strauss, 1966). While medical schools are highly selective in regard to the preprofessional qualifications of the students they accept, the variety of nursing programs and the lack of centralized control of these programs by organized nursing has meant that practically any person can gain admission to some type of nursing program. Usually only a high school education is necessary for admission to most programs leading to the R.N.; only two years of high school are often required to enter programs of practical nursing. Most professions obtain some degree of control over who is accepted and allowed to graduate into the profession's ranks in order to ensure that only the most desirable candidates are able to represent the profession. While such controls are never perfect, they nevertheless represent a profession's standards. That nursing has relatively low standards of recruitment thus lowers its claim to professional status.

Nursing Students

In 1976–1977, 1,349 schools of nursing offered programs leading to the R.N., with a total of 249,541 students enrolled in their courses. Over 50,000 of these students graduated annually through the 1970s, with their total number increasing by a few thousand each year. Nursing students have traditionally been characterized as having lower-middle-class and working-class social origins, often from small towns or rural areas, who are attracted to nursing as a means of upward social mobility (Hughes et al., 1958). Although this pattern still persists today, there have been increasing numbers of students from upper- and upper-middle-class families and urban areas entering nursing schools (Davis, 1972; Mauksch, 1972), with the result that nursing, like teaching, has become a distinctly middle-class occupation.

There have been several studies of student nurses and their reasons for seeking training as a nurse. These studies, as summarized by Mauksch (1972), suggest that the objectives of a majority of nursing students are to be needed and to be engaged in personal helping relationships. However, some studies have suggested that a serious conflict often develops within new students concerning the lay image of the nurse as mother-surrogate (an image the students usually bring with them to the school) and the refusal of the nursing faculty to reinforce this image (Davis, 1972; Olesen and Whittaker, 1968; Psathas, 1968; Warnecke, 1973). Nursing faculties have tended to insist on students viewing their patients objectively, which has operated to deemphasize an intimate nurse-patient relationship. The prevailing reward system also places greater emphasis on removing the nurse from patient care and placing her in a supervisory position over auxiliary nursing workers.

In his study of nursing students in a major university school of nursing on the West Coast, Fred Davis (1972) observed that nursing students passed through six distinct stages of socialization. First was the stage of *initial innocence,* which consisted of the nursing students wanting to do things for patients within a secularized Christian-humanitarian ethic of care and kindness consistent with the lay (mother-surrogate) image of nursing. This stage was characterized, however, by feelings of inadequacy, worry, and frustration, as the nursing instructors failed to support the lay image of the nurse. Instead, the students were directed toward seemingly inconsequential tasks of patient care such as making beds and giving baths. These feelings of frustration, which usually came during the first semester of training, generated the second stage, which Davis called *labeled recognition of incongruity.* In this stage, the nursing students began collectively to articulate their disappointment and openly to question their choice of becoming a nurse. At this point a number of the students resigned from the school because they did not or could not adjust to the incongruity between lay expectations and actual training.

For those that remained, the third stage of *"psyching out"* began, in which the nursing students, like the medical students in the Becker et al. (1961) study, attempted to anticipate what their instructors wanted them to know and to concentrate upon satisfying these requirements. Whereas some students may have attempted to "psych out" the instructors from the very beginning, it now became a group phenomenon with the entire class collectively participating in the process. The fourth stage, termed *role simulation*, was characterized by students performing so as to elicit favorable responses from the instructors. The approved mode of behavior was the exhibition of an objective and "professional" (detached) attitude toward patient care, which included an understanding of the principles behind nursing techniques as well as mastery of those techniques. Many of the students felt they were "playing at acting like a nurse" and they questioned their lack of conviction about the role. But Davis points out that the more successful they became at convincing others that their performance was authentic, the more they began to gain confidence in themselves as nurses. This stage usually came at the end of the first year. The last two years of their program were characterized as the fifth stage of *provisional internalization* and the sixth stage of *stable internalization*. During these final two stages, the nursing students took on a temporary self-identity as a "professional" nurse, as defined by the faculty, and finally settled into a stable and consistent identification of self by the time of their graduation.

The same type of socialization was apparent in another study at a large midwestern hospital school of nursing conducted by George Psathas (1968). Psathas found that while freshmen nursing students entered training with people-oriented attitudes, senior nursing students were more technique oriented. For example, when shown cards depicting situations concerning nurses and patients, freshmen were much more likely to respond that the patients needed emotional support, while the seniors were much more likely to see the situation involving simple technical or physical problems. All in all, the freshmen were considerably more idealistic about patient care than the seniors, who saw their work in a more unemotional and routine fashion. Psathas observed that as the work became more routine, it became less attractive and the training program took on the aspects of "something to get through." Psathas (1968:64) said, "that this result could occur in three years and while the girl is still in school—does not speak well for the development of an academic or professional interest or an increased dedication to the role."

Another problem with respect to the professional status of nursing is that, unlike medical students, who desire a medical education as a terminal career, not all nursing students, perhaps not even a majority, view a career in nursing as their primary life goal. Davis (1972; Davis and Olesen, 1963) observed that many nursing students did not, either upon entry into nursing school or upon graduation, see themselves as being committed to a career in nursing. Their major life goal was that of marriage and family. This was so despite the influence of women's liberation and the encouragement of the nursing faculty to view nursing as a lifelong career. Davis (1972:46) found that the majority of students sought nursing training "as a kind of life insurance," should marriage and having a family not occur or should the marriage be less than ideal and result in "childlessness, divorce, premature widowhood, excessive financial burdens, or boredom with the home."

Therefore, the contingency of marriage became the decisive factor upon which all other career decisions were based. Davis noted that a student's announcement of an engagement to be married was a great occasion for both the student and her classmates. Not only did it indicate that the major concern was resolved in a positive manner for the engaged girl, but it also served to remind those not engaged of their less positive circumstances. Davis (1972:46) found that during the senior year there was "a veritable marital sweepstakes," in which the announcements of some engagements acquired the "theatrical overtones of a last minute rescue." Davis concluded:

> In sum, the life perspective of these students was predominantly one in which a rather unpredictable set of contingencies lying well outside their sole determination and control—whether they would marry, when, to whom, with what resultant gains or losses—was seen as ruling over matters about which they could, if they chose, much more nearly exercise determination and control, that is, what to do about their careers in nursing.[1]

Other studies (Davis and Olesen, 1963; Psathas, 1968) have found that many nursing students anticipate that nursing school will provide them with the opportunity to meet physicians, medical students, or other young men working in health-related fields. This situation is further emphasized in the most readily available accounts of nurses in popular fiction, where marriage to the young doctor, not a commitment to a career, is portrayed as the heroine's ultimate goal (Richter and Richter, 1974).

On the West Coast, Davis and Virginia Olesen (1963) noted that many nursing students have difficulty adjusting to their categorization by male medical students primarily as "nurses" rather than as young, pretty, intelligent, and attractive females. In fact, nursing students had nothing to do with medical students in class or on the hospital wards. Friendships were formed largely around occupational lines, with the medical students tending to socialize with each other, leaving the nursing students to do likewise.

Psathas (1968) found similar trends in his study. Many freshmen nursing students arrived with the expectation of meeting and marrying a physician. Often they would describe themselves as having a "typical high school crush" on doctors and being satisfied just to be able to work beside them. Seniors, however, had a much greater interest in heterosexual activity and saw relationships with men, physicians or otherwise, as romantic or dating relationships to be consummated by marriage or an "affair." Relationships with interns and staff doctors were primarily described as "affairs," which Psathas interpreted as reflecting the reality of age and status differences between doctors and student nurses. It was unlikely that such relationships would lead to marriage. Instead, nursing seniors were much more likely than freshmen to describe orderlies and laboratory technicians, with equal or lower social status than themselves, as probable romantic interests.

The overall image of nursing projected by these studies is that of an occupation dominated by a small group of older, career-oriented R.N.s who serve as leaders, policy makers, and educators for a large and transient mass of younger nurses whose career aspirations are greatly weakened by outside influences such as marriage (see Freidson, 1970b). Thus nursing, like many other work roles for women, has been defined as a contingent role that can be assumed only to the extent that it does not interfere with the primary roles of wife and mother (Warnecke, 1973).

[1]Fred Davis, *Illness, Interaction, and the Self* (Belmont, Cal.: Wadsworth, 1972), p. 46.

Furthermore, the motivation to work in such a role and to train for it often appears to be based on factors (marriage and subsequent satisfaction) that are tangential or irrelevant to the intrinsic content of the role itself. Research by Richard Warnecke (1973) shows that a lack of commitment to the nursing role is the major nonintellectual factor of attrition from collegiate nursing programs; Davis (1966, 1972) has shown that among student nurses who graduate there is often a lack of commitment to the actual practice of nursing. The nursing degree thus often becomes an end in itself rather than the basis for a lifelong career, and this lack of professional commitment remains a most serious problem for the future development of nursing.

National Associations

Nurses have sought to improve the conditions of nursing practice and to gain professional status through the organization of national associations representing nursing interests. The most prominent of these organizations have been the National League of Nursing and the American Nurses' Association.

The National League of Nursing is composed mainly of nursing educators and formal agencies interested in nursing education. Its primary aim is to promote quality standards for nurses' training. The American Nurses' Association has become the major organization for registered nurses and is the official representative of nursing in relations with outside organizations. The ANA has not had the control over its membership, currently about 160,000 registered nurses, that has characterized the American Medical Association. Nor has membership in the ANA played an important role in the ability of individual nurses to establish important relationships with nursing colleagues. The overall effectiveness of ANA has been hampered by internal power struggles and lack of support of a unified membership. Only during the last few years has the ANA enjoyed the increasing support of a number of concerned nurses, who see in it the potential for positive group action (Bowman and Culpepper, 1974).

The "Doctor–Nurse Game"

It might be assumed from the literature examined thus far that nurses have generally been powerless and dependent practitioners. Some studies clearly suggest that nurses perceive themselves as pawns in most power struggles, that they have perhaps internalized the attitudes of subordination projected by physicians and hospital administrators. The attitudes of all participants are no doubt reinforced by the stereotypical roles of male dominance and female passivity. Mauksch (1972:223) has suggested, for example, that physician–nurse interaction "might be the last vestigial remains of the nineteenth-century relationship between the sexes."

Sex roles, however, are not the only social–psychological factors affecting the physician–nurse relationship. As Barbara Bates (1970) has noted, the full development of the nursing role has been limited both by pressures from without (physicians) and by timidity from within. In her review of the literature, Bates observed that few nurses have openly rebelled against physician authoritarianism and most have accepted a position of deference toward the physician. This attitude is also prevalent in nursing traditions, where obedience to the physician has been emphasized (Strauss, 1966; Bates, 1970; Mauksch, 1972). Additionally significant in this regard is that physicians are often older than the nurses they work with, come from a higher socioeconomic background, are the socially recognized experts on medicine, and have been accorded greater rewards and higher prestige by the general public (Bates, 1970; Freidson, 1970a). Nor have medical schools provided experiences for medical students concerning the potential contribution of nurses (Becker et al., 1961).

Certainly the formal lines of authority that exist in the medical setting do operate to place nurses at a disadvantage in exercising and acting upon their judgments regarding medical treatment. Yet there are times when nurses do go ahead and exercise their own judgment in opposition to the orders of physicians. An example of this situation is found in the experiment conducted by Steven Rank and Cardell Jacobson (1977) in two hospitals in a large midwestern city. The experiment consisted of having an assistant, using the name of a little known staff surgeon at the hospital who had given permission to use his name, telephone eighteen nurses who were on duty and order them to administer a nonlethal overdose of Valium to appropriate patients. The call was made in a self-confident manner, using medical terminology and familiarity with hospital routine. None of the nurses questioned the telephone request and all but one suspicious nurse entered the request on a medication chart. One of the experimenters, posing as a contractor working on a bid to install some new equipment on the ward, was present at the time of the call with the duty of terminating the experiment should the nurse actually proceed to administer the drug, refuse to comply, fail to take action after fifteen minutes, or try to call the "doctor" back. As a further safeguard, nursing supervisors were stationed in each of the patient's rooms to prevent the medication from being administered. Sixteen out of eighteen nurses refused to administer the Valium. One nurse (Rank and Jacobson, 1977:191) said, "Whew! 30 mg.—he [the doctor] doesn't want to sedate her [the patient]—he wants to knock her out." Twelve of these nurses tried to recontact the doctor: only two appeared ready to comply with the order. Rank and Jacobson suggest that the high rate of noncompliance was due to an increased willingness among hospital personnel to challenge a doctor's orders in contemporary medical practice (a 1966 study had found twenty-one out of twenty-two nurses willing to give an overdose), rising self-esteem among nurses, and a fear of lawsuits for malpractice.

However, rather than challenge physicians' orders directly, which can have unpleasant consequences for the nurse (being "chewed out," fired), most nurses have been able to develop an extremely effective informal interactional style with physicians. This interaction has been described by Leonard Stein (1967) as the "doctor–nurse game" because it has all the features of a game—an object, rules, and scores. The object of the game is for the nurse to be bold, show initiative, and make significant recommendations to the doctor in a manner, however, that appears passive and totally supportive of the "super-physician." The central rule of the game is to avoid open disagreement between the players. This requires the nurse to communicate her recommendation without appearing to do so, while the physician, in seeking a recommendation, must appear not to be asking for it. Stein notes that the greater the significance of the recommendation, the more subtly it must be conveyed. Both participants must therefore be aware of each other's nonverbal and verbal styles of communication.

Stein illustrates the doctor–nurse game with an example of a nurse telephoning and awakening a hospital staff physician who is on call with a report about a female patient unknown to the doctor. The nurse informs the doctor that the patient is unable to sleep and had just been informed that day about the death of her father. What the nurse is actually telling the doctor is that the patient is upset and needs a sedative in order to sleep. Since the doctor is not familiar with the patient, the doctor asks the nurse what sleeping medication has been helpful to the patient in the past. What the doctor is actually doing is asking the nurse for a recommendation; however, the sentence is phrased in such a way that it appears to be a question rather than a request for a recommendation. The nurse replies that pentobarbital 100 mg has been effective for this particular patient, which Stein interprets as a disguised recommendation statement. The doctor then orders the nurse to administer pentobarbital 100 mg as needed and the nurse concludes the interaction by thanking the doctor for the order. The nurse has been successful in making a recommendation without appearing to do so, and the doctor has been successful in asking for a recommendation without appearing to do so.

While all of this may seem silly to persons unfamiliar with the physician–nurse relationship, it nonetheless represents a significant social mechanism by which the physician is able to utilize the nurse as a consultant and the nurse is able to gain self-esteem and professional satisfaction from her work. A successful game creates a doctor–nurse alliance and allows the doctor to have a good "score" by gaining the respect and admiration of the nursing staff; the nurse, in turn, scores by being identified by the physician as "a damn good nurse." If the doctor fails to play the game well, pleasant working relationships with the nurses may become difficult and the doctor may have problems of a trivial yet annoying nature when it comes to getting his work done. Nurses who do not play the game well (are outspoken in making recommendations) are either terminated from employment if they also lack intelligence, or are tolerated but not "loved" if they are bright. Nurses who do not play the game at all, according to Stein are defined as dull and are relegated to the background in the social life of the hospital.

NURSING: FUTURE TRENDS

According to William Goode's (1957, 1960) analysis of the features of a profession (discussed in Chapter Six), the two core characteristics of a profession were those of a service orientation and control over a specialized body of abstract knowledge. Nursing, of course, has traditionally had a service orientation, which is inherent in the mother-surrogate role. But nursing's claims to a specialized body of knowledge do not seem to be justified in light of physician-defined and -created practices. Goode (1960), in fact, excluded nurses from consideration as professionals because he believed nursing training was nothing more than a "lower-level medical education." This same type of reasoning has prompted Freidson (1970a) to describe nursing as a paramedical occupation.

However, despite their lack of control over a unique body of specialized knowledge, nurses have continued to strive for a true professional position within the status and work hierarchy of medicine. The result has been a definite separation of nursing tasks; bedside care is accomplished by lower-echelon workers, while "professional" nurses, especially those R.N.s with baccalaureate degrees, have abandoned the mother-surrogate role in favor of roles as administrators and primary-care healers. This trend, which shows every sign of continuing, suggests that nurses may be likely to achieve a partial degree of professional status in the future social structure of medical care.

Hospital Administration

One significant change in the work role of nursing has been the evolution of the R.N. into an administrative role. Wilson (1970) has indicated that this development may be viewed as a response to blocked mobility. Competent nurses cannot be rewarded by promotion to the higher rungs of the medical profession; if the nurse is to reach the top of the medical structure, she is forced to leave nursing altogether and become a doctor. Since this is usually impractical, many nurses have sought a career in hospital administration because it allows them to be less subordinate to physicians and to assign traditional nursing tasks to less qualified health workers. Also, from the perspective of hospital administrators, registered nurses can be used more economically in managerial and supervisory positions because lower paid personnel are available for bedside tasks (Schulman, 1972).

The paradox in this development, however, is that while it allows the nurse to gain a somewhat more secure claim of professional status, it greatly reduces or eliminates the contact with patients for which nursing was organized in the first place. Yet it has been suggested that patients usually cannot tell one type of nurse from another and generally do not overtly request emotional support (Elder, 1963). Instead, patients typically request simple tasks—such as medications to ease pain or assistance in moving to a more comfortable body position—which can be accomplished by less qualified nursing aides. As Sam Schulman (1972:236) points out, in hospitals "mother-surrogateness is seldom encountered: in large measure, it is not asked for by patients nor is it given by nurses." Schulman concludes that, in an indirect sense, patients are supportive of the removal of most professional nurses from their bedsides because they want the most professional persons in charge of their care. Whether or not patients do approve of removing the best qualified nurses from their bedside is an arguable point; nevertheless, it is happening.

The Nurse Practitioner

The most recent change in nursing has been the emergence of another kind of nurse—the nurse practitioner or nurse clinician. This change is not intended to create a new type of health worker, but instead to use more fully the skills and capabilities of the well-trained nurse. The nurse practitioner is intended to occupy a work position similar to that of the new physician assistant role. The nurse practitioner is trained to assume many of the primary and routine tasks of patient care normally handled by the physician, such as giving physical examinations, taking medical histories, ordering laboratory tests and x-rays, providing health education to patients and their families, and making the decision as to whether or not the patient needs to consult with a physician. This role for the nurse allows the physician to assume the more realistic position of a highly trained specialist. It frees physicians from the routine tasks of medical practice and allows them to concentrate more fully on the complex medical problems for which their training has prepared them.

Although the role of nurse practitioner has not been fully conceptualized in terms of the training, qualifications, and responsibilities, existing studies (Merenstein et al., 1974; Taller and Feldman, 1974) suggest that nurse practitioners have met with a high degree of acceptance among patients who have used their services, and that patient care can indeed be made more efficient by involving paramedical personnel.

Hence, a formal role for nurses who practice medicine as well as nursing is beginning to develop within the context of patient care. In the future, nurse practitioners may even provide most or even all primary care for patients, leaving physicians to further consolidate their role as specialists. Although this would not effect a change in nursing's subordinate work role, it would allow the practitioners at least some share of the characteristics of professionalism. The primary concern, however, with this projection of an expanded role is that the nurse practitioner may simply be "consumed" by the medical profession as a "lesser" doctor or given only a more complex form of tasks delegated by the physician (Bates, 1970). Certainly this result is a distinct possibility and it relates to the point made earlier in this chapter by Wilson (1970) that nursing represents a case of blocked mobility; if "professional" nurses are to become anything more than supervisors of nursing care or practitioners of lower level medical care, they must leave nursing because the work role is inherently subordinate to the physician.

Current trends suggest that the new generation of R.N.s will play an expanded role in medicine through increased decision making and direct responsibility for decisions made as either administrator or practitioner. They will do so, however, within the overall structure of medical practice, and their position will remain subordinate to that of the physician. Direct bedside care of patients will increasingly come to be the domain of the practical nurse and the nurse's aide.

PHYSICIAN'S ASSISTANT

While the concept of the nurse practitioner derives from the expansion of a traditional occupation, that of physician's assistant represents a new form of paramedical practitioner. This new occupation results from the recognition by American physicians that specialization has reduced them to narrower and narrower competencies and that the pressure of increasing case loads has reduced the time available for attending to many minor and routine patient demands. It has been charged that some physicians have relied upon excessive use of laboratory and diagnostic tests (thus increasing the costs of medical treatment) as a partial substitution for physician–patient interaction. It has also been suggested that decreased physician–patient time per visit has contributed to patient dissatisfaction and thus to malpractice suits. Ideally physician's assistants will handle many routine medical problems, thereby releasing the physician for increased physician–patient contact and more attention to difficult and complex problems. Although the exact duties and responsibilities of the physician's assistant have yet to be standardized, a general job description would be to provide a level of primary patient care similar to or higher than that of nurse practitioners.

In a survey of graduates of the eighteen physician's assistant training programs extant in 1972, Richard Scheffler and Olivia Stinson (1974) found that members of this new occupational group were primarily young white males, between the ages of twenty-five and thirty, who had a background in health care services prior to their qualification as physician's assistant. Their training was either in general medicine or in specialties, especially ophthalmology and orthopedics. Typically, they worked directly for physicians, either in private medical practices or in hospitals providing in-patient services. They indicated that they spent the largest part of their workday providing direct patient care, which was divided about equally between those tasks directly supervised and those indirectly supervised by physicians; considerably less time was spent in technical or laboratory work or in the supervision of other health workers.

However, the lack of a definitive role for physician's assistants has resulted in a problematic acceptance by other members of the health occupations, particularly nurses. Rodney Coe and Leonard Fichtenbaum's 1972 study of a small midwestern group practice and community hospital found that those persons who were initially supportive of the physician's assistant role had a clearer understanding of his duties than those opposed to the role. Physician's assistants viewed themselves as a "limited extension of the physician," but nurses ranked them below their own position but somewhat higher than practical nurses in the status hierarchy of the hospital. Nurses questioned the need for even having physician's assistants, especially in the hospital, and they were most concerned about those duties of the physician's assistant that overlapped their own assignments. Many nurses felt physician's assistants could be better utilized in rural communities that did not have a doctor in residence. Physicians, in contrast, generally agreed that the overall idea of a physician's assistant was a good one, but they expressed concern about the possible legal liabilities. They favored physician's assistants working under direct supervision in their own private offices. In sum, Coe and Fichtenbaum observed that in the beginning:

> The general attitude held by most hospital personnel (except physicians and administrators) was, at best, ambivalent. Much of it was negative. The ambivalence stemmed from "envy" of the physician assistant's close relationship with the physician, his freedom to make decisions (which most felt were the sole responsibility of the physician) and greater financial rewards with less formal training than most of the personnel with whom he worked.[2]

[2] Rodney M. Coe and Leonard Fichtenbaum, "Utilization of Physician Assistants: Some Implications for Medical Practice," *Medical Care*, 10 (Nov.-Dec. 1972), 500.

Yet, in a follow-up study six months later, Coe and Fichtenbaum detected the emergence of increasingly favorable attitudes toward physician's assistants (due in large measure, they believed, to the positive support of physicians). Earlier vehement criticisms were replaced with discussions about hiring more physician's assistants, and various other health personnel—registered nurses and laboratory technicians—were obviously motivated to become physician's assistants by the higher status and higher salaries. Coe and Fichtenbaum concluded that as long as physicians were willing to accept the responsibility for physician's assistants, problems were minimal.

Thus, it appears that if problems of role definition can be solved, the physician's assistant is likely to become an established occupation within medicine. Although the new occupation is composed primarily of men, it may become increasingly attractive to women not only because the status and pay are inviting, but also because the work role is asexual. It currently avoids both the female stereotype of nursing and the male stereotype of physicianship. (This may change, however, if males continue to dominate the ranks.) Most important for patient care, the physician's assistant, in conjunction with the nurse practitioner, may be able to resolve the significant issue of providing more primary care practitioners in the American system of health care delivery.

OTHER HEALTH PRACTITIONERS

In the United States there are other practitioners who are not under the direct authority of physicians, but who nonetheless provide health care in some form to certain people. One such class of practitioners is the *osteopath*. Among all the alternative health practitioners, the osteopath is the closest to being like a physician. Osteopathy began in the 1860s in Kirksville, Missouri as little more than a pseudoscientific cult (New, 1958; Coe, 1978; Wardwell, 1979; Wolinsky, 1980). Its founder, Andrew Taylor Still, had a "divine inspiration" that illness was caused by a dislocation of one or more bones in the spinal column. For many years, osteopathy was viewed by physicians and much of the general public as a form of quackery. But gradually osteopathy achieved respectability by moving away from its early focus on spinal manipulation. By the mid-twentieth century, osteopaths were receiving scientific medical training in such areas as surgery and drug therapy. Training for osteopaths takes place at five osteopathic colleges in the United States, which are affiliated with universities and whose graduates are awarded the Doctor of Osteopathy Degree (D.O.). Further training as an intern and resident are required. Osteopaths have also formed their own professional organization, the American Osteopathic Association, which serves to promote professionalism, although it is not as large or powerful as the American Medical Association.

In 1953 the American Medical Association recognized osteopaths as another medical specialty and they now enjoy the rights and privileges of physicians, even though their status is decidedly inferior to that of medical doctors. To be fully accepted by the medical profession, osteopaths will probably have to give up entirely what made it unique—spinal manipulation—and be submerged into medicine. There is some evidence that this is happening, as in 1961 the California College of Osteopathic Physicians and Surgeons was reorganized as the University of California College of Medicine at Irvine. Previous graduates were offered the M.D. degree to replace the D.O. degree. To date, however, osteopaths have been able to maintain their separate identity, yet the trend is toward absorption into medicine. In 1975 some 14,000 osteopaths received over 46 million visits from patients for pain, injury or swelling of the back region, physical examinations, the treatment of fatigue, influenza, pains in the lower extremities, and a variety of similar ailments. In 1980 there were an estimated 17,700 osteopaths (HEW, 1980).

Another alternative health practitioner is the *chiropractor*. The chiropractic approach to healing also involves manipulation of bones in the spinal column. This type of treatment originated with Daniel Palmer in Davenport, Iowa in 1895. It is based on the idea that manipulation of the spine can relieve pressure on the nerves and thereby alleviate illness, pain, and suffering. While there is some dispute over whether the osteopathic and chiropractic approaches evolved independently of each other in terms of initial conceptualization, chiropractors today are restricted solely to nonmedical techniques. In 1978 there were seven accredited chiropractic colleges in the United States, three that are candidates for accreditation, and seven that are not accredited by the Council on Chiropractic Education of the American Chiropractic Association. There are also chiropractic colleges in Canada, England, and Australia. Training is four years in duration, three in the classroom and one in practice at the college. There are no internships or residencies to serve.

While there is some evidence that chiropractic techniques do help patients with certain neuromusculoskeletal problems (Wardwell, 1980), the medical profession has traditionally opposed the extension of professional status to chiropractors. Rather than attempt to absorb the chiropractor into medicine, physicians have preferred to eliminate the field altogether. Nevertheless, chiropractors are licensed to practice in all fifty states and are authorized to receive Medicare payments for treatments rendered to patients over the age of sixty-five. In 1976 about 18,000 chiropractors provided services to approximately 7.5 million people. Chiropractors are often favored by people with low incomes because they charge less than physicians ($11 for a routine office visit and $56 for an initial examination, including laboratory tests and x-rays in 1977), were friendly, gave more time to patients, and explained difficulties in words easily understood (Bauwens, 1977; Wardwell, 1980). In fact, chiropractors have been known as the "poor person's doctor" (Koos, 1954:93).

However, chiropractors have been hampered in their attempts at professionalization not only by physicians but also because of conflicts among themselves. Some chiropractors favor a more expanded role, using a variety of techniques, in which a wider range of health problems would be treated. Others prefer a more "pure" approach, in which chiropractors would limit themselves to spinal manipulation. Chiropractors must often compete among one another for patients and have little control over who should be licensed to practice. Moreover, two organizations, the American Chiropractic Association and the International Chiropractor Association, have differing positions, although most chiropractors agree they should merge. Walter Wardwell summarized the overall chiropractic situation as follows:

> To the extent that they reject the basic conceptions of medical science as fundamentally wrong, and propound chiropractic as a completely different philosophy and science capable of treating nearly the entire range of human ailments, they inevitably find great difficulty in convincing the mass of informed citizens that medicine's evaluation of chiropractic is wrong. Such citizens, unless persuaded by personal experience, are unlikely to view chiropractic as scientific or chiropractors as qualified doctors. Lack of acceptance by the public and rejection by orthodox medical authorities explains why the word "marginal" has been used to describe the chiropractic profession ever since 1952. . . . However, from being "marginal," chiropractic could evolve, as has osteopathy, to being "parallel" to medicine if it becomes the equal of medicine in education, scientific research, public acceptance, and success in therapy.[3]

Among the remaining practitioners are quacks, folk healers, and faith healers. *Quacks* are people posing as physicians or some type of formally certified "doctor" or are physicians who have lost their license to practice medicine. Thus, their claims at expertise are fraudulent, although they might obtain some successes and attract patients. However, their practices may be harmful at worst or accomplish nothing at best. A current example of quackery, according to the medical profession, is those physicians who are no longer licensed in the United States but provide laetrile treatments and "special" diets to cancer patients at clinics in northern Mexico. To date, laetrile has not been scientifically confirmed as an effective mode of treatment for cancer despite claims to the contrary.

Folk healers were discussed in Chapter Three (The Process of Seeking Medical Care). Folk healers are not used to any significant extent in the United States except by some racial and ethnic minorities. Low-income blacks in Chicago (Snow, 1978) and Mexican-Americans in the Southwest (Kiev, 1968) are examples of people who frequent folk healers. Apparently few Anglos go to folk healers, although some elderly people living in poverty and rural areas may be prone to use "folk" remedies in treating ailments (Bauwens, 1977). Common ingredients in folk remedies are such substances as whiskey, honey, sugar, lemon juice, baking soda, aspirin, kerosene, salt, butter, mustard, sassafras, and so forth (Denton, 1978).

Finally, there are *faith healers*. These are people who use the power of suggestion, prayer, and faith in God to promote healing. According to John Denton (1978), two basic beliefs are prevalent in religious healing. One form of belief supports the idea that healing occurs primarily through psychological processes and is effective only with psychophysiological disorders. The other belief is that healing is accomplished through the intervention of God and constitutes a present-day miracle. Denton offers five general categories

[3]Walter I. Wardwell, "The Present and Future Role of the Chiropractor," in *Modern Developments in the Principles and Practice of Chiropractic*, S. Haldeman, ed. (New York: Appleton-Century-Crofts, 1980), pp. 36–37.

of faith healing: (1) self-treatment through prayer; (2) treatment by a lay-person thought to be able to communicate with God; (3) treatment by an official church leader, for whom healing is only one of many tasks; (4) healing obtained from a person or group of persons who practice healing full-time without an affiliation with a major religious organization; and (5) healing obtained from religious healers who practice full-time and are affiliated with a major religious group, such as Christian Science healers. A common theme running though each of these categories is an appeal to God to change a person's physical or mental condition for the better.

An example of faith healing is found in the study conducted by Gillian Allen and Roy Wallis (1976) of members of a small congregation of a Pentecostal church, the Assemblies of God, in a city in Scotland. Members of the church subscribed to a belief that the devil caused illness and that even for such afflictions as mental illness, blindness, dumbness, and epilepsy a person could be possessed by evil spirits. Accepting the Bible as the literal truth, the Assemblies of God officially support the idea of *divine healing* based upon Biblical passages indicating that (1) some people have the power to transmit the healing forces of the Holy Spirit or to exorcise demons and (2) healing can be obtained through faith the same way as salvation from sin. The healing procedure was described in this manner:

> Prayer for healing in the Assembly of God occurs at the end of normal services when those who need healing or help and advice, are asked "to come out to the front." There the pastor and the elders perform the laying on of hands and sprinkling with holy oil and pray simultaneously: "Oh Lord, heal this woman! Yes, Lord. We know you can heal her." The occasional case of demon possession is dealt with in a similar way when the pastor or evangelist addresses the demon along these lines: "Get out, foul demon! In the name of Jesus, leave her!"[4]

Although the Pentecostal church used divine healing as a central aspect of church dogma, it did not prohibit members from seeking professional medical care. Use of divine healing, however, was preferred because it offered the advantage of providing both spiritual and physical healing. It was also believed to work in many cases where orthodox medical practices failed. The members had a fund of knowledge attesting to spectacular cures, either through the specific effect of the emotional healing services or through the power of prayer in general. Yet since church members also believed that "God's methods are sometimes through men" and that "God put doctors in the world and gave them their skills," it was permissible to seek physician assistance. For serious illnesses in particular, divine healing was used in conjunction with professional medicine. Hence, church members held both religious and scientific beliefs about the causation and treatment of illness simultaneously, without any apparent conflict. "In serious illnes-ses," state Allen and Wallis (1976:134–135), "members were not faced with the choice between breaking their religious principles by fetching the doctor and refusing medical treatment altogether." Consequently, Pentecostalists

---

[4]Gillian Allen and Roy Wallis, "Pentecostalists as a Medical Minority," in *Marginal Medicine,* R. Wallis and P. Morley (eds.) (New York: Free Press, 1976), p. 121.

were usually able to avoid the dilemma of whether to use *either* a religious *or* a medical curing process.

In the United States, some faith healers hold services in a church or in their homes, others travel from city to city holding meetings, perhaps in tents, and some appear on television or radio. The number of people who frequent such healing services and who are actually helped by this method is not known. But faith healers tend to be readily available and most cities and towns are visited by such healers at least once a year.

One reason why not only faith healers but also other marginal practitioners like chiropractors and folk healers have been more competitive with professional medicine in the United States than in other countries, like Great Britain, is that Great Britain offers free medical care for the mass population (Wallis and Morley, 1976). This type of care, in concert with effective forms of medical treatment, gives the British medical profession an almost complete monopoly over the delivery of health services. The high cost of care, lessened availability of physicians, and social psychological barriers inherent in welfare medicine have encouraged the poor in the United States to use marginal practitioners in many cases.

SUMMARY

Nursing as an occupation has evolved from being an informal exercise of charity ("sisterhood") into a formal occupational role subordinate to the authority and control of the physician. Many social factors have contributed to the maintenance of this situation, especially the stereotype of the mother-surrogate. It has also been noted that nurse's training is not necessarily viewed by nursing students as a means to a career, but as a kind of "life insurance" should they be disappointed in their primary goals of marriage and family. Nevertheless, nurses have continually struggled to achieve formal colleagueship with the physician and they may, to a certain extent, reach this goal as a result of their movement toward hospital administration and the nurse practitioner role.

The role of nurse practitioner seems particularly promising because it would enable nurses to gain some autonomy over what they do and to share more fully in medicine's specialized body of knowledge. Both the nurse practitioner and the physician's assistant roles result from a trend toward physician specialization that has made doctors less accessible to patients with minor and generalized ailments who nonetheless demand attention. Moreover, the emerging paramedical practitioners represent evidence that physicians have begun to modify their position in the medical work hierarchy by sharing once jealously guarded tasks of primary medical care. Perhaps the time may come, as Wilson (1970) has suggested, when the physician will lead a balanced team of health personnel who are involved in decision making and limited independent action.

Other health practitioners—osteopaths, chiropractors, quacks, folk healers, and faith healers—were discussed. The osteopaths were found to be the most like physicians of any other type of practitioner and, in fact, are threatened with absorption into the medical profession. The other practitioners remain on the margin of health care delivery.

PART III

HEALTH
INSTITUTIONS

chapter **8**

THE HOSPITAL

Since many health problems require a level of medical treatment and personal care that extends beyond the range of services normally available in the patient's home or in the physician's office, modern society has developed formal institutions for patient care intended to help meet the more complex health needs of its members. The hospital, the major social institution for the delivery of health care in the modern world, offers considerable advantages to both patient and society. From the standpoint of the individual, the sick or injured person has access to centralized medical knowledge and technology that will render treatment much more thorough and efficient. From the standpoint of society, as Talcott Parsons and Renée Fox (1952) suggest, hospitalization both protects the family from many of the disruptive effects of caring for the ill in the home and operates as a means of guiding the sick and injured into medically supervised institutions where their problems are less disruptive for society as a whole.

The purpose of this chapter is to consider the social role of the hospital. Besides serving the prescribed social function of providing medical treatment, hospitals can be viewed from the perspective of a functionally specific world. This chapter will examine the organizational aspects of that world in the following order: (1) development of the hospital as a social institution; (2) the hospital system in the United States; (3) social organization of hospital work, including its effect on the patient role; and (4) rising cost of hospital services.

THE DEVELOPMENT OF THE HOSPITAL
AS A SOCIAL INSTITUTION

The development of hospitals as institutions providing medical services for the general public proceeded in pace with the prevailing needs, beliefs, values, and attitudes of the societies they served (Knowles, 1973; Coe, 1978; Rosen, 1979). Historically, hospitals have passed through four distinct phases of development: (1) as centers of religious practice, (2) as poor-houses, (3) as deathhouses, and (4) as centers of medical technology.

Hospitals as Centers of Religious Practice

Although the Romans were the first to establish separate medical facilities (for economic and military reasons) which have been described as hospitals, the origin of the institution we know today as the hospital has usually been associated with the rise of Christianity. Christian theology emphasized that human beings were duty bound to provide assistance to the sick and needy; this belief was reinforced by the notion that spiritual salvation could be obtained by whoever provided such a service. Consequently, the Roman Catholic Church encouraged its clergy to found hospitals and to locate these hospitals near churches as an integral feature of Christian religious endeavor. Furthermore, during the period of the Crusades between 1096 and 1291, many hospitals were established along the routes taken to the Holy Land by the Christian armies. Secular benefactors, such as kings, queens, other members of the nobility, wealthy merchants, artisan and craftsmen's guilds, and municipalities also founded hospitals. By the end of the fifteenth century, an extensive network of hospitals was known to have existed throughout Western Europe (Rosen, 1979).

The medieval hospital, however, was not a hospital by any modern standard. True, these hospitals were community centers for the care of the lower-class sick; yet the medical care, supervised and largely performed by clergy and nuns, consisted primarily of a rudimentary form of nursing. The primary functions of the medieval hospital were the exercise of religious practices and the extension of charity and welfare services to the poor, including both the able-bodied and the sick. These early hospitals, therefore, provided a wide spectrum of social tasks for the benefit of the lower classes, especially the provision of food, shelter, sanctuary, and prayer as well as nursing.

During the Renaissance and the Reformation, the religious character of the hospital began to disappear as increasing numbers of hospitals were placed under the jurisdiction of secular authorities. Nevertheless, as Rodney Coe (1978) has observed, three basic features of the modern hospital are derived from the influence of the Church. First, the concept of a service oriented toward helping others has become a guiding principle for the manner in which hospital personnel are required to approach their work. Second, hospitals are supposed to have a "universalistic" approach—that is, to accept for treatment all people who may be sick or injured. And third, the custodial nature of hospital care has been facilitated by housing patients within the confines of a single location.

Hospitals as Poorhouses

The secular control of hospitals marked a period of decline for the development of Europe's hospital system. Even though monks and nuns continued to work in hospitals, the removal of the centralized authority of the church left hospitals under many separate administrations, usually those of municipal governments. Without general regulations pertaining to hospital administration, individual hospitals were free to pursue any course of action they desired. This situation encouraged abuse, particularly in regard to neglect of facilities, misappropriation of funds, and the lowering of prevailing standards of patient care. In England the suppression of the monastery system in the mid-1500s led to the collapse of the English hospital system as many hospitals, left without personnel or money, were forced to close. The few remaining hospitals limited their services to people who were actually sick and who could be cured. While this policy relegated the poor, both the incurably ill and the able-bodied, to poorhouses or to the streets for their support, it marked the beginning of a new definition of hospitals as institutions active in curing the sick and injured so that they could return to society.

However, by the end of the sixteenth century, as George Rosen (1979) explains, the economic and social conditions of the poor worsened to a considerable degree. Unemployment, higher prices, and the loss of land created a serious problem of vagrancy throughout Europe. Many vagrants likewise claimed to be sick or crippled, and they crowded whatever hospital facilities were available. In accordance with the new definition of social welfare as a community rather than a church responsibility, measures were eventually taken by city and national authorities to provide public assistance. Many hospitals were reopened, but they soon acquired the characteristics of boarding houses because they offered food and shelter to the poor, regardless of whether they were sick or healthy. Those persons living in hospitals who could work were required to pay for their lodging, while hospitals received further financial support through public taxation. Hospitals became little more than social "warehouses," where invalids, the aged, orphans, and the mentally defective could be sent and thus removed from the mainstream of society. Even today in the United States, people with chronic health problems requiring long-term hospitalization—the insane, the incurable, and individuals suffering from highly infectious diseases—tend to be sent to public institutions, while private hospitals tend to accept patients with acute disorders.

Hospitals as Deathhouses

Following the Renaissance and the Reformation, the outward character of hospitals appeared to change very little from that of a public institution whose purpose was to provide welfare services for the lower social classes on behalf of the communities in which they were located. Nonetheless, changes were taking place as physicians discovered that hospitals contained large numbers of sick and injured (and also generally powerless) people whose health problems could be studied and upon whom the various evolving techniques of medical treatment could be practiced.

Physicians had first begun to associate themselves with hospitals during the fourteenth century; initially they had little influence because they were not members of the hospital staff and provided their services on a purely voluntary basis. By the seventeenth century, however, physicians acquired a virtual monopoly over the existing body of medical knowledge that placed them in the position of first advising and eventually directing all patient care within the hospital. As physicians became increasingly influential, nonmedical hospital tasks gradually disappeared. By the early nineteenth century, hospitals had clearly assumed their present-day role as institutions for medical care, for medical research, and for the education of medical students.

Although medical treatment was recognized as the primary function of the hospital in the eighteenth century, the primitive level of that treatment produced few cures. Trained physicians were unable to achieve consistent results with their techniques and, accordingly, neither they nor hospitals were held in high esteem by the general population. Because so few patients survived treatment despite occasional heroic efforts, hospitals acquired an image as places where the poor went to die.

According to Coe (1978), the high death rate in hospitals was also related to the appalling living conditions provided patients. Typically, hospitals were dirty, poorly ventilated, and filled to capacity. Often more than one patient was placed in a single bed regardless of the patient's disorder, and treatment was usually carried out publicly on the ward itself. Surgery, which Coe points out was limited at that time mostly to amputations and childbirth, plus the purging of fevers with various potions, bloodletting to eliminate "excess" blood, and the removal of the dead all occurred in the same general area where patients ate and slept. Nor did the attending physicians and surgeons practice even the most rudimentary standards of sanitation, moving from bed to bed and treating a great variety of disorders, including those that were infectious, without washing their hands or changing their clothes. Thus, it is not surprising that hospitals were regarded by most people as places where only the lower social classes went to die.

Hospitals as Centers of Medical Technology

Since the end of the nineteenth century, a new image of hospitals evolved as institutions where patients of all social classes could generally expect to find the highest quality medical care and could reasonably expect to be cured of their disorders. Three major factors were responsible for this change. First was the fact that medicine had indeed become a science in terms of employing the scientific method to seek out accurate medical knowledge and to develop successful techniques that could be employed in a consistent manner. Of particular importance was increased knowledge about human physiology and the development of the science of bacteriology; also important was the perfection of ether as an anesthetic, which allowed surgery to be performed in a relatively painless fashion. Since the new medical technology required extensive and often expensive facilities, these facilities were centralized in hospitals so that they could be available to most physicians. Hospitals eventually became places where physicians also referred their upper- and middle-class patients, since the most advanced medical technology was located there. While the poor generally remained in a charity status as hospital patients, a new type of patient came into being—the private patient—who required private accommodations, usually had a private physician, and who paid for hospital services.

A second important factor, concomitant with the development of medical technology, was the discovery and use of antiseptic measures in the hospital to help curtail infection. Hospitals were not only properly cleaned and ventilated, but patients with infectious diseases were isolated in special areas of the hospital, and hospital staffs were required to wash their hands and change their clothing after working with these patients. The use of such items as surgical masks, rubber gloves, and sterilized surgical instruments became commonplace. These procedures not only reduced the number of deaths among hospital patients, but also reduced the amount of time required for patient recovery.

Third, there was a significant improvement in the quality of hospital personnel. Especially important was the entry on the scene of the trained nurse and the laboratory technician, whose specialized skills were able to support the physician in his or her primary role of diagnostician and practitioner. In the twentieth century, the hospital has become the major institutional resource available to society for coping with problems of health and illness.

HOSPITALS IN THE UNITED STATES

The first hospitals were founded in the United States over two hundred years ago. Generally their development paralleled that of Western European institutions in the 1700s. The first such hospital was established by William Penn in Philadelphia in 1713, with the care of the sick being incidental to the main purpose of providing shelter for the poor. The well-known Charity Hospital in New Orleans was founded by the Catholic Church in 1737 for similar reasons. The first hospital to be established in the United States solely for the purpose of treating the sick was the Pennsylvania Hospital, founded by Benjamin Franklin and a group of interested citizens in 1751. These early hospitals were not governmental undertakings, as Rosen (1979) points out, but were largely based on voluntary initiative by private citizens who wanted medical care available on a nonprofit basis. They were generally intended to provide treatment for those patients who had curable disorders.

Federal government participation in health care did not actually begin until 1798 with the U.S. Public Health Service hospital program for merchant seamen. State governments did not enter into health care delivery until the 1800s, and their efforts were largely confined to the establishment of state mental institutions. By 1873 there were only 178 hospitals of all types in the United States; this number grew to 7,271 hospitals in 1976.

Hospital Ownership

The ownership of hospitals in the United States may be classified into three major types: (1) voluntary (nonprofit), (2) proprietary (profit-making), or (3) government (federal, state, or local). Table 8–1 shows that of the total of 7,271 hospitals in 1976, the largest single type was the voluntary hospital.[1]

[1]A hospital is defined as a facility with at least six beds that is licensed by the state as a hospital, or that is operated as a hospital by a federal or state agency and is therefore not subject to state or local licensing laws (National Center for Health Statistics, 1978:297).

TABLE 8-1.   Ownership of Hospitals, 1976

Ownership	Total Hospitals	General Medical and Surgical	Specialty				
			Total	Psychi-atric	Chronic disease	Tuber-culosis	Other[1]
TOTAL	7,271	6,361	910	502	63	21	324
Government	2,653	2,220	433	296	40	19	78
Federal	380	352	28	25	—	—	3
State-local	2,273	1,868	405	271	40	19	75
Proprietary	996	800	196	117	4	—	75
Nonprofit	3,622	3,341	281	89	19	2	171
Church	776	734	42	13	4	—	25
Other	2,846	2,607	239	76	15	2	146

[1] Includes eye, ear, nose, and throat hospitals; epileptic hospitals; alcoholism hospitals; maternity hospitals; orthopedic hospitals; physical rehabilitation hospitals; and other hospitals.
SOURCE: U.S. National Center for Health Statistics, *Health Resources Statistics* (Washington, D.C.: U.S. Department of Health, Education and Welfare, 1978).

This figure of 3,622 voluntary hospitals represents over 50 percent of all American hospitals.

Controlled by a board of trustees, nonprofit hospitals are exempt from federal income taxes and many other forms of state and local taxes. These hospitals have generally been characterized as emphasizing high quality care for the upper and middle social classes, while also allowing access to their facilities to lower-class patients primarily through clinics and teaching programs (Elling and Halebsky, 1961). Voluntary hospitals are highly dependent on community physicians for membership on their staffs and for the referral of patients. According to data obtained from a 1969 American Hospital Association survey, Noralou Roos and her associates (1974) project that 59 percent of all capital funds for voluntary hospitals are derived from internal resources, mostly income from patient services. Other sources of capital funds for voluntary hospitals are philanthropic (24 percent) and government (17 percent). Large voluntary hospitals, however, are somewhat less dependent than smaller hospitals on local physicians because of their greater prestige, more extensive facilities, and higher ratio of doctors requesting staff positions (Roos et al., 1974).

Table 8-1 shows that 996 hospitals (14 percent of the total) are classified as proprietary. These hospitals are usually small and are also highly dependent on local physicians for staff membership and patient referrals. The referral system is especially critical because generally the proprietary hospital's only source of capital funds is internal.

The number of government-owned hospitals shown in Table 8-1 is 2,653, which is 36 percent of the total. Roos estimates that government hospitals receive 56 percent of their capital funds from government sources, 36 percent from internal sources, and 8 percent from philanthropic contributions. Government hospitals tend to lack prestige in comparison to volun-

TABLE 8–2.   Hospital Beds by Ownership of Hospitals, 1976

Ownership	Total Beds	General Medical and Surgical	Total	Specialty			
				Psychi- atric	Chronic disease	Tuber- culosis	Other[1]
TOTAL	1,381,267	1,069,828	311,439	244,358	19,933	3,546	43,602
Government	584,218	316,471	267,747	226,434	16,460	3,368	21,485
Federal	126,916	100,478	26,438	24,768	—	—	1,670
State-local	457,302	215,993	241,309	201,666	16,460	3,368	19,815
Proprietary	95,993	82,519	13,474	9,507	38	—	3,629
Nonprofit	701,056	670,838	30,218	8,417	3,135	178	18,488
Church	192,182	188,611	3,571	1,319	261	—	1,991
Other	508,874	482,227	26,647	7,098	2,874	178	16,497

[1] Includes eye, ear, nose, and throat hospitals; epileptic hospitals; alcoholism hospitals; narcotics hospitals; maternity hospitals; orthopedic hospitals; physical rehabilitation hospitals; and other hospitals.
SOURCE: U.S. National Center for Health Statistics, *Health Resources Statistics* (Washington, D.C.: U.S. Department of Health, Education and Welfare, 1978).

tary hospitals, perhaps because they fill the majority of their staff positions with interns and residents. They are the major source of health care for people with low-incomes, particularly in urban areas. Roos describes government hospitals as "hospitals of last resort" because they place their greatest emphasis on public access to their facilities rather than on the quality of their care. Yet the increased affiliation of government hospitals with medical schools portends a shift in emphasis toward quality care and superior facilities.

Table 8–2, a tabulation of the number of hospital beds by type of ownership in 1976, offers a further illustration of the distribution of hospital facilities in the United States. The figure reveals that voluntary hospitals have 701,056 hospital beds, with most of these beds (670,838) located in general medical and surgical hospitals. Thus, voluntary hospitals (representing 50 percent of all hospitals) have approximately 51 percent of all hospital beds. Government hospitals (representing 36 percent of the total) have 584,218 beds or 42 percent of the total number of beds. Proprietary hospitals (13 percent of the total number of hospitals) have 95,993 beds or 7 percent of the total. These beds are primarily in general hospitals.

The General Hospital

At this point it is important to distinguish between general and specialty hospitals, the two major categories of hospitals according to the type of service they offer. General medical and surgical hospitals provide diagnostic and treatment services for patients who have a great variety of health disorders. Most general hospitals are short-term care facilities. According to the U.S. Center for National Health Statistics (1978), there were approximately 6,361 general hospitals with over one million beds in 1976 (as shown in Tables 8–1 and 8–2). Although general hospitals are located throughout the United States, the South has the largest concentration of them. By state, California has the largest number (641) of general hospitals, followed by Texas (578). In 1976 there were over 36 million admissions to general hospitals, representing a ratio of about 168 admissions for every 1,000 Americans. Approximately 34 percent of these admissions were in the South, but two states, California and New York, had 16 percent of the total U.S. admissions to general hospitals. The U.S. Center for National Health Statistics also reports that in 1976 over 3.1 million people were employed either full- or part-time in general hospitals, with the majority (80 percent) working full-time. This figure represents a national average of 3.5 full-time general hospital workers for each hospital patient.

The Specialty Hospital

Specialty hospitals typically restrict their services to patients with specific disorders. Specialty hospitals are generally long-term care facilities, and the majority are either psychiatric, chronic disease, or tuberculosis hospitals. The U.S. National Center for Health Statistics classified approximately 910 hospitals in the United States as specialty hospitals in 1976. Table 8–2 indicates that psychiatric hospitals were the largest single type of specialty hospital, with a total of 502 hospitals. New York and Massachusetts are the two states with the largest number of specialty hospitals. Northeastern United States has more admissions to specialty hospitals than any other region of the country. There were 1.2 million admissions to specialty hospitals nationally in 1976 and nearly 79 percent of these admissions were to psychiatric hospitals. The number of patients in specialty hospitals during 1976 averaged 255,641, or 1.2 patients per 1,000 citizens. About 390,400 persons, some 92 percent of them full-time, were employed in these hospitals. This figure represents an average of 1.4 full-time specialty hospital employee per patient.

THE ORGANIZATION OF THE GENERAL HOSPITAL

Certainly not all hospitals are alike in their organiztion of services, but general hospitals, as the most common single type of hospital in the United States, exhibit organizational features similar to most other types of hospitals. Figure 8–1 shows the typical organization of large general hospitals. As a social organization, the general hospital has been described as being formal, highly stratified, quasibureaucratic, and quasiauthoritarian (Croog and Ver Steeg, 1972; Georgopoulos and Mann, 1972). General hospitals have also been described as "multipurpose institutions" in that they provide a variety of health-related functions for society such as: (1) treating patients, (2) conducting medical research, (3) training health practitioners, (4) providing laboratories and other medical facilities to the community, and (5) sponsoring health education and preventive medicine programs for the general public (Heydebrand, 1973; Coe, 1978). Robert Wilson (1963), for example, describes the hospital as a hotel, a school, a laboratory, and a stage for treatment. The *primary* goal of the hospital, however, is that of providing medical treatment to its patients within the limits of contemporary medical

FIGURE 8–1. Typical Large General Hospital Organized into Five Divisions

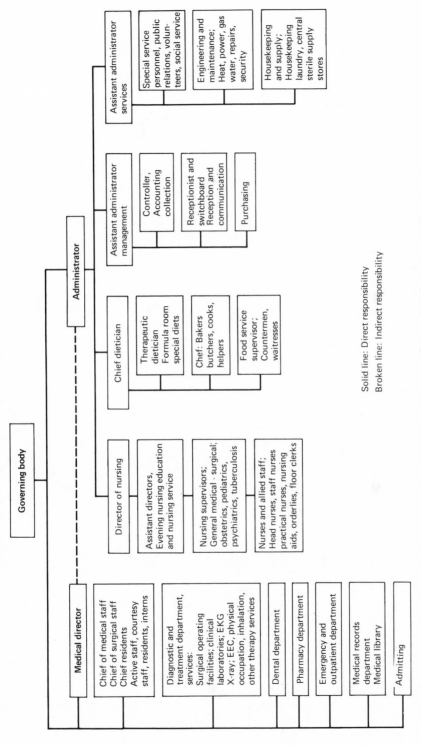

SOURCE: *Technology and Manpower in the Health Service Industry*, Manpower Research Bulletin, No. 14 (Washington, D.C.: U.S. Department of Labor, Manpower Administration, May 1967).

Solid line: Direct responsibility
Broken line: Indirect responsibility

knowledge and technology and the hospital's available resources. The hospital thus qualifies as a formal organization in that it has developed to coordinate scarce resources to achieve stated goals as efficiently as possible (Becker and Gordon, 1966).

To accomplish its tasks and coordinate its various activities, the hospital relies on a prescribed hierarchy of authority (as shown in Figure 8–1), which is operationalized through formal rules, regulations, and administrative procedures. The key to hospital efficiency and overall effectiveness is coordination of the various departments and individuals. They represent a complex and highly specialized division of labor that is both interlocking and interdependent.

Consider what happens when a staff doctor prescribes medication for a patient. The doctor's order for medication is written in the patient's medical records by a floor clerk, and the clerk, or a nurse's aide or orderly, takes the request to the pharmacy. When the medication is sent by the pharmacy, it is most likely administered by a nurse. A record is then forwarded to the accounting office so that the proper charges for the drug can be entered on the patient's bill; another written order might be sent from the pharmacy to purchasing (through the appropriate administrative channels) to reorder the medication and replace it for future use by another patient. So the rather routine activity of one particular member of the hospital staff (in this case a doctor) initiates a chain of events that affects the work of several other hospital employees.

The Hospital: Dual Authority

According to Figure 8–1, the overall supervision of the general hospital comes under the auspices of its governing body. In most nonfederal hospitals, that governing body is a board of trustees. Figure 8–1 also shows that whereas the medical director and the hospital administrator are linked to the governing body by a direct line of responsibility, they are only indirectly responsible to each other. What this type of arrangement indicates is that the authority system of the general hospital operates on a dual level (see Smith, 1955; Coser, 1958; Goss, 1963; Durbin and Springall, 1974). This system is an outgrowth of the organizational conflict in the hospital between bureaucracy and professionalism.

Several sociologists (see Goss, 1963; Heydebrand, 1973) have noted that Max Weber's (Gerth and Mills, 1946) concept of bureaucracy appears incompatible with the norms of professional authority. Weber described bureaucracy as a rational and impersonal division of labor characterized by the principles of *office hierarchy* and levels of graded authority (lower offices are supervised by higher ones), and by *fixed and official areas of jurisdiction* governed by laws or administrative regulations. The essence of the conflict between bureaucracy and the professional consists of the professional's insistence on exercising an autonomous individual judgment within the limits prescribed by the profession itself. As Mary Goss (1963) points out, the work norms of the professional (in this case, the medical doctor) emphasize self-determination for each practitioner, that is, exclude control by those outside the profession. The bureaucrat (here, the hospital administrator), on the other hand, seeks to follow a rationalistic management approach that favors the efficient coordination of the hospital's activities through formal rules and impersonal regulations applicable to all persons in all situations.

Charles Perrow (1963) has traced the evolution of this conflict in his study of one voluntary general hospital he believes to be representative of most other hospitals of this type. Perrow noted that in the late 1800s and early 1900s the voluntary general hospital was dominated by its board of trustees, because this was an era when securing capital funds and gaining community recognition were critical hospital goals. Since community involvement was the pivotal factor, individual members of boards of trustees were usually laypersons selected at large from the community. Legally they were responsible for protecting the community's interests, but they also sought to incorporate hospital services into the general pattern of community life. Perrow believes this approach ultimately derives from seventeenth-century attitudes toward hospitals as state institutions operated on public funds, that is, as community welfare agencies and poorhouses.

In the 1930s trustee domination succumbed to medical domination. Perrow (1963) cites three major reasons for this change: first, the emphasis on free care declined significantly as hospital services became oriented toward patients who could pay; second, the facilities to support a complex system of medical technology were developed and the quality of care provided patients was improved; and third, the hospital sought prestige through medical research in terms defined by physicians. Hence, medical domination went hand in hand with increasing medical knowledge. During this period, however, Perrow also noted the appearance of several abuses which could be attributed to the great personal power of the medical director and his department heads. Especially deficient was the out-patient care afforded to people with low-incomes; also conspicuous was the favoritism shown toward certain physicians in the use of hospital facilities and staff promotions. Perrow observed:

> There was little to prevent such abuses. The doctor is an individual entrepreneur, selling his services for a profit. His income is affected by the facilities he commands in the hospital, his freedom from scrutiny, and by the price he must pay in the form of reciprocal duties such as teaching or committee work. Reliance upon professional ethics, even buttressed by the atmosphere created by teaching and research activities, is not sufficient in itself to guarantee a disinterested, ethical non-economic point of view. Nor will it prevent abuses stemming from the enormous concentration of power in the hands of the chief of staff and department heads who also control the hospital.[2]

What was needed, said Perrow, was a system to limit these powers, to establish objective criteria for promotion, and to provide for more effective representation of patient and organizational interests. That system gradually emerged during the 1940s and 1950s as the role of hospital administrator gained in importance; through a constitutional system, the administration

[2] Charles Perrow, "Goals and Power Structures: A Historical Case Study," in *The Hospital in Modern Society*, E. Freidson, (ed.) (New York: Free Press, 1963), p. 123.

was able to define the medical staff's official power, standardize the hospital's administrative procedures, and establish a level of quality for the hospital's medical services. These early administrators were often physicians who could be expected to further the interests of the medical staff, but in doing so began to curtail their power. As authority became centralized in the administrator's office, there often developed a blockage of communication between the staff and the board of trustees. This period, according to Perrow, was characterized by a complex power struggle which eventually led, in the 1950s, to a system of multiple leadership common among general hospitals today.

Multiple leadership, at least in its hospital version, is actually a system of dual authority, one administrative and the other medical. Perrow notes the high probability of such a system developing in the hospital, because goals are generally multiple (trustees, administration, and medical staff often have diverse interests), the criteria for achieving them broad, and the power of each group to protect its interests is considerable. Since the physician's professional norms can set specific limits on the hospital administrator's authority and vice versa, the result has been to reconcile the physician-professional with the administrator-bureaucrat by establishing a system of dual authority.

The board of trustees still remains the nominal center of authority in the general hospital. It usually meets on a periodic basis, weekly or monthly, to review the hospital's operations and act upon those matters brought to its attention. Generally the trustees themselves are people who are influential in the wider community and who tend to use their hospital board membership as a power base in the community and/or as a symbol of their contribution to the community's welfare (Perrow, 1963; Holloway et al., 1972). But despite their position as the hospital's ultimate source of authority, the trustees have only limited de facto authority over the medical staff, who usually make all health-related decisions (Georgopoulos and Mann, 1972). The board of trustees typically concerns itself with administrative matters and public relations while working closely with the hospital administrator, who acts as their agent in exercising authority and supervising the day-to-day routine of the hospital.[3]

The medical staff maintains control over medical matters. As Basil Georgopoulos and Floyd Mann (1972) point out, physicians are subject to very few nonmedical restrictions because (1) private physicians are not employees of the hospital (they are "guests" with the privilege of practicing medicine there); (2) they have considerable social status and prestige in American society; and (3) they have supreme authority in all matters of patient care and medical professionalism. Nowhere in a hospital's bylaws are there statements denoting the responsibility of medical staff members to the

---

[3] However, as Morton Creditor (1971:135) points out, large urban voluntary hospitals have problems defining the community (usually a polyglot of racial, religious, and socioeconomic groups originating from the hospital neighborhood, the broad metropolitan area, the suburbs, and beyond). Since its trustees cannot be truly representative of this undefinable community, there is considerable difficulty in setting hospital policy in response to community needs. Instead, hospital policy is usually most influenced by whatever is "good for the hospital."

administration; medical staff members are responsible to each other and to their patients, but not to the hospital (see Creditor, 1971). Thus occurs a rather curious situation where the primary function (medical treatment) of an organization (a hospital) is carried out by people (nurses and other health professionals) employed by the organization, but who are supervised by self-employed individuals (private practitioners). The primary "customer" of the hospital is the physician, who does not pay for its services. Eliot Freidson describes this situation by making the following comparison:

> It is as if all professors were self-employed tutors, sending individual pupils to universities where they can themselves administer some special training, but most particularly where they can count on having their pupils trained specially by lesser personnel employed by the university rather than by the professor.[4]

The occupational group in the hospital most affected by its system of dual authority are the nurses and auxiliary nursing workers who perform health care tasks on the hospital's wards. Nurses are responsible to the physician for carrying out the physician's orders, but they also are responsible to the nursing supervisors and the upper echelons of the hospital's administration. Even though the communication and allegiance of ward personnel tend to be channeled along occupational lines within and toward the "administrative channel of command," medical authority can and does cut across these lines (Wesson, 1972). While this system can at times cause interpersonal stress, inconsistency, overlapping of responsibility, and inadequate coordination (Henry, 1954, 1957), it also allows ward personnel to "play off" one authority against the other if one appears unreasonable (Wessen, 1972) and acts to reduce organizational inflexibility and authoritarianism (Georgopoulos and Mann, 1972). In fact, Georgopoulos and Mann further argue that the hospital's system of dual authority is virtually inevitable in light of its high degree of functional specialization and professionalism. Nonetheless, hospital personnel share a common goal of providing quality patient care through competency, devotion to duty, and hard work, qualities Georgopoulos and Mann suggest have had the effect of producing many common norms, values, and complementary expectations. The hospital's normative system, they argue, underlies its administrative structure and:

> . . . enables the hospital to attain a level of coordination and integration that could never be accomplished through administrative edict, through hierarchical directives, or through explicitly formulated and carefully specified organizational plans and impersonal rules, regulations, and procedures.[5]

In a separate study of a psychiatric hospital, Anselm Strauss and his associates (1963) noted a similar process wherein the hospital rules governing the actions of the professionals who worked within its setting were far from

* Eliot Freidson, *Professional Dominance* (Chicago: Aldine, 1970), pp. 174–175.
[5] Basil F. Georgopoulos and Floyd C. Mann, "The Hospital as an Organization," in *Patients, Physicians and Illness*, 2nd ed., E. Jaco (ed.) (New York: Macmillan, 1972), p. 308.

extensive, clearly stated, or clearly binding. These researchers contended that the social order of the hospital was not fixed or automatically maintained, but was the result of continual negotiation between the administration, the medical staff and other hospital employees, and patients. The individuals involved had varying degrees of prestige and power, were at different stages in their careers, and had their own particular goals, reference groups, and occupational ideologies. In addition, hospital rules governing physicians' conduct were not clearly stated, extensive, or binding. The hospital administration tended to take a tolerant position toward institutional rules in the belief that good patient care required a minimum of "hard and fast" regulations and a maximum of "innovation and improvisation." Thus, there was continual negotiation of the medical rules—what they were and whether or not they applied in a particular situation. What held the hospital staff together was the sharing of a common goal to return their patients to the outside world in a better condition than when they entered the hospital. Strauss and associates explained:

> This goal is the symbolic cement that, metaphorically speaking, holds the organization together: the symbol to which all personnel can comfortably, and frequently point—with the assurance that *at least* about this matter everyone can agree! Although this symbol . . . masks a considerable measure of disagreement and discrepant purpose, it represents a generalized mandate under which the hospital can be run—the public flag under which all may work in concert.[6]

Although it might appear from the Strauss study that the hospital was in a state of chaos, held together by only a single, idealistic agreement, actually the process of negotiation was observed to have a definite pattern. In following their own particular approach to their work, the physicians were able to originate relatively stable understandings with the nurses and other hospital employees; this resulted in efficient and standardized forms of behavior not dependent on special instructions for all contingencies. Consequently, the process of negotiation not only created new meanings, but also reinforced the significance of the more formalized rules through a process of periodic appraisal.

In summary, the hospital's organization consists of a varied group of professionals and allied health workers with different functions, training, and occupational values. To make this social organization function effectively, it has been necessary to construct a decentralized system of authority organized around a generally acceptable objective of service to the patient. While the administrator directs and supervises hospital policy, the medical staff retains control over medical decisions.

However, the reader should realize that the dual system of authority that currently exists in the hospital may be in jeopardy as a result of the

---

[6] Anselm Strauss, Leonard Schatzman, Danuta Ehrlich, Rue Bucher, and Melvin Sabshin, "The Hospital and its Negotiated Order," in *The Hospital in Modern Society*, E. Freidson (ed.) (New York: Free Press, 1963), p. 154.

precedent-setting Darling case in Illinois.[7] The Darling case involved a suit for damages sought by the plaintiff for alleged medical and hospital negligence. The patient, Dorrence Darling, broke his leg while playing football and was taken to the emergency room of Charleston Community Hospital. A general practitioner put the leg in the cast. The leg became discolored, pulseless, and a foul odor developed. The nursing staff complained to the administrator and the physician in charge. The cast was ventilated but the odor continued. Ultimately the leg was amputated. The physician settled out of court. The nurses were not held negligent because they followed the accepted guidelines and procedure. The hospital bylaws provided for the consultation of another physician upon the request of the administrator. The administrators maintained that the hospital had provided the "brick" and "mortar" (the facilities) in which health care took place and that they had acted as all other hospital administrators would have done. The court found the administrators negligent in their relationship to the patient by not requiring a consultation as provided in the hospital bylaws. It held that hospitals do much more than just furnish treatment facilities; they also assume certain responsibilities for the care of the patient.

Therefore, as Richard Durbin and W. Herbert Springall (1974) have pointed out, if the hospital is going to be held liable for professional medical decisions, the administration will probably attempt to gain greater control over the practice of medicine within its facilities. Durbin and Springall predict that liability for patient care will result in the hospital's imposing more of its rules and regulations on the physicians, raising the standards of qualification required for staff privileges, and generally reducing the amount of professional discretion and autonomy physicians have traditionally been allowed to exercise. Moreover, research by Ann Barry Flood and W. Richard Scott (1978) found that the greater the power of the hospital administration, the greater the quality of surgical care rendered to patients. "The strongest and most consistent factor related to quality of care," state Flood and Scott (1978:251), "was the power of the hospital administrators to influence decisions within their own domain." Thus, control by hospital administrators may not only affect professional discretion, but also professional effectiveness as the practitioners within the hospital are provided with better coordination of services and staff support.

THE HOSPITAL–PATIENT ROLE

While hospital services are oriented toward a supportive notion of patient welfare, hospital rules and regulations are generally designed for the benefit of hospital personnel so that the work of treating large numbers of patients can be more efficient and easier to perform (Freidson, 1970a; Lorber, 1975; Coe, 1978). Consequently, the sick and the injured are organized into various patient categories (maternity–obstetrics, neurology, orthopedics,

---

[7] See *Darling v. Charleston Community Hospital*, 33 Ill. 2d 326, 211 N.E. 2d 253 (1965), 50 Ill. App. 2d 253, cert. denied, 383 U.S. 946 (1966).

urology, pediatrics, psychiatry) that reflect the medical staff's definition of their disorder, and are then usually subject to standardized, staff-approved medical treatment and administrative procedures.

While it can be argued that standardizing patient care results in increased organizational efficiency—and ultimately serves the best interest of the patient—a prominent theme of the hospitalization experience noted by medical sociologists has been that of depersonalization. Erving Goffman (1961), for example, describes the status of mental hospital patients as akin to being a "nonperson," while Coe (1978) believes that patients in general tend to be devalued by hospital personnel even before they are admitted to the hospital because they are old, sick, or defective in some way. In other words, hospital patients are more than just dependent upon other people, but they are also less than "ideal." H. Jack Geiger, an M.D., illustrates the feelings of depersonalization in hospital care by commenting on his own experience as a patient:

> I had to be hospitalized, suddenly and urgently, *on my own ward.* In the space of only an hour or two, I went from apparent health and well-being to pain, disability, and fear, and from staff to inmate in a total institution. At one moment I was a physician: elite, technically skilled, vested with authority, wielding power over others, affectively neutral. The next moment I was a patient: dependent, anxious, sanctioned in illness only if I was cooperative. A protected dependency and the promise of effective technical help were mine— if I accepted a considerable degree of psychological and social servitude.[8]

Geiger was subsequently placed in the ward's only private room, which he believed was more for the benefit of the staff than for himself. He felt that had he been placed among the other patients, lending objective credence to physician "mortality," the patients might have used the situation to reduce status and role barriers between themselves and the staff. Furthermore, Geiger learned what he now believes is the major reason why physicians make such "notoriously terrible patients." It was not because their technical knowledge caused them to be more fearful of the consequences of their disorder or more critical of the way it was treated. Instead it was the loss of their professional role and authority in the medical setting, which Geiger surmises is an integral part of their self-concept.

Personnel in hospitals do not necessarily have the express goal of making their patients feel depersonalized, but the organization of the hospital's work does favor rules and regulations that reduce patient autonomy and encourage patient receptivity of the hospital routine. Another important factor is the work situation itself. Jeanne Quint Benoliel (1975:180) has pointed out that nurses who had difficulty tolerating the work in intensive or coronary care hospital units felt oppressed by "repetitive exposure to death and dying, daily contact with mutilated and unsightly patients, formidable and demanding work loads, limited work space, intricate machinery, and

---

[8] H. Jack Geiger, "The Causes of Dehumanization in Health Care and Prospects for Humanization," in J. Howard and A. Strauss (eds.), *Humanizing Health Care* (New York: Wiley-Interscience, 1975), p. 13.

communication problems involving physicians, staff, and families." The intensive care ward is thus an example of a work situation that generates pressures of a dehumanizing nature as a result of staff attempts to cope with inherently intense psychological stress. Furthermore, Benoliel adds that on the surgical wards patients are so concerned about themselves that if the nurses do take a personal interest in them, they demand increasing amounts of the nurses' time and energy.

Yet it should be noted that the process of depersonalization is not just a result of the manner in which large numbers of patients are managed or the work conditions, but it is also related to the patient's subjective experience of feeling sick. Howard Leventhal (1975) has explained that most reports of depersonalization commonly cite the experience of one's self as a physical object or thing. A second common experience is the feeling that one's own psychological self is isolated from other psychological selves (other people). Furthermore, Leventhal suggests that bodily symptoms such as pain can create a sense of separation within the individual of the physical self from the conscious psychological self. This inner alienation, in addition to the feeling of isolation from others, compounded by the doubt, uncertainty, and confusion that often accompany feelings of illness, can create for patients a sense of inadequacy and inability to control their lives. Leventhal's argument is that this attitude of incompetency is further intensified by the patient's having to assume an institutional role like the sick role, in which he or she is officially dependent and excluded from decision making (see also Bloom, 1963). The process of depersonalization is undoubtedly enhanced by the need of the physician or nurse to have access to the patient's body. However legitimate this may be, Coe (1978) points out that the exposure and giving over of one's body to strangers can be a degrading and humiliating experience, even though it is intended to be therapeutic.

Stripping, Control of Resources, and Restriction of Mobility

Coe (1978) states that patients are alienated from their usual lives and reduced to a largely impersonal status in the hospital through three basic mechanisms of hospital processing: (1) stripping, (2) control of resources, and (3) restriction of mobility. Coe explains that when patients present themselves for treatment in a hospital, they bring with them a particular social identity, what Goffman refers to as a "face" (see Chapter Three); this represents their attitudes, beliefs, values, concept of self, and social status, all of which form the basis for their manner of presenting themselves to the world. *Stripping* occurs when the hospital systematically divests the person of these past representations of self. The patient's clothes are taken away and replaced with a set of pajamas; regardless of whether the pajamas are the property of the hospital or the patient, the simple fact of wearing pajamas serves as a uniform that identifies that person as sick and restricts movement to those areas of the hospital in which pajamas (patient dress) are authorized. Personal belongings of value are taken away and locked up for safekeeping by the staff. Visiting regulations control not only when patients are allowed to have visitors, but also who is allowed to visit (children under age fourteen are typically excluded). In addition, the staff supervises the patient's diet, decides when the patient should be asleep or awake, and in essence controls the general conduct of the patient's social life in the hospital. The hospital routine for one patient is very similar to the routine of others having the same or similar health problems.

Another important feature of hospitalization is the *control of resources* by the staff. Coe includes under the control of resources not only physical items, like bedclothes and toilet paper, but also the control of information about the patient's medical condition. For example, patients are normally not aware of their prognosis or the results of laboratory tests and x-rays unless the physician decides to inform them. On occasion doctors and nurses will even deliberately limit communication with patients if it interferes with their work or might lead to patients' discovering their mistakes and shortcomings (Roth, 1963; Brown, 1966; Lorber, 1975). Several studies indicate that a major complaint of patients is the difficulty they have in obtaining information about themselves from their doctors (Shiloh, 1965; Duff and Hollingshead, 1968; Davis, 1972; Coe, 1978), including patients who were dying (Glaser and Strauss, 1965; McIntosh, 1974; see also Chapter Twelve).

Fred Davis (1972) found, in a study of the interaction between the parents of children who were victims of paralytic poliomyelitis and their physicians, that four communication modes were possible: (1) communication, where the doctor could make a reasonable prognosis and communicated it to the parents; (2) dissimulation, where the doctor could not make a reasonable prognosis, but communicated one to the parents anyway; (3) admission of uncertainty, where the doctor could not make a reasonable prognosis and admitted this to the parents; or (4) evasion, where the doctor could make a reasonable prognosis, but chose not to communicate it. The most common form of communication was evasion; the doctors tended to answer the questions of the parents in terms that were either evasive or unintelligibly technical. One staff member rationalized that it was better for the parents to find out for themselves in a "natural sort of way." The "natural way," Davis (1972:97) observed, was often a painfully slow and prolonged reduction of the parents' expectations about a complete recovery for their children. The reason the physicians in the Davis study did not explicitly inform the parents that their child was likely to be crippled or significantly impaired was apparently fear of being confronted with an "unmanageable" emotional reaction on the part of the parents. Other physicians rationalized that the parents would not be able to understand the prognosis even if they were informed. Davis (1972:98) concluded that in being evasive, equivocating, and abruptly ending an interview with the parents, the doctor was able to avoid a possible "scene," in having to confront them. Such tasks were generally viewed by hospital personnel as unpleasant and time consuming.

Inability to understand what they are told and negative effects of the threatening information are the two most common reasons given by medical professionals for not communicating fully with their patients (see Howard and Strauss, 1975:238–239). However, even if patients are able to comprehend the medical ramifications of their disorder, should they always be told the full story? As Robert Cooke has pointed out, physicians need to know what the knowledge will do to the patient and the patient's family:

> I'm worried about the problem of the patient's knowing when he or she can't do anything about it, as is true for Huntington's Chorea. You may have a child who at 12 has serious deterioration of the central nervous system. . . . We can now make the diagnosis on this newborn sib, age one week; and you say to the family: "I can tell you with 100 percent certainty this child is going to be just like your older child and be deteriorating and dead in 5, 6, 7, 9, 10 years." [9]

The situation Cooke describes could cause considerable anguish, worry, frustration, and anxiety within a family. Most likely the hopelessness of this type of health disorder would compound the emotional trauma resulting from knowledge of the condition. Cooke implies, then, that perhaps in some circumstances it is better not to make a full disclosure and to spare a family's feelings for as long as is realistically possible. Thus, the dilemma remains unresolved. In general, however, all patients are entitled to full knowledge about their medical condition, and it is incumbent upon the doctor to help them cope with this information. Coe indicates that the denial of this information contributes to a sense of uncertainty among patients and lessens their perceived ability to control their own lives.

The third aspect of depersonalization outlined by Coe is the *restriction of mobility*. In most hospitals patients are not allowed to leave their wards without the permission of the head nurse, who is usually required to know the location of all patients at all times; when patients do leave the ward to travel to another area of the hospital, they are generally accompanied by a nurse, nurse's aide, or orderly. When patients are admitted to the hospital and also when discharged, they are taken in a wheelchair between the ward and the hospital entrance regardless of their ability to walk because the hospital is "responsible" for them whenever they are inside its walls. The result is that even the ability of patients to move about is supervised and controlled.

Conforming Attitudes

Some patients may be so seriously ill that feelings of depersonalization do not enter the picture. All they desire is to get well and they are very happy to do or experience whatever is necessary to accomplish that goal. That is, they are quite willing to conform to the situation.

Yet this assumption may not be entirely correct. In a recent study of hospital patients in New York City, Judith Lorber (1975) found that conforming attitudes were common among cancer patients but not among patients hospitalized for very serious surgery. Lorber suggests that the cancer patients may have been scared by the ambiguities of the information they received. One woman, for example, refused to believe her doctor was

[9] As quoted in Jan Howard and Anselm Strauss (eds.), *Humanizing Health Care* (New York: Wiley-Interscience, 1975), p. 239.

telling her the truth after she had a tumor removed and it was found to be benign. Serious surgery patients, on the other hand, were much better informed about their illnesses, yet they behaved more "deviantly" (were troublesome, uncooperative, and complaining) than the cancer patients. Their somewhat lengthy stays in the hospital had not generally resulted in their complete acceptance of the staff's model of the "good" (obedient) patient. Thus, seriousness of a patient's illness was not a good predictor of whether or not a patient would conform to hospital routine.

The best attitude predictors, according to Lorber, were age and education: the younger and better educated the patient, the less likely was the patient to express highly conforming attitudes. Conversely, the older and more poorly educated patients were the least likely to express deviant attitudes. Yet among college-educated patients, Lorber found those patients over sixty years of age to be moderately conforming, while those under sixty tended to adopt "deviant" attitudes. This latter finding is consistent with other studies (Coser, 1956; Cartwright, 1964), which suggest that younger patients tend to be more aggressive about seeking information in the hospital and less conforming, while older patients tend to be more submissive to hospital rules.

Lorber (1975:220) also examined the attitudes of the doctors and nurses toward the patients, and her analysis of staff evaluations suggested the important finding that "ease of management was the basic criterion for a label of good patient, and that patients who took time and attention felt to be unwarranted by their illness tended to be labeled problem patients." "In short," Lorber (1975:220) says, "the less of a doctor's time the patient took, the better he or she was viewed." Patients who had a tendency to complain or be uncooperative or overemotional were generally considered to be a problem only by the particular staff member who had cause to interact with them. The key variable, therefore, in how the doctors and nurses defined the patients was the amount of time from the staff that the patient demanded. Interestingly enough, Lorber reported that some staff members labeled certain patients as "good" if they couldn't remember them too well.

A question remains as to what actions physicians and nurses take to deal with troublesome hospital patients. Some studies (Daniels, 1960; Glaser and Strauss, 1965) suggest that staff members tend to avoid patients who are not liked or who are uncooperative; sometimes particularly bothersome patients will be reprimanded or scolded. Lorber found that the usual method of handling difficult patients in a New York City hospital was to prescribe tranquilizers or sedatives. If drugs did not accomplish the desired cooperation, then disruptive patients might on occasion be sent home or transferred to a convalescent center with trained psychiatric nurses. Lorber's general impression was that the hospital staff tended to treat the short-term, paying patients in a permissive fashion and put up with the problems they caused. It remains to be seen if the staff would have been as tolerant had the patients been hospitalized on a long-term, charity basis.

The Sick Role for Hospital Patients

To Parsons' (1951) concept of the sick role, which emphasizes patient cooperation and striving to get well (see Chapter Five), we may now add that of the hospitalized sick role, which apparently includes an obligation to accept hospital routine without protest (Tagliacozzo and Mauksch, 1972). Lorber (1975:214) notes the similarities between Parsons' sick role and the role of the hospital patient. Both are universalistic, affectively neutral, functionally specific, and collectivity oriented. However, a major difference between them, Lorber observes, is that the idea of voluntary cooperation, one-to-one intimacy, and conditional permissiveness (being temporarily excused from normal social activities on the condition of seeking medical advice and care) applies primarily to the relationship between an out-patient and a private physician. In-patient care subjects the hospital patient to a role additionally characterized by submission to authority, enforced cooperation, and depersonalized status.

Coe (1978) has suggested that acquiescence is the most common form of patient adjustment to hospital routine and the most successful for short-stay patients in terms of the quality of their interaction with the hospital staff. Basically, all the attitudes of the hospitalized sick role are results of the necessity for a well-established work routine for hospital staff. As Rose Laub Coser (1956) has pointed out, in meeting the medical needs of patients the hospital demands that its patients give up substantial rationality about the direction and nature of their personal activities in favor of the functional rationality of organizational life.

THE RISING COST OF HOSPITALIZATION

Any discussion of American hospitals would be incomplete without considering the financial cost of hospitalization, which has risen more sharply in recent years than any other aspect of medical care. For purposes of comparison, John Knowles (1973) indicates that in 1925 the cost of one day's stay as a patient at the Massachusetts General Hospital in Boston was $3.00, and the bill was paid entirely by the patient. By 1977, however, the average one-day cost of hospitalization had risen to nearly $225, with most of the expense paid by a third party such as a private health insurance company— Blue Cross, Blue Shield, or some other hospital-medical plan—or Medicare, Medicaid, or a state welfare agency. Not only did costs increase significantly, but the manner of payment has also changed, as about 90 percent of all expenses for hospital services are now paid by third-party sources. In some cases, third-party coverage has led to increased hospital admission rates, since health needs which are met in the physician's office are often not covered by insurance. Hospitalization can therefore reduce the patient's direct cost of health care.

But this does not mean that patients escape paying hospital bills. Government expenditures are paid out of tax revenues, while private health insurance costs must also be covered and private companies are set up to make a profit. In 1969, health insurance companies paid $14 billion in benefit payments in return for $17 billion they received in insurance premiums from policy holders. In 1974, health insurance companies paid nearly $28 billion out of approximately $34 billion in premiums.

About sixty-one cents of every insurance claim dollar goes for hospital bills, thirty-one cents for physicians' services, three cents for dentists, three cents for drugs and drug sundries, and the remaining two cents for private-duty nursing, eye care, nursing home care, visiting nurse service, and other types of care.

Although most private health insurance payments are for hospital expenses, insurance benefits are not the largest source of hospital income. In 1976, public funds, primarily Medicare and Medicaid monies, accounted for 55 percent of all hospital care expenditures. Private insurance companies paid for an additional 36 percent, leaving the individual consumer to be responsible for direct payments covering 8 percent of hospital costs. Overall health expenditures in the United States in 1978 amounted to $192.4 billion, of which $76.6 billion was spent on hospital care. Thus, about 40 percent of all the money spent on health in the United States is spent on hospital services.

What does the hospital do with its income? Knowles explains that hospital expenses are categorized as either routine or ancillary costs. Routine costs are those expenses of providing room and board, including the provision of several different diets of three meals a day served in bed; the cost of nonmedical supplies and equipment; the salaries of all members of the hospital's nonmedical staff; and the salaries of medical technicians, nurses, auxiliary nursing workers, interns, and residents who are available to patients on a twenty-four-hour basis, seven days a week. Ancillary expenses include the cost of laboratories, the pharmacy, operating rooms, x-ray rooms, cast rooms, and other specialized hospital facilities, plus the cost of all medical supplies. Even though patients do not get to see or even use all of a hospital's facilities, the cost of maintaining and operating these facilities for those patients who do use them continues regardless.

The most expensive hospitals in the United States are located in New England and on the Pacific Coast, while the least expensive are found in the South and in some of the Rocky Mountain states. Supposedly, regional differences in the cost of hospitalization are related to regional differences in the overall cost of living. Other factors (see Berry, 1974) that have been found to be important in determining hospital costs are the ratio of personnel to total expenses (the cost of labor is higher in high-cost hospitals) and the patient occupancy rate (low-cost hospitals tend to have relatively high occupancy rates). Even the type of hospital administrator may be a significant factor, as administrators with medical qualifications (M.D.s) may be able to negotiate to the administration's advantage in controlling the staff's demands for more and/or improved equipment and facilities.

It has also been found that one of the most significant factors affecting costs is the structure of the decision-making process. Edward Morse and his associates (1974) argue that decentralization of decision making tends to facilitate a hospital's adoption of modern medical technology. But while the application of new technology usually reduces the average length of stay and may increase the average occupancy rate, it has little direct impact upon the hospital's total expenses. Instead, Morse suggests that the more centralized the hospital's decision-making structure, the more efficient it will be in controlling expenses by selecting those organizational practices that facilitate goal achievement at the lowest cost. Inefficient hospital management has, needless to say, been a major factor in the rise in hospital costs.

Two other factors contributing to higher hospital expenses have been inflation and increased costs of hospital labor. Between 1967 and 1978, the overall cost of medical care in the United States rose by 119.4 percent, which was the highest increase of any category in the Consumer Price Index— higher than even the rise in the cost of food (106.2 percent), housing (102.6 percent), and transportation (85.8 percent). The increase in the cost of all consumer items combined was 95.3 percent. Moreover, inflation has not only affected the cost of medical equipment, supplies, and new construction, but has also served to intensify the demands of hospital employees for higher salaries to meet the rise in the cost of living. Labor constitutes about 70 percent of a hospital's total expenses, and increased labor costs are therefore a highly significant component of rising hospital expenses (Andersen and May, 1972).

On a national average, it cost about $198 for one day's stay in a hospital in 1977. Since a patient remains in a hospital for an average of 7.6 days, the average total cost of being hospitalized in the United States is approximately $1500 (Health Insurance Institute, 1979). This amount represents almost a 70 percent increase over 1973, when the average hospital stay was 7.8 days, but the average cost was $890. In 1968 a patient remained in the hospital for an average of 8.4 days with the cost being about $520. Thus, while the average length of stay in the hospital has declined somewhat since 1968, the cost of that stay has tripled.

What can be done about controlling increases in hospital costs? Several measures might prove effective. For one thing, inflation is not the only cause. Knowles (1973) states that the decisive factor in controlling hospital costs is the full and appropriate utilization of hospital beds. Also important are improved management techniques, maximum use of computers, automatic machines, industrial engineers, and reduced turnover rates for hospital employees. Knowles states, for instance, that it costs the hospital between $1000 to $2000 to break in a new nurse, yet turnover rates for nurses in the United States today are as high as 70 percent per year. Knowles also urges the adoption of regional planning in order to utilize hospital facilities to their fullest and to avoid overduplication. In addition, he points out that health insurance programs are needed to promote low-cost services, health education, and programs of preventive medicine; especially helpful would be the further development of more health maintenance organizations, such as the Kaiser-Permanente system on the Pacific Coast.

One new measure undertaken to control hospital costs is the National Health Planning and Resources Development Act of 1974 (Public Law 93–641. This act divides the United States into 202 Health Services Areas, each of which contains a Health Systems Agency (HSA). The HSAs are directed by a governing body of ten to twenty members with 50 to 60 percent of the members being health care consumers. The remaining members are composed of health care providers and at least some locally elected government officials, as stipulated in the act.

The Health System Agencies are intended initially to survey hospital systems in their respective areas and to originate health care plans to eliminate the costly duplication of hospital services. The act also contains provisions to eventually give the HSA widespread authority over all the hospitals in its area, both public and private. The primary objective of this new legislation is to prevent the kind of proliferation of medical care facilities that occurred in a number of metropolitan areas fifteen or twenty years ago. At that time, many hospitals were able to procure funds locally from various private and municipal sources, money that could be used to buy expensive technology or to expand facilities. Every hospital had to have a cobalt machine or a large modern maternity ward, or whatever. Thus a goal for planning agencies like HSAs is to bring about a consensus of which hospitals in large communities should be responsible for what. The idea is not to police the provision of hospital services but to coordinate all available services through efficient planning, thereby reducing the cost of having expensive specialized facilities at all hospitals. HSAs can tell hospitals whether to expand or close down services, how much to charge, and possibly even to shut down altogether.

There is currently some question as to whether HSAs will be responsive to local needs and issues, since they report directly to the U.S. Department of Health and Human Services, and what their authority will be in relation to county governments that currently provide much of an area's hospital services. It remains to be seen exactly whether the HSAs will be effective in controlling hospital costs; the concept does, however, reflect the public's demand that something be done to contain the rising costs of health services in the United States. As this book goes to press, the Reagan Administration's budget proposals eliminate federal funding for HSAs by 1984. Yet an alternative proposal in Congress provides support for HSAs at current funding levels. Should the program not survive, it is doubtful that the concept will disappear. Hospitals will likely continue their own planning efforts, perhaps in coordination with other area hospitals, in order to avoid unnecessary duplication of services and remain effective in a competitive market.

Yet, as Herman Somers (1970) pointed out, it would be illusory to believe that health care costs can be prevented from rising. So long as the prices of goods and services in general continue to increase, the cost of health care and hospitalization may be expected to rise accordingly. The principal issue is whether or not increases can be contained in such a way that hospital care is kept within a reasonable relationship to the rest of the economy and that the highest quality of care can be provided for all Americans for the amount of money spent for that care. More satisfactory means of financing health services must be found, and this topic will be considered in the next chapter.

SUMMARY

This chapter has reviewed the hospital's evolving role as a community institution intended to serve the needs of sick and injured people as a form of social responsibility. Passing through stages of being a center for religious practice, a poorhouse, and a deathhouse, the hospital has finally come to be a center for medical technology designed to handle the health problems of all members of society, not just the lower classes.

Today in the United States hospitals can be classified in terms of their type of ownership (voluntary or nonprofit, proprietary or profit-making, or government owned) and by their type of service (general medical–surgical or specialty). The largest single type of hospital in the United States is voluntary and general medical–surgical. These hospitals are nominally supervised by a governing body, such as a board of trustees, but actually exhibit a dual system of authority: administrative and medical. Although hospitals are supposedly oriented toward the welfare of the patient, a significant body of literature in medical sociology is concerned with the fact that treating large numbers of people has resulted in organizational procedures that tend to depersonalize the individual patient. The final section of the chapter dealt with the rising cost of hospitalization, which has become a major social issue.

chapter 9

HEALTH CARE DELIVERY
AND SOCIAL POLICY

The central issues in the public debate about health care delivery in the United States are those of inflated costs and maldistribution of services. No other single issue in medicine has attracted more public attention in recent years than the rising cost of health care and the diminished ability of certain segments of American society to obtain health services adequate for their needs. The paradoxical nature of this situation, as Rodney Coe (1978) points out, is that the United States—one of the wealthiest countries in the world—has developed a technology to provide high quality health care and has the resources to implement it on a large scale; yet a substantial portion of the population does without even minimally adequate health care. The Americans most affected by the sharply escalating costs of medical services are the white rural and urban poor, ghetto blacks, the lower-middle class above the Medicaid income maximum, and middle-class families unable to contend with rising costs.

An illustration of the increase and the magnitude of the cost of health care in American society can be found in an examination of the U.S. Consumer Price Index. As in most other nations of the world, the cost of goods and services has been steadily rising. Table 9–1, however, shows that between 1935 and 1978 the cost of medical care increased *faster* than any other major category of personal expense. Between 1967 and 1978 alone, medical costs rose by 119.4 percent, higher than any other major category of personal expense.[1]

[1] Health expenditures for Americans increased an average of 12 percent annually between 1970 and 1978. In 1970, Americans spent a total of $69.2 billion on health needs, as compared to fiscal year 1978 health expenditures of $192.4 billion. Also, in 1970 an average of $334 per person in the U.S. was spent on health; by 1978 this figure had risen to $863. Preliminary figures available for 1979 show that the nation's health bill for that year was $212.2 billion (12.5 percent over 1978). This represents nine percent of the Gross National Product. The average cost per person in 1979 was $920.

TABLE 9-1.   Consumer Price Index in the United States

Year	All Items	Food	Apparel	Housing	Transpor- tation	Medical Care
11935	41.1	36.5	40.8	49.3	42.6	36.1
1940	42.0	35.2	42.8	52.4	42.7	36.8
1945	53.9	50.7	61.5	59.1	47.8	42.1
1950	72.1	74.5	79.0	72.8	68.2	53.7
1955	80.2	81.6	84.1	82.3	77.4	64.8
1960	88.7	88.0	89.6	90.2	89.6	79.1
1965	94.5	94.4	93.7	94.9	95.9	89.5
1966	97.2	99.1	96.1	97.2	97.2	93.4
1967*	100.0	100.0	100.0	100.0	100.0	100.0
1968	104.2	103.6	105.4	104.2	103.2	106.1
1969	109.8	108.9	111.5	110.8	107.2	113.4
1970	116.3	114.9	116.1	118.9	112.7	120.6
1971	121.3	118.4	119.8	124.3	118.6	128.4
1972	125.3	123.5	122.3	129.2	119.9	132.5
1973	133.1	141.4	126.8	135.0	123.8	137.7
1974	147.7	161.7	136.2	150.6	137.7	150.5
1975	161.2	175.4	142.3	166.8	150.6	168.6
1976	170.5	180.8	147.6	177.2	165.6	184.7
1977	181.5	192.2	154.2	189.6	177.2	202.4
1978	196.3	206.2	159.5	202.6	185.8	219.4
Percent of Change 1967–1978	96.3	106.2	59.5	102.6	85.8	119.4

* 1967 = 100.0
SOURCE: U.S. Department of Labor, as quoted in *Source Book of Health Insurance Data, 1978–1979* (New York: Health Insurance Institute, 1980).

Within the general category of medical care, Table 9–2 shows the increase in the costs of various subcategories of items. The greatest single increase has been in semiprivate hospital room rates, which includes only the basic charge for room and board; this category is followed by increases in physicians' fees. Since 1967, the cost of a semiprivate hospital room has tripled and physicians' fees have more than doubled.

Besides the increased cost of health care, the maldistribution of existing health services is also a significant problem in American society. It is a problem felt not just by the poor, but also by individuals and families who have enough income or health insurance to pay for the services they desire. For this group of people the problem is to get the kind of care they need when they need it (Fuchs, 1974). What prevents them from accomplishing this has to do with (1) the geographical dispersion of physicians and (2) the decline in number of primary care practitioners.

A major factor in obtaining adequate medical care for some people is the numerical shortage of physicians serving patients in rural areas and urban slums. Physicians generally prefer to practice medicine in urbanized settings where they are close to cultural, educational, and recreational facilities. Another advantage of an urban practice is its proximity to extensive technological resources in the form of well-equipped hospitals, clinics, and

TABLE 9–2.   Consumer Price Indices for Medical Care Items in the United States

Year	All Medical Care Items	Physi- cians' Fees	Dentists' Fees	Opto- metric Examina- tion and Eye- glasses	Semi- private Hospital Room Rates	Prescriptions and Drugs
1947	48.1	51.4	56.9	67.7	23.1	81.1
1950	53.7	55.2	63.9	73.5	30.3	88.5
1955	64.8	65.4	73.0	77.0	42.3	94.7
1960	79.1	77.0	82.1	85.1	57.3	104.5
1965	89.5	88.3	92.2	92.8	75.9	100.2
1966	93.4	93.4	95.2	95.3	83.5	100.5
1967*	100.0	100.0	100.0	100.0	100.0	100.0
1968	106.1	105.6	105.5	103.2	113.6	100.2
1969	113.4	112.9	112.9	107.6	128.8	101.3
1970	120.6	121.4	119.4	113.5	145.4	103.6
1971	128.4	129.8	127.0	120.3	163.1	105.4
1972	132.5	133.8	132.3.	124.9	173.9	105.6
1973	137.7	138.2	136.4	129.5	182.1	105.9
1974	150.5	150.9	146.8	138.6	201.5	109.6
1975	168.6	169.4	161.9	149.6	236.1	118.8
1976	184.7	188.5	172.2	158.9	268.6	126.0
1977	202.4	206.0	185.1	168.2	299.5	134.1
1978	219.4	223.3	199.3	—	331.6	—
Percent of Change						
1967–1978	119.4	123.3	99.3	68.2	231.6	34.1

* 1967 = 100.0
SOURCE: U.S. Department of Labor, as quoted in *Source Book of Health Insurance Data, 1978–1979* (New York: Health Insurance Institute, 1980).

laboratories staffed by well-trained personnel. Also important are the relationships with colleagues, which tend to enhance professional life, and these
relationships are more readily available in urban areas where there are
greater opportunities for professional recognition. And finally, it should be
recognized that the more financially rewarding medical practices are those
in large cities.

The maldistribution of physicians in the United States can be illustrated by comparing differences between predominantly urban and rural
states. In 1979, 205 doctors were involved in patient care for every 100,000
people in New York State, while South Dakota had eighty-nine doctors per
100,000 people. . Differences within states are even larger. One out of every
twenty counties in the United States does not have a single doctor and more
than half of all counties do not have a pediatrician, according to 1978 U.S.
Bureau of the Census data. Even though small communities often advertise
and try actively to recruit physicians, many doctors remain attracted to
urban life.

The physician shortage is not limited to rural areas, however; it also
extends into certain urban locales. Physicians in private practice are seldom
found in neighborhoods characterized by large numbers of poor and non-

white residents. Areas whose residents have relatively low levels of education and income tend to have proportionately fewer medical doctors in private practice. Consequently, shortages of physicians may exist in parts of New York City as well as in rural Texas and South Dakota.

But there are a few signs that the distribution of physicians is beginning to improve. Part of this development is due to market conditions. Some areas have an oversupply of doctors, which encourages others to look elsewhere for establishing their practice. Also, rural areas with only one physician for every 3,500 or more people and poverty areas with only one doctor per 3,000 or more are eligible to apply for doctors under the National Health Service Corps. The National Health Service Corps (NHSC) is a federally funded program designed to recruit and help organize the practices of health providers such as physicians, osteopaths, dentists, and physician's assistants for isolated and low-income areas. Physicians who volunteer for NHSC service are paid financial incentives for joining and medical students are given scholarships in return for participation in the program after graduation. For every year of support, the medical student is required to serve a year in the Corps. In addition, other programs exist, like the Rural Practice Project funded by the Robert Wood Johnson Foundation and administered by the School of Medicine at the University of North Carolina. This project, which has pilot programs in several states, matches a physician in a rural area with a health care administrator to provide improved services to medically deprived people.

Another factor that presents an intriguing situation for medical economists is the projection that the United States will have more physicians than it needs by 1990. The Graduate Medical Education National Advisory Committee predicted in 1980 that in 1990 there will be 536,000 physicians, a surplus of 70,000. By 2000, the number of physicians is likely to increase to 634,000, or 145,000 more than are needed if present trends continue. The ratio of physicians to the general population, which was 171 per 100,000 in 1978, will grow to 220 per 100,000 in 1990 and 247 per 100,000 in 2000. Some economists suggest that the impact of larger numbers of physicians will be increased competition, possibly leading to reduced fees, more doctors in inner-city and rural areas, and more general practitioners as specialties become crowded. Yet others argue that more doctors will mean more medical spending—possibly without a noticeable improvement in the overall health of the population. An attempt may be made to offset the projected doctor surplus by limiting medical school enrollments and restricting the number of foreign medical school graduates who are allowed to practice medicine. For the present, however, there is a shortage of doctors in general and in rural and urban poverty areas in particular.

Shortages in the number of physicians in certain areas are not the only factor contributing to physician maldistribution. The overspecialization of medical doctors has further reduced the access of patients to primary care or general practitioners. The number of general practitioners has declined substantially from 112,000 in 1950 to under 55,000 in 1977. In 1979, there was one physician for every 580 Americans, but there is only one general practitioner for about every 5,000 people. A major reason for the trend in specialization has to do with the complexities of modern medicine. At Cornell

Medical School, Patricia Kendall and Hanan Selvin (1957) noted that as the medical students progressed through medical school, more and more of them began to express a preference for specialized training. Kendall and Selvin found that the reason for the tendency to specialize was the students' desire to restrict themselves to a particular area of knowledge with which they could be highly skillful, rather than trying to deal with an insurmountable body of knowledge. In addition, a specialized and more manageable area of medicine may be less demanding of personal time, has more prestige, and provides a greater income (Fuchs, 1974; Magraw, 1975).

There are twenty-two specialty boards affiliated with the American Medical Association that certify physicians to practice in some fifty-two medical specialties such as internal medicine, pediatrics, anesthesiology, obstetrics, gynecology, dermatology, psychiatry, general surgery, orthopedic surgery, urology, ophthalmology, and neurology. While medical specialization has produced positive benefits by allowing physicians to concentrate their efforts upon treating certain parts of the body, it has produced negative side effects in that it has become increasingly difficult to find a physician to take on continuing responsibility for the "whole" patient. Victor Fuchs describes the situation as follows:

> What the typical patient wants is easy, quick, reliable access to a source of care seven days a week, twenty-four hours a day. Morever he wants this source of care to know him, have all his records, care about him, take continuing responsibility for him, and guide him through the labyrinth of whatever specialty care may be available. Such access is indeed rare. Instead, the medical care industry offers him a multitude of highly trained specialists, each of whom can provide better care then was previously available—but only within his specialty and only during office hours.[2]

It is clear that the continuing decline in the number and availability of primary care practitioners inhibits the access of patients to the health care delivery system in the United States (Rogers, 1973). Hospital emergency rooms are increasingly becoming centers of primary care because of the lack of general practitioners, the reluctance of physicians to make house calls, and the unavailability of private physicians in the urban innercity (Gibson et al., 1970). Also significant is the fact that hospital emergency rooms are accessible, have a minimum of administrative barriers, and have the resources of an entire hospital behind them (Satin and Duhl, 1972). The people who tend to utilize emergency rooms for primary care are the underprivileged who have minimal social ties and no other regular source of medical care (Satin, 1973).

The medical specialty that has drawn the greatest amount of criticism in recent years is surgery. About 25 percent of all beginning physicians enter surgical training programs which, in the face of the growing shortage of primary care physicians, is too large a percentage. Not only are there too many surgeons, but the question has also arisen whether all the surgical operations ordered are necessary. John Bunker (1970), writing in the *New England Journal of Medicine*, compared the number of surgeons and surgical

[2] Victor R. Fuchs, *Who Shall Live?* (New York: Basic Books, 1974), pp. 68–69.

operations performed in the United States, England, and Wales. He found that there are twice as many surgeons in proportion to the population in the United States as in England and Wales, and that they perform twice as many operations. He could not determine if American surgeons operated too often and British surgeons too infrequently, yet he noted that surgery in Great Britain was closely regulated, involved more frequent use of consultants, and included restrictions in facilities and in the number of surgeons.

Another study by Rita Nickerson et al. (1976) found that too many nonspecialist physicians perform surgery, while the work loads of surgical specialists tend to be relatively modest. This study, based on hospital operations performed in 1970 by some 2,700 practitioners, noted that approximately one-half of the physicians performed one operation or less a week. Only one percent of the total physician population operated ten or more times a week. The obvious conclusion of this study was that there are far too many physicians of all kinds who perform surgical operations.

OVERVIEW OF HEALTH CARE DELIVERY

The existing health care delivery system in the United States is a conglomerate of health practitioners, agencies, and institutions, all of which operate more or less independently. The greatest portion of all patient services, approximately 80 percent, is provided in the offices of private physicians, who sell their services on a fee-for-service arrangement. About two-thirds of the 313,000 active nonfederal physicians involved in direct patient care work in an office-based practice, while the remainder are mostly interns, residents, or full-time staff members of hospitals. Of these office-based physicians, 80 percent are either solo practitioners or are part of a two-physician partnership. The other 20 percent are organized into group practices which usually comprise three to four physicians each. Thus, the predominant organizational form of private medical practice in the United States is the solo or two-person office-based partnership providing services to patients in return for a monetary fee. In 1978, direct payments by patients represented 35 percent of all expenditures for physicians' services; private insurance paid 39 percent, and the government paid 26 percent. The total amount of expenditures for physician services in 1978 was $35.3 billion or about $135 for every man, woman, and child in the United States.

The next most prominent form of health care delivery consists of services provided by hospitals. With the exception of tax-supported government institutions, hospitals, like physicians, charge patients according to a fee-for-service system. Voluntary (nonprofit) hospitals charge patients for hospital services from the standpoint of recovering the full cost of services provided, the determination of which, as economist Uwe Reinhardt (1973:172) has observed, "is at best an imprecise matter." Proprietary hospitals calculate not only the cost of services rendered, but also function to realize a profit from those services. Voluntary and proprietary hospitals rely heavily on third-party sources, either private health insurance or government agencies, to pay most or all of a patient's bill. Americans spent $76 billion or about $310 per person on hospital services in 1978.

Besides office-based medical practices and hospitals, the other types of organizations involved in the delivery of health care to the American public are official agencies, voluntary agencies, health maintenance organizations, neighborhood health centers, and allied health enterprises in the business community.

Official agencies are public organizations supported by tax funds, such as the U.S. Department of Health and Human Services, the U.S. Public Health Service, and the Food and Drug Administration, which are intended to support research, develop educational materials, and provide services designed to minimize public health problems. Official agencies also have the responsibility for the direct medical care and health services required by special populations like reservation Indians, the military, veterans, the mentally ill, lepers, tuberculosis patients, alcoholics, and drug addicts.

Voluntary agencies are charitable organizations, such as the Multiple Sclerosis Society, the American Cancer Society, and the March of Dimes, who solicit funds from the general public and use them to support medical research and provide services for disease victims.

Health maintenance organizations (HMOs) are prepaid group practices, like the Kaiser-Permanente program, in which a person pays a monthly premium for comprehensive health care services. HMOs are oriented toward preventive and ambulatory services intended to reduce hospitalization. Under this arrangement, HMOs derive greater income from keeping their patients healthy and not having to pay for their hospital expenses than they would if large numbers of their subscribers were hospitalized. There is some evidence that HMOs do reduce hospital use and produce lower overall medical costs than the traditional open-market fee-for-service pattern (Roemer and Shonick, 1973; Newman et al., 1979). Most of the savings are due to lower rates of hospitalization, but surgical rates are also especially low for HMO populations. Physicians participating in HMOs are not usually paid according to a fee-for-service schedule, but are paid a salary or on a capitation (set amount per patient) basis. In 1980 it cost an individual about $50 per month to belong to an HMO, while families paid between $100 and $150 monthly. Membership entitled them to receive physician services, hospitalization, laboratory tests, x-rays, and perhaps prescription drugs and other health needs at little or no additional cost.

There are some disadvantages to HMOs, namely that they are difficult to organize (Saward, 1973), a patient (especially at nights or on weekends) may be treated by whoever is on duty rather than their "own" doctor, and little is known about the quality of HMO care—although supposedly it is similar to that of usual fee-for-service practice. Currently, HMOs have attracted considerable attention in the United States because of their cost control potential. The number of HMOs and their enrollment has been rapidly increasing in the last few years, but as of 1978 only 4 percent of the population belonged to a health maintenance organization (HEW, 1978).

Neighborhood health centers (NHCs) are clinics financed by the federal government to provide ambulatory care in low-income areas where health services are either nonexistent or inadequate. NHCs are supposed to provide health care that is financially and physically accessible to all members of the community and to be particularly sensitive to meeting the health needs of the poor. NHCs have apparently been able to reduce the barriers to access among poor people and blacks; however, their drawbacks include inequitable distribution of service among poor communities, difficulty in attracting physicians and other health personnel (thereby implying a substandard level of care), and suspicion of promoting a two-class health care system by segregating the poor from other channels of health care (Reynolds, 1976).

Allied health enterprises are the manufacturers of pharmaceuticals and medical supplies and equipment; these enterprises belong to an industry whose business totals over $20 billion per year.

Despite the existence of HMOs, NHCs, and direct patient care programs supported by official agencies, the majority of patient care services in the United States are still delivered on the traditional fee-for-service system. This is the case whether the consumers pay the bill themselves or whether the bill is paid indirectly through a third party. Reinhardt (1973:172) points out that Americans probably accept this arrangement as quite normal within the total pattern of consumerism in the United States. However, this method has resulted in a number of undesirable side effects, the most undesirable of which is, according to Robert Alford (1975:1), that health care in the United States is fragmented, unresponsive, uncoordinated, costly, and inefficient. All of this is consistent with the charge that the American system of health care delivery is actually a "nonsystem."

David Rutstein illustrates the American "nonsystem" of health care delivery by depicting it as a "tangled web." Rutstein says:

> The catch-as-catch-can structure of our unplanned medical care system is comprised of conflicting and duplicating activities on one hand and gaps in service on the other. Doctors settle where they will with large numbers in the suburbs and few, if any, in the country or in the slums of our large cities. Hospital centers tend to be self-centered. Their growth in buildings and equipment is usually not determined by community need but by financial resources, the interest and demands of the medical staff, and the pride and drive of the board of trustees. Public health and social service resources appear to grow with the social outlook of the community, with more and better services in the wealthier communities and fewer and poorer services in the low-income areas where they are most needed. All of these discrepancies persist even though our federal government through legislation and financial allocations attempts to equalize services throughout the country.[3]

The Argument for the Fee-for-Service System

Advocates of the fee-for-service system of health care delivery agree that under that system there is no single pathway to health care nor any determination by a single coordinating authority as to the extent of health care services and the placement of health personnel and facilities. However, as James Appel (1970) argues, an organized system of health care delivery has developed nonetheless and is based on the voluntary decisions of both health care providers and consumers. Appel says that a "line of drift" exists in which people in need of medical treatment are attracted to private physicians on the basis of their reputations within specific geographic areas. These private physicians represent "portals of entry" into the health care

[3] David Rutstein, *The Coming Revolution in Medicine* (Cambridge, Mass: MIT Press, 1967), p. 49.

delivery system, as they either provide the needed services in their offices or direct the patients into hospitals or to other health practitioners where those sevices can be obtained.

Furthermore, advocates of the fee-for-service system propose that if the quality of American health care is to be improved, an expansion should be undertaken in the diversity of medical facilities, the number of physicians, the competition between health facilities, and the quantity and quality of private health insurance (Alford, 1975:1-3). This notion derives from the concept of the open market, in which the consumers of health care, like the consumers of other products, are supposedly free to choose which health care provider offers the best services at the best price. The assumed benefit is an improvement in services as a result of competition between the providers. Theoretically, physicians who are incompetent or who charge excessive prices and hospitals with inferior or duplicated facilities would be driven out of the market by the more competent, reasonably priced, and more efficient physicians and the better hospitals. The fee-for-service system also includes the proviso that the cost of quality health care for the indigent will be assumed by the government.

Thus, the open-market fee-for-service thesis rests on the belief in free choice both for the physician as provider and the patient as consumer. To eliminate or reduce free choice would, according to this argument, undermine the incentive of the physician to satisfy the patient; the eventual result would be treatment that is not only inferior but also depersonalized.

The fee-for-service system is a highly attractive situation for physicians, and it is obviously no coincidence that it is the dominant form of private practice. It allows physicians to decide what branch of medicine they should specialize in, where they should practice medicine, how many patients they should have, how many hours they should work per week, and how much money they should charge for their services. Professional ethics are supposed to block any desire they might have to try to make as much money as possible.

The Argument Against the Fee-for-Service System

But, as Reinhardt (1973) explains, health care delivery is not a good example of a perfectly competitive marketplace because of the very nature of the physician-patient relationship. Physicians define what patients need and then provide the service; patients themselves do not select those services with fully knowledgeable consent. In addition, Alford points out that critics of the prevailing system argue that:

> ...the choices allegedly provided by the plurality of health care providers are not real for most people, that the economic incentives to physicians result in much over-doctoring, over-hospitalization, and over-operating, and that the alleged intimate and humane quality of most doctor–patient relationships is a myth.[4]

Specific misgivings about the fee-for-service system have been summarized by Reinhardt (1973:172–174) into four principal arguments.

[4] Robert R. Alford, *Health Care Politics* (Chicago: University of Chicago Press, 1975), p. 3.

1. The existing system of health care delivery lacks effective planning and coordination. This has resulted in
    a. widespread duplication of expensive facilities that unnecessarily increase the cost of health care
    b. maldistribution of medical resources with a relative abundance of resources in affluent urban areas and a corresponding lack in poorer urban and rural areas
    c. a lack of comprehensiveness and continuity of care.
2. While current licensure laws and restrictions on medical practice protect consumers from unqualified personnel, this benefit is dubious because they also
    a. tend to discourage the use of paramedical personnel for tasks they could accomplish as well as and cheaper than physicians
    b. tend to discourage entry of candidates into the paramedical occupations because of the lack of opportunity for upward mobility.
3. The fee-for-service system, combined with the fact that consumers are usually more fully insured for in-patient rather then outpatient care, tends to
    a. deter consumers not covered by private health insurance or other third-party sources from seeking out preventive care in the early stages of a health problem
    b. encourage consumers and physicians to use insured hospital services rather than uninsured ambulatory care
    c. block some consumers, particularly the lower-middle class, from access to health care
    d. encourage physicians to overtreat those consumers who can afford to pay for the treatment.
4. Hospital reliance on the full-cost recovery formula, combined with the fact that a hospital's prestige increases in relation to the more complex types of cases it handles, tends to encourage the purchase of expensive and "superfluous" equipment. The result of unwarranted capital outlays is higher cost passed on to the consumer.

Reinhardt concludes:

Even a cursory reading of the literature on health care, both academic and popular, convinces one that there is widespread disenchantment with the nation's existing health-care system. It is argued that the present system fails to deliver what is needed, where it is needed, and at the right time. Furthermore, there is persuasive empirical evidence that such services as are made available to consumers are often produced inefficiently and are therefore unnecessarily costly. As a result, even those individuals who can afford the price of normal health-maintenance services are constantly exposed to the risk of financial ruin through illness.[5]

At the very least, Reinhardt contends that existing health care delivery be consolidated and coordinated, that less expensive paramedical personnel be substituted for more expensive physicians, and that the fee-for-service system be replaced with a system of prepaid capitation (per capita) fees for comprehensive health care.

[5] Uwe E. Reinhardt, "Proposed Changes in the Organization of Health-Care Delivery: An Overview and Critique," *Milbank Memorial Fund Quarterly*, 51 (Spring 1973), 208–209.

In sum, the United States is the only major industrial country that has no comprehensive program for making health care available to all its citizens. The suggestion of Appel (1970) of the merits of a "line of drift" of consumers to health care providers based upon the "reputation for excellent perform-ance" by those providers is clearly idealistic, oversimplified, and fails to account for the needs of consumers whose economic and social disadvantages preclude them from drifting toward the best health care available in Amer-ican society. If such a "line of drift" does exist, it appears that affluent patients drift toward the better physicians and facilities, leaving the less affluent to drift toward less adequate sources of care, while physicians themselves tend to gravitate toward well-to-do urban areas featuring a wide range of prestigious social activities. Moreover, rising costs of medical care have not resulted in improved quality of care, and the growth of public resentment in this regard has forced and is forcing regulation in the Amer-ican system of health care delivery, despite the opposition of the medical profession.

SOCIAL LEGISLATION IN HEALTH CARE

The medical profession in the United States, as Ernest Saward (1973) has pointed out, has a consistent record of resistance to social legislation seeking to reduce the authority, privileges, and income of physicians. With the exception of some individuals, the profession as a group has opposed work-men's compensation laws, social security and voluntary health insurance in their initial stages, Medicare and Medicaid, and the creation of Professional Standards Review Organizations (PSROs) to review the work of those physi-cians involved in federally funded programs. The medical profession has also opposed the expansion of health maintenance organizations and strongly resisted proposals for national health insurance, even in the light of overwhelming evidence of their inevitability. "In short," Saward (1973:129) states, "the organized medical profession has repeatedly been on the nega-tive side of social issues where the general public has been on the affirmative side."

Medicare and Medicaid: Passage and Programs

For more than forty years, the American Medical Association fought successfully to block the passage of any federal health care legislation that threatened the fee-for-service system or that advocated national health insurance. By the early 1960s, however, it was clear to most segments of society that private health insurance had not met the needs of the aged and the poor (see Saward, 1973:131). A considerable portion of the literature in medical sociology during the 1950s and 1960s, for instance, documented the disadvantaged position of the elderly and the poor in obtaining adequate health care in American society. Several sociological and political factors thus combined to influence the drafting of laws to provide hospital insurance for the aged—the commitments of Presidents John F. Kennedy and Lyndon B. Johnson; the changed composition of the U.S. Senate in 1962 and the U.S. House of Representatives in 1964; the lack of past effective health care legislation; the continuing increase in the cost of medical care; and perhaps the lessening credibility of the AMA, which claimed that "physicians cared for the elderly" and "knew their health needs better than anyone else" or that federal health insurance was incompatible with "good" medicine (Stevens, 1971:438–439).

Despite the strong resistance of the medical profession, Congress passed the Medicare and Medicaid amendments of the Social Security Act in 1965. Although these amendments were compromises between what was ideal and what was politically feasible, their passage marked a watershed in the history of medical politics in the United States as the general public for the first time emerged as a dominant voice in health care delivery and demonstrated that the direction of medical practice might no longer be the sole prerogative of organized medicine (Stevens, 1971; Marmor, 1973; Saward, 1973). In addition, the resistance of the medical profession to Medicare brought home the point to the general public that the medical profession could not always be relied upon to place the public's interest ahead of the profession's interest.

Medicare. Medicare is a federally administered program providing hospital insurance (part A) and supplemental medical insurance (part B) for people sixty-five years or older, regardless of financial resources; disabled people under the age of sixty-five who receive cash benefits from social security or railroad retirement programs and certain victims of chronic kidney disease. Hospital insurance benefits include (1) in-patient hospital services for up to ninety days for an episode of an illness, plus a lifetime reserve of sixty additional days of hospital care after the initial ninety days have been used; (2) care in a nursing home for up to one hundred days after a period of hospitalization; and (3) up to one hundred home health visits after hospitalization.

Supplementary Medicare insurance benefits include (1) physicians' and surgeons' services, certain nonroutine services of podiatrists, limited services of chiropractors, and the services of independently practicing physical therapists; (2) certain medical and health services, such as diagnostic services, diagnostic x-ray tests, laboratory tests, and other services, including ambulance services, some medical supplies, appliances, and equipment; (3) out-patient hospital services; (4) home health services (with no requirement of prior hospitalization) for up to one hundred visits in one calendar year; and (5) out-patient physical and speech therapy services provided by approved therapists.

There are specified deductible and coinsurance amounts for which the beneficiary is responsible. The current deductible on the hospital insurance (part A) is $84 and on the medical insurance (part B) is $60, with a 20 percent coinsurance amount also required for most part B services. The hospital insurance is financed primarily through social security payroll deductions, while the medical insurance plan, whose participation is voluntary, is financed by premiums paid by the enrollees and from federal funds. The medical insurance premium in 1977 was $7.70 a month.

The Medicare program is under the overall direction of the Secretary of Health, Education and Welfare and is supervised by the Bureau of Health Insurance of the Social Security Administration. Most of the day-to-day operations of Medicare are performed by commercial insurance companies and Blue Cross/Blue Shield plans that review claims and make payments. Requests for payment are usually submitted by the provider of services and signed by the beneficiary; reimbursement is made on the basis of reasonable charges as determined by the private insurance companies who issue the payments. In 1974, a total of $12.4 billion in Medicare benefits were paid under coverage that extends to about twenty-two million people.

Medicaid.   Medicaid, as Rosemary Stevens (1971) points out, is technically a welfare program. It provides for the federal government sharing in the payments made by state welfare agencies to health care providers for services rendered to the poor. Medicaid provides, to the states, federal matching funds ranging from 50 to 83 percent, depending on the per capita income of the states involved. Each state is required to cover all needy persons receiving cash assistance. Eligible health care services include in-patient and out-patient hospital services, laboratory and X-ray services, skilled nursing home services, and physicians' services, plus other forms of health care covered at the option of the individual states. For instance, it permitted states to include not only the financially needy, but also the medically needy, the aged, blind, and disabled poor, as well as their dependent children and families. Medicaid is administered by the states, not the federal government, and as such is subject to wide variation.

Medicare and Medicaid: Evaluation

Medicare and Medicaid were not designed to change the structure of health care in the United States. These programs did not place physicians under the supervision of the federal government nor attempt to control the distribution or quality of medical practice. Instead they were based on preexisting patterns of insurance coverage, involving the participation of private health insurance companies, and they allowed physicians to continue to set their own fees and conduct business as usual.

In fact, Medicare and Medicaid turned out to be a financial boon to organized medicine and to hospitals as they channeled federal monies into health care and helped the industry become a $206 billion a year business in the United States, grossing five times more in 1979 than it did in 1965. It can also be argued that Medicare and Medicaid contributed to rising prices in health care as they provided the opportunity to pass excessive demands for payment on to insurance companies instead of to the patients themselves. Of course, the general public does not really escape from paying higher prices, as the costs of the insurance companies have to be met. And to make matters worse, in some states the Medicaid program was beset by serious problems of fraud, abuse, scandal, and administrative inefficiency. In 1976 in New York City, for example, it was estimated that 10 to 20 percent of a total $2 billion annual Medicaid benefits were overpayments.

However, as Stevens (1971) notes, if the only problems in American health services were poor management and high incomes for physicians, there would not be the sense of massive urgency that has pervaded the United States health care situation in recent years. The problems in fact go to the very core of medical practice—its purpose to provide quality medical care for the entire population. What Medicare and Medicaid have accomplished on a national scale is basically two highly important measures. First, these programs may have been expensive and may not have met all the needs of the aged and the poor for which they were intended, but they have provided needed health services for the old and poverty-stricken where these services were not previously available.

Second, Medicare and Medicaid established the precedent of the federal government's involvement in the administration of health care, and this involvement is the key to future health care planning and reorganization. And, according to Stevens, the time has long passed in the United States when the question of whether or not the federal government should intervene in health care delivery is debated. Federal government involvement in health care is now an important and substantial reality, and whatever happens in the future organization and scope of health care services in the United States is now dependent on federal government decisions.

As for the present effects of Medicare and Medicaid on the elderly and indigent, two studies, one by Karen Davis (1975b) and one by Lu Ann Aday (1976), provide relevant indicators. Davis, in a study of U.S. Department of Health, Education and Welfare data pertaining to Medicare services provided in 1968, concluded that Medicare had helped some elderly persons but had not been sufficient to guarantee equal access to health care for all. She found that the poor, blacks, and residents of the South tended to use the program least frequently; these people also tended to have the poorest health. Elderly people with incomes above $15,000 annually received twice the payments for physician services (and were also more likely to seek care from higher priced physicians) than those received by people with family incomes below $5,000. Whites received 30 percent more payments for hospital services than blacks, 60 percent more payments for physician services, and more than twice the payments for posthospital extended care services. This disparity between the races was particularly evident in the South. The South as a whole received the lowest proportion of payments of any region of the country, some 40 percent lower than the West, the highest recipient.

Davis explains that geographical variations in Medicare benefits are primarily a reflection of regional patterns of availability of medical resources and differences in the cost of medical care. Thus, greater uniformity among geographical regions is not likely without a better distribution of medical resources, particularly physicians. But since Medicare payments are based on prevailing costs and charges, physicians practicing in scarcity areas and charging lower prices will continue to receive lower levels of payment, thus discouraging the new generation of physicians from opening practices there.

Davis also found that differences in Medicare utilization were not solely attributable to those aspects of higher income associated with having more education and living near a greater concentration of medical resources. Conversely, the lower utilization of services by blacks was not attributable to a lower average income or poorer education. Instead, the data suggested that the structure of the Medicare program itself was largely responsible for the greater use of its services by people with higher incomes (who also tended to be white) because of the requirement for cost-sharing. Davis found that the deductible and coinsurance provisions of the medical insurance portion (part B) of Medicare were a significant deterrent for many poor elderly people.

Davis suggested four improvements in Medicare:

1. adjusting the cost-sharing structure according to income, with all elderly people below the poverty line exempted from deductible and coinsurance amounts
2. improving the access of minorities to medical care
3. reforming the financing of Medicare
   a. to eliminate the premium for supplementary medical insurance
   b. to extend coverage of both parts of Medicare to all elderly people even if they are not eligible for social security benefits
   c. to change the structure of payroll deductions to help lower income workers
4. improving reimbursement policies, not the least of which would be to set a nationally uniform reimbursement schedule for physicians to ensure that physicians working in underserved areas would be paid the same as those in affluent areas.

Aday's (1976) study was based on 1963–1970 nationwide surveys of access to medical care, before and after the introduction of Medicare and Medicaid. Aday suggested that there should be "guarded optimism" in regard to the success of Medicare and Medicaid in narrowing the differential between income groups. She found that people with low incomes, in contrast to previous patterns, now visit a doctor more often than do those with a high or middle income (see Chapter Four). In 1970, 65 percent of people with low incomes saw a physician compared to only 56 percent in 1963. However, considering the use of services by the poor relative to their needs, they were still found to be at a disadvantage because of their higher ratio of disability.

Aday concluded: "Changes in the financing of care have apparently enhanced low-income people's ability to get care when the need arises—especially among those who have a regular point of entry to the system. For those who do not, however, significant inequities in access persist."[6]

National Health Insurance

The major public issue now in health care delivery is to move beyond Medicare and Medicaid toward the development of some form of national health insurance that would provide coverage to all Americans. At the present time several different plans for national health care are before Congress, but regardless of whether one of these plans is adopted or a new plan is envisioned as more satisfactory, most of these programs are concerned with three important goals: (1) ensuring that all people have financial, geographic, and social access to medical care; (2) eliminating the financial hardship of medical bills; and (3) limiting the rise in health care costs (see Davis, 1975a).

Exactly how these goals should be pursued, however, is a matter of serious disagreement and debate. The form of national health insurance to be adopted may be either one or a combination of several major proposals.

[6] Lou Ann Aday, "The Impact of Health Policy on Access to Medical Care," *Milbank Memorial Fund Quarterly*, 54 (Spring 1976), 228.

The plans most commonly discussed are the Kennedy-Mills proposal, the Kennedy-Griffiths Health Security Act, and the Long-Ribicoff Catastrophic Insurance Plan. The Kennedy-Mills proposal is a two-part bill that provides a national health insurance plan for the general population and a revised Medicare program for the aged and disabled. The plan would abolish Medicaid and would be funded on the basis of a graduated payroll tax on the first $20,000 of earned income. All persons eligible for social security benefits, working full-time or covered under other programs now in existence, would be extended coverage under this plan. The Kennedy-Griffiths Health Security Act would cover all Americans, regardless of income or age, and would be financed by payroll deductions and general federal revenues. The entire cost of care would be covered, and there would be no limit on the number of claims that could be made. A person would have the option of being insured by a consortium of commercial insurance companies, Blue Cross-Blue Shield, independent group health insurance plans, or HMOs. Employers would be liable for the premium payments, but would require workers to pay up to 35 percent of the total. The federal government would pay the bills for the elderly and the poor. The Long-Ribicoff Catastrophic Insurance Plan would (1) cover the general population with a provision for catastrophic cost coverage when medical expenses exceed a certain limit, and (2) provide an assistance plan for the poor and the medically indigent. This plan would cover people of all ages who are covered by social security and would be financed by a special tax on wages.

None of these plans appears to be totally adequate when its coverages, costs, and system of administration are carefully reviewed (for an extensive discussion of current national health care plans, see Davis, 1975a; HEW, 1976). The most pressing issue does not concern coverage and implementation but finance: how to keep the costs down and obtain the money to pay for the services. It is idle to speculate at this time about which plan is best or which will probably be adopted because as this book goes to press, many of the key issues in the formulation of a national health insurance plan have yet to be decided.

Finally, it should be noted that national health insurance will probably not change the structure of medical care. Organized medicine still has a professional monopoly over medical knowledge, techniques, and procedures and can define most clearly and authoritatively what health care should entail in the United States. Therefore, regardless of what program is chosen, public control of medical practice in the United States will probably remain relatively indirect unless there is a fundamental reconstruction of the social and economic structure of American society—which seems rather unlikely.

A RADICAL CRITIQUE OF AMERICAN HEALTH CARE

There is, of course, a radical critique of the American system of health care delivery based on liberal and Marxist views. This approach suggests that Americans would best be served by adopting a national health service modeled after Great Britain or Sweden (Krause, 1977) or that of some other type of socialist system (Ehrenreich, 1978). The standard critique follows political and economic lines. It holds that medicine is a commodity that is inherently *good* and the problem is that not everyone in American society has equal access to it. What is needed therefore is a redistribution of health services on a more equitable basis. What the standard critique leaves out, according to John Ehrenreich (1978), is that certain things about American medicine are inherently *bad*. Ehrenreich's position is that while medicine does accomplish some good, it is not administered by doctors who are morally neutral and who use essentially benign and effective techniques for helping people. He argues that some medical techniques are harmful (such as unnecessary surgery, prescription of inappropriate or dangerous drugs, and the use of oral contraceptives for women), yet the medical profession promotes dependency on its decisions. Moreover, the doctor–patient relationship is regarded as racist, sexist, and discriminatory on a socioeconomic basis.

This argument is similar to that proposed by Ivan Illich (1976) in a well-known radical critique of the 1970s. Illich maintained that medicine caused harm not only through the use of questionable procedures, but also because the medical bureaucracy strove to manage the responses to more and more critical life events. Whether it managed them well or badly was not the issue for Illich as much as it was that medicine was taking more control over social problems and reducing the ability of people to handle their own lives. Ehrenreich and others (Navarro, 1976), however, believe Illich was focusing on the wrong target—medical bureaucracy—and that the real culprit is the American class system. The upper class is seen as perpetuating the present mode of health care delivery as part of its power base. Medicine helps to maintain the social status quo by managing the personal difficulties of people who come to it as patients. Ehrenreich calls for a mass movement, similar to that of Women's Liberation and the civil rights movement of the 1960s, to reduce the power of professional medicine and make medicine more responsive to the public. As part of this change, he argues, medicine must be reoriented toward a stronger ethic of service and selfless caring— with the profit motive eliminated.

It is unlikely that a mass movement will evolve in the near future to bring on the kind of socialist change advocated by Ehrenreich. There is no evidence that indicates the existence of any widespread support in the United States for such a political activity. Marxist and socialist programs have traditionally not had great appeal for the American people. In addition, American medicine is slowly becoming somewhat more responsive to the public interest as it has come under increasing attacks from the mass media and politicians seeking to achieve reform of the current system of health care delivery. For example, a majority of delegates to the 1979 American Medical Association meeting approved guidelines that supported programs of voluntary private health insurance for major medical expenses and an expansion of Medicare and Medicaid to cover catastrophic illnesses for the American public. Such a position would not have been adopted a few years ago.

According to a 1978 Louis Harris poll, Americans do not want any major changes in the nation's health care system. But there is growing support for some form of government-sponsored, comprehensive national health insurance. As Stevens (1971) points out, it would be unrealistic to assume that a total sweep of traditions and institutions will take place over night; instead any future health care system is likely to be profoundly influenced by the pattern of American medicine developed over the past three centuries. The result is likely to be a compromise of public interests and medical professional interests, with organized medicine retaining direct control over medical practice, education, research, and health care delivery, but with sizable inroads on professional autonomy that should render the medical profession more responsive to public needs.

HEALTH CARE: A RIGHT OR A PRIVILEGE?

In the final analysis, what we are really talking about is the issue of whether medical care is a *right* of all Americans or whether it is a *privilege*. Some people have maintained that health care is a privilege, not a right, and if people want medical treatment they should pay for it. This type of statement should not necessarily be construed to mean that the poor are unworthy of receiving medical care. Behind this argument is a generalized opposition to the welfare state; it is felt that the best way to help the poor is to provide them with jobs so that they can *buy* medical care like everybody else. To give the poor the highest quality of medical care available without improving the conditions of poverty within which they live is thought to be an exercise in futility. Although it does make sense to increase the overall purchasing power of the poor and to bring medical care within their reach financially, this utopian view would also allow the medical profession to maintain its current system of fee-for-service oriented toward financial gain.

A more socially responsible argument is that medical care does represent a special case. More in the nature of an opportunity rather than a commodity, quality health care should be available as a right of all Americans, regardless of living conditions or financial status. But, as Victor Fuchs (1974) points out, the "right" to health is a misleading concept. It implies that society has a supply of "health" on hand, which it can pass on to those individuals who have access, either privately or publicly secured, to the system of health care providers. Fuchs suggests that the notion that we can spend our way to health is an oversimplification. There is very little that medical care can accomplish for some conditions, for example, fatal wounds resulting from homicide or automobile accidents, or advanced cases of cirrhosis of the liver resulting from an excess of alcohol, or lung carcinoma due to smoking. In fact, we may be reaching the point where there is no longer a significant relationship between spending money on health and getting improved results (Forbes, 1967; Burger, 1974). It has been suggested that the complete eradication of heart disease, cancer, and stroke would extend the average life expectancy at birth by only six or seven years (Kass, 1976). Thus, medicine's contribution to longer life may reach a natural limit. William Forbes (1967) points out that when life expectancy is considered, cultural factors may now be more important than medical factors in countries where infectious diseases are no longer the major causes of death.

Forbes states that:

> . . . improvement in our average remaining lifetime is more likely to result from the study and control of factors not commonly thought of as medical ones than from further efforts along strictly medical lines. Examples of such factors

follow the organization of modern life as determined by urbanization, the automobile and television; diet as determined by industrial pressures and requirements; and interpersonal relations as influenced by crowding and by industry.[7]

What Forbes is telling us is that we may be reaching the point of diminishing returns with regard to health care expenditures. More significant for the future than medical technology may be the effects of life style and physical environment on our health, especially such things as chemical pollution and insecticides in our food. Forbes may be correct in his assessment of the limitations of medicine to provide the American public with "health," but at this point, the central issues are finding answers to the questions of how we can stop rising health care costs and how we can see that every American at least has the opportunity to obtain quality health services. Until such time as there is a major change in our present system of health care delivery, certain preliminary measures should be taken to reach these goals. These measures include:

1. Provide universal comprehensive health insurance for all Americans, with a variety of plans available so that a person can choose the plan which best meets his or her needs.
2. Encourage medical schools to train more primary care and family practice practitioners.
3. Make greater use of physicians' assistants and nurse practitioners to offset shortages of primary care practitioners.
4. Train physicians to be more sensitive to the needs of women, the poor, and members of racial/ethnic minority groups.
5. Require public and private health insurance agencies to be more critical in assessing physician and hospital fees; refuse to pay unreasonable charges and set lower maximum payments for services.
6. Stimulate cost-containment policies among hospitals.
7. Expand preventive medicine programs and hospital out-patient facilities in order to prevent illnesses or detect and treat them at earlier stages.
8. Insure that adequate health care facilities and practitioners are readily accessible to all members of the community, including rural areas and urban slums.

HEALTH POLICY IN SELECTED INDUSTRIAL COUNTRIES

The remainder of this chapter will review the policies and organization of health care delivery in selected industrial countries. To varying degrees, all nations of the world are faced with increased pressure of demands for quality health care and faced with rising costs of providing that care. This pressure has led to a renewed search for alternatives, among both developed and underdeveloped countries, with the result that interest and scholarship in the field of cross-national studies of health systems has significantly increased in recent years (Elling, 1980).

Three types of health care systems will be discussed: (1) the *socialized* forms of medicine common to Sweden and Great Britain, (2) *decentralized national health programs* in West Germany and Japan, and (3) *socialist* medicine in the Soviet Union and China.

[7] William H. Forbes, "Longevity and Medical Costs," *New England Journal of Medicine*, 277 (July 13, 1967), 77.

Sweden

Sweden, along with Great Britain, has demonstrated that a socialized system of health care delivery can be effective in a capitalist country through the formation of a national health service. A national health service is created by a government nationalizing or taking over the responsibility for a nation's health care. Thus, the government becomes the employer for health workers, maintains facilities, and purchases supplies and new equipment through the use of funds collected largely by taxation. Little or no money is exchanged between the patient and the provider of services. Except for paying taxes, health services are essentially free to those who use them. However, taxes in Sweden are among the highest in the world, so health care is not actually free—rather its cost is spread out over the entire population, thus reducing the financial burden on those who need it the most. In Sweden, people in the upper income brackets are taxed more than 50 percent of their income and, if a person makes enough money, it is possible to be taxed *more* than one's income.

Still, on practically every measure, the Swedes must be considered one

TABLE 9–3.   Infant Mortality Rates in Selected Countries, 1972–1977

Country	Infant Mortality Rate	
	1972	1977[1]
	Infant deaths per 1,000 live births	
Canada	17.1	14.3
United States	18.5	14.1
Sweden	10.8	8.0
Great Britain[2]	17.2	13.7
Netherlands	11.7	9.5
West Germany	22.7	17.4
France	16.0	11.4[3]
Switzerland	13.3	10.7
Italy	27.0	17.6
Israel	21.3	22.9
Japan	11.7	9.3
Australia	16.7	14.3

[1] Data for Canada, Israel, and Australia refer to 1975; data for West Germany, Switzerland, and Japan refer to 1976; all 1977 data are provisional, except for United States.
[2] Data for England and Wales only
[3] Excludes infants who have died before registration of birth.
SOURCE: U.S. Department of Health, Education and Welfare, *Health United States, 1979* (Washington, D.C.: U.S. Government Printing Office, 1980).

TABLE 9–4.   Life Expectancy at Birth for Selected Countries, According to Sex, 1970 and 1976

Country	Male		Female	
	1970[1]	1976[2]	1970[1]	1976[2]
	Remaining life expectancy in years		Remaining life expectancy in years	
Canada	69.3	69.6	76.2	77.1
United States	67.0	69.0	74.6	76.7
Sweden	72.3	72.2	77.4	78.1
Great Britain[3]	68.8	69.7	75.2	75.8
Netherlands	70.9	71.6	76.6	78.1
West Germany	67.3	68.1	73.6	74.5
France	69.1	69.5	76.7	77.6
Switzerland	70.3	71.7	76.2	78.3
Italy	68.5	69.9	74.6	76.1
Israel[4]	69.9	71.0	73.4	74.7
Japan	69.5	72.3	74.9	77.6
Australia	67.4	69.3	74.2	76.4

[1] Data for the United States refer to the average for the period 1969–1971; data for Switzerland refer to the average for the period 1968–1973.
[2] Data for Canada, France, and Italy refer to 1974; data for West Germany, Israel, and Australia refer to 1975.
[3] Data for England and Wales only.
[4] Jewish population only.
SOURCE: U.S. Department of Health, Education and Welfare, *Health United States, 1979* (Washington, D.C.: U.S. Government Printing Office, 1980).

of the world's healthiest populations. As shown in Table 9–3, which contains the infant mortality rates for representative countries of the world's healthiest nations, Sweden had the lowest rates of infant mortality for both 1972 and 1977. In 1977, the infant mortality rate for Sweden was 8.0 per 1,000 live births, followed by Japan (9.3) and the Netherlands (9.5). Switzerland, France, East Germany, and Great Britain all had infant mortality rates lower than the United States. As for life expectancy, perhaps the best overall measure of a nation's health, Table 9–4 shows that in 1970 Sweden had the highest life expectancy of both males (72.3 years) and females (77.4 years). In 1976, for males, Sweden was barely second only to Japan (72.2 years as compared to 72.3 years); for females, Sweden's total of 78.1 years was equaled by the Netherlands and slightly behind that of Switzerland (78.3 years). For males, Table 9–4 also shows that, of the countries being compared, the United States in 1976 had an average life expectancy exceeding only that of West Germany. For females, life expectancy in the United States in 1976 is shown in Table 9–4 as less than that of Switzerland, Sweden, the Netherlands, France, Japan, and Canada.

In Sweden, the national health service is the responsibility of the Ministry of Health and Social Affairs, which was established in its present form in 1964. Only particularly important health issues are decided by the

Ministry. Most decisions pertaining to health policy are made by the National Board of Health and Welfare, which was established in 1968. This board plans, supervises, and regulates the delivery of health services at the county level (Navarro, 1974). Physicians are employed by county councils and are paid according to the number of hours worked rather than the number of patients treated. Physicians are obligated to work a fixed number of hours per week, usually about forty-five to fifty hours although this amount may decrease shortly to about forty to forty-two hours weekly. It is generally left up to the doctor to decide what percentage of his or her time is to be spent on treating patients, doing research, or teaching. Physicians' salaries are standardized by specialty, place and region of work, and seniority.

A major characteristic of the national health service in Sweden is that general hospitals are owned by county and municipal governments. These local governments are responsible for maintaining and providing services. The state pays the general hospitals a relatively small amount of money from a health insurance fund, leaving the balance to be paid from local tax revenues. Enrollment in the government sponsored health insurance program is mandatory for the entire population. Most of the money to support the insurance program comes from the contributions of employers and payroll deductions of employees. This insurance, a form of national health insurance, is used primarily to pay the salaries of physicians and other health workers. There are also some general practitioners in private practice whose fees are paid by the insurance fund and token payments from patients. Fees for all physicians, however, are set by the government and paid according to their schedule.

The Swedish health care system has some additional benefits other than generally free medical treatment. Excessive travel expenses to physicians and hospitals are paid by the government, and there is a cash sickness fund designed to protect a person's standard of living against losses of income due to illness or injury. Under this program people may receive up to 80 percent of the income they would be earning if they were able to work at their job. Drugs are either free or inexpensive, and financial supplements are paid to each woman giving birth to a child and to families with children under the age of sixteen regardless of income.

It would be misleading to consider the funding of Sweden's health care delivery system as an example of national health insurance. Most of the revenues for health care comes from county councils. The total health bill in Sweden is met by contributions of approximately 70 percent from county taxes, 13 percent from the national government, 7 percent from health insurance, 1 percent from patients' fees, and 8 percent from miscellaneous sources (Navarro, 1974).

While there is much to be admired about Sweden's system of welfare in general and health care in particular, the Swedes are heavily taxed to pay for it. And, like the situation in most other countries, the cost of health care is rising. In 1965, Sweden spent 5 percent of its Gross National Product on health services. In 1974, health costs had risen to 9.5 percent of the G.N.P. and reached 11.3 percent in 1978. The Swedish Government is attempting to hold costs down and is routinely denying some services—such as expensive organ transplants to people seventy years of age or older.

Great Britain

The British National Health Service was formed in 1948 after it was recognized that attempts spanning over thirty years had failed to finance health care by means of a national health insurance program. Prior to this time, the quality of health care one received in Britain clearly depended on one's financial resources; the poor suffered from a decidedly adverse situation. Thus, the Labor Party, which was in power after World War II, undertook to insure that everyone would be able to receive medical treatment free of charge. To accomplish this the government had to take over privately owned hospitals. The National Health Service Act of 1948 reorganized British health care into three branches: (1) the Executive Councils, which are responsible for administering the system; (2) the Local Health Authority Services Branch, which is responsible for public health, out-patient care, home nursing, community care for the mentally ill, and homes for the aged; and (3) the Hospital and Specialist Services Branch, which is responsible for the management of all hospitals (except for a few private specialty hospitals) and physician specialists, who constitute the medical staff in British hospitals.

The first line of medical care in Great Britain remained the general practitioner who worked out of an office or clinic as part of either a solo or group practice. General practitioners are paid an annual capitation fee for each patient on their patient list as part of a contractual arrangement with the National Health Service. The general practitioner may have up to 3,500 patients on his or her list if a solo practitioner or up to 4,500 if the doctor is a member of a partnership and the average for the partnership does not exceed 3,500 (Maynard, 1975). The general practitioner is required to provide medical services free of charge. The patient has the right to select his or her doctor (if over the age of sixteen) and the doctor is free to accept or reject anyone as a full-time patient. But if a potential patient is rejected from joining a doctor's list, the doctor must still provide treatment if the person is not on any physician's list or if the person's physician is absent. A higher capitation fee is paid for patients who are sixty-five years of age or older, and additional sums are paid by the government to meet certain basic office expenses, to join a group practice, for additional training, seniority, and for practicing medicine in areas that are underserved by physicians.

Except for emergencies, if treatment by a specialist (called "consultants" in the British system) or hospitalization is warranted, the general practitioner must refer the patient to a specialist. Generally, specialists are the only physicians who treat patients in hospitals. Specialists are paid a salary by the government. About 10 percent of the funds to support the National Health Service are derived from payroll deductions and employer's contributions; most of the revenue comes from general taxation.

However, because of strong opposition from physicians when the National Health Service was first organized, physicians are also allowed to treat private patients and a certain number of hospital beds ("pay" beds) are reserved for this type of patient. Private patients are responsible for paying their own bills and most of them have health insurance from private insurance companies. The advantage of being a private patient is prestige, less time spent in waiting rooms and obtaining appointments, and, of course, privacy.

In addition to the medical care provided by the National Health Service, the British have a sickness benefit fund to supplement income while a person is sick or injured, death benefits paid to survivors, and maternity benefits.

The National Health Service has been marked by controversy and subject to considerable criticism. The mode of capitation payments to general practitioners meant that the more patients seen by a physician, the more money the physician was able to make. Hence, there was a serious concern and some evidence that medical care was being provided in quantity rather than quality. A measure was introduced to pay physicians less for treating more patients, but as the population has increased the doctors have found it difficult to reduce their patient load. Also, the government and physicians have disputed the amount paid for capitation fees, with the physicians arguing that it is not enough. Disputes have taken place between general practitioners and specialists as well, and a division of labor has emerged that limits specialists to hospitals and places general practitioners outside of them. Specialists have more prestige and draw higher incomes. On occasion, cooperation, even in patient care, between the two groups has been questionable. General practitioners have claimed that the NHS favors specialists in regard to not only income but also fringe benefits (vacations, retirement, etc.) and have demanded that administrators and politicians become more sensitive to their needs. Alan Maynard describes the situation as follows:

> By placing medical care outside the market place and inside the public sector the British have removed one set of problems and replaced them with another set. Whilst students of foreign health usually have to study the interaction of financers and providers of health care, the student of the NHS has to study the interaction of politicians, administrators, and pressure groups. The institutions differ and the respective problems differ accordingly. However, behind each set of problems lies the basic question of what medical care, how much medical care, how should it be produced and to whom should it go. The nationalisation of medical care facilities and their finance out of general taxation does not solve these problems.[8]

The central problem faced by the British NHS is its lack of financial resources. Great Britain is less affluent than Sweden and therefore is unable to spend as much money on welfare and medical services. Moreover, the NHS has worked hard to hold down medical costs and only 5.6 percent of Britain's G.N.P. was spent on health care in 1977. Though relatively successful in combating rising expenses, this policy has had its drawbacks. There is currently a doctor shortage since many physicians have left the country, believing they are unable to earn enough money under the NHS. Consequently, certain services like elective surgery have been reduced.

Nevertheless, the NHS has accomplished what it set out to do: provide free comprehensive medical care to the residents of Great Britain. It has shown significant results: the general health profile of Britain is among the highest in the world. In comparison to the United States, Table 9–3 and 9–4 show, for example, that the British have a lower rate of infant mortality and a slightly higher rate of life expectancy for males. Most studies agree that the British have come to accept their system of health care delivery and generally

[8] Alan Maynard, *Health Care in the European Community* (Pittsburgh: University of Pittsburgh Press, 1975), pp. 209–210.

approve of it (Maynard, 1975; Denton, 1978; Atkinson et al., 1979). The number of private patients and hospital beds devoted to private cases is rapidly declining. While part of this trend is undoubtedly due to the rising costs of private care, a significant factor is the widespread acceptance of the NHS.

West Germany

The structure of health care delivery in the Federal Republic of Germany (West Germany) has not changed significantly since 1883 and the reforms instituted by Bismarck's administration in old imperial Germany. The program established at that time was based on three principal components: (1) compulsory insurance, (2) free health services, and (3) sick benefits. Employees, self-employed, unemployed, old-age pensioners, and certain categories of female workers providing infant and child care, home help, and the like are all required to be insured by one of some 1,800 sickness funds. These sickness funds are coordinated by the National Federation of Sickness Funds and the money used to pay benefits is obtained from contributions made by all employers and employees. About 8 percent of an individual's income will go to pay for membership in a sickness fund. The sickness fund will issue a medical certificate to members and their dependents periodically. This certificate is presented to a physician when services are rendered. The physician then submits the certificate to his or her association of registered doctors, which all physicians are required to join. Payment is made to the physician through the doctors' association according to a fee schedule agreed upon by the association and the sickness funds. During the first six weeks of an illness or injury all workers receive full wages from their employer; after that sickness funds pay up to 75 percent of the person's wages if the person is either hospitalized or remains at home but is unable to work. Maternity and death benefits are also paid through the sickness funds.

As the above discussion indicates, the West German government does not play a major role in the financing of health services. The government's primary function is one of administration. The Federal Ministry of Labor and Social Affairs exercises general supervision of the health care delivery system through state ministries and local health boards.

Approximately 56 percent of West Germany's physicians are general practitioners, which is a relatively high percentage compared to the United States. Most West German doctors practice medicine in private offices or clinics on a solo basis. Few work in a group practice. West German physicians are also especially well-paid. Incomes averaged $100,000 in 1978, far higher than their American counterparts, whose median income for that year was $65,000. Health care costs in West Germany have risen about 20 percent annually in recent years and the government has attempted to control costs by putting pressure on physicians and hospitals to hold charges down. In 1978, West Germany spent 12.8 percent of its G.N.P. on health care.

Japan

The Japanese spend only half as much of their G.N.P. on health care as the West Germans, but have achieved striking results. For example, in 1955 the average life expectancy of a Japanese was more than four years less than that of an American. By 1967, Japan's life expectancy had passed that of the United States and in 1976, as shown in Table 9–4, life expectancy for

Japanese males surpassed Sweden's to become the longest of any nation in the world. Life expectancy for females is among the highest in the world. Japanese rates for infant mortality, listed in Table 9–3, were lower than any other country in 1977 except Sweden.

In comparison to other major industrialized nations, Japan has a relatively low rate of coronary heart disease. This trend undoubtedly influences higher levels of life expectancy among the Japanese, especially among adult males. While diet is an important factor, traditional Japanese culture and the manner in which modern Japanese society is organized to reduce stress also seems significant in lessening the risk of heart disease. For example, in a study of first and second generation Japanese Americans living in Hawaii (the Honolulu Heart Study), 2,437 men were divided into two groups; (1) those men who had thoroughly adopted a Western style of life and (2) those who followed more traditional Japanese customs and values (Cohen et al., 1979). The men in each group were also assessed as having either a Type A or Type B personality. The Type A individual, as discussed in Chapter Three, is someone who tends to be very competitive, impatient, and time-oriented and is thought to be more prone to stress-related illnesses like heart disease as a result. The Type B person is more easygoing and less impatient. Less than 20 percent of the men were Type A, a percentage much lower than that usually found among samples of white Americans. The central research problem pursued in this study was to determine if those men who were both Type A and Westernized were more likely to manifest higher rates of coronary heart disease than those who were Type B and more traditionally Japanese in their attitudes and behavior. It was found that the most significant variable was degree of Westernization. Those Japanese Americans who were the most Westernized had the highest prevalence of heart disease. This was particularly true if they were also Type A.

Y. Scott Matsumoto (1971) found that Japanese living in the continental United States had a higher mortality rate from heart disease than Japanese living in Hawaii and a much higher rate than Japanese living in Japan. The more removed from Japanese culture, the higher the mortality rates for heart disease. Matsumoto suggested that the difference was largely due to the stronger feelings of group solidarity in modern Japan among workers, strengthened by the extensive paternalism of Japanese corporations and stress-reducing activities like after-work socializing and periodic group vacations.[9]

A significant group activity among Japanese male workers is the after-work socializing on a daily or weekly basis with close friends in bars or tea and coffee shops. These drinking places are designed to encourage relaxation and to allow temporary escape from the tensions of modern living. The

---

[9] Ezra Vogel (1979:137) describes the paternalism of Japanese corporations in the following manner:

> . . . an ordinary employee remains in the firm from the time he first enters after leaving school until he retires, which in most firms averages about fifty-seven or fifty-eight. The firm is committed to the employee and provides a sense of belonging, personal support, welfare and retirement benefits, and increased salary and rank with age. Barring serious long-term depression, the employee expects that he will never be laid off, and even if the company were to disband or be absorbed by another company, he expects a new job elsewhere will be arranged.

activity seems to have been fully incorporated into the life style of industrial Japan.

Japan has a national health insurance plan but its benefits are low by Western standards. Japanese patients pay 30 percent of the cost of health services, with the national plan paying for the remainder. People over seventy years of age have all of their costs covered. Patients are allowed to choose their own doctors and are encouraged to visit their doctors regularly. Thus, there is opportunity to diagnose health disorders at earlier stages. Physician fees for office visits and examinations are low, which further stimulates frequent visits. Also, hospital costs tend to be low because the government refuses to pay high costs. Japanese doctors, however, receive a substantial income from the drugs they prescribe and the Japanese use more drugs than patients in most other countries (Vogel, 1979).

The Japanese national health insurance plan does not cover all Japanese. Instead, the government adopted the example of Bismarck's system in Germany and encouraged private organizations to keep government involvement at a minimum by setting up their own welfare programs. Part of the normative structure of the Japanese business world is that companies are responsible for taking care of their own employees. In Japan this responsibility includes providing retirement plans, helping retired employees find post-retirement work, arranging vacations, offering low-cost loans for housing, and providing medical care. Consequently, there are separate programs of health services for employees of large companies, small and medium-sized companies, and public and quasipublic institutions. There is also a program for citizens who are not covered under other plans. Some large companies even have their own doctors and hospitals.

The concept of having a decentralized system of health care based largely on occupation is supported by Japanese businessmen, who generally provide more benefits than they are required to by law. "Businessmen oppose the government's assuming heavy welfare burdens," states Ezra Vogel (1979:191), "for they want to pay less in taxes and to avoid the large governmental administrative overhead required for a large public welfare system." The tax burdens in welfare states like Sweden and Great Britain are undesirable, as is the type of welfare system in the United States. But an even more attractive reason for Japanese businessmen is that providing security to employees helps to maintain their loyalty and, hence, is thought to improve their productivity. This system also gives large Japanese corporations a distinct advantage in attracting workers because of the greater benefit packages they can offer. This, of course, means that the Japanese do not share equally in health benefits and some, in fact, are discriminated against. Vogel states:

> There are many in Japan, including the leaders of the Japanese Medical Association, who would argue that the system of having different welfare schemes for different companies and other groups of the population is a feudalistic holdover that should be rationalized by having a more unified standardized national welfare program for everyone. Clearly, the individual does not receive as complete a coverage of various benefits as those attached to the largest companies. The large company's health and pension funds thrive

and grow while government sponsored funds for self-employed individuals are in chronic deficit. Certain groups in Japan suffer from these disparities to an extent that many civic-minded Japanese consider undesirable and that the vast majority of Americans would consider undesirable.[10]

These groups include Koreans, descendants of the old outcast caste in feudal Japan, widows and divorcees, and middle-aged job seekers from small businesses. The long-term trend in Japanese welfare, says Vogel, is to attempt to provide adequate coverage for such people.

Soviet Union

Although citizens of the Soviet Union are not free to select their own doctors (they are assigned by district) and they receive health services in a highly regimented system, there does not appear to be widespread dissatisfaction with the services available. In fact, the provision of free and comprehensive medical care is considered one of the greatest achievements of the Soviet system (Field, 1967; Kaser, 1976; Roemer, 1977). The government finances all health services with income derived from the nation's economic production. About 4 percent of the national income (the Soviets do not use the concept of a G.N.P.) is spent on health care. This percentage is much lower in comparison with similar measures in the other industrialized countries discussed in this section.

The ownership and operation of all health facilities is the responsibility of the Ministry of Health, which is also charged with the training of health workers. Management duties are delegated from the Ministry of Health to subordinate agencies in the Soviet Union's republics, provinces, and regions down to local neighborhoods and rural areas. Most of the population receives health care at polyclinics located in cities or in rural health centers. A particular health practitioner will be responsible for a designated number of people. A physician who gives primary care, for example, will be assigned about 2,000 people on the basis of what district they live in. Priority of care in the Soviet Union goes to industrial workers and children.

The Soviet Union had about 32.5 physicians per 10,000 people in 1975, which is approximately twice the proportion found in the United States. Soviet doctors also work fewer hours, about six hours a day, because medicine is considered to be a highly stressful occupation. The majority of Soviet physicians are women, a trend which holds true for other health workers as well. The reason for this is apparently not so much the result of any government policy, but because Soviet men have traditionally been more attracted to other fields such as engineering. Soviet doctors do enjoy some status and prestige, yet the highest prestige in Soviet society goes to such occupations as airline pilots. Soviet doctors are all paid salaries by the state that differ according to training, skill, seniority, and level of responsibility. Salaries are in the same range as those paid to high school teachers and skilled manual workers; physicians are not among the best-paid professionals

[10] Ezra F. Vogel, *Japan as Number One* (Cambridge: Harvard University Press, 1979), pp. 197–198.

in the Soviet Union. Physicians are supported in their work by large numbers of nurses and *feldshers*, who are similar in training and duties to physician's assistants and nurse practitioners in the United States. The Soviet Union did not abolish private medical care after the 1917 Revolution, but private medicine died out once health services were available to the general population following massive training programs for physicians and other health workers, which continue to this day. Nevertheless, Soviet citizens do not show a striking advantage in levels of health as compared to citizens of other advanced societies. Life expectancy for Soviet males, for instance, was 66.5 years and for females was 74.3 years in 1975. These are lower averages than any of the countries shown in Table 9–4 for 1976.

The People's Republic of China

In ancient China, a doctor was paid to keep patients well. If a person became sick, the doctor was supposed to pay the patient. And, if the patient died, a lamp was hung outside the doctor's home as a warning to other patients. This method is, of course, no longer employed today, but a strong sense of social responsibility still pervades contemporary Chinese medical practice. That responsibility has not always been present in Chinese history, however. Prior to the 1949 Revolution, there were few Western trained physicians in China and these doctors generally lived in major cities where they commanded high fees for their work. Except for a few missionary doctors in the countryside, the bulk of the Chinese population received medical care from folk practitioners and shamans. There was a heavy death toll from disease, poor sanitation, and widespread ignorance about health matters. In 1949, the average life expectancy of a Chinese was only thirty-two years.

Improvement in health became one of the major goals of the Red Chinese government after it came to power following the civil war with Nationalist forces. One of the first public health measures was the "Patriotic Health Movement," in which millions of Chinese killed flies, removed trash, and worked to improve sanitation. Two other measures were also important. First, traditional Chinese medicine was revived, featuring the use of herbal medicines and techniques like acupuncture, in which pain is controlled by the insertion of needles into certain designated points in the body. Even though its therapeutic value is not fully understood, traditional Chinese medicine is still used today throughout China with considerable effectiveness for many health problems. Often traditional medicine is used in conjunction with Western medicine, and while Chinese physicians are trained largely in either the traditional or the Western approach, all receive some training in both disciplines. Second, the so-called barefoot doctors movement was begun, in which over 150,000 paramedical personnel were trained in rudimentary medicine and sent to rural areas to provide basic medical treatment and assist in efforts at preventive medicine and public health. Through this movement, the majority of the population was able to have at least some routine access to medical care.

Red China's attempts at improving its health care system suffered a serious setback during the Cultural Revolution of 1966–1977. The Cultural

Revolution was intended by China's leaders to be a mass movement of the people that would expose corruption and rid the government of unnecessary bureaucracy. Many influential people were subjected to severe public criticism and even persecuted by revolutionary groups such as the Red Guards, whose membership included thousands of young students. Schools and universities were closed as young people abandoned their studies to participate in revolutionary activities. Factions developed within the movement itself, and this period of Chinese history is marked with great confusion as power struggles were waged even within the hierarchy of the government and the Communist Party. There was a widespread disruption of work and education, and many people lost their lives in the turmoil that followed. For nearly four years, there was virtually no medical research or training of medical students. Thousands of doctors were forced to leave their positions and were sent into the countryside to work with peasants in agricultural communes. When medical education was resumed in 1970, the time for training was cut from eight years after high school to three years, with emphasis on practical and applied medicine. Almost anyone could gain admission to medical school and few or no examinations were given during training. The quality of Chinese doctors declined accordingly and the old system has now returned. But many valuable years were lost in regard to both medical education and research.

Today an extensive network of health care facilities exists in China. Clinics providing preventive medicine, birth control measures, and first aid are readily available in both rural areas and urban neighborhoods. People with serious illnesses or injuries are quickly referred to district and regional hospitals. Many communes and factories have their own clinics or hospitals. Medical care for workers is paid for by welfare funds which the communes and factories set up with money obtained by the sale of goods and crops. Funds to support public employees and others are derived largely from income at the national level generated by economic production as in the Soviet system. For the individual, medical care is therefore essentially free, except for small charges for food when hospitalized or for some drugs which are generally inexpensive and easily obtained. China is completely self-sufficient in the manufacture of drugs and costs have gone down considerably since 1950.

In 1980, the average life expectancy of a Chinese male had risen to 66.9 years and for females the average was 69.5 years. Acute infectious diseases have been brought under control or eliminated and effective treatment of parasitic diseases has greatly improved the overall health of the Chinese people. Heart disease and cancer are now the major health problems in most parts of the country. By modern standards, medical science in China is still not highly developed and much of its medical technology is outdated. Improvement in health care delivery, however, remains a major goal of the society.

Comparative Health Policy

This review of the organization and social policy of health care in selected major countries suggests that no one nation has an ideal system of dealing with health problems. All nations are faced with rising demands for quality health care in the face of limited resources, and in most countries the high cost of care has presented special problems in achieving a desired outcome. Exact comparisons between nations in terms of the effectiveness of their respective health care delivery systems are difficult because of varying political structures, diet, climate, degree of technological advancement, social commitment to national health care, and cultures, which have an impact on the overall health profile of a particular country. Sweden, for example, appears to have a much more effective approach to the provision of medical care than the United States as measured in terms of infant mortality and life expectancy. Yet Sweden has a much smaller and more homogeneous population than the United States and fewer social class differences. It is much easier for the Swedes to focus on health care and mobilize their financial resources to cope with it. Generally speaking, it can be said that the United States has an overall level of health comparable to that of other industrialized nations.

Yet some obvious worldwide trends seem to be appearing and are likely to have an effect on health care policy in future. These trends are: (1) more attention is being paid to the cost of health care and controls over such costs are beginning to emerge; (2) preventive medical services are receiving increasing emphasis as more attempts are being made to keep well people healthy; (3) efforts are being made to design a more effective administration of large health care systems; and (4) there is more demand and increased responsiveness on the parts of governments and policy makers to provide a health care system that meets national needs. While different countries are taking different approaches to solve health problems, most countries appear to be moving toward a system that will eliminate inequities.

SUMMARY

This chapter has examined the significant social debate regarding the rising cost of health care and the unequal distribution of health services in the United States, which has been a focal point of concern in the interaction between medicine and society. Although organized medicine has consistently opposed social legislation that might affect the fee-for-service system of medical practice and the entrepreneurial role of the physician, the passage of Medicare and Medicaid signified the emergence of public awareness that the medical profession's interests were not always those of the general public. It now appears to be a foregone conclusion that in the near future there will be some form of national health insurance. It is likely, however, that such an insurance plan will not be a radical departure from the past, but will reflect a compromise of medical and public interests.

The health care delivery systems of Sweden, Great Britain, West Germany, Japan, the Soviet Union, and the People's Republic of China were also reviewed. To date, no one nation has achieved an ideal system of providing health care to its citizens.

PART IV

HEALTH
AND SELECTED
SOCIAL PROBLEMS

chapter 10

MENTAL DISORDERS

Mental disorders rank with heart disease, cancer, and accidents as the greatest threats to health for Americans. Fully reliable statistics describing the incidence and prevalence of mental disorders in the United States do not exist, but the best evidence to date suggests that about 15 percent of the American population, about thirty-two million people, suffer from some form of mental illness (HEW, 1978). Because of its immense importance and because of the significant relationship between mental disorder and social conditions, the study of mentally disturbed behavior is a major area of sociological inquiry and analysis.

It is the purpose of this chapter, accordingly, to examine the social processes involved in the onset, experience, and consequences of being mentally ill in American society. The discussion will focus on four selected topics as an introduction to the field: (1) theoretical models of mental disorder; (2) the social epidemiology of mental disorders; and (3) the social process of mental hospitalization—pre-patient, in-patient, and post-patient phases; and (4) community mental health.

THEORETICAL MODELS OF MENTAL DISORDER

Attempts to understand and explain disordered mental behavior and to cope with the psychological and social problems that result from such behavior have been confounded by a pronounced inability to define mental disorder in accurate and scientific terms. Generally, mental disorders are considered a form of deviant behavior. However, as Robert Spitzer and Paul Wilson (1975:827) explain, the lack of consensus among psychiatrists about what actually constitutes a mental disorder concerns three issues: (1) whether a given mental condition is undesirable; (2) the degree of undesirability; and

(3) whether the condition, no matter how undesirable, is a problem properly treated by psychiatry or by some other discipline. Noting that none of the standard psychiatric textbooks and neither the first nor second edition of the American Psychiatric Association's *Diagnostic and Statistical Manual of Mental Disorders* define mental disorder, Spitzer and Wilson (1975:831–833) point out that psychiatrists have worked since the mid-1800s to formulate an objective diagnostic system in an area that is inherently subjective and not amenable to precise explanations of cause and effect that apply to many physical illnesses. Before discussing the five major theoretical approaches to mental disorder—the medical model, the psychoanalytic model, the societal reaction model, the social learning model, and the social stress model—the reader should first take a glimpse at the present classification system employed by psychiatry to conceptualize mental disorders.

Major Types of Mental Disorders

The American Psychiatric Association's *Diagnostic and Statistical Manual of Mental Disorders* (DSM-III) published in 1980 lists the following major classifications of mental disorders:

1. *disorders usually first evident in infancy, childhood, or adolescence* (mental retardation, attention deficit disorder, anxiety disorders of childhood or adolescence, etc.)
2. *organic mental disorders* (brain dysfunction caused by a specific organic disturbance related either to the effects of aging or the ingestion of alcohol or drugs)
3. *substance use disorders* (maladaptive behavior accompanying the use of substances like alcohol or drugs)
4. *schizophrenic disorders* (disturbance in mood, thinking, and behavior, manifested by distortions of reality that include delusions and hallucinations)
5. *paranoid disorders* (strong delusional system of thought emphasizing notions of persecution or jealousy)
6. *affective disorders* (fundamental disturbance in mood consisting of either prolonged depression or elation)
7. *anxiety disorders* (conditions in which anxiety is the main characteristic)
8. *somatoform disorders* (symptoms of physical illness for which there are no demonstrable physical causes but which are apparently due to psychological factors)
9. *dissociative disorders* (sudden and temporary loss of motor behavior, consciousness, or identity)
10. *psychosexual disorders* (sexual dysfunctions caused by psychological factors)
11. *personality disorders* (inflexible, maladaptive patterns of behavior that pertain to perceiving and thinking about the social environment and one's own self in relation to that environment in such a way that behavior is impaired; manifested as personality traits and seldom results in hospitalization)

The Medical Model

The medical model conceives of mental disorder as a disease or disease-like entity that can be treated through medical means. It seeks to attribute all mental dysfunctions to physiological, biochemical, or genetic causes. The medical model can be said to have originated from the efforts of physicians during the Renaissance and post-Renaissance to combat the notion, prevalent during the Middle Ages, that mental disorder was caused by supernatural forces: the devil, demons, and spirits of the underworld. People exhibiting bizarre or unorthodox behavior were often considered to be possessed by or under the influence of the devil. Many of these people were persecuted and even put to death because of strong popular beliefs in demonology and witchcraft, when in actuality they were nonconformists, victims of religious persecution, or were suffering from a mental disorder.

Yet by the end of the seventeenth century, considerable progress had been made by the medical profession in separating explanations of mental disorder from the realm of theology and placing them instead within the field of medicine. Physicians looked to the study of human anatomy for evidence that abnormal behavior was caused by pathological organic processes within the body, but with exceptions, such as syphilis of the brain, such evidence was not forthcoming. Nevertheless, in the latter half of the nineteenth century the idea that mental disorders were caused by mental diseases had been widely accepted by the medical profession, despite the lack of proof to support this assumption. Since physicians were held responsible for the treatment of mental disorders, their views were generally shared by the lay public.

However, in the twentieth century, it has become clear that most mental disorders cannot be attributed to physiological factors. As Spitzer and Wilson (1975:826–827) note, most psychiatric conditions do not meet the four presumed criteria for a physiological dysfunction: (1) having a specific etiology (such as a germ); (2) being qualitatively different from some aspect of normal functioning; (3) showing a demonstrable physical change; and (4) being internal processes which, when once initiated, proceed somewhat independently of environmental conditions outside the body.

In defense of the medical model as it applies to mental disorder, Spitzer and Wilson point out that some physical disorders, such as essential hypertension, endocrine disorders, and vitamin deficiencies, likewise fail to meet all the criteria for the medical model and that these disorders are treatable through medical means. They argue that the appropriateness of the medical model cannot be derived from the requirements of logic but should be based upon how well the model works in practice. And even when it works poorly, they insist that it should not be abandoned until another model is shown to be more effective.

In some situations, the medical model has proven effective. Several studies have shown, for example, that the use of psychoactive drugs like the phenothiazines has promoted greater improvement among mental hospital in-patients than among similar patients administered a placebo or given no treatment at all (Ray, 1978). Furthermore, the introduction of psychoactive drugs into psychiatric treatment programs on a large scale in the mid-1950s has been regarded as the major factor in the decline of the United States mental hospital population. Prior to that time, the mental in-patient population in this country had been steadily increasing.

In addition, current research on brain chemicals, focusing upon those compounds responsible for neurotransmission, has shown that an increase in the supply of norepinephrine (believed important in the control of emotions) can have a significant effect on increasing the rate of recovery from the depressive disorders. Haloperidol, chlorpromazine, and the tranquilizing drugs of the phenothiazine group have been found to be effective in the treatment of schizophrenia. These latter drugs apparently are able to block the action of dopamine, another neurotransmitter, whose hyperactivity is thought to be important in the production of paranoid delusions and auditory hallucinations.

Other research in the area of behavior genetics has produced strong evidence that genetic factors are important in the transmission of schizophrenia, thus providing an explanation of why certain people appear to be prone to schizophrenia and why schizophrenia tends to be prevalent in certain families and not in others. The exact genetic factors involved in this process are not fully understood at present, and it is also not known what conditions actually "trigger" schizophrenia in a genetically susceptible person, but the evidence does indicate that a genetic mechanism has something to do with the onset of schizophrenia in some individuals (Kohn, 1974; Kety, 1975; Rainer, 1975; Gershon, 1979).

While such research efforts as these offer considerable promise for the understanding and treatment of mental disorders, the emphasis of the medical model on drug therapy can be severely criticized. This approach, as Albert Bandura (1969:16) has explained, has "led to heavy reliance upon physical and chemical intervention, unremitting search for drugs as quick remedies for interpersonal problems, and long-term neglect of social variables as influential determinants of deviant response patterns." Therefore, while they may provide an effective short-term solution to many mental problems, drugs obviously cannot change social situations that act to precipitate a mental disorder. Studies of patients diagnosed as acute schizophrenics have shown that drug therapy provides better short-term results in the hospital setting than psychotherapy alone, and that treatment by drugs combined with effective planning for the patient's future after discharge from the hospital is more effective than drugs alone; after discharge, however, psychotherapy, public health nursing, and social case work may be more effective than drug therapy (May, 1975:972).

Despite its inadequacies, the medical model of mental disorder has been and continues to be a pervasive influence on the practice of psychiatry. This should not be too surprising since all psychiatrists are first trained as medical doctors and are thereby socialized into a medical perspective. The medical profession, of course, regards medical training as the optimal preparation for working with mentally disturbed persons.

The Psychoanalytic Model

The psychoanalytic approach to mental problems is analogous to the medical model in that it also focuses attention on internal factors that affect the human being. In its concern with psychic rather than physiological conditions, however, the psychoanalytic model views human beings as driven in a seemingly irrational manner by powerful internal forces. Not only is the individual unable to control these forces, but he or she is even unaware of their existence.

The psychoanalytic model is based upon the work of Sigmund Freud (1856–1939), who lived most of his life in Vienna, and upon the work of others whom he influenced, such as Erik Erikson, Carl Jung, Alfred Adler, Adolf Meyer, Karen Horney, Otto Rank, and Wilhelm Reich—to name only a few of the important figures in psychoanalytic literature. The scope of this chapter does not permit an extensive discussion of Freud's theories, which psychoanalysts regard as the most comprehensive and profound explanation of human behavior (Meissner et al., 1975) and which many behavioral scientists, particularly sociologists, view as interesting, but theoretically incorrect (Swanson, 1972). Despite conflicting assessments of Freud's life work, the reader should be aware that the psychoanalytic approach has dominated the training and practice of psychiatry in that it constitutes a fundamental aspect of psychiatric terminology, ideology, and understanding of human behavior.

Freud's Concept of the Personality.   Briefly stated, Freud views the human organism as a complicated energy system with all of the energy needed to perform the work of the personality being obtained from instincts, which Freud defines as mental stimuli arising from within the organism itself. However, instincts are seen as a special type of stimulus because they do not have a single or momentary impact, but are a constant force within the personality. The *id*, one of the three major components in Freud's structure of the personality, functions as the discharger of any energy or tension brought about by internal or external stimulation. It is guided by the primary process which produces a memory image of the tension-reducing object. The id uses its energy for instinctual gratification by fulfilling the pleasure principle (avoiding pain and finding pleasure) through the means of reflex action—eating, having sex, wish fulfillment.

The failure of the id to obtain satisfaction gives rise to the *ego*, the second major part of the personality, which represents the energizing of new processes of memory, judgment, perception, and reason that are intended to bring harmony to a person's psychological system by synchronizing the subjective inner world with the objective outer world of social reality. The ego is governed by the reality principle, whose function is to postpone the release of energy until the actual object has been located that will satisfy the need; the ego tolerates or opposes tension until it can be discharged by an appropriate form of behavior. Thus, to the primary process of memory is added the secondary process of finding the correct solution (reality) through thought and reason. Sometimes the solution is not found until various realities have been tested and discovered to provide suitable fulfillment. Hence, the ego is primarily a product of interaction with the external environment.

The third major aspect of the personality, the *superego*, can be described as the moral or judicial branch of the personality. Freud hypothesizes that the superego evolves from the ego as the child assimilates the moral authority of his or her parents by patterning behavior after the parents' own overt behavior or motives and the parents' aspirations for the child. The internalization of parental values in the child is accomplished through fear of punishment and desire for parental approval, which cause the child to control his or her own behavior in accordance with the wishes of the parents. The super-ego represents what is ideal rather than what is real, and its aim is to strive for perfection instead of reality (the function of the ego) or pleasure (the function of the id). Through its two subsystems, the ego-ideal and the conscience, the superego has the power both to reward and to punish the organism psychologically through feelings of pride (ego-ideal) or of guilt and inferiority (conscience).

Seen in its basic form, Freud's concept of the personality is a system of psychic energy consisting of the id striving for pleasure in order to satisfy fundamental instincts and the superego striving for perfection while leaving the ego to balance the two drives with a sense of reality. Obviously, the personality would be maladjusted should the ego fail and either the id or the superego become dominant.

Psychosexual Development and Adult Ego Defense. A basic premise of psychoanalytic theory is that "the child is psychologically father to the adult." What Freud means by this is that the events of infancy and childhood persist in the personality throughout all subsequent life. The impairment of adult behavior can therefore be systematically traced to early childhood experiences, particularly the manner in which sexually oriented urges for bodily pleasure were resolved by the parents during the oral, anal, phallic, latency, and genital stages of psychosexual development. These stages last from birth through adolescence and present the child with a series of developmental crises such as obtaining oral gratification, developing trust and a sense of external reality, becoming toilet trained, acquiring the appropriate sex role identity, and gaining a sense of social competency. Successful resolution of these tasks results in a mature adult.

Freud's concept of ego defense is based upon the premise that at each stage of psychosexual development the ego builds up appropriate defense mechanisms to defend against the conflicts, anxieties, and frustrations that disturb normal psychological functioning. The ego is responsible for this defense because, as the personality's center of narcissism or self-love, it attempts to escape from any situation that threatens its sense of well-being and integrity. Threats that summon up the ego's defenses come from essentially three sources: (1) the id as it tries to overwhelm the ego with pressure for instinctual gratification, (2) the superego as it attempts to punish the ego through feelings of guilt, and (3) external danger perceived as being directed toward the ego. All ego defense mechanisms operate at an unconscious level and are activated on a more or less automatic basis; therefore, the individual is not even aware of their existence. Some of the most common ego defense mechanisms are sublimation, repression, projection, denial, rationalization, regression, and reaction formation.

Psychoanalysis and Psychoanalytic Therapy. According to psychoanalytic theory, emotional problems are likely to be revealed in one of four general ways. The person (1) develops a personality disorder (displaces conflicts toward the external world), (2) becomes neurotic (develops excessive ego defenses), (3) develops a psychophysiologic disorder (tension is experienced within the body and eventually produces an organic pathology), or (4) becomes psychotic (the ego disintegrates with a loss of the ability to cope with reality).

The forms of treatment used to eliminate or reduce the effects of unconscious pressures upon the personality are psychoanalysis and psychoanalytic therapy. Psychoanalysis is a one-to-one relationship between the therapist and the patient which utilizes free association as its primary technique. In free association the patient is encouraged to say whatever comes to mind, while the analyst ensures that the sequence of the undirected thought remains unchanged and that the patient does not withhold any information, no matter how trivial or distressing. Psychoanalysis is a lengthy process and takes about two to five years to complete, but its proponents believe that sooner or later the patient will direct the underlying disorder toward the therapist in a process known as transference. Once this happens and the unconscious tendencies are revealed, the patient can be made aware of the source of the problem and counseled upon ways to deal effectively with it.

Psychoanalysis is used most often with patients who are suffering from anxiety and who have some ego strength. Besides being time-consuming, it is expensive and does not lend itself to the treatment of large numbers of patients simultaneously. In addition, there is evidence that anxiety tends to be self-limiting, that psychoanalysis is no more successful than other psychotherapeutic methods, and that recovery obtained through ordinary life experiences and nonspecific treatment may work as well for anxiety as all other forms of psychotherapy, including psychoanalysis (Eysenck, 1961).

Psychoanalytic therapy is a modified form of psychoanalysis. The major difference is that psychoanalytic therapies focus on current conflicts instead of attempting to work through the entire history of a person's psychosexual development; however, prior to treatment, an extensive psychiatric diagnosis seeks to obtain as much information as possible about the patient's history. This therapy also involves a moderately superficial transference reaction and relies more upon interviewing and discussion than upon free association. The principal types of psychoanalytic therapy are insight therapy (resolution of selected conflicts), relationship therapy (assisting growth of an immature personality), and supportive therapy (assistance in adjusting to difficult situations).[1]

Assessment of the Psychoanalytic Model. One of the most striking criticisms of the psychoanalytic model is that it is based largely upon myth. Advocates of the model are required to accept as dogma the unproven assumptions of Freudian thought in much the same way that people living in the Middle Ages accepted on faith the idea that mental disorder was caused

[1] Another type of treatment influenced by the psychoanalytic model includes group therapy. Group therapy is popular in the United States and consists of gathering selected mentally disordered patients together with a trained therapist for the purpose of the patients helping each other to confront problems and achieve personality change. Group therapy emphasizes values of rugged individualism and a collective approach to problems, while at the same time allowing for the expression of deviant behavior. There are many different types of group therapy, but most of them rely on a psychoanalytic perspective (Sadock, 1975).

by the devil. There is no evidence that the human personality has a tripartite structure consisting of an id, ego, and superego. A second major criticism of the psychoanalytic model is that it portrays human beings as being propelled by instincts without taking into account the individual's ability to will his or her own behavior. Some behavioral scientists argue, for example, that the mind is not a structure but a process. This concept arises from the unique human ability to engage in reflexive thinking, an ability that makes possible the control and organization of conduct by the individual in relation to the environment. Third, most research does not support the view that "the child is psychologically father to the adult." There is no conclusive evidence linking personality problems of adults with specific experiences of pleasure or frustration during a particular developmental stage of childhood. Fourth, the psychoanalytic approach has been accused of underemphasizing the importance of cognitive development and overemphasizing emotional development. Alfred Lindesmith and his associates (1975:319) point out that the separation of emotional experience from cognition neglects "the fact that emotional experiences do not exist as pure states, but are shot through with cognitive elements." And the fifth major criticism of psychoanalytic theory is that it is vague, difficult to test empirically, and does not lend itself to predictive assessments. For instance, it does not offer any guidance to parents about what they can do to protect their children from experiencing an inadequate psychosexual development in advance of that development.

Why then has the psychoanalytic perspective been so influential? Primarily for two reasons: First, no other theoretical approach has provided so many insights into the development and functioning of the human personality.[2] Even though the central propositions of psychoanalytic theory are not empirically verifiable, neither are many of the theories of the classic masters of sociological thought—Emile Durkheim, George Herbert Mead, Georg Simmel, and Max Weber among others—or, ultimately, other branches of human behavior. "Freud is provocative," states Guy Swanson (1972:41), "because he provides a rich set of differentiations readily interpretable as variations in mind which, in turn, are particularly significant consequences of social organization's impact on individuals." Furthermore, psychoanalytic theory proposes explanations for some of the subtle features of human behavior that have been overlooked elsewhere in psychology and addresses itself to the presence of unconscious influences on the individual.

Second, psychoanalytic theory is important because it offers a model that is inseparable from physiological concepts and is therefore an ideal psychology for the physician. It provides the physician with an objective structure of the personality and a prescribed mode of treatment, as well as a nosology by which physicians can communicate about, attempt to control, and comprehend mental disorders. In the absence of other models that can be proven more effective *when applied to the care and treatment of patients*, the quasimedical psychoanalytic model and the medical model dominate the practice of psychiatry.

---

[2] For a more comprehensive discussion of Freud's work, see Freud, 1953–1966; Meissner et al., 1975.

The Societal Reaction Model

Szasz: The Myth of Mental Illness.   The societal reaction model of mental disorder is derived from the suggestion by Thomas Szasz that mental illness is clearly not an "illness" and should not be regarded as such. In his book *The Myth of Mental Illness* (1974), Szasz proposed the following argument: (1) only symptoms with demonstrable physical lesions qualify as evidence of disease; (2) physical symptoms are objective and independent of sociocultural norms, but mental symptoms are subjective and dependent on sociocultural norms; (3) mental symptoms result from problems in living; therefore, (4) mental disorders are not diseases, but are conflicts resulting from differing social values that the medical profession disguises as illnesses through the use of medical terminology.

For example, Szasz says that a man's belief that he is Napoleon or is being persecuted by communists cannot be explained by a defect or disease of the nervous system. Statements such as these are considered to be symptoms of a mental disorder only if the observer (the audience) believes that the patient is not Napoleon or is not being persecuted by the communists. Thus, the statement that X is a symptom of a mental disorder involves rendering a social judgment. The observer must match the person's ideas and beliefs with those held by the observer and the rest of society. In other words, a person's behavior is judged by how well his or her actions "fit" a concept of normality held by a social audience. It is upon this basis then that Szasz insists that mental illness cannot be defined in a medical context. Mental illness should be defined within a social and ethical context, with psychiatrists recognizing that in actual practice they are dealing with problems in living rather than illnesses.

In rebuttal, David Ausubel (1961) has disputed Szasz's perspective by arguing that (1) mental symptoms do not have to be physical lesions to be defined as a disease (subjective pain, for instance, can be regarded as a disease state); (2) psychological symptoms can be classified as evidence of disease if they impair the personality and adversely affect behavior; (3) there is no contradiction in regarding psychological symptoms both as evidence of illness *and* problems in living; and (4) deviant behavior (such as engaging in an immoral act) and mental illness are clearly different types of conditions.

As a result, Szasz's argument is regarded by many psychiatrists as representing a radical position in psychiatry—interesting but not terribly relevant to actual psychiatric practice, since it is not more useful in treating mental disorders than the medical model Szasz attacked (Spitzer and Wilson, 1975). However, among behavioral scientists and laypersons who object to the medical orientation toward mental disorder, and especially among sociologists who subscribe to the approach of labeling theory, Szasz's work has become very influential.

Scheff: A Societal Reaction Theory of Mental Disorder.   The leading spokesman of the societal reaction or labeling theory approach to mental disorder in sociology is Thomas Scheff (1966, 1974, 1975). Scheff (1966) agrees with Szasz that the social situation is of primary importance in understanding mental disorders; he further suggests that social stereotypes profoundly shape the symptoms of mental disorder in American society. Scheff maintains that the stereotyped image of mental disorder is learned in early childhood. The meaning of "crazy" is grasped by grade school children and becomes part of our culture, as illustrated by the general understanding of phrases like "The boogie man will get you." Scheff goes on to point out that the cultural stereotype of insanity stays with us even in adulthood and is continually reinforced through social interaction; in fact, it is often the basis for our manner of reacting to people who have already been labeled insane. Furthermore, this stereotype is available to the patient and becomes part of the patient's orientation for guiding his or her own "crazy" behavior. Thus, in brief, Scheff considers mental disorder a social role whose behavior conforms to society's expectations about people who are "crazy."

Scheff argues that for various reasons some people will occasionally engage in residual rule-breaking. Residual rule-breaking is based upon the idea that most social conventions are fairly clear-cut. Violations of these social conventions tend to be regarded as violations of morality—people who kill are murderers, people who steal are thieves, people who think they are better than others are called snobs. But Scheff says there is a residual area of social convention that goes beyond just violating norms and is assumed to be so natural that it is part of "human nature." These residual social conventions include such behaviors as looking at the person you are talking to or responding to someone who calls your name. To violate these residual norms, that is, to act "unnatural," is to do something that is very disturbing. People can understand why someone would kill under certain circumstances, like a war, or why someone might steal or be a snob, but to break residual rules is considered to be doing something for which there may be no other explanation than a mental disorder.

Depending upon certain contingencies, such as the identity of the rule breaker, the rule broken, and the social context in which the rule-breaking behavior takes place, the residual rule breaker may be publicly labeled as being "mentally ill." Once a person has been so labeled, society reacts to stabilize the abnormal behavior. The process of stability results from the stereotype of mental disorder, learned and culturally reinforced since childhood, which governs the expectations about being "mentally ill" both for the rule breaker and for the social audience. The rule breaker is thus constrained to behave as a crazy person in order to conform to the popular conception. Also, once labeled as mentally ill, the rule breaker is rewarded for playing the stereotyped deviant role because, as will be discussed, one of the first actions of psychotherapy in mental hospitals is to get patients to recognize that they are mentally ill and need help. If patients conform to the stereotype of what their mental problems are supposed to represent, then they are regarded as "good" patients. If the labeled person tries to return to a conventional role instead of accepting the stereotyped deviant role, he or she is punished for it; witness the 1972 case of a U.S. Senator who was not allowed to continue as a vice-presidential candidate after it was publicly disclosed that he had once been under psychiatric care. Once the labeling of a person as deviant (in this case, being mentally ill) has taken place and society responds to the person in accordance with that particular label, Scheff contends that a deviant has been created by society. And this process is confirmed for both society and the individual when the person accepts the label of mental illness as correct. Through the agency of labeling, such a person "is launched on a career of 'chronic' mental illness" (Scheff, 1975:10).

In a subsequent article, Scheff (1974) refuted criticism from Walter Gove (1970) that certain existing studies did not clearly support Scheff's explanation of mental illness. Scheff showed that a majority of studies dealing explicitly with the societal reaction or labeling theory approach did provide supportive evidence of his views. Scheff's defense, however, rested on the assumpton that only those studies that explicitly test labeling theory can provide relevant evidence, and this may not necessarily be a correct assumption (see Gove, 1975). Nevertheless, additional criticisms have been forthcoming that point to serious weaknesses in the labeling theory of mental illness as proposed by Scheff. These criticisms argue (1) that Scheff has not adequately taken into account the implications for labeling theory of recent advances in drug therapy (Gove, 1975), and (2) that a person may not be irreparably stigmatized ("launched on a career of chronic mental illness") by friends and family as a result of once being labeled mentally ill (Gove and Howell, 1974; Clausen and Huffine, 1975; Huffine and Clausen, 1979). Nor for that matter does the labeling theory of mental illness explain what actually causes mental disorders other than societal reaction to residual rule breaking. It likewise fails to offer a systematic model of therapy for mentally disordered people.

The merit of Scheff's work is that it emphasizes the common conceptions of mental disorder shared by people and that these ideas significantly affect the manner in which members of a society regard mental abnormality. This process can thus have very definite social consequences for the person being so labeled.

The Social Learning Model

Another alternative to the medical and psychoanalytic models of mental disorder is the social learning model, based chiefly upon theories of learning and techniques of behavioral conditioning derived from the classical conditioning experiments of Ivan Pavlov and Edward Thorndike. The underlying premise of this model is that social behavior is learned and that what can be learned can also be unlearned and replaced with more appropriate behavior (Bandura, 1969; Brady, 1975). The therapeutic technique of the social learning model, known as behavior modification, emphasizes that treatment should be centered on behavior that is externally observable and measurable. Preferred techniques include those of symptom desensitization (learning to approach feared situations or objects without anxiety), positive reinforcement (reward), aversive conditioning (punishment), extinction (eliminating a stimulus), conditioned avoidance (electric shocks or drugs paired with situational stimuli), and contingency contracting (agreeing with others to engage in certain behavior in return for a similar response).

Social learning theory, like labeling theory, overlooks those mental disorders related to genetic and physiological factors; unlike labeling theory, social learning theory does suggest specific forms of therapy. However, behavior modification appears to be subject to four major limitations. First, there are serious questions as to whether human beings can actually be "conditioned" to the extent that they respond more or less automatically to the play of stimuli upon their cerebral functions. Second, even if such conditioning is possible, there are questions concerning the duration of the effects and their strength in real world, nonclinical settings. Third, behavior modification may not be a totally sufficient form of therapy for many types of mental disorders in which the complexity of the disorder may require much more than just learning new behaviors. And fourth, behavior modification requires that patients be willing and able to learn, have a certain amount of willpower, and recognize and cope with reality at least somewhat consistently—prerequisites many mental patients may not have.

Still it can be argued that behavior modification does have certain strengths. Its grounding in experimental psychology lends itself more readily to verifiable research techniques, and some studies have shown it to be an effective approach (see Bandura, 1969), especially for short-term results and simple symptom configurations such as bedwetting. This therapy may also be more appropriate for the treatment of lower-class people, both because it is less expensive than psychoanalysis and because it does not demand a high degree of self-analysis. Just how effective behavior modification actually is has yet to be determined.

The Social Stress Model

A particularly active line of research, incorporating aspects of both medical and sociological concepts, is found in current investigations of the relationship between mental disorder and social stress. The medical factors in this situation pertain to the possible predisposition of some individuals toward mental disorder when they are psychologically stressed because of genetic inheritance and/or some triggering of biochemical abnormalities. The social factors relevant to this condition arise from the majority of studies on stress, which indicate that most, if not all, stress is socially induced as a result of interaction between people. Thus, the impressive body of evidence accumulated in genetics that supports a genetic role in mental disorder looks to social situations as the determining factors in explaining the activation of these genetic tendencies. "The most likely model of schizophrenic illness," according to Herbert Weiner (1975:887), "is that given a genetic predisposition, which may very likely be polygenic, stressful life events elicit schizophrenia."

Sociological research such as that of Lloyd Rogler and August Hollingshead (1965), which uncovered a series of mutually reinforcing life crises as being the significant difference between schizophrenic and nonschizophrenic lower-class families in Puerto Rico, and M. Harvey Brenner (1973), who traced the relationship between economic downturns and mental hospitalization in New York State for a period of 127 years, lends strong support to a social stress model of mental disorder. Chapter Three (The Interaction of Mind, Body, and Society) contains an extensive discussion of stress research and the reader is invited to review this material, especially the section on life events research, for a fuller understanding of the manner in which stress promotes health problems in general and mental disorder in particular.

Defining Mental Disorder

The intent of this section has been to give an overview of the various definitions of mental disorder based on the competing perspectives of the medical, psychoanalytic, societal reaction, social learning, and social stress models. None of these models provides a satisfactory overall explanation of mental disorder, but if one such model were to be selected for its potential significance for future psychiatric practice, it is likely that model would be the medical model. This is so because the medical profession has high expectations for drug therapy and studies of brain chemistry. This trend seems likely even though such an approach ignores most psychological and sociological correlates of mental disorder and does not adequately deal with the nonchemical causes or the external environments that foster behavioral abnormalities. The psychoanalytic model will also remain some-what influential, though less influential than in the past, because its defini-tions, terms, and conceptualizations still dominate the psychiatric perspec-tive of mental disorder. The social learning and social stress models, perhaps in combination with the medical model, are likely to remain important, but the societal reaction model appears to have the least influence outside sociology itself.

Spitzer's (Spitzer and Wilson, 1975:829) definition of a mental dis-order appears to offer mental health professionals the most realistic assess-ment of such conditions in terms of both adequately explaining and treating them. Spitzer defines mental disorder as follows: (1) it is a condition that is primarily psychological and that alters behavior, including changes in physiological functioning if such changes can be explained by psychological concepts, such as personality, motivation, or conflict; (2) it is a condition which, in its "full-blown" state, is regularly and intrinsically associated with subjective stress, generalized impairment in social functioning, or behavior the person would like to stop voluntarily because it is associated with threats to physical health; and (3) it is a condition distinct from other conditions and responds to treatment.

Of the three criteria described by Spitzer, the first separates psychiatric from nonpsychiatric conditions. The second specifies that the disorder may be recognizable only in a later stage of its development ("full-blown") and that its identification depends on consistent symptomatology ("regularly associated with"). Spitzer also says that the disorder must arise from an inherent condition, and not from the manner in which society reacts to the condition, and that the impairment in functioning not be limited to a single form, such as heterosexual relationships, but include an inability to function in several social contexts ("generalized impairment in social functioning"). Criterion two also includes "behavior one would like to stop voluntarily," for example, compulsive eating or smoking. The third criterion places the definition within the confines of the medical model as a distinct condition that is treatable.

Even though the locus of the pathological condition is defined by Spitzer as existing within the individual, the basis for determining whether or not a person is mentally disordered includes criteria that are distinctly sociological. To a large extent, a finding of generalized impairment in social functioning derives from an understanding of sociological concepts such as norms, roles, and status that set and give meaning to normality in particular social situations. The disruption or disregard of these concepts, like every-day taken-for-granted understanding of how people should conduct them-selves in a particular society or social group, causes a person's mental state to be questioned. Although mental disorder arises not from society's reaction to such a person but from within the person, as Spitzer points out, the expression of one's disordered psychological condition as social behavior ultimately determines the need for psychiatric treatment.

SOCIAL EPIDEMIOLOGY OF MENTAL DISORDERS

One of the major contributions of medical sociology to the practice of psychiatry has been its investigation of the extent of mental illness in the general population and the identification of significant sociodemographic variables. Since many of these studies have focused on patients admitted to psychiatric treatment facilities, they have helped to describe the relationship between social factors and rates of mental disorders. Although studies of admissions to psychiatric treatment programs are important in the planning of such services, rates of patients in treatment fail to indicate the "true" distribution of mental disorders, which includes both treated and untreated cases. In an extensive review of the literature, Bruce and Barbara Dohren-wend (1974; also see Bruce Dohrenwend, 1975) have noted that since 1900 some sixty investigators in eighty different studies conducted in several countries have attempted to assess the "true" prevalence of mental disorders among their respective populations. Most of these studies were based upon large samples of the general public and included few people who had ever been mental patients. Although direct comparisons were difficult because of differences in methodology, cultures, time periods, locations, and contrasting definitions of mental disorder, the most impressive feature of all these studies was the consistent finding of significant relationships between mental disorder and three specific sociodemographic variables: sex, rural versus urban location, and social class. Race, which is often a significant factor in explaining human behavior, is apparently not a strong predictor of mental disorder (see, for example, Warheit et al., 1975).

Sex

The majority of studies of the "true" prevalence of mental disorder by sex clearly indicate (see Dohrenwend and Dohrenwend, 1974, 1976; Bruce Dohrenwend, 1975) that: (1) there are no consistent differences by sex in rates of psychotic symptoms in general and schizophrenia in particular; (2) rates of affective and anxiety disorders are consistently higher for women regardless of time and place; and (3) rates of personality disorders are consistently higher for men regardless of time and place.

Obviously, then, these findings refute contentions that more mental disorder is found among women than men and that changing sex roles in American society promote more mental disorder among women. Instead, as the Dohrenwends indicate, sexual differences are consistent and apparent only in specific types of mental disorders—women being more likely to have manic-depressive psychoses and neuroses, and men being more likely to have personality disorders. Significant also is that these findings apply throughout the twentieth century, regardless of changing sex roles. According to the Dohrenwends, we should

> ... discard undifferentiated, unidimensional concepts of psychiatric disorder and with them false assumptions about whether women or men are more prone to "mental illness." In their place we would substitute an issue posed by the relatively high female rates of neurosis and manic-depressive psychosis, with their possible common denominator of depressive symptomatology, and the relatively high male rates of personality disorders with their possible common denominator of irresponsible and antisocial behavior. The important question then becomes, What is there in the endowments and experiences of men and women that pushes them in these different directions?[3]

Differences by sex in certain types of mental disorders seem to relate to both biological and sociocultural factors. States of depression and neuroses in women may possibly be influenced by hormonal changes in the body, such as those occurring during menstruation and menopause. Research on animals has suggested that the male hormone androgen stimulates aggression (Mazur and Robertson, 1972), while there is limited and inconclusive evidence that the Y (male) sex chromosome is an "aggression" gene. Data supporting such a premise are derived from studies of XYY genotypes (males with an extra male chromosome), who tend to be somewhat over-represented in penal and mental institutions; nevertheless, the number of such individuals is quite small in relation to the total population and the theory is unproven (Hook, 1973).

There is also evidence that the sexes may differ in the way they think, perceive, aspire, daydream, experience anxiety, and play competitive games (Hochschild, 1973). A recent study by Janet Lever (1978) of the complexity of children's play and games found significant differences between the sexes. Using school-playground observations, interviews, written questionnaires, and diary records maintained by the children, Lever studied some 180 predominantly white and middle-class ten- and eleven-year-olds at three schools—two urban and one suburban. Boys' play was found to be more complex than girls' play as illustrated by greater role differentiation, interdependence between players, size of play group, explicitness of goals, number of rules, and team formation. Lever suggests that the boys' games are a valuable learning experience. Boys, more than girls, learn to deal with diversity in group membership in which each person is required to perform a specialized task, to coordinate actions and maintain cohesiveness among group members, to cope with impersonal rules, and to work for collective as well as personal goals. Lever states:

> Team sports furnish the most frequent opportunity to sharpen these social skills. One could elaborate on the lessons learned. The rule structure encourages

---

[3] Bruce P. Dohrenwend and Barbara Snell Dohrenwend, "Sex Differences and Psychiatric Disorder," *American Journal of Sociology*, 81 (May 1976), 1453.

strategic thinking. Team sports also imply experience with clear-cut leadership positions, usually based on universalistic criteria. The group rewards the individual who has improved value skills, a practice which further enhances a sense of confidence based on achievement. Furthermore, through team sports as well as individual matches, boys learn to deal with interpersonal competition in a forthright manner. Boys experience face-to-face confrontations—often opposing a close friend—and must learn to depersonalize the attack. They must practice self-control and sportsmanship; in fact, some of the boys in this study described the greatest lesson in team sports as learning to "keep your cool."

Girls' play and games are very different. They are mostly spontaneous, imaginative, and free of structure or rules. Turntaking activities like jumprope may be played without setting explicit goals. Girls have far less experience with interpersonal competition. The style of their competition is indirect, rather than face-to-face, individual rather than team affiliated. Leadership roles are either missing or randomly filled.

Perhaps most important, girls' play occurs in small groups. These girls report preferring the company of a single best friend to a group of four or more. Often girls mimic primary human relationships instead of playing formal games, or they engage in conversation rather than play anything at all.[4]

The differences in the complexity of the children's play as reported by Lever are most likely due to socialization as much as or more than biological factors. Lever notes that male children are quick to learn that displays of athletic skills earn the praise of adults, especially fathers. Girls, in contrast, may be discouraged from participation in sports in order to avoid the "tomboy" label. Whether the sexes develop different social skills through play in childhood that carry over and influence adult behavior is primarily speculation, as Lever mentions. Nevertheless, the differences in play are striking and are similar to adult behavior patterns for each sex.

In the classroom, girls seem to start out ahead of boys in nearly all subjects, and then fall behind boys in some subjects, beginning in the late high-school years. Studies comparing sex differences in intelligence, for example, show that despite a more or less equal distribution of boys and girls in terms of superior performance, there are substantial differences between the sexes in specific abilities (Boocock, 1972). Males tend to outperform females on mathematical reasoning, judgment, manipulation of spatial relations, and mechanical aptitudes. Females tend to outperform males on vocabulary, verbal fluency, and memorization tasks. Eleanor Maccoby (1966) has found that sex differences in scholastic performance may be attributed to boys' more aggressive and active behavior, whereas girls exhibit greater dependency, anxiety, and passivity. These tendencies could be significantly related to more depression and anxiety disorders among women and to more personality disorders, which are often characterized by active and antisocial behavior, for men. However, whether these behavioral differences between males and females are mostly the result of innate biological qualities or of sociocultural influences is not known.

[4] Janet Lever, "Sex Differences in the Complexity of Children's Play and Games," *American Sociological Review*, 43 (1978), 480–481.

When sociocultural factors are considered, sex-based differences in behavior appear to be the result of socialization into the socially prescribed roles for men and women. Sex-specific behavior in human society is strongly influenced through the process of sex typing, in which boys are taught to be men, and girls to be women, with all that these roles imply in terms of masculine or feminine attributes. The sex role for men clearly offers an advantage in self-direction and professional opportunities, yet may lend itself to increased susceptibility to personality disorders. Conversely, the sex role for women may lend itself to increased depression and anxiety. Walter Gove and Jeannette Tudor (1973), for instance, have summarized some pertinent assumptions concerning the role of adult American women: (1) most women are restricted to a single occupational and social role—that of being a housewife—and this severely limits their sources of gratification; (2) being a housewife is frustrating because it requires limited skill and has low prestige; (3) the role of the housewife is relatively unstructured and invisible; (4) when a woman is employed outside the home, she is typically in a less satisfactory position than a male; and (5) expectations for women are unclear. Thus, we see that to be a housewife is to have limited involvement with people outside the home. The activities themselves also may be boring and lonely for many women. Many married women who work outside the home are viewed as working primarily to supplement the family income rather than as working toward specific career goals. Employed women may also be discriminated against in terms of salaries and promotions when competing with men in the same company. And working wives usually have to maintain the house as well as perform satisfactorily on the job, which, in essence, is tantamount to having two full-time jobs. It may be that working wives are under greater strain than their husbands, although not all studies agree that this is true (Northcott, 1980). Nevertheless, whether in the home or on the job, the lives of women are often dependent on what others (usually men) do; hence they cannot control the possibilities for satisfaction as much as men can.

These sociocultural differences, combined with biological differences, undoubtedly contribute to the varying incidence between men and women of certain mental disorders. The task currently before sociologists, as the Dohrenwends (1976; Bruce Dohrenwend, 1975) point out, is to assist in isolating the relative contributions of male–female biological differences and social differences in those mental disorders in which gender is an important variable.

Rural versus Urban Living

The widely held assumption that the stress of urban living is responsible for high rates of mental disorder and that rural areas are relatively free of such problems is not entirely accurate. In their review of relevant studies, the Dohrenwends (1974; Bruce Dohrenwend, 1975) found that psychoses in general and manic-depressive psychoses in particular are more prevalent in rural areas. Schizophrenia was an important exception in that it appears to be much greater in urban areas. Anxiety and personality disorders are also more common in urban areas.

Although these trends are clearly evident in the bulk of the research investigating the relationship of residence upon mental disorder, it is not at all certain what causes them. The relatively high incidence of manic-depressive psychoses in rural areas may be related to feelings of physical isolation. Schizophrenia, the neuroses, and personality disorders, on the other hand, may be related to the stress of urban living, but this is also a purely speculative conclusion. One of the most significant demographic shifts in the United States during this century has been the move from rural to urban areas, so perhaps some of these rural migrants brought their mental disorders with them to the city. Obviously this would inflate the rate of mental disorder for urban areas. Whatever the exact cause(s) of the urban-rural differences in the proportion of certain mental disorders, the differences seem to be there nonetheless.

Another factor relevant to our discussion of mental disorder in urban areas is the well-established finding that schizophrenia tends to be more prevalent in the inner city (Faris and Dunham, 1939; Eaton, 1974). Studies tracing the ecological distribution of schizophrenia consistently find higher rates of it in the central areas of large cities, and the rates drop significantly as the pattern of schizophrenic residencies is followed to the suburbs and rural areas. This finding is presumably tied to that of social class, with the lower class most likely to be both schizophrenic and residents of the inner city.

Socioeconomic Status

The basic finding of most studies that the highest overall rates of mental disorder are found among members of the lowest socioeconomic group has, according to Bruce Dohrenwend (1975:370), "remained remarkably persistent in the 'true' prevalence studies conducted since the turn of the century." The lower social class has been observed to have both the greatest prevalence of mental disorder in general and personality disorders and schizophrenia in particular. Anxiety and affective disorders, however, tend to be more prevalent among the upper classes (see Dohrenwend and Dohrenwend, 1974; Bruce Dohrenwend, 1975).

Three of the best known studies of the relationship between social class and mental disorder have been those of Robert Faris and H. Warren Dunham (1939), August Hollingshead and Frederick Redlich (1958), and Leo Srole et al. (1962). The first systematic study of the distribution of mental disorder in a community was conducted in Chicago by Faris and Dunham in the mid-1930s. Using large maps to trace the addresses of some 35,000 people who had received psychiatric care from both public and private mental hospitals, Faris and Dunham found that the highest rates for psychoses, especially schizophrenia, were clustered in the slum areas of town. They hypothesized that people living in conditions of poverty were more isolated from "normal" social contacts and therefore more vulnerable to developing a "seclusive" personality, which they believed was the key trait of schizophrenia. Although impaired social relationships are a characteristic of schizophrenia, we know now that they are usually the result of the disorder rather than its cause. Nevertheless, the Faris and Dunham study does point to isolation from significant others as an important factor in the experience of becoming schizophrenic, and the process of isolation apparently becomes more pronounced as the progress of the disorder becomes more advanced.

The Hollingshead and Redlich study was conducted in New Haven, Connecticut, in the 1950s and involved a comparison of public and private mental patients with a sample of the general nonpatient population. The study employed Hollingshead and Redlich's influential Index of Social Position, which correlated race, ethnicity, and religion with location of residence, occupation, and education to determine a person's socioeconomic status. The study found that upper- and upper-middle-class people were more aware of psychological problems and more perceptive of conflict and the nature of personal difficulties. This was in direct contrast to lower-class people, who were much slower to attribute personal problems to mental disorder or to label someone as "crazy" because of the serious consequences of such a label (arrest, confinement in a mental hospital). This study likewise found that the lower the social class, the greater the prevalence of mental disorder. Particularly significant was the finding that the prevalence of schizophrenia was over eleven times greater in the lower class than in the upper class.

The Srole study, also conducted in the 1950s, involved an investigation of the "true" prevalence of mental disorder among a cross-section of people living in the midtown Manhattan area of New York City. 1,660 people were interviewed and data were obtained on their personal background, past history of psychopathology and psychotherapy, and their acknowledgment of current symptoms of mental disorder. The respondents were also rated by the interviewer in terms of their level of tension at the start of the interview. All of the information was then provided to a team of psychiatrists who assessed the respondent's psychiatric status. Once again mental disorders were found to be more prevalent among the lower class than among the other socioeconomic groups. In addition, it was found that those people who were socially upward mobile showed fewer signs of emotional disturbances than those remaining at the same socioeconomic level or who were downwardly mobile.

The Faris and Dunham study in Chicago and the Hollingshead and Redlich study in New Haven can, of course, be criticized for investigating only treated cases of mental disorder, and the midtown Manhattan study of Srole and associates can be faulted for relying upon subjective and somewhat incomplete judgments by psychiatrists. Yet the results of these three studies relating mental disorder to social class position have been confirmed by several other investigators to the extent that the trend is clear: there is greater prevalence of mental disorder among the lower class. However, once having established this point, it is necessary to move beyond a description of what seems to exist to an explanation of why it exists.

Three rationales have generally been advanced to explain this significant relationship. First is the *genetic* explanation, which holds that there is a greater predisposition to mental disorders among the lower social classes as a result of genetic inheritance. But recent studies of monozygotic twins and adopted twins have shown that genetics alone cannot account for the onset of schizophrenia, a mental disorder prevalent among the lower classes. It is therefore apparent that, while genetic mechanisms are significant, sociocultural factors are also important (Dohrenwend, 1975; Kohn, 1972, 1974). Second is the *social stress* explanation, which notes that members of the lower class are subjected to greater stress as a result of living in a deprived life situation and having to cope with this deprivation with fewer resources. This explanation may also contribute much to our understanding of mental disorders if its validity can be determined. However, in a review of studies of individual reactions to extremely stressful situations (war and natural disasters) and a review of studies dealing with the relationship between mental disorder and ordinary stressful life events, Barbara Dohrenwend (1975) has indicated that the existing evidence is inconclusive. Third is the *social selection* explanation, which maintains that more mental disorder is located in the lower class because mentally ill people tend to "drift" downward in the social structure (the "drift" hypothesis) or, conversely, mentally healthy individuals in the lower class tend to be upwardly mobile, thus leaving behind a "residue" of mentally ill (the "residue" hypothesis). While there is evidence to support a relationship between social mobility and mental disorder (see Srole et al., 1962; Kohn, 1972, 1974; Bruce Dohrenwend, 1975), social mobility in itself does not seem to be a fully adequate explanation. As Melvin Kohn explains in the case of schizophrenia, the weight of the evidence

> . . . clearly indicates either that schizophrenic individuals have been no more downwardly mobile (in fact, no less upwardly mobile) than other people from the same social backgrounds, or at minimum, that the degree of downward mobility is insufficient to explain the high concentration of schizophrenia in the lowest socioeconomic strata.[5]

The social selection approach, along with the genetic and social stress explanations, are all very likely contributing factors in the prevalence of mental disorder among the lower classes. Considered separately, none of these hypotheses has at present sufficient explanatory power, but all appear to warrant serious consideration in future research.

Kohn's (1974) alternative explanation to the class–schizophrenia relationship appears to be a highly promising line of inquiry. His hypothesis is that the constricted conditions of life experienced by people in the lower socioeconomic classes encourages the formation of limited and rigid conceptions of social reality that inhibit such people's ability to deal effectively with problems and stress. His earlier research (Kohn, 1969) noted that the lower a person's social class position, the more likely that person was to value conformity to external authority and to believe that such conformity was all that his or her own capacities and external resources would allow. The social-psychological orientation of the lower-class person was therefore one that appeared to feature a rigidly conservative view of life involving fear, distrust, and "a fatalistic belief that one is at the mercy of forces and people beyond one's control, often, beyond one's understanding" (Kohn, 1974:129).

[5] Melvin L. Kohn, "Social Class and Schizophrenia: A Critical Review and a Reformulation," in *Explorations in Psychiatric Sociology*, P. Roman and H. Trice (eds.) (Philadelphia: F. A. Davis, 1974), p. 118.

Kohn does not argue that this orientation is held by all members of the lower class or that it is a philosophy to which lower-class people subscribe exclusively, but simply that the perception of social reality he has described is more prevalent in the lower class. Kohn suggests that the family is particularly important in this scheme because of its role in transmitting its unique conception of social reality to the young. By transmitting a learned conception of reality that is too limited and too rigid to deal effectively with complex and changing stress-inducing situations, lower-class families may well contribute to the onset of schizophrenia among those genetically susceptible persons who experience great stress.

Ronald Kessler (1979), however, claims that lower-class people are more flexible and less rigid than upper-class people in dealing with comparable stresses. This, of course, goes against Kohn's thesis that the lower class has a more rigid outlook. Kessler's argument is that the poor are more flexible but go under because they are hit much harder with more stress. "The greater exposure of the poor to stressful experiences," says Kessler (1979:265), "cancels out their relative advantage in effectively buffering stress impacts."

Whether or not lower-class people have more rigid or more flexible patterns of coping with stress is unresolved. The crucial variable appears to be the amount of personal resources, social or economic, available to contend with stressful conditions—a situation that clearly goes against the poor (see, for example, Rushing, 1978). Socialization is still important because it is the means by which the young are taught to perceive social reality and use whatever resources they have to reduce threats to their well-being. Therefore, it is apparent that future investigations of social class and schizophrenia should look at the social psychology that underlies class-based conceptions of social reality. This suggestion appears to be highly appropriate when it is remembered that (1) most schizophrenia occurs in the lower class, (2) the lower class contends with the harshest and most discomforting forms of social reality, and (3) schizophrenia is a mental disorder characterized by *withdrawal from reality*, accompanied by delusions, hallucinations, ambivalence, and bizarre activity.

THE SOCIAL PROCESS OF MENTAL HOSPITALIZATION

Another focal point of medical sociology's investigation into mental disorders has been the examination of the social processes by which an individual becomes committed to a mental institution and the effect of this experience upon the patient. This literature will be discussed from the standpoint of the pre-patient, in-patient, and post-patient phases of hospitalization.

The Pre-patient Phase

The initial decision that a particular person is mentally disordered usually takes place within the context of the social groups such as family or friends in which that person participates. The lack of clear guidelines for defining mental illness, both among mental health professionals and laypersons in the United States often creates a problem. Generally a person is started on the route to becoming defined as "mentally ill" when that person's inability to respond "normally" in a given situation becomes a consistent pattern of behavior; at other times the person himself or herself recognizes a dysfunction when comparing his or her performance or behavior with that of others. Usually, however, the person's behavior is defined as abnormal by others in the community; the difficulty here is not only the lack of objective guidelines, but also the fact that there are vast differences among people, both individually and as a group, in their capacity to tolerate difficult behavior. The strong tendency of others, particularly relatives, to "normalize" difficult behavior patterns through rationalization until those patterns can no longer be tolerated is a major reason why delay in psychiatric treatment often occurs.

The reluctance to label a family member as having a mental problem is aptly illustrated in studies of the wives and husbands of mental patients. M. Yarrow and associates (1955), in their study of the process by which wives attempted to cope with their husband's mental illness, found that it usually involved five major stages: (1) an initial recognition that the husband's behavior was not understandable or was unacceptable; (2) the wife would adjust her own expectations about her husband to account for his deviant responses; (3) the wife's interpretation of the husband would vary, sometimes seeing the husband as normal and at other times abnormal; (4) the wife would try to adapt to the husband's behavior and would become very defensive about it with other people; and (5) finally the wife would no longer be able to sustain a definition of normality or be unable to cope with the husband's behavior. The fifth stage would generally be the prelude to intervention by outside authorities.

A study by Harold Sampson and associates (1964) found that husbands displayed a somewhat similar series of responses to their wife's abnormal behavior. First was the development of a pattern of accommodation by the husband to the wife's behavior. Often a husband would simply withdraw from his wife and develop new interests elsewhere—another woman, a second job, a hobby, or sports. Second, this pattern of accommodation would eventually be disrupted as the pattern of withdrawal by the husband became intolerable to one or both of the parties involved. Either the husband would suggest that the wife seek help or the wife would realize that she could not go on as things were. Sometimes the husband would just get rid of the "problem" by divorcing his wife. This was particularly true for men about the age of forty who looked at the future and decided they did not want to spend the remainder of their active years with their present spouse. Some husbands would develop a pattern of resistance to their wife's demands for involvement. These husbands would either appear indifferent if the wife sought help from a minister or psychiatrist or, if other people became interested in their wife's problems, they would usually respond negatively. Often the husband did not become involved as a responsible party in the wife's mental condition until the wife was actually hospitalized, and usually this event would result from some extreme act of deviance on the part of the wife, such as burning the house down, that called attention to her needs.

Sampson and associates point out that many mental patients come to the attention of mental health professionals only during the course of an unmanageable crisis. Without such an emergency, the wife's problem was likely to continue to be ignored. This situation is consistent with Howard Becker's (1973) assertion that many people are willing to tolerate deviance or ignore it until someone actually makes a complaint about it and forces society to act against the deviant.

Erving Goffman (1961) explains that when a person is launched on a "career" of being a mental patient, that career involves a round of agents and agencies that mark the progress of the individual's passage from the status of a "civilian" to that of a mental patient. Goffman identifies the agent roles involved in this process as next-of-relation, complainant, and mediators. The next-of-relation, usually a relative, is the person whom the patient expects to be the last to doubt his or her sanity and the first to save the patient from being committed to a mental hospital. The complainant is the person who actually starts the patient on his or her way to the mental hospital. Since this person may also be the next-of-relation, the emotions the patient experiences during the commitment sequence are compounded. The mediators are a sequence of agents and agencies through which the individual is relayed until he or she is actually committed to the mental hospital. These persons are typically lawyers, police, social workers, clergy, physicians, and psychiatrists. Eventually, one agent (the judge in proceedings for involuntary commitment) will have the legal mandate to sanction commitment and may exercise it. If this happens, all of the mediators will retire and the pre-patient now becomes an in-patient.

Goffman points out that this passage to the mental hospital is often characterized by feelings of betrayal on the part of the patient. Goffman found that the potential patient is encouraged to cooperate with others to the extent that it was possible for the patient to travel the whole circuit from home to hospital without forcing anyone to look directly at him or her or to deal with raw emotion. Upon reflection, the patient may realize that everybody else's comfort was being maintained while his or her long-range welfare was being undermined. Often the next-of-relation will handle the patient's affairs while he or she is in the hospital. This person thus serves as a useful identity to whom the hospital can point for justification for its method of treatment. The staff's action is therefore in the patient's best interest both because of their superior training and knowledge *and* because of the authorization by the next-of-relation (who supposedly has the patient's best interests at heart) to work on behalf of the patient. Paradoxically, as Goffman notes, the next-of-relation is the person to whom the patient turns for support in being discharged from the hospital and also the person to whom the hospital turns for authorization to treat the patient.

The passage to commitment as a mental patient as described by Goffman may not apply to all potential mental patients, especially those who seek voluntary admission to a mental hospital or those who are arrested by the police and for whose commitment the state assumes responsibility. However, the import of Goffman's research is that in many cases passage to the mental hospital is a process of alienation; the patient is removed from "normal" society to a setting in which he or she is clearly regarded as being mentally unacceptable.

Voluntary Commitment.   Voluntary commitment results when individuals present themselves for admission to a mental hospital on their own accord. Elliot Mishler and Nancy Waxler (1968) have found that the most important variable in whether a mental hospital will accept a person who volunteers for treatment is a referral by a physician. Physician requests to admit a person were viewed as more "legitimate." Other significant factors were the presence of a relative at the admission interview, the age of the patient (younger patients were preferred), and the patient's past history of mental hospitalization (there was a low acceptance rate of ex-patients).

A well-publicized study of voluntary admission procedures conducted by David Rosenhan (1973) consisted of a group of eight supposedly normal persons—a psychiatrist, a pediatrician, a painter, a housewife, a psychology graduate student, and three psychology professors—who presented themselves for admission as schizophrenics at twelve different mental hospitals located in five different states on both the East and West coasts. All were admitted, and once in the hospital they immediately reverted to their usual normal behavior. Yet despite their show of sanity after some initial nervousness over actually being a mental patient, the pseudopatients were never detected by the hospital staffs as being "fakes." Rather it was the "real" patients who correctly identified the pseudopatients as imposters. For example, all of the pseudopatients took extensive notes about their confinement experiences in an obvious fashion. This writing was viewed by the staffs as being just another aspect of their pathological behavior, while the real patients accused the pseudopatients of being either journalists or college professors who were "checking up" on the hospital.

Goffman (1961) makes the highly significant point that there are no objective and universally applicable standards for admission to mental hospitals, and such studies as those by Mishler and Waxler (1958) and Rosenhan (1973) seem to confirm Goffman's observation. Mishler and Waxler found that factors external to the mental disorder itself, such as the presence of a relative or a letter of referral by a physician, were relevant in being admitted to a mental hospital on a voluntary basis. The Rosenhan study suggests that practically anyone, sane or insane, can in fact gain admission to a mental hospital; once in the hospital, what appeared to be important was not so much the patient's behavior, but the general acceptance by the staff of the diagnosis given at admission. There was even evidence that the history of past behavior taken during interviews was somewhat distorted to be consistent with theories of mental disorder held by the interviewer. *Thus, past circumstances did not shape the diagnosis, but instead the diagnosis appeared to shape the diagnostician's perceptions of past circumstances.* Rosenhan believed that the failure of the hospital staffs to discover the pseudopatients (length of hospitalization ranged from seven to fifty-two days, with an average of nineteen days) illustrates the power of labeling in psychiatric assessment. Once labeled as a schizophrenic, there was nothing the pseudopatients could do to overcome an identification that profoundly affected the perceptions of other people about them and their behavior. Their release from the mental hospital was contingent upon the staff's accepting the idea that the nonexistent schizophrenia was in "remission."

This discussion is not intended to convey the impression that all mental hospitals are unable to tell real patients from phony ones or that factors not directly relevant to a person's mental status are always highly significant in admission procedures. But it is intended to convey the idea that without objective standards for admission, decisions made by mental hospital staffs concerning admissions are subjective and are clearly prone to error—yet result in significant consequences for the person who becomes a patient.

Involuntary Commitment.   Involuntary commitment results when a state uses its power and authority to involuntarily confine an individual to a mental hospital. Involuntary commitment proceedings are of two types: those dealing with criminal offenses, in which insanity is claimed as a defense, and those which are civil (noncriminal) in nature. Scheff (1964) observed the legal psychiatric screening procedures for civil cases in a midwestern state. There were five steps in this procedure, which consisted of (1) three citizens making an application to the court, (2) an intake examination conducted by a hospital psychiatrist, (3) an examination conducted by two court-appointed psychiatrists, (4) an interview by a court-appointed lawyer to represent the patient, and (5) a judicial hearing conducted by a judge. The primary legal rationales for depriving patients of their civil liberties was that they represented a danger to themselves, to others, or to property. Scheff found that a majority (63 percent of the patients) were not necessarily dangerous. He concluded that the evidence in such cases was somewhat arbitrary (there were no objective standards for admission); that the patients were often prejudged (it was assumed that all who appeared were in need of being admitted, otherwise they would not have been there); that the examinations were both careless and hasty (the interviews by the lawyer and the examinations by psychiatrists lasted about ten minutes on the average); and that sometimes there was really no "evidence," but people were committed anyway (there was an assumption that psychiatric treatment would either help or was neutral—it would not hurt—and that it was better to risk unnecessary hospitalization than have the patient be in a position to hurt himself or herself or others).

In criminal cases, the claim of mental disorder is employed as an excusing condition that relieves the individual from criminal responsibility for his or her act. The logical model for an excusing condition in Anglo-American law is the accident, and it defines a class of people who fall outside the boundaries of blame (Szasz, 1963; Goldstein, 1967; Simon, 1967). A finding of insanity by a judge or jury, based upon the testimony of psychiatrists as expert witnesses, is a matter of opinion, as the law, like psychiatry, does not have objective standards for ascertaining mental disorder. A verdict of insanity does not release the individual to return to society, for in most jurisdictions that person is involuntarily committed to a mental hospital.

For civil commitment of an involuntary nature, the mere designation of a mental disorder is not sufficient justification for the confinement of an individual to a mental hospital. There usually must also be a finding that the mental disorder is of such degree or character that if the individual in question were allowed to remain at large, that person would constitute a danger to self, others, or property. Despite the fact that these criteria for civil commitment are widely recognized, few concepts in the law are as elusive and undefined as dangerousness. Decisions are normally rendered by judges on a case-by-case basis, based on the opinions of psychiatrists who assess the probability of the individual's committing a dangerous act. Actions ranging from murder to writing bad checks have all been found to be dangerous enough to warrant confinement. To determine dangerousness, courts look to the severity of the harm, the likelihood that the action will occur, and the behavior of the person that gave rise to the prediction of dangerousness. There is no judicial consensus on any but the most obvious acts of dangerousness, such as murder and direct physical harm, and the issue remains one of the most unsettled areas of the law.

As in the Mishler and Waxler study of voluntary commitment, a study of the assessments used to determine dangerousness in cases of involuntary commitment by Richard Levinson and M. Zan York (1974) also found evidence that factors external to the disorder itself were influential in the decision-making process. This study, based on the files of a large mental health program in Atlanta, Georgia, found that being male, young, unmarried, with a past history of previous psychiatric treatment, and a person for whom help was solicited by a caller outside the person's household were all factors contributing to a diagnosis as dangerous, provided the person demonstrated disorderly behavior in the presence of the mental health professional making the assessment. Levinson and Zan York concluded that since standards are imprecise, criteria unrelated to the pathological condition may unduly influence the attribution of dangerousness to a particular person and the decision to commit that person to a mental hospital.

Therefore, as Goffman explains, whether or not a person is actually launched on a career as a mental patient depends upon a number of contingencies—for example, the visibility of the offense, the socioeconomic status of the patient, the availability of treatment, the convenience of authorities, the opinion of judges and perhaps jurors (in criminal proceedings), and so forth. Becoming a mental patient is a highly arbitrary process.

The In-patient Phase

The last step in the pre-patient phase is the recognition by the individual that he or she has been turned out by society and subjected to the restrictions of living in an institution under the authority of others. Goffman (1961:xiii) has described the mental hospital as being a "total institution," which he defines "as a place of residence and work where a large number of like-situated individuals, cut off from the wider society for an appreciable period of time, together lead an enclosed, formally administered round of life." The central feature of the total institution, which also includes prisons, monasteries, homes for the blind, and military camps, is a breakdown of barriers normal to most people. All aspects of life are conducted in the same place, under the same authority, and in the immediate company of others who are treated alike and who do the same thing together. All phases of activities are scheduled to fulfill the aims of a rational plan supposedly designed to meet the official goals of the institution, which in the case of the mental hospital is therapy and/or custodial care.

Goffman explains that a major characteristic of all total institutions is the existence of some form of deference between or among its group members. In mental hospitals this deference refers to the status of the staff as superior and righteous and the status of the patients as inferior and guilty of failure in the so-called normal world. This type of perspective, however, lends itself to a process of dehumanization that makes it easier for the staff to tend to disregard the inmates to achieve greater efficiency without a great expenditure of personal energy and emotional involvement. While not all mental patients in all mental hospitals may experience depersonalization, the dependent status of the patient does lend itself to that type of situation. Furthermore, Goffman points out that the ease with which an inmate can be managed by the staff is likely to increase the degree to which that inmate is dehumanized.

In his study of normal people posing as patients, Rosenhan (1973) found that being a mental patient involved the recognition that powerlessness was evident everywhere. Mental patients lacked credibility in what they said by virtue of their mental disorder. They could not initiate contact with the staff but could only respond to overtures from them. Furthermore, there was only minimal personal privacy, and personal thoughts and history were open to inspection by any staff member, no matter what the reason. Rosenhan stated:

> At times, depersonalization reached such proportions that pseudopatients had the sense they were invisible, or at least unworthy of account. Upon being admitted, I and other pseudopatients took the initial physical examinations in a semipublic room, where staff members went about their own business as if we were not there.
>
> On the ward, attendants delivered verbal and occasionally serious physical abuse to patients in the presence of other observing patients, some of whom (the pseudopatients) were writing it all down. Abusive behavior, on the other hand, terminated quite abruptly when other staff members were known to be coming. Staff were credible witnesses. Patients are not.
>
> A nurse unbuttoned her uniform to adjust her brassiere in the presence of an entire ward of viewing men. One did not have the sense she was being seductive. Rather, she didn't notice us. A group of staff persons might point to a patient in the dayroom and discuss him animatedly, as if he were not there.[6]

Rosenhan attributed the origins of depersonalization to two major factors: (1) the attitudes held by society toward the mentally ill, including those who treat them, as "some*thing* that is unattractive" despite benevolent intentions toward them; and (2) the hierarchical structure of the mental hospital, which facilitated depersonalization in that those at the top had the least contact with patients and their behavior was a model for the rest of the staff. Rosenhan found that patients spent very little time with hospital physicians (an average of 6.8 minutes a day for six pseudopatients over a total of 129 days of hospitalization) and that the physicians, in turn, influenced the behavior of the nurses and ward attendants, who likewise tended to reduce the time they spent with patients. Heavy reliance on drug therapy also seemed to contribute to the process of depersonalization by allowing the

[6] David L. Rosenhan, "On Being Sane in Insane Places," *Science*, 179 (January 19, 1973), 256.

staff to rationalize that treatment was being conducted and that additional contact with the patient was not needed.

Goffman has pointed out that mental patients actually have very little choice but to adapt to the social environment of the hospital. He identifies four different types of adjustment to the total institution: (1) situational withdrawal, (2) intransigence (rebellion), (3) colonization (using experiences of life in the outside world to demonstrate the desirability of life on the inside), and (4) conversion (living up to the staff-sponsored ideal model). Goffman tells us that typically the inmates will not follow any one particular mode of adaptation completely, but will most likely adopt a somewhat opportunistic combination of conversion, colonization, and loyalty to the inmate group. Instead of making what Goffman calls a primary adjustment of "giving in" to the system, the patient will make a secondary adjustment, which is to appear to conform to the system while gaining hidden satisfactions wherever possible. One of the primary functions of inmate society is to help maintain a sympathetic and supportive atmosphere in the hospital ward and to serve as a vehicle by which the patient can assert a self-identity and perhaps some independence within an overall context of dependence and forced association (Smith and Thrasher, 1963). Apparently one of the prominent activities that takes place in these patient "societies" is the expression of face-saving rationalizations for each other's presence in the hospital. Goffman explains that such stories as the following are given:

> I was going to night school to get an M.A. degree and holding down a job in addition, and the load got too much for me.

> I got here by mistake because of a diabetes diagnosis and I'll leave in a couple of days. (The patient had been in seven weeks.)

> The others here are sick mentally but I'm suffering from a bad nervous system and that is what is giving me these phobias.[7]

As Goffman notes, an entire social role in the patient community may be constructed on the basis of these fictions; thus what we see in these exchanges is the classic function of a network of equals to serve as audiences for each other's self-supportive statements. But while the patient may be denying that he or she is mentally ill, that same patient may at other times show evidence of mental disorder. And, as Goffman indicates, there is still that official sheet of paper to confirm the patient's illness. Regardless of the patient's attempts to rationalize his or her fate, being admitted as a mental patient seriously inhibits the credibility of the rationalizations. Goffman states:

> Certainly the degrading conditions of the hospital setting belie many of the self-stories that are presented by patients, and the very fact of being in the mental hospital is evidence against these tales. And of course there is not always sufficient patient solidarity to prevent patient discrediting patient, just as there

[7] Erving Goffman, *Asylums* (New York: Anchor, 1961), pp. 152–153.

is not always a sufficient number of "professionalized" attendants to prevent attendant discrediting patient. As one patient informant repeatedly suggested to a fellow patient:

If you're so smart, how come you got your ass in here?[8]

Thus, despite the possible supports provided by inmate society, the influence and power of the hospital staff is pervasive. Sometimes the staff will even deliberately discredit a patient's story to encourage the patient to adopt the hospital's view of himself or herself. What is that view? Generally, the "good" patient is expected to (1) believe that recovery is possible, (2) recognize that he or she is mentally ill and needs treatment, (3) trust and have faith in the therapist, (4) conform willingly to hospital life, and (5) accept the treatment that is prescribed (Denzin, 1968). If a patient follows this prescription, then, to use Goffman's terminology, that patient is "converted." And since the patient's release from the hospital (in cases of non-criminal confinement) depends on the staff's assessment of how well he or she conforms to their expectations of behavior, the staff have tremendous leverage in their influence over the patient.

Recent studies, however, indicate that many mental patients do not necessarily think of themselves as mentally ill and that conversion is mostly an acceptance of hospital life and the status of mental patient—not an acceptance of the institution's definition of themselves (Braginsky et al., 1969; Townsend, 1976). As Goffman explains in his general approach to institutionalization, inmates, over time, will make opportunistic adjustments to the institution. Townsend (1976) points out that mental patients are in a special situation. They know that their subjective and personal feelings are under observation and that the outcome of this observation helps determine their fate. Thus, they adjust their behavior to the situation, depending on what they perceive is the purpose of that situation. Townsend explains:

> . . . Given the mental patient's special situation, it may not be a meaningful question to ask what he "really" thinks of himself. His responses will not necessarily match his actual feelings at the moment and, in any case, both feelings and responses tend to vary with context. At times the patient may feel good about himself; at other times, bad. Some may suspect at times that they are insane and yet not admit these suspicions. At other times, things may be going well and they consequently feel healthy. Even so, they might still fear leaving the hospital, and, as a result, do poorly during a staff evaluation. Patients, like anyone, are also capable of deceiving themselves. They may inwardly suspect they are insane, yet ward off confrontation with these feelings by rationalizing their presence in the hospital and denying that they are mentally ill.

> It thus appears that it is difficult to define exactly what a patient thinks of his condition at any one time, and it may be that this is not an empirically useful question.[9]

[8] Goffman, *Asylums*, p. 154.
[9] J. Marshall Townsend, "Self-Concept and the Institutionalization of Mental Patients: An Overview and Critique," *Journal of Health and Social Behavior*, 17 (September 1976), 269.

Nevertheless, a number of medical sociologists and other people interested in the treatment of mental patients have expressed concern about the effects of the mental hospital as a total institution on the attitudes and self-concepts of the inmates. The major focus of this concern has to do with the effect of prolonged living in a state of enforced dependency. It is feared that this process may influence the patient to become so dependent on the hospital and its routines that it becomes well-nigh impossible for the patient to leave. As William Eaton (1974:252) describes it, the patient "gradually learns to play the chronic sick role, to reduce aspirations, and to find friends within the hospital instead of outside." The literature is clear that the longer a person stays at a mental hospital, the less likely that person is to leave (Eaton, 1974; Townsend, 1976). One of the focal points of Ken Kesey's popular novel on a mental hospital, *One Flew Over the Cuckoo's Nest*, is the effort of the patient McMurphy to organize inmate society and to literally force it to recognize that life outside the hospital is much more attractive. Two of the studies most often cited to depict the effects of institutionalization are those of Ailon Shiloh (1971) and John Wing (1968). Shiloh investigated the attitudes of mental patients toward the outside world in a veterans' hospital in Illinois and found basically two groups, whose goals were diametrically opposed. He classified about 40 percent of the patients as being "institutionalized" and not wanting to leave the hospital, while 25 percent were classified as "noninstitutionalized" patients in that they had a reasonable expectation of getting out. The remaining 35 percent of the patients could not be classified either way. The key difference between the institutionalized and noninstitutionalized patients was that the former group was generally poorly educated, single or divorced, and lower class; the noninstitutionalized patients were mostly middle-class, married, and well educated. Noninstitutionalized patients saw being hospitalized as a temporary but unfortunate state. In contrast, the institutionalized patients considered themselves as simply cut off from the outside world, yet were well aware of the hospital's comforts—food, warm beds, television, movies. The goal of the institutionalized inmates was very plainly that of security.

Wing studied the patients in two mental hospitals in London and found that the syndrome of institutionalization is dependent on three factors. First is the social perspective of the patient. Patients who lacked strong family and community ties were usually not too concerned with restrictions on personal liberty. Second, the disease process itself may be significant, as many mental disorders foster social withdrawal. And third, the influence of the institution itself, particularly over a long period of time, may gradually affect the patient by making him or her more dependent on institutional life and unable to adapt to other living situations.

Eaton (1974) has investigated the influence of the mental hospital on institutionalization by proposing four theoretical models to account for the number of times a person is hospitalized for schizophrenia. The positive reinforcement model holds that the hospital positively reinforces the individual at each episode and is consonant with institutionalization. The negative reinforcement model takes the opposite position, that the hospital experience causes individuals not to want to return. The heterogeneity model proposes that individual differences between people explain the variation, and the pure random model assigns a strictly random cause for recurrent stays in mental hospitals. Eaton suggested that all four models represent processes that occur to some degree; however, the heterogeneity model was found to be the most satisfactory in explaining the data.

Although institutions may be able in some cases to positively reinforce an individual's attitudes toward accepting hospital life, the most relevant factor, as suggested by Eaton's work, is apparently that people exhibit psychological and social characteristics that lend themselves in different degrees to acceptance of enforced dependency. Some people are apparently very attracted to situations in which their needs are provided for with little effort or risk on their part.

Although this discussion thus far would suggest that life in mental hospitals is generally a dehumanizing and oppressive experience, Raymond Weinstein (1979) tells us that this is not necessarily the case. Weinstein argues that most mental patients have a positive attitude toward the hospital. He reasons that (1) the hospital can be a "temporary haven"; (2) the environment of the hospital may be more attractive than living in conditions of poverty, deprivation, and inactivity; and (3) hospitalization represents an opportunity for self-improvement.

The answer to whether or not mental patients generally perceive hospitalization as either positive or negative probably lies somewhere between the two extremes of "good" and "bad." For some patients, the experience no doubt is positive, especially for those who, as noted by Weinstein, have severe mental problems. The mental hospital can provide a better environment than some alternative living situations, particularly if the facilities are good and adequately staffed and if the staff is generally supportive of the patients. For other patients, the experience may be unpleasant, as they must cope with depersonalization, restrictive rules, lack of privacy, confinement, unpleasant associates, and a schedule of activities that is not of their own choosing. Moreover, they may have been alienated from friends and family on the way to being hospitalized, have had their identity placed in circumstances in which they are viewed by others as less than desirable, and have been forced to exhibit their most private thoughts in the attempt to treat them. For most people there is a better way to live than being a patient in a mental hospital.

The Post-patient Phase

A considerable portion of the research on the post-patient phase of the mental hospital experience has been concerned with the effect of stigma upon these individuals. Charles Whatley (1959) found, for example, that strong tendencies to shun mental patients were most prevalent in personal situations. ("Would you want your daughter to marry an ex-mental patient?") The greatest tolerance was exhibited in impersonal situations. More recently, however, it has been found that if former mental patients manage to function well in their work and get along well with their family, feelings of stigma apparently diminish over time and neither patient, family, nor friends will tend to characterize them as former mental patients (Clausen and Huffine, 1975). Americans may tend to reject persons classified as mental patients, but they also may tend to accept the authoritative judgments of psychiatrists that a person has recovered and is "normal" (Olmsted and Durham, 1976).

Generally, people who have had close relationships with former mental patients seem to be less prejudiced against them than those who have not had such contact. Research by Howard Freeman and Ozzie Simmons (1961), for instance, found that although some upper-class and middle-class families tended to be sensitive about having a former mental hospital patient in the family, these feelings were not strong among most of the families. In another study, Freeman and Simmons (1963) investigated the experiences of 649 adults in Massachusetts over a one-year period after hospitalization. A close relative, usually the wife or mother, was interviewed twice after the patient returned home from the hospital. The first interview came about six weeks after discharge, and the second followed one year later. The relatives had rather high expectations of how well the former patients would do socially and on the job. And there was little change in these expectations over the year. Although recent research shows that family expectations of the mental patient do not necessarily influence the expressions of psychiatric symptoms (Greenley, 1979), such studies also suggest that often families initially regard the family member as more or less cured after hospitalization and give that person the benefit of the doubt until there is evidence to the contrary.

It seems likely that the label of "mental patient" does not necessarily carry over into the future of former mental patients if over time their behavior does not correspond to the label. Evidence that it is possible for a former mental patient to resume his or her past role in the community without irreversible stigma is found in the study of a small group of thirty-six married men whose occupational careers were followed by Carol Huffine and John Clausen (1979) between the 1950s and 1972–1973. Because all of these males were married, they are not typical of all male ex-patients, since the ability to sustain a marital relationship is an important indicator of a positive outcome for the mentally disturbed person. Yet, as Huffine and Clausen (1979:1052) note, "the stigmatizing aspect of confinement to a mental hospital should be no less for a married man than for a single one." Hence, examining the occupational careers of this group of males (most of whom were under the age of forty at the time of admission to a mental hospital, and all of whom were first admissions and suffering from a severe disorder—schizophrenia) can provide useful information about the post-hospitalization experience.

Of the original thirty-six men, twenty-nine survived until 1972–1973. Nine men had been symptom-free for at least five years prior to the follow-up, and most had been symptom-free since their initial hospitalization. All nine were working at jobs of equal or higher status than those they held before their hospitalization. Nine others had been mildly symptomatic over the years or had experienced infrequent recurrences of serious symptoms. Five of these men worked at jobs equal to or higher than their jobs before admission to a mental hospital, and four had slipped to lesser jobs. There were sufficient data to assess the outcome for an additional nine men. These men had suffered serious symptoms and had been rehospitalized frequently (the average number of readmissions was four) following their initial admission. Interestingly, all of these last nine men, despite the severity of their problems, had worked at jobs during the period of the study. Four of them had kept jobs equal to or better than those held at first admission, but the remaining five men had had lesser jobs. Of the four men who had maintained or improved their job status, Huffine and Clausen (1979:1059) comment that their ability "to continue to work effectively and to retain their jobs in spite of recurrent or persistent severe symptomatology is impressive indeed." Two of these men, in fact, had jobs requiring considerable skill. However, among the men who worked at lesser jobs after hospitalization, most were unable to work at all by the time of the follow-up interview. Thus, not all of them were "success" stories. Some were clearly failures.

Many former mental patients, principally those who have families who care for them and jobs either awaiting them or readily available, are able to make a relatively smooth transition from the mental hospital to life in the outside world—providing their symptoms are not too severe. And if a good family life and job are available, the former patient may still be able to have a satisfactory life outside the hospital even if severe symptoms recur, according to the Huffine and Clausen study. Yet many mental patients face an uncertain and bleak existence in the outside community, particularly if they have been hospitalized for a long period of time. These patients may have become elderly, have seen their family likewise grow old or die, or perhaps have lost contact with them. Thus, they are alone in facing their problems, except for help from community mental health programs and social welfare agencies. It is this group of patients that has particular difficulty in getting reestablished in a community. Often they end up living meagerly in slum area housing, and their mental condition is compounded by living in poverty. Therefore, although public attitudes in general may be "easing up" or becoming less negative, many ex-patients are nonetheless condemned to live in unsatisfactory circumstances because of their symptoms and lack of family, friends, and income.

The key to adequate readjustment to the outside world for most mental patients probably is being able to construct a social-psychological framework in which the ex-patient can show a strong degree of competence. In a study of over one thousand former mental patients in California, Dorothy Miller (1971) identified four elements as being significant factors in the patient's ability to stay out of the mental hospital. First, an adequate source of material support was needed. Second, the presence of someone who cared about the patient and provided close support for the patient's attempts to cope with the outside world was very important. Third, the patient needed to experience a series of spontaneous positive relationships with other people. And fourth, the ability to define a new situation as one in which the patient was able to exercise some degree of control was helpful. If any of the above four elements was missing, Miller believed that ex-patients were likely to fail outside the hospital.

COMMUNITY MENTAL HEALTH

Since the mid-1950s there has been a steady decline in both the number of people admitted to mental hospitals in the United States and the average length of confinement. The most significant change in mental health policy in recent years has been the development of community mental health centers to provide therapy in the community setting. In 1963, Congress passed the Mental Retardation and Facilities and Community Mental Health Centers Construction Act as a commitment on the part of the federal government to help support easily accessible and locally controlled mental health centers. This law reflected the philosophy that the objective of modern treatment should be to support mental patients in their own communities as much as possible so that they can lead relatively normal lives. Advocates of community mental health cite four major concerns as the rationale behind community mental health programs (Cohen, 1974). First is the idea that the mental patient's entire social environment be viewed as a "therapeutic community" that offers resources for treatment to mental health professionals. The second concern, clearly related to the first, is that some means must be found to use the patient's relationships with family and friends to improve therapy and to prevent recurrence of a mental disorder. The third concern is to develop and organize local community control over these mental health centers so that center policies are both community based and oriented. Fourth is the desire to reduce the patient "load" at state mental hospitals by providing prompt response and twenty-four-hour service.

In 1979 there were 647 community mental health centers in the United States and the number has steadily increased since. To meet federal funding requirements, community mental health centers are required to provide both in-patient and out-patient services, day care services, a twenty-four-hour emergency service, and educational services for community agencies and professional personnel.

Several studies have confirmed the utility of home treatment (see, for example, Freeman and Simmons, 1963; Segal and Aviram, 1978). When this method works, it provides the advantage of being more personalized and less expensive than hospitalization. But is home treatment the answer? It all depends upon which environment—hospital or community—is best for the patient. David Mechanic (1980) has observed that when mental patients do show impressive signs of remission during hospitalization these symptoms often reappear when the patient returns home. This seems to be indicative of difficulties in the home environment, which may remain unchanged. Also, one of the benefits of hospitalization is that it affords a respite—both to the patient and to the family—from the turmoil that may have been a major causal factor in the onset and progress of the disorder. This respite can provide a period of reassessment and redefinition leading to a hopeful outlook. Sampson and associates (1964) have found that a significant effect of hospitalization upon marital ties is to separate the disputants, block final action, and defer formalization of the end of the marriage so that other solutions can be attempted. Often hospitalization may create conditions under which a relationship can be resumed.

However, although community mental health programs have had some success in working with patients who can be helped best in the community and in providing prompt crisis intervention services, they have been handicapped by funding shortages and overburdened by client demand. They also have contributed to a new problem, which is the presence of mental patients living in the community who are ill equipped to deal with life outside an institution. Many of these patients do not live with their families for various reasons and tend to congregate in ghettos of the mentally ill where some live lonely, disorganized, frustrated lives in slum environments.

The decision of whether to opt for hospital care or community (home) care, therefore, seems to depend on the situation. Merely to conclude that institutional life is dehumanizing, and therefore necessarily bad, is to overlook those situations in which it may be the better alternative.

SUMMARY

This chapter has reviewed selected aspects of the sociology of mental health from the standpoint of theoretical models of mental disorder, social epidemiology of mental disorder, and social processes of mental hospitalization. The medical model has been enhanced in recent years by successful research in brain chemistry, which the medical profession believes will offer the greatest potential for treating abnormal behavior. Although the medical model will, in all probability, retain its preeminent position in determining theory, therapy, and policy, the contributions of sociology toward our understanding of what mental disorders are and what causes them are gaining ever greater acceptance. Research in the social epidemiology of mental disorder has clearly pointed to three variables—sex, rural versus urban location, and social class—that demonstrate significant differences among groups of people. Because the relationships among these variables have remained consistent over time, they will prove useful in clarifying causes of mental difficulties. Studies of hospitalization in mental institutions have illustrated some of the problems; and one important reaction has been the development of community mental health to provide a more humane treatment situation.

chapter 11

AGING

A number of health-related factors, including improved medical care, nutrition, sanitation, and housing, have combined in the twentieth century to help promote longer lives for most Americans. In 1977, for example, the average infant at birth in the United States could expect to live 73.2 years. This figure represents an increase in longevity of nearly 50 percent since 1900, when life expectancy at birth in the United States was 47.3 years. Furthermore, in the decade between 1960 and 1970, the number of people aged seventy-five and over increased three times as fast as the number in the 65–74 age category. Today, there are over 20 million people in the United States age sixty-five and over, of whom about one-third are seventy-five and over.

Thus, the present century in the United States can be described as a period of exceedingly rapid growth of the aged population. Not only are more people living to reach older ages, but also since 1958 the fertility rate in the United States has been in a period of decline. The lower death rate coupled with the lower birth rate has thus produced a much higher proportion of older Americans in relation to the total population. Table 11–1 illustrates this trend by showing that in 1900 only some 4 percent of the total United States population was age sixty-five or over. By 1970, however, older Americans constituted 9.7 percent of the total population and by 2050 it is projected that 17.5 percent of all Americans will be in this age bracket.

Another way to illustrate the growing proportion of elderly people in America is to recognize that in 1980 about one in ten Americans was over sixty-five; by the year 2050, this ratio will have increased to almost one in five.

The increasing longevity of Americans has helped foster a growing interest among both social and medical scientists in the biological and behavioral aspects of the aging process and the social role of the elderly person.

TABLE 11–1.   Percent of Total U.S. Population Age 65 and Over for Selected Years

	1900	1930	1950	1970	1980 (projected)	2000 (projected)	2050 (projected)
Percent Age 65 and Over	4.0	5.4	8.1	9.7	11.2	12.2	17.5

SOURCE: U.S. Department of Health, Education and Welfare, *Facts and Figures on Older Americans: An Overview, 1971* (Washington, D.C.: U.S. Government Printing Office, 1971); U.S. Bureau of the Census, *Current Population Reports: Projections of the Population of the United States, 1977–2050* (Washington, D.C.: U.S. Government Printing Office, 1977).

Accordingly, the study of gerontology has increased in scope and importance in recent years, and many medical sociologists are specializing in social gerontology, that is, the study of aging as a social and psychological experience.

AGING AND THE LIFE CYCLE

In the United States, age sixty-five has generally marked that point in life when a person is "officially" old—largely because of its arbitrary selection by the Social Security Administration as the age of eligibility for old age benefits. Except for its bureaucratic significance, however, being sixty-five has no other particular relevance. This is because chronological age is an inconsistent indicator of the aging process. Just as physical and intellectual capabilities mature at different times in different people so can aging be said to begin at different points in time for different people. It is possible to be a "young" sixty-five or an "old" fifty-five.

Also, it is interesting to note that individual perceptions of whether or not a certain age is "old" can vary. Gordon Bultena and Edward Powers (1978) studied 611 people in Iowa in 1960 and returned in 1970 to restudy 235 of the original respondents. Most of the remainder had either died or moved away. The median age of people in the restudy group was seventy-six years and more than one-fourth of the sample was over eighty years old. About three-quarters of the respondents were women. Bultena and Powers found that a majority rejected the idea that they were old. Instead, many defined themselves as being middle-aged; some said they were simply elderly. This finding is consistent with other studies that identify the variables of age and sex as having a significant impact upon perception of the aging process. In general, older people and women tend to perceive middle and old age as occurring chronologically later in life than do younger people and men (Drevenstedt, 1976). Or as one senior citizen once put it: "To me old age is always fifteen years older than I am" (Rosow, 1974:11).

One way to "explain" the social and psychological aspects of the aging experience is to categorize that experience into phases or stages denoting the human life cycle (Birren, 1964; Neugarten and Moore, 1968; Atchley, 1977;

Ward, 1979; Decker, 1980). Although the stages of the life cycle are based on chronological age and do not account for variations among individuals, they are nevertheless indicative of the general life course most people follow. Implicit in the idea of a life cycle is a common set of social experiences through which all members of a society are expected to pass. For instance, childhood is the time when a person generally receives a primary education; adolescence and young adulthood are usually the time of courtship and marriage; the period of later maturity is typically the time of retirement.

Thus, as Vern Bengston (1973) points out, age is a dimension of social organization because the divisions of the life cycle are those prescribed by the culture of a society in order to lend stability and predictability to the typical sequence of life events. Implied in this arrangement is the idea that individuals also undergo a change in behavior as they pass from one stage of life into a subsequent stage. Infants, children, young adults, middle-age adults, and older persons are all expected by other people to behave in a manner characteristic of their age group; social judgments of their maturity depend on how close their behavior approximates the corresponding age-related norm. Furthermore, at each stage of life a person takes on new social roles and the responsibilities that accrue to those roles, while the person's status and relationships with other people are modified accordingly.

The typical stages of the human life cycle and the approximate ages they represent are shown in Table 11–2. Although a person can be regarded as aging from the moment of conception or from the moment the individual reaches full maturation (there is some disagreement on this point), for the purposes of our discussion, the stages of middle age, later maturity, and old age are most relevant.

As previously noted, the onset of old age varies among individuals. Although aging is known to occur as a result of changes in the body's cells, the exact cause of the process is still a mystery. The two most widely accepted theories state that aging may be due in large part to deterioration in the integratory homeostasis that exists between cells of the same tissue and those of other tissues, or it may be the result of some form of preset genetic program for cell aging. Whatever the cause, the interaction of biological, genetic, and social-psychological factors seems to be involved. Aging can also

TABLE 11–2.   The Life Cycle

Stage	Approximate Age
Infancy	2
Preschool	2–5
Childhood	5–12
Adolescence	12–17
Early Maturity	17–25
Maturity	25–40
Middle Age	40–55
Later Maturity	55–75
Old Age	75

be of a primary or a secondary nature. Primary aging occurs over time, while secondary aging occurs through disease or trauma and may be temporarily premature. The single most obvious indication of aging is the appearance of the skin, which tends to dry out and wrinkle. The person's capacity for sight and hearing are reduced and the brain begins to shrink, losing about 100,000 cells a day. Muscles also shrink and become weaker, joints stiffen and swell, while the heart, lungs, kidneys, and bladder begin to operate at reduced levels of effectiveness, and the body's output of hormones begins to diminish. The body becomes increasingly susceptible to stress, infection, and especially to the degenerative diseases of cancer, arteriosclerosis, and diabetes.

According to Robert Atchley (1977), *middle age* is the period of life when a person initially becomes aware of the fact that he or she is aging. Middle age is the time when the person recognizes a reduction of energy and often begins to favor intellectual activities over physical endeavors. Usually the person's work career more or less reaches a plateau, and the great majority of a couple's children will have left home to lead their own lives. As Atchley explains, middle age is when most people realize that they are aging and that death is very real, not just something that happens to somebody else. Robert Kastenbaum (1971), for example, has found that a characteristic of old age is a foreshortened time perspective. The older person avoids thoughts of the future because of the limited time left and instead dwells on the past. Kastenbaum suggests that a majority of people are past-oriented by the age of forty and virtually all people are by age fifty-five.

Later maturity is characterized by a marked reduction in energy, vision, and hearing. Chronic health disorders are commonplace and poor health can join with reduced income, retirement, and the deaths of friends and relatives to curtail social interaction. By the time they are in their mid-sixties, most women are widows. But, as Atchley notes, the period of later maturity can be a pleasant one for those people who plan for it, retain a good measure of physical vigor, and perhaps wish to enjoy a time of lessened responsibilities. Also, the aged individual may continue to be a highly productive member of society. Charles Bowden and Alvin Burstein (1974:212) point out, for example, that the "myth that age necessarily involves an inability to produce is challenged by the numbers of second careers and examples of influence maintained by prominent individuals late into their lives."

Old age, in contrast to other stages of life, is more likely to be a rather unpleasant period as there is a higher probability of loneliness, boredom, and loss of self-esteem. Also it can be a time when mental processes are diminished. Whereas it seems clear that the aged brain takes longer to respond to a stimulus and the recall of recent events may be impaired (probably due to the older person's tendency toward increased distractability), remote memory of past events is usually quite good. If there is considerable memory loss, it can be a sign of organic brain damage. But it should be realized that while such brain damage may be likely to occur with increasing age, it does not occur in all elderly people. Besides reduced mental activity in very old age, another problem peculiar to the elderly is that of physical frailty and the possibility of being so disabled that physical mobility is highly restricted or denied.

Physical and mental infirmities and the reality of being tired, ill, and less able to cope with problems—all set in a framework of the recognition of impending death—can and do produce severe problems of adjustment and depression for the elderly. With reduced resources, the elderly person is less able to cope with stress and adapt to new conditions. Old age is thus a period in life many people fear and wish to avoid, yet, as in the period of later maturity, the key to success in old age is obviously to maintain an optimal level of physical strength and mental awareness.

SOCIAL GERONTOLOGY: THEORIES OF AGING

There are several theories of aging in social gerontology, but four of these—disengagement, activity, continuity theory and age stratification theory—that have generally been accepted as the most influential to date will be considered here.

Disengagement Theory

Disengagement theory stems from the functionalist perspective in sociology. According to two of its proponents, Elaine Cumming and William Henry (1961), disengagement theory contains three basic propositions: (1) a process of mutual withdrawal of aging individuals and society from each other is a usual occurrence; (2) this process of withdrawal is inevitable; and (3) it is also necessary for "successful" aging. Disengagement theory tells us that all people die eventually, yet for society's institutions to survive they must maintain social stability and cohesive social functioning. It follows then that it is necessary to have an orderly means of transferring power from the older members of society to the younger. Disengagement theory supports the notion that it is to society's benefit to phase out those individuals whose deaths would disrupt the smooth functioning of the social order. The process of phasing out older people from the mainstream of society thus becomes institutionalized, as stable and routine norms are developed to indicate which individuals should be disengaged and what forms of behavior should occur at this time. Accordingly, societies develop norms requiring that an individual retire from work at a certain age and a rite of status passage—for example, a retirement ceremony—often marks the occasion. However, as Atchley (1977) explains, disengagement is not usually a single event, but instead a gradual process that involves the separation of an individual from several of his or her regular social roles and activities.

As a functionalist perspective, disengagement theory is similar to the Kingsley Davis and Wilbert Moore (1945) theory of social stratification. Davis and Moore held that to attract the best qualified people to compete for the positions that fill society's most important needs, it is necessary to offer society's greatest rewards and inducements (money, power, prestige, status) to those people. Disengagement theory extends the Davis-Moore thesis by explaining that the work of people in key positions must continue uninterrupted if social order is to be preserved. Therefore, society must be able to replace people whose ability to perform adequately in an important position becomes questionable through old age or otherwise. If old age is a problem (which disengagement theory says it is), then it is necessary for society to be able to move the aged person out of the key position and into a less important one.

However, the disengagement of society from the individual is only half of disengagement theory. The other half of the theory, according to Cumming and Henry (1961), maintains that individuals themselves select to withdraw from certain social roles when they become old. The more roles an older person withdraws from, the less that person is bound to society's norms. The disengaged person is thus able to play a particular social role (the retired person) that allows him or her to become increasingly more self-centered and more preoccupied with personal interests. To the extent that the disengagement process allows the aged person to assume such a role, the more successful the aged person will be in retirement.

There are, as should be obvious to the reader, some significant weaknesses in disengagement theory. As Atchley (1977) points out, societal disengagement does not seem to occur in all social institutions. He explains that if societal disengagement were a functional necessity, it should apply to political officeholders as well. However, the relatively older ages of U.S. senators and particularly U.S. Supreme Court justices (who have an average age of sixty-four) seem to bespeak a flaw in the propositions advanced by Cumming and Henry.

Additionally, as Atchley notes, disengagement theory does not adequately account for individual disengagement. From this perspective, there are essentially three major difficulties with disengagement theory: (1) individual disengagement is most probably a much more complex process than the theory allows; (2) preliminary research has shown that once an individual has internalized a norm, more than simply the absence of interaction is required to extinguish it; and (3) the assumption that people will desire to be disengaged (to pursue their own self-centered world) does not explain the desire that many individuals have toward continued engagement.

In a study of university and college professors emeritus, Paul Roman and Philip Taietz (1967) were able to observe a post-retirement position that allowed retired professors to continue working in their pre-retirement activities of research, teaching, administration, or public service. Roman and Taietz believed that disengagement was not a feature of all social systems, and they questioned the assumption of disengagement theory that individuals naturally want to disengage as they perceive themselves getting old. Roman and Taietz found that, given the opportunity to continue their activities, most of the professors emeritus remained engaged. What is indicated by this study and others (Carp, 1968; Tallmer and Kutner, 1969; Atchley, 1977) is the importance of the social situation. Some people may disengage because the rules of the institution force them to or because of the impact of physical and social stress. But given the opportunity and the means to remain engaged, they might well choose to do so. The assumption of disengagement theory that disengagement is both natural and positive for the aged person cannot be conclusively demonstrated.

Why then is disengagement theory important? Chiefly because it is able to describe the social processes that occur when older people withdraw from their usual roles as a result of age. The theory is particularly applicable to situations of forced disengagement according to predetermined rules of an institution or organization and to situations of mutual disengagement, where both society and the individual define disengagement as positive. The strength of disengagement theory lies in the realization that at some point in time the interests of society intersect with the role performance of older people in key positions, and the result is often the disengagement of that older person. By setting a specific age, usually sixty-five, as the time of retirement, disengagement becomes institutionalized and orderly and inevitable, just as aging itself is inevitable. Some degree of disengagement appears to be inherent in the aging process for many people and disengagement theory helps to explain what happens in certain specific situations. Overall, then, disengagement theory can be described as a promising theory that remains to be reformulated if it is to attain a greater measure of universal validity.

Activity Theory

Activity theory, as suggested by Robert Havighurst (1963), is primarily an action theory for successful aging. It consists of three basic premises: (1) that the majority of normally aging people will maintain fairly constant levels of activity; (2) that the amount of engagement or disengagement will be influenced by past life styles and by socioeconomic considerations rather than by some intrinsic and inevitable process; and (3) that it is necessary to maintain or develop substantial levels of social, physical, and mental activity if the aging experience is to be successful (see Palmore, 1969).

What constitutes successful aging? According to Havighurst, the norms for old age are the same as those for middle age; therefore, successful aging is how close a person in the stages of later maturity or old age approximates the norms and activities of middle-aged persons. In other words, activity theory is an approach to understanding the social behavior of elderly people in terms of how well they deny the fact that they are elderly. Successful aging consists of being or behaving as much as possible like a middle-aged person.

There is research that clearly supports the basic propositions offered by activity theory. In a longitudinal study at Duke University carried out over a ten-year period, Erdman Palmore (1968, 1969) found that older men tended to show almost no overall reduction in their activities or in life satisfaction, while older women tended to have a small (but statistically significant) reduction in both activities and life satisfaction. Temporary decreases in activities due to illness were usually followed by subsequent increases so that there was little or no overall change.

Palmore noted that his data were obtained from people who were relatively healthy and, therefore, disengagement may be more typical of the less healthy. His point was, however, that disengagement by the elderly is not an inevitable product of aging. The respondents showed consistently high levels of activity throughout the ten-year period of the study. Furthermore, it was found that activity was significantly related to high morale and life satisfaction. The more active a person was, the more likely that person was to be happy. Palmore concluded that continued engagement rather than dis-engagement was typical of the normal, healthy older person, and the amount of that person's activity was strongly related to his or her past life style. If disengagement occurred among these elderly people, it usually did so only just prior to death.

What activity theory essentially tells us is that some people (perhaps a majority) do not disengage from society when they become old. If they do retire from their occupational role, they compensate for its loss by engaging in some other type of activity which provides satisfaction. Bernice Neugarten (1971), for example, cites the case of a seventy-five-year-old retired school teacher who made the most money of his life selling insurance as a second career after retirement. This is not to forecast, however, that most elderly people will seek a second career, but rather that they are likely to remain active in some fashion if their past lives were characterized by being active.

Yet as a theory explaining the social behavior of the aged, activity theory suffers from two basic inadequacies. First, it rests on the assumption that older people judge themselves according to norms common to middle-aged activity and behavior, but it does not explain what happens when the elderly do not subscribe to such norms. And second, it does not explain what happens to those older people who cannot, for physical, mental, or socio-economic reasons, maintain a middle-aged standard of living regardless of how they judge themselves. Thus, activity theory, like disengagement theory, fails to account for the behavior of all individuals.

Continuity Theory

Continuity theory, a third major theoretical approach to the social experience of aging, is somewhat more recent than the others (Neugarten, 1964; Atchley, 1977). It is based on the premise that the various stages of the life cycle are characterized by a high degree of continuity. As a person grows to maturity and passes on to the stages of later maturity and old age, continuity theory holds that the individual develops rather stable values, attitudes, norms, and habits that become an integral part of his or her own personality. The manner in which an individual will react to the aging process will thus be influenced by that person's attempts to maintain char-acteristic traits and predispositions.

Continuity theorists do recognize, however, that predispositions to act in certain ways are always subject to change or modification because of the ongoing and sometimes complex forms of interaction people have with others and with the environment during all stages of the life cycle. Although there will be a tendency toward consistency, continuity theory admits that people also change by adapting to new situations. For instance, a person who looked forward to retirement might not like it after all, and might instead be forced to accommodate to an unwelcome situation. Continuity theory thus admits of a wide range of different reactions to the aging experience, each dependent on a variety of factors.

The merit of continuity theory is that it might be able to explain several aspects of aging in a much fuller sense than disengagement or activity theory is now able to do. But conversely, the theory seems extremely difficult to conceptualize, to make operational for research studies, and to analyze in ways that indicate its relevance for our understanding. It is too early to tell what contributions continuity theory may produce to explain aging, but the theory does offer considerable promise.

Age Stratification Theory

Age stratification theory is based largely on the work of Matilda White Riley (1971; Riley et al., 1971). It takes the position that society is stratified into various age classes. Each age class has both life course and historical dimensions. The life course dimension is somewhat like the stages of the life cycle. People belong to different age groups depending on how long they have lived and, as a result, they share similar social roles and experiences. At approximately the same point in their lives, they have all been infants, elementary school children, high school students, workers, parents, grand-parents, and so forth. They have had similar roles in their respective pasts, are occupying similar roles in the present, and are likely to have similar roles in the future as members of the same age cohort. As they grow older, everyone else grows older as well and younger people fill their former roles while they move on with others of their age to assume roles consistent with their age class. The historical dimension pertains to the fact that people experience distinct historical periods together and share particular events on the basis of age. For example, the Vietnam War is likely to have had a different meaning for Americans who were children at that time, or who were draft age, or who perhaps were older and had lived through World War II and the Korean War. Each shared an event, but brought a different perspective to it because of age. Thus, age stratification theory holds that relationships must be studied not only among members of the same age group, but also between age groups. As David Decker (1980:145) points out, "this approach has the advantage of allowing us to look at each age group in terms of its distinctive characteristics and history, and also to view any particular age group within the context of a set of age groups."

Age stratification theory does offer a method by which both the characteristics *within* age groups and *between* age groups can be analyzed. An age group can be seen as a particular generation in relation to other living generations and one that brings its own attitudes and beliefs to bear on situations held in common. Individuals can also be seen as members of a generation working out its problems within the context of particular historical circumstances. People can, accordingly, be viewed as living in a world already constructed for them and as active participants in shaping that world to meet their needs. This approach is apparent, for example, in the work of social gerontologists like Russell Ward (1979), who suggests that an individual's experience with the aging process is influenced at the "macro" level by the age stratification system of society and at the "micro" level by the person's own characteristics and personality. In sum, age stratification theory is attractive because it is logical, appears comprehensive, and points the way toward which a researcher can analyze the interplay between macro and micro level social processes as they relate to aging. Unfortunately, this theory may also be difficult to operationalize for empirical research and it awaits more extensive use before its strengths and weaknesses can be fully determined.

Theories of Aging: An Overview

For the present, two theoretical approaches—disengagement theory and activity theory—dominate the research literature in social gerontology. These theories have attempted to systematize the existing social and psychological data on aging so as to serve as a predictive model of the behavior that accompanies old age. Disengagement theory views old age as a distinct phase of life decidedly different from middle age; it is a time when specific social and psychological forces come to bear upon the person to make him or her aware of a reduced ability to contend with stress. Furthermore, disengagement theory suggests that disengagement of the elderly from society's important functions is not only beneficial for society, but also for the elderly person, who is freed from the stresses of the pre-retirement role. While an overall decrease in social activity is generally observable in old age, disengagement theory does not account for the fact that many older people remain active (engaged) in some fashion and that such activity is significantly related to life satisfaction. So it is not at all clear that disengagement is inevitable nor is it as personally satisfying an experience as the theory would suggest.

Activity theory, on the other hand, strongly supports the notion of a positive relationship between activity and life satisfaction. Yet its weakness lies in not explaining what happens to people who cannot be active or who do not believe that being active is the only way to keep happy in old age. The proposition that high levels of activity are necessary for "successful" aging has not been conclusively demonstrated. The promise of continuity theory is that it tells us people age according to a general life pattern which, with adaptations, continues to the end of life. Thus, aging people may not necessarily be dependent on the social environment, but are seen as capable of making adaptations to social and biological changes in their lives. Continuity theory is, however, still in the nature of a hypothesis. As for age stratification theory, it, too, is underdeveloped. Yet the theory is promising. It describes the manner in which age classes develop their own class "consciousness" and relate to other age groups, and discusses how individual behavior is affected by large scale (macro) and small scale (micro) processes in the aging experience.

It is obvious that all theories of social gerontology are still in the formative stage. There are two major reasons for this situation. First, social gerontology is a relatively new field that marks its beginning with a study of aging conducted by Robert Havighurst and Ruth Albrecht in 1953; as such it awaits the accumulation of an extensive body of research data that can only come with a considerable amount of work in the field. Second, research concerning the aging experience should include studies of people as they age if social gerontology is going to be able to explain and perhaps to predict the changes in behavior that come with aging. Such research is not only expensive, but, if done correctly, is going to take several years of data collection before adequate theories can be formulated.

IMAGE OF THE AGED:
SELECTED RESEARCH FINDINGS

Society's View of the Aged

A major theme underlying the social psychology of aging is the anxiety with which many adults face old age. According to Neugarten (1971), most people have an irrational fear of aging based on negative stereotypes of what it is like to be old. Palmore (1971), for example, studied attitudes toward aging as suggested by humor. Humor can be an important indicator of social attitudes since it often reflects widely held social stereotypes. Some 264 jokes were singled out and analyzed to indicate prevalent societal attitudes. Over half of the jokes reflected a negative view of aging, the most disparaging being those whose principal subject matter was physical ability, appearance, age concealment, mental abilities, and being an "old maid." The majority of jokes about being a male "old-timer" and still having sexual ability were either positive or ambivalent. Jokes dealing with old men generally tended to be much more positive than those dealing with old women; in fact, most of the age concealment jokes referred to women. In addition, jokes that could be related to the activity theory of aging were more positive than those related to disengagement theory. This study suggested: (1) the popular culture generally devalues old age, and (2) a double standard may exist in which aging women are viewed more negatively than aging men.

The common stereotypes of old age in American society are that it is characterized by economic insecurity, poor health, loneliness, rigid attitudes, and failing physical and mental powers (Tuckman and Lorge, 1953; Neugarten, 1970, 1971). Despite the fact that many elderly people are not lonely, poor, and in bad health, nor do they become overtly senile or mentally ill (Neugarten, 1970, 1971), negative stereotypes of aging are both pervasive (Atchley, 1977; Ward, 1977, 1979; Larson, 1978) and highly resistant to change (Tuckman and Lorge, 1952). The end result of these stereotypes is their use as a psychological barrier by the young to separate themselves from the old and to ascribe an inferior social status to being elderly.

The group in society that appears to hold the most negative views of old people is young and middle-aged adults. By contrast, studies involving children find little evidence of devaluation of old age. In a review of children's literature between 1870 and 1960, Mildred Seltzer and Robert Atchley (1971) found little evidence of negativity toward aging. More recently, Elizabeth Thomas and Kaoru Yamamoto (1975) have found a rather positive attitude toward the aged in a study of children and adolescents. There was general agreement that older people were "good" and "wise," while the qualities of being "pleasant," "happy," and "exciting" were seen to decrease with age but were nonetheless present in old age. Only on the qualities of being "active" and having "power" were the elderly rated negatively. Thomas and Yamamoto suggest that rather than developing negative attitudes toward aging in childhood, what apparently happens is that people acquire negative stereotypes of aging as they themselves begin to feel threatened by old age.

Thus, older people must not only confront the fact of biological decline, but they must also cope with being relegated to a relatively inferior social status. In pointing out that perhaps the most important impact of aging is that it may cause an individual to lose eligibility to occupy a valued social position. Atchley aptly summarizes society's view of the aged:

> To put the position of older person into proper perspective, one need only to ask: do people get wealthy, revered, or influential simply by growing old? The answer must be a resounding "no." As a matter of fact, if anything happens to a person as a result of getting old, it will probably be that wealth, influence, or prestige of his other positions will *decrease*. Being defined as old may cause him to be *removed* from some of his other positions.[1]

The above discussion, however, pertains to conditions in Western society. In China, Korea, and Japan, the elderly typically occupy a position of respect and honor largely because of the lingering influence of Confucianism and the tradition of ancestor worship. In the Confucian system of social relations, a clearly defined order of superiority-subordination guided behavior. This system subordinated the young to the old, females to males, and subjects to rulers. While the Confucian system was overturned in China and North Korea by communism and in South Korea and Japan through rapid industrialization and capitalism, the cultural traditions it fostered still persist. In China today the old are not left to live alone but are expected to remain in the family setting and serve in an honored role. To be old is to be accorded greater respect in Chinese society, for age is equated with wisdom (Fairbank, 1979). Japan has a national holiday, *Respect for the Elders Day*, that honors the aged; the sixty-first birthday is also a time to be honored by the family; while the young are taught to be respectful to the old and seats are reserved on buses and trains for aged citizens. Since 1973, all people over age seventy in Japan have been eligible for free medical care. According to Palmore (1975), some 79 percent of all Japanese couples over the age of sixty-five in 1973 still lived with at least one of their children, compared to figures of 14 percent in Denmark and 18 percent in the United States and Great Britain. Among widows and widowers over age sixty-five, more than 80 percent of both groups lived with children. While the reality of actual living conditions for many of the elderly in Asia may be less than ideal, their social role is equated with much higher status than in the West.

The Aged's View of Themselves

A review of the research literature comparing the way the aged view themselves with societal stereotypes of the elderly both supports and refutes the proposition that older people view themselves in a negative context. For example, in a comparison of institutionalized older people and noninstitutionalized older and younger people, Evelyn Mason (1954) found that the aged institutionalized group viewed its self-worth in a significantly more negative fashion than did either of the noninstitutionalized groups. Within

---

[1] Robert C. Atchley, *The Social Forces in Later Life* (Belmont, Cal.: Wadsworth, 1977), p. 100.

this latter group, however, the noninstitutionalized aged viewed their self-worth more negatively than a similar group of young adults. Irving Rosow (1967) has suggested that the stress of daily living, especially alienation resulting from the loss of preferred adult statuses, tended to lower feelings of self-worth and well-being among the aged. In a later work, Rosow (1974) held that the ambiguity associated with the role of older people affects psychological stability and promotes depression, anxiety, anomie, and refusal to view one's self as old. This condition is attributed to role loss and society's failure to develop clear norms pertaining to the role of the elderly.

Other research, however, has indicated that older people have a generally positive impression of themselves. In a comparison of the attitudes of retired and nonretired older people, Caroline Preston (1967) found no significant differences between the two groups in terms of life satisfaction and suggested that the aged may indeed feel more positive about themselves than had been previously assumed. In a study of teachers and telephone company employees, Atchley (1976) found that the great majority of his subjects liked retirement. Atchley (1977) noted that retirement per se had little psychological effect on the individual (the greatest problem may be reduced income), and other research (Riley and Foner, 1968) suggests that negative orientations toward the self tend to decrease with age.

Why is the research about the self-perceptions of the elderly so contradictory? A basic problem has to do with the attempts of many researchers to generalize that most old people are either unhappy or happy. These gross generalizations fail to take into account considerable variance among individuals in the manner in which they cope with the aging experience. Neugarten (1971) has made the important point that the aged in American society are not a homogeneous group. As Neugarten explains, a consistent finding of studies of happiness, intelligence, personality, and the health of adults have shown that age is a poor index of the way in which people differ from each other. At the University of Chicago, for instance, Neugarten and her colleagues carried out a longitudinal study lasting fifteen years of the adaptational patterns of about 2,000 people aged seventy to seventy-nine. Three principal areas of life among the aged were examined—personality, life satisfaction, and extent of social-role activity. As a result of their data, they were able to construct four major types of personalities common to the aged: (1) integrated, (2) defended, (3) passive-dependent, and (4) disintegrated.

The majority of these respondents were classified as having an *integrated* personality, that is, they were characterized as being high in life satisfaction, mature, open to new experiences, having good cognitive abilities and a view of themselves as competent. The integrated personality consisted of three subtypes, each of which was based upon the person's role activity. One subtype, termed the *reorganizers*, included those who engaged in a wide variety of activities, such as business and community affairs. The second subtype was classified as the *focused*; these were people who remained active, but only in a few select roles. The other subtype was the *disengaged*, people with well-integrated personalities who experienced satisfaction with their lives but demonstrated low activity. Members of this latter group had high self-esteem and appeared to be complex, self-directed individuals, yet they had voluntarily withdrawn from role commitments to be content with the "rocking-chair" approach to old age.

The second major personality category was the *defended*. These were hard-driving, ambitious, achievement-oriented individuals who were very defensive about aging. The defended personality consisted of two major subtypes. First was the *holding-on* group, which continued to work hard and maintain relatively high levels of activity as a means of obtaining satisfaction from life. Next were those defended personalities described as *constricted*. Constricted individuals combated aging by trying very hard to maintain their health through diet and general activities, while also being oriented toward maintaining a youthful physical appearance.

The third major personality was identified as *passive-dependent*. There were two subtypes common to this group. *Succorance-seeking* individuals had strong needs to be dependent and have other people respond to them. They were somewhat active and seemed to adjust to aging in a positive manner so long as they had some other person or persons to depend on for assistance and support. The second subtype, of whom only a small number were found, was the *apathetic*. The primary characteristic of this person was passivity. These people had little interaction with others, engaged in few activities, and seemed to have little interest in what went on around them.

The fourth major personality type was the *disintegrated*. Very few people qualified for this category. The disintegrated personality consisted of people who demonstrated gross psychological disorganization and who were generally only able to maintain themselves outside an institution because of family arrangements or the tolerance of other people in their social network.

While recognizing that other personality types common to patterns of aging may exist, Neugarten has suggested two important conclusions about aging in American society. First, she has pointed out that older people deal with aging in a number of ways. She is impressed by the fact that variation rather than similarity seems to be the rule among the aged, and she further indicates that such variation may become even more pronounced in the future. This is so because current data on the aged are derived from people who tend to be poor, foreign-born, and poorly educated. As Americans who have enjoyed the financial affluence and higher standards of education characteristic to the mid-twentieth century become old, she believes these people will have even greater freedom in selecting their lifestyles. And second, as an advocate of continuity theory, she suggests that people age in accordance with the behavior that is generally typical of lifelong patterns of responses. Though lacking conclusive data, she believes that the general image of aging is one of personality continuance over time.

However, besides personality, some other variables have been found to affect the way in which older people view themselves. The most significant of these variables, which seem to be related to each other as well as important in themselves, are: (1) level of health, (2) sex, and (3) socioeconomic status.

Regardless of one's personality, a most significant variable affecting an individual's adjustment to old age is level of health. George Maddox (1962), for example, has found that the most important single determinant of an elderly person's self-assessment is that person's health status. Pessimism about one's health was associated with anxiey and poor adjustment to the environment, while optimism about one's health was associated with an absence of these problems. Preston (1968) studied older people who were about to retire. She found that those who reported more chronic health disorders and more incapacity due to illness showed a greater tendency to think of themselves as being "old" than those who did not report such health problems. In another study, Arthur Schwartz and Robert Kleemeier (1965) examined two groups of elderly people and two groups of young people who were categorized by age and state of health (sick or well). They noted that among those who were sick, illness tended to have a greater effect on the self-perceptions of the aged than the young, but the relationship was due to the effects of illness and age, and not just to age alone.

Sex-based differences in attitudes toward aging constitute another important variable. A past assumption in some of the research literature on aging has been that the retired role is much more difficult for men than for women because men are considered to be more strongly attached to their occupational role and relationship with the external social structure (see Cumming and Henry, 1961). In Atchley's (1976) sample of aged school teachers and telephone company employees, however, it was the women rather than the men who had the most difficulty facing retirement. In comparison to the men (who seemed reasonably content with retirement), the women were more likely to be lonely, anxious, unstable in self-concept, highly sensitive to criticism, and highly depressed; the men were more susceptible to anomie and more likely to identify themselves as "old."

Denial of aging appears to be a characteristic more typical of women than men. As noted earlier (Drevenstedt, 1976), women generally perceive the onset of old age later than men. This tendency may be related to sex role stereotypes in American society which equate female beauty and sexuality with youth. With very few exceptions, aged women are not generally depicted in the popular culture as "beautiful," but aged men can be considered "handsome" or "distinguished." Instances of older men marrying young women, for example, tend to be more common than older women marrying young men. All in all, the fact that women live longer than men does appear to be a mixed blessing, as old age for women presents serious difficulties of adjustment.

The third variable that needs to be mentioned is socioeconomic status. As Arlie Russell Hochschild (1973a) has observed, the assumption that old age is the great leveler because it affects the rich and poor alike is not necessarily true. It is much better to be old and rich than to be old and poor. Chapter Two on social epidemiology showed that the upper social classes tend to have a longer life expectancy than the lower classes and, in effect, what Hochschild is saying is that the shorter a person's life expectancy, the poorer that person's health and morale. Therefore, lower-class people may begin to "feel" old at progressively earlier ages than upper-class people. For instance, Caroline Preston and Karen Gudiken (1966) have found that indigent older people expressed significantly more negative than positive traits about themselves when they compared themselves to "others my age." Negative self-reporting among the indigent aged appeared to be a manifestation of depression. Maddox (1962) also noted that social class position is related to optimism and pessimism about health. Older people of high social status were much more likely than other people to be optimistic about their health. Older people of low social status tended to be pessimistic about their health, even when they were medically assessed to be in good health.

Besides the effect of poverty on the health status and general outlook of the aged, the aged poor are more likely to be socially isolated. Rosow (1967) found in Cleveland that middle-class older people tended to have more good friends in old age than working-class older people. Hochschild summarizes this situation as follows:

> Removed from the economy, the old have been cast out of the social networks that revolve around work. Lacking work, they are pushed down the social ladder. Being poor, they have fewer social ties. Poverty reinforces isolation. To eliminate enforced isolation, we have to eliminate poverty, for the two go together.[2]

The significance of race in the aging experience is generally a result of the fact that aged people who belong to racial minority groups are also more likely than aged whites to be poor. There has been a suggestion (see Palmore, 1969) that perhaps old age provides some relative advantage to blacks because aged blacks do not suffer as great a reduction in income as whites (whether or not this is an advantage is certainly questionable, because the income of blacks is more likely to be low anyway) and because older blacks receive more acceptance and support from their children. This latter assumption has been challenged, however, in a study of black and white widowed women by Helena Znaniecki Lopata (1973) in a large northern metropolis. Contrary to the common belief that older black widows live rich and full lives surrounded by their kin, Lopata found that black widows appear to be just as isolated in old age as white widows. In fact, it may be that the psychological stresses of being a member of a racial minority group in the United States is further compounded when that person becomes old. Regardless of race, old age itself seems to confer no particular advantage upon the elderly person in the United States except that of lessened responsibilities.

The Aged as a Minority Group

A controversial issue in social gerontology is whether or not the aged in American society constitute an emerging minority group (see Palmore, 1969). It has been pointed out that many older people experience negative stereotyping, relegation to an inferior social status, discrimination, and segregation. A common reaction of people exposed to these social and psychological stresses is the formation of a group identity with a specific

---

[2] Arlie Russell Hochschild, *The Unexpected Community* (Englewood Cliffs, N.J.: Prentice-Hall, Inc., 1973), p. 140.

group-oriented belief and value system reflecting the needs and goals of group members. It has therefore been proposed that such a group identity in the form of a distinct subculture has been developing among the aged. This subculture is thought to be an increasingly important phenomenon as the proportion of older people in American society increases (Rose and Peterson, 1965).

One of the most engaging studies on the subculture of the aged is Hochschild's (1973a) research among the residents of Merrill Court, a small apartment building in San Francisco, comprised mostly of sixty-, seventy-, and eighty-year-old widows. The forty-three residents of Merrill Court had developed their own social community, which Hochschild suggested was founded on a particular kind of relationship—the "sibling bond." What was special about this community was not that it was an old age subculture, but that membership in the sisterhood at Merrill Court offered these social siblings a full and meaningful social life based on adult autonomy. Unlike the institutionalized elderly, the widows at Merrill Court took care of themselves and made their own decisions. By sharing a social life of coffees, lunches, shopping, activities in the service club, bowling, and by being related to the other residents in terms of belonging to the same age stratum with its common rewards, problems, desires, and abilities, the widows were tied to each other by a bond characteristic of siblings.

Hochschild believes that certain periods of life, specifically adolescence and old age, are better for forming sibling bonds as they are times when people seem to be in particular need of "back-up" social relationships. In these periods—just before and after raising a family and entering and leaving the economy—many people tend to forge friendship solidarity within their own generation. These are also times when social change is most pronounced in a person's life. Hochschild explains that the sisterhood at Merrill Court was no substitute for the love of children and family, but that it did provide a social life independent of the family and added a measure of meaningful and enjoyable activity not otherwise obtainable. While recognizing that the residents of Merrill Court may not be typical of most old people, Hochschild suggests that this type of community may be a forecast of what is to come among the aged because it is a positive adjustment to an unpleasant social condition: the tendency of aged people in modern, industrialized societies to be socially isolated.

To describe elderly people in general, however, as constituting a genuine minority group is a dubious assumption. The best description (Barron, 1961) is that the aged represent a "quasiminority group" because they do not currently function as a socially organized subgroup in American society. Yet as Palmore (1969) explains, the extent to which the aged represent a distinct minority group is apparently a matter of degree, as elderly people organize and develop social and political power to reduce discrimination and win benefits for their specific needs. Social action groups for the aged are becoming more commonplace in the United States, and the future may see the aged emerge as a powerful interest group in American society mobilized to effect social changes in favor of the elderly. At present the aged subculture in retirement communities appears to be retreatist in content rather than activist, as their distinctive pattern of life is the preference for interaction with other elderly people in the retirement setting (Longino et al., 1980).

SUMMARY

This chapter has reviewed the major theories and selected research findings that currently constitute the field of social gerontology. The most influential of these theories is disengagement theory, which views the withdrawal of the older person from society as being beneficial both to society and to the individual. Disengagement theory encounters a serious challenge, however, in activity theory, which holds that activity itself keeps older people happy. A relatively recent theory, continuity theory, offers another perspective. People act in accordance with their past activities and personalities, but are amenable to a certain degree of change in new situations. Thus, the elderly person may have a wider range of choice than had previously been recognized. Age stratification theory, another relatively new approach, explains how particular age groups develop a sense of themselves in relation to other age groups in their society. However, further refinement of these theories is needed before their validity can be fully assessed.

A major problem confronting older people is their devaluation by the young, as reflected in numerous negative stereotypes ascribed to the elderly. Yet older people do not necessarily agree with these stereotypes; in fact, research was cited by Neugarten (1971) to suggest that most older people are relatively happy and satisfied with their lives. Life satisfaction in old age, however, seems to be affected by the variables of health, sex, and socio-economic status. At the present time, it cannot be claimed that a distinctive subculture appears among the elderly or that they constitute a genuine minority group in terms of political and social organization to benefit group membership. However, the number and proportion of older people in the United States is continuing to increase and the time may come when the aged represent a much greater social force in American society than they currently do. Overall, the literature has revealed that there is no homogeneous self-concept among the aged; older Americans do not all think alike about aging and themselves as aged people.

chapter 12

DEATH AND DYING

Death is a characteristic of human existence and all societies have developed social arrangements for containing its impact. Yet despite the obviousness of this personal and social phenomenon, it has only been in the last decade that the study of death as a social process has been given considerable attention in medical sociology and also in psychology, medicine, psychiatry, and law. Death as a topic of investigation had been generally avoided because of the unpleasantness of the subject matter. Yet attempts to define death as something so indeterminate that it can be denied or easily avoided have not been successful strategies in coping with both the meaning and process of dying, either on an individual or societal level. Death is an inevitable biological and social experience of all people and as such is a dominant part of the process of living. Its effect on human behavior cannot be ignored.

Beginning in 1965 with Barney Glaser and Anselm Strauss' seminal work, *Awareness of Dying*, medical sociologists have become increasingly interested in studying the process of death and dying in contemporary society. The result has been that the study of death has become one of the most active areas of research in medical sociology. The study of attitudes toward death have also made that topic one of the most recent sources of significant theoretical and applied insight into human behavior.

Initially, most of the research concerning death dealt with the problem of death as a solitary and perhaps cruel experience in modern hospitals where the dying patient was often found to be socially and psychologically isolated. Hospital staff and the dying patient's family appeared inhibited in their attempts to interact with the patient in an open and socially meaningful manner. The process of dying was itself hidden as much as possible to minimize the effect of death on all concerned, especially the living. Now it seems that our attitudes toward death may be changing, not only in the academic disciplines, but in American society generally. While it remains to be confirmed that we are actually in a period of a "death revolution," which some writers suggest will see the elimination of the fear of death in advanced industrialized societies, the contemporary approach toward death is to deal with it as a natural part of the human condition. It is hoped that this approach will help us to understand our own lives and ease our fears about the inevitability of mortality in a more open, honest, and satisfying manner.

DEATH AND THE INDIVIDUAL

The basic problem that humans have in dealing with death is fear. In a review of traditional attitudes toward death, Elisabeth Kübler-Ross (1969) points out that death has been and remains a fearful and frightening event to human beings and that fear of death is universal throughout the human species. Many studies in psychology and psychiatry have documented the fact that this strong, deep-rooted fear motivates many people to seek secure environments and to avoid activities and situations that could result in premature death. Sigmund Freud, for example, believed that fear of death was a primary motivation for social cohesion as people sought security and strength from group membership. Even though some people may not overtly express a fear of death and dying, Herman Feifel and Allan Branscomb (1973) have suggested that nearly everyone fears death. In a survey, Feifel and Branscomb noted that over 70 percent of their respondents verbally denied they were afraid of death. However, at a second level of testing, which involved reactions to images of death, the respondents began to demonstrate ambivalent attitudes. At a third level of testing, involving word and color-word associations, nearly 95 percent of the respondents revealed a subconscious fear of death. Even people who characterized themselves as extremely religious indicated "a demonstrable fear of death" on the subconscious level.

Fear of Death

Although many fears have been identified in connection with death, the primary fear is fear of the unknown—the dread of not knowing what happens when you die and after you die. Barney Glaser and Anselm Strauss (1968) say that when death occurs slowly, the dying patient is forced to cope with death by overcoming the fear of loss of self and the fear of dying as physical, and perhaps mental, disintegration. No one can share his or her experiences of death with the living; yet reports are available from people who have nearly died of a heart attack or from an accident of some kind. Although such reports do give clues about the experience of life's final moments, the reader should be cautioned about accepting the validity of such accounts because they obviously cannot be verified.

A study by Russell Noyes, Jr. (1972) of the process of dying found that many people who report being close to death have similar experiences. Using descriptions of dying experiences, both autobiographical and clinical, Noyes developed a model of the death experience consisting of three stages: resistance, review, and transcendence.

The initial stage of *resistance* to death begins when a person struggles for survival, realizing that death may be imminent. This resistance is characterized by marked anxiety but not disabling panic. If even the slightest possibility of survival remains, the person often feels an enormous surge of energy that may enable him or her to survive by alert mental activity and possible feats of strength. But, conversely, this upsurge of energy is countered by a powerful desire to surrender and the person is caught between the impulse to fight and the impulse to surrender. If the person is dying gradually, Noyes claims that as energy wanes, life seems to be dependent on an inner struggle to maintain it. He (1972:177) states: "It is as though their will to live sustains them and as though without it they might simply let themselves go and, in a sense, will their deaths."

The second stage of *review* appears after all hope of survival has apparently disappeared and the person surrenders to his or her fate. Death is faced calmly, perhaps with a sense of tranquility. At this particular point, Noyes says that the person begins to review past life experiences from a detached perspective, as if the ego had become an entity capable of observing itself act out the past. The present author has interviewed people who reported similar experiences after being close to death as a result of automobile and industrial accidents. These people believed that they, in fact, left their hospital beds and "hovered" about the room, able to view themselves and others as a detached consciousness. Parapsychologists term this experience an "out-of-the-body" phenomenon, which may be a negation of death on the part of the dying person. Here the subject views his or her body as near death, but exists outside it, thus becoming a detached witness. Some people, according to Noyes, report viewing scattered scenes or all the important events in their lives in this "detached" state. He suggests that the certainty of loss of future may necessitate a return to the past to make their existence real in a final grip on life. The phenomenon of the ego splitting from the body may also lessen personal anxiety by reducing death to solely bodily annihilation.

The final phase is *transcendence.* Here the person's perspective becomes more distant and they experience themselves as outside of time or beyond the past and future. This altered sense of time represents complete immersion in the present moment. Another characteristic feeling is a sense of loss of control as if held by a superior power. At this point the person experiences feelings of oneness or unity with other human beings and the universe. Death is near.

While providing some interesting insights, Noyes' analysis of the death process cannot be considered conclusive by any means. His descriptions were rendered by people generally in good health who were suddenly threatened with death. We do not know if these experiences are typical or how accurately most people identify their dying moments. Then, too, the mystical state of consciousness reported during transcendence may not be shared by all dying people, but just those who have a tendency toward such modes of perceiving. Other variables, such as age, sex, personality, and culture, may also be very important. Still, the similarities among those cases reported by Noyes seem to suggest important guidelines for future research into the experience of dying.[1]

The first stage of resistance in Noyes's typology raises an important sociological question regarding death. This question concerns the extent to which the "will to live" is responsible for length of life. Although researchers are not aware of what physiological mechanisms may be at work in this process, a body of literature in psychology suggests that perhaps rats, chickens, monkeys, human beings, and even cockroaches become unusually susceptible to death when they discover that they have no control over what is happening to them and that further action is futile (Seligman, 1974). The experience of American prisoners-of-war during the Korean and Vietnam wars who simply lay down and died, although apparently in good physical health, are examples of this phenomenon.

Research by David Phillips and Kenneth Feldman (1973) has found evidence that there are fewer deaths than usual before important ceremonial occasions such as a birthday, a presidential election, and the Jewish Day of Atonement. According to data derived from biographies of famous people, Phillips and Feldman suggest, in accordance with Emile Durkheim's (1961) description of social integration and ceremonies, that people who are strongly integrated into a society feel an obligation to participate in the ceremonies of that society. Thus, people strongly attached to society postpone death in order to participate in meaningful social ceremonies; people detached from society and uninvolved with its ceremonies may die prematurely by committing suicide or by just "letting go." Admittedly speculative, this hypothesis does offer interesting possibilities for future sociological

---

[1] Research by Raymond Moody, reported in his book *Life After Life* (1976), suggests that the out-of-the-body phenomenon and the review of one's past life are especially common elements of the dying process. Moody, a physician, interviewed several people who were supposedly near death at some time in their lives and he described the typical experience of death as follows:

> A man is dying and, as he reaches the point of greatest physical distress, he hears himself pronounced dead by his doctor. He begins to hear an uncomfortable noise, a loud ringing or buzzing, and at the same time feels himself moving very rapidly through a long tunnel. After this, he suddenly finds himself outside of his own physical body, but still in the immediate physical environment, and he sees his own body from a distance, as though he is a spectator. He watches the resuscitation attempt from this unusual vantage point and is in a state of emotional upheaval.

> After a while, he collects himself and becomes more accustomed to his odd condition. He notices that he still has a "body," but one of a very different nature and with very different powers from the physical body he has left behind. Soon other things begin to happen. Others come to meet and help him. He glimpses the spirits of relatives and friends who have already died, and a loving, warm spirit of a kind he has never encountered before—a being of light—appears before him. This being asks him a question, nonverbally, to make him evaluate his life and helps him along by showing him a panoramic, instantaneous playback of the major events of his life (Moody, 1976:121–122).

> Moody goes on to explain that the dying man is caught up in intense feelings of joy and peace. But somehow he realizes that it is not time for him to die. Reluctantly, he returns to his physical body and lives.

research concerning the will to live and the social processes that might either reinforce or possibly negate that will.[2]

The other major fear of the unknown is fear of what happens after death. Beliefs about existence after death are common in most cultures, and one of the primary functions of religion is to reduce anxiety by providing answers concerning life after death. However, research to date about the effects of religion in allaying fear of death has been inconclusive (Dumont and Foss, 1972). Kübler-Ross (1969) found in her research with terminally ill patients that religious patients seemed to differ little from those who were not religious. Very few patients could be identified as being truly religious or as confirmed atheists. Most held beliefs somewhere between the two extremes and their philosophical perspectives were usually not strong enough to relieve them of the fear of dying. Kübler-Ross observed that people with less education, little sophistication, and few professional obligations or social ties had the least difficulty in facing death. Those persons experiencing the greatest difficulty were characterized as ambitious, attempting to strive for control of their environment and for accumulation of material goods. Although they had many social ties, they exhibited few meaningful personal relationships and usually faced death alone.

But fear of the unknown is not the only fear related to the experience of dying. At least five other significant fears have been identified: (1) fear about not being able to pursue or to complete certain goals; (2) fear of what will happen to dependents; (3) fear of the loss of self-mastery or control over one's destiny; (4) fear of punishment for sins; and (5) fear of isolation and separation from loved ones and treasured objects. All of these fears, either singly or in combination, can produce a considerable degree of anxiety in an individual concerned about death.

Strategies for Dealing with Death: Childhood, Adolescence, Adulthood

Since fear of death is universal—defined by existentialist philosophers as the human being's "most profound awareness"—numerous strategies have been employed by individuals and society for coping with death anxieties. In very early *childhood*, there is generally no conception of what death means, and the discovery of the phenomenon of death is not usually accompanied by great emotion (Anthony, 1968, 1972). Often the child's discovery of death occurs as a simple incident in day-to-day living when the child explores his or her environment and perhaps finds a dead object such as a bird or insect. Sylvia Anthony (1968) tells us that usually there is a definite interval between a child's first questions about death and the arousal of

[2] An interesting example of the possible relationship between a significant social event in a person's life and the will to live is found in the biography of Thomas Jefferson. Jefferson died on July 4th, fifty years to the day after he signed the Declaration of Independence. Jefferson's physician described the scene as follows:

About seven o'clock of the evening of that day, he [Jefferson] awoke, and seeing my staying at his bedside exclaimed, "Oh Doctor, are you still there?" in a voice, however, that was husky and indistinct. He then asked, "Is it the Fourth?" to which I replied, "It soon will be." These were the last words I heard him utter (Peterson, 1970:1008).

emotion connected with the idea of dying. Death is commonly associated with the child's understanding of his or her world and may be viewed as going to sleep, going on a trip, or going up in the sky.

Relevant research suggests that anxieties regarding death do not appear until around the ages of three to five, when the child realizes the possibility of loss of someone upon whom the child depends or the loss of one's own self (Prugh et al., 1953; Knudson and Natterson, 1960; Natterson and Knudson, 1960; Anthony, 1968; Spinetta, 1974). D. G. Prugh and associates found that among hospitalized children, types of death anxiety varied according to age; children under the age of six were thought to be highly anxious about separation from other people. The other studies cited above agree that death disturbs the very young child mostly in regard to the thought of separation, loneliness, or abandonment.

Many young children, however, do not develop death anxieties. They are usually able to control their fears about death because they do not perceive death as the end of life. The dead may be viewed as being simply another category of the living who are less than alive or who live somewhere else, such as in heaven. Many children are taught that there is an after-life as a defense against death anxiety. Often the perception of young children regarding death may involve a close relationship between death and birth— someone dies and then returns as a baby. Many games that children play also include a death theme in which death is not defined as a permanent or finite state. Children who are "killed" while playing "soldier" or "cowboys and Indians" are expected to come back to life at an appropriate time. This view of death is reflected in children's literature, where death is seen as an event that can be undone; the dead hero can be returned to life by magic or the intervention of good fairies and spirits (Wahl, 1965).

While there is general agreement in the research literature concerning three- to five-year-olds' fears of death as separation, there has been serious disagreement about the characteristics of death anxieties in the six- to ten-year-old age group. Much of the initial research consisted of data collected from observations of terminally ill children that found that this age group lacked the intellectual ability to develop an extensive concept of death (see, for example, Evans and Edin, 1968; Debuskey, 1970; Ingalls and Salerno, 1971). These children apparently experienced little anxiety about dying unless adults intervened to point out to the child the seriousness of the illness. Other research suggested that while six- to ten-year-olds could not fully conceptualize death, nonetheless they were aware that something very serious was wrong with them (see, for example, Binger et al., 1969; Easson, 1970). John Spinetta (1974) has strongly criticized this research, however, on the grounds that their conclusions rested largely on observations of parents and hospital staff rather than on direct observation of the children; also, when they were based upon observations of the child, the studies lacked objective measures, with little or no use of control groups for comparison.

Recent studies, however, strongly suggest that six- to ten-year-olds are aware of what death means. E. H. Waechter (1971) asked a set of four matched groups of children—children who were fatally ill, children with chronic but not fatal illnesses, children with temporary illnesses, and normal, nonhospitalized children—to construct stories about themselves using a set of pictures. Waechter found a greater number of overtly expressed death themes among the fatally ill children. She concluded that this age group is not only subjectively aware of dying, but also able objectively to express that awareness.

Spinetta and associates (1974) tested Waechter's conclusion in an experiment involving a group of twenty-five children fatally ill with leukemia with a control group of twenty-five chronically ill children with nonfatal diseases. The six- to ten-year-olds were matched not only by age group, but also by sex, race, grade in school, and amount of medication. The children were asked to tell a story about a sick friend in the hospital by placing dolls representing a sick child and significant adults (nurse, doctor, mother, father) in their *usual* places in a model of a hospital room. Later the children were asked to repeat the story by putting the dolls in places they would *like* them to be. Since the dying children placed the adult dolls at such a significantly greater distance from the doll of the sick child, Spinetta and associates inferred that the placement of the dolls by the dying children was reflective of a growing sense of psychological separation from both the people and the circumstances of the hospital environment. In interviews with parents and hospital staff, they found additionally that adults reported a decrease in the frequency, intensity, and quality of interaction with the dying child. Although the parents wished for the child's recovery and attempted to provide great affection, they also wished to withdraw from the child to protect themselves emotionally when the child died. The hospital staff likewise reported a reluctance to become emotionally involved for similar reasons.

Accordingly, Spinetta and associates ask some important questions: Does the dying child reflect the unresponsive feelings of adults or does the child try to prepare for death by separating from parents? Does the dying child prefer to be left alone for reasons of his or her own choosing or because he or she senses embarrassment on the part of adults?[3] Spinetta does not provide answers to these questions, but he does suggest that whatever the reason, the fatally ill child is aware of death and perhaps dies psychologically isolated from other people.

Spinetta concludes:

> It seems clear . . . that the fatally ill 6–10-year-old child is concerned about his illness and that even though this illness may not always take the form of overt expressions about his impending death, the more subtle fears and anxieties are nonetheless real, painful, and very much related to the seriousness of the illness that the child is experiencing.[4]

[3] Judith Miller (1975), reporting on the research of Richard Lansdown, a British child psychologist, notes that the most difficult problem for the dying child was the anxiety of the child's parents. Although considered as "callous" by those who were not intimately familiar with the situation, Lansdown found when the parents stopped visiting the child, the child was happiest, sensing that the parents were no longer worried or extremely upset about him. This finding is counter to the implications of Spinetta et al. (1974) regarding the unpleasantness of the dying child's psychological isolation.

[4] John J. Spinetta, "The Dying Child's Awareness of Death: A Review." *Psychological Bulletin*, 81 (April 1974), 259.

Jean Piaget (1959), the noted Swiss psychologist, has observed that children do not recognize the generality and impersonality of death until somewhere between the ages of six and twelve. Piaget considers this recognition of major importance in the development of mature concepts of causality. It signifies that the child is changing his or her perception from the idea that all events and existence can be attributed to personal motivation to an acknowledgement of the action of impersonal causal forces.

Once children near *adolescence*, around the age of ten or so, they develop adult concepts of death which recognize that death is not only inevitable, but also final. Yet adolescents generally fear death less than other age groups because death is not an immediate threat and they are reasonably sure of a full life ahead of them (Dumont and Foss, 1972). Actually, the outward aspects of death often appear very funny to them. They construct jokes and rhymes about death and enjoy laughing at movie and television scenes containing exaggerated expressions of bloody mayhem. Anthony (1968) calls the adolescent's mockery of death "a half-way house" to the defenses against death anxiety available to the adult.

Human beings like to think that somehow the individual personality is not meant to die and that something personal about themselves is able to survive death. However, the strategies that exist for use by the *adult* in the desire for eternal survival are limited to those of (1) sexual reproduction, (2) belief in an after-life, or (3) belief in reincarnation. Sexual reproduction allows adults at least to imprint themselves genetically upon succeeding generations. Belief in an after-life is derived either from religion or a personal philosophy of existence. Some people embrace religion and try to live the kind of life that "qualifies" for life after death in heaven. Other people have their own perhaps nonreligious belief in a life or existence of some type after death, perhaps as a spirit or energy form in the cosmos, or the adult may believe in reincarnation. Several accounts have been written by people who are convinced they were born, lived, and died at a time in the past and have returned to the present to live another life. Otherwise, the adult must cope with the idea of death as the total end of experience and an eternity of nothingness.

Strategies for Dealing with Death:
The Dying Patient

Despite the particular strategy an individual selects to contain the fear of death, the time arrives for most people (except for infants, comatose patients, or those persons dying sudden and unexpected deaths) to confront the process of dying. Two of the most noted studies describing this process are those of Kübler-Ross (1969) and Glaser and Strauss (1965). Kübler-Ross has identified five stages of coping with dying: (1) denial and isolation, (2) anger, (3) bargaining, (4) depression, and (5) acceptance. The first stage of *denial and isolation* consists of the patient's shock and dismay at the disclosure of impending death. Often the initial awareness of death is accompanied by resentment against other people who are not dying or against fate itself. Sometimes patients in the stage of denial will "shop around" for another physician to disprove a previous diagnosis of terminality.

Most patients, according to Kübler-Ross, demonstrate at least partial denial of their deaths at some point in their efforts to cope with the dying process.

Glaser and Strauss also found attempts at denial in their study of terminal patients. Some of these attempts included refusal to seek further information from physicians, refusal to discuss their illness and death with anyone, favorable comparisons of themselves with other dying patients, emphasis upon the future, resumption of activity with a passion, and juggling time. This last strategy consisted of setting a particular point in time as a survival goal and, after reaching that time, selecting another future time, and so on.

Throughout all of the stages outlined by Kübler-Ross, dying patients expressed hope that death could somehow be averted. Usually this hope was based on the possible discovery of a new drug or sometimes upon the skill of physicians. Stewart Alsop (1973), a journalist dying of cancer, said that such hope allowed the dying person to die more easily. While the patient may be told he or she *may* die or *probably* will die, Alsop thought that the patient should not be told he or she *will* die.

Kübler-Ross observed that very few patients are able to maintain a "make-believe world" in which they are healthy up until the final moments of living. When denial of one's death can no longer realistically be maintained in the face of medical evidence, the second stage of anger appears. Often this anger is displaced on family, friends, the hospital staff, or God. Kübler-Ross said this can be a very difficult time for those who must interact with the dying patient. The next stage, *bargaining*, usually does not last very long. This stage represents an attempt to postpone death by good behavior or good deeds. Perhaps in return for some special service, dying patients hope they will be granted an extension of life. The fourth stage, *depression*, occurs usually prior to the acceptance of death. Here the patient knows definitely that absolutely nothing can be done to change his or her fate. The great majority of patients, according to both Kübler-Ross and Glaser and Strauss, come to terms with their depression sufficiently to go on to the final stage of *acceptance*.[5]

If the patient has had enough time and perhaps assistance in working through the other stages of reaction to dying, Kübler-Ross found that the patient usually reaches the stage of acceptance. During this stage the patient is no longer angry or depressed, but recognizes the inevitability of death. This is not a happy period, but one characterized by Kübler-Ross as "almost devoid of feelings." Pain and struggle may be over and all that usually remains is the wait for death. Glaser and Strauss, however, tell us that acceptance may be either active or passive. Passive acceptance consists of calm

---

[5] Lansdown (Miller, 1975) discovered in his research with children dying of leukemia that the parents of these children underwent a stage of mourning during the acceptance of death. This "anticipatory mourning" occurred prior to the death of the child and was similar to post-death mourning. He also found that since leukemia is a disease characterized by remission periods during which the children appeared healthy, parents who had reached the stage of acceptance sometimes returned to the stage of denial, and the entire process of accepting death was repeated several times. Remissions, according to Lansdown, make leukemia "one of the more psychologically complex diseases."

resignation as described by Kübler-Ross, but active acceptance involves preparing for death by becoming philosophical about life and death, settling personal and financial affairs, becoming very religious, or eliminating the distressing prospect of dying a painful and lingering death by committing suicide. Some patients accept the fact of their dying, but decide to fight it by intensive living, seeking out marginal or "quack" doctors for miracle cures, or by volunteering to participate in medical research and experiments that might produce a cure.

Alsop (1973) has provided a particularly insightful account of the acceptance of death in his book *Stay of Execution*. Although he did not welcome the prospect of dying, it was difficult to accept a life of pain and weakness with a dependency upon medication and blood transfusions. To be without the possibility of ever returning to a normal life and to feel very, very sick made the thought of death far less terrible to him. Alsop (1973:23) finally reached the point where he believed that just as a sleepy man needs to sleep, a dying man needs to die, and that a time comes when it is both wrong and useless to resist.

DEATH AND SOCIETY

Like individuals, societies develop attitudes toward death which are reflected in the establishment of normative practices designed to contain death's presence. To assess the contemporary American perspective regarding death, it is useful to compare its evolution from the social thought of Western Europe during the Middle Ages to the present. According to Philippe Ariés (1974), the French social historian, death in Western society in the twelfth century could be characterized as "tamed death" because it seemed to lack the anxieties common to the twentieth century. People in the Middle Ages did not desire to die, or at least they were in no hurry to do so, but when they realized that death was near, the art and literature of the period suggests that they usually died very simply, as if death was a familiar aspect of living. Death was supposedly viewed as the collective destiny of the species and the simplistic, perhaps naive, acceptance of death was acceptance of the order of nature.

Except for sudden or unexpected death, the deaths that occurred during the Middle Ages usually involved a familiar ritual. First, the dying person was supposed to lie down in bed, if at all possible, in order to die. Then, the actual process of dying consisted of a ceremony organized by the dying person, who was expected to follow a prescribed sequence of behaviors intended to conclude life. The dying person was supposed to express sorrow about the end of life and to recollect beloved persons, events, and things. He or she was expected to pardon the usually numerous companions who gathered around the deathbed for any disapproved acts, followed by a final prayer in which the dying person requested forgiveness of sins. After a priest administered absolution, all that remained was the wait for death. Dying was a public and familiar act, and the dying person's room was a social setting to be entered freely by relatives, friends, and neighbors. For example, as Ariés points out, no portrayal of the deathbed scene between the twelfth and eighteenth centuries failed to include the appearance of children. Usually there was no great show of emotion at the deathbed because behavior was guided by the dying person in the formally prescribed death ritual.

In modern society people no longer experience death in this simple, ceremonial manner. Instead the modern version of dying has been characterized by fear, anxiety, and social isolation. What happened? What caused our attitudes toward death to change? Ariés claims that from the Middle Ages on, death in Western society was subtly modified into a pervasive dread. One source of this change, as noted by Ariés and others, is found in Christianity. Walter Kaufmann (1959:61) states that "although some early Christian martyrs died fearlessly, in eager anticipation of eternal bliss, Christianity has on the whole used its vast influence to make men dread death." Inspired by the book of Matthew, the Christian death scene during the Middle Ages emphasized the idea of judgment; that is, the weighing of souls by Christ the Judge according to the deeds, both good and bad, committed during a person's lifetime. The eternal destination of heaven or hell for the dying person was at issue and, notwithstanding its cosmic essence, judgment was peculiar to each individual. Thus, the security of death as a collective rite was joined by the anxiety of interrogation and personal trial.

Medieval Christianity was certainly not wholly responsible for the changing attitudes toward death, but it was influential. During the eighteenth century, romanticism, with its emphasis on love of nature and the expression of strong emotion, viewed death as a painful rupture from the beauty of nature and the joy of living things. Acute anxiety over death was a norm sanctioned by a society strongly aware of the pain of separation from persons and objects that were loved and valued. Another important attitude that first emerged full-blown in the nineteenth century, the Age of Rationalism, was the notion of guilt about personal failure to accomplish certain goals. Ariés (1974:105) summarizes this latter attitude as "a passion for being, an anxiety at not sufficiently being."

The twentieth century marked the efforts of society to control death by making it as unobtrusive a social process as possible. Emphasis was placed on the "acceptable" death, which was a death that could be tolerated by the survivors. This idea had its origin in the belief of the Middle Ages that there was a close relationship between death and an individual's personal biography. It was thought that each person's life flashed before his or her eyes at the moment of death; the dying person's attitude at that time would thus provide his or her biography with its conclusion and final meaning. Death was believed to be the occasion when human beings were most able to know themselves. Consequently, to die well or to experience a good death became very important. The twentieth century interpretation of this attitude, however, was concerned not with the benefit of the individual but with society. The antithesis to an "acceptable" death was the graceless, fearful, and embarrassing death that caused strong emotions and revulsion among other people and a disruption of social life. Therefore, modern society sought to control death and to make it as acceptable as possible by hiding it.

Societal control of the impact of death was significantly assisted by two contemporary phenomena: (1) the occurrence of dying generally among people furthest removed from the mainstream of social life and (2) the displacement of the traditional site of dying from the home to the hospital. Approximately two-thirds of all deaths in industrialized societies are the result of biological decay and the infirmities of old age. Deaths associated with the aging process occur largely among people who have retired from work and who no longer have parental responsibilities. These deaths rarely interrupt the smooth functioning of society.

Hospitals have become the places to die because the care provided there is usually not possible in the home. Today in American society only a minority of people die at home and the number is decreasing rapidly. Exact figures on the number of persons actually dying in hospitals are difficult to obtain, but a review of available data suggests that about one-half of all deaths occur in large general hospitals and a smaller but increasing number occur in nursing homes (Morison, 1973). Probably fewer than one-third of the deaths in American society take place at home, at work, or in public places. The removal of most deaths from the home has caused the traditional death ritual to disappear. Death in the hospital is controlled not by the dying person or his or her family, but by the physician and the hospital staff, who define not only the circumstances of death, but the exact moment of dying.[6] Access by family and friends to the dying patient can also be controlled by the hospital, so that death occurs under the jurisdiction of relative strangers to the dying person. Such a controlled death is disruptive neither to the general functioning of the hospital nor to society at large.

The Social Organization of Dying

Two major studies on death in medical sociology, those of David Sudnow (1967) and Glaser and Strauss (1965), provide illustrations of the death environment in contemporary American society. Sudnow (1967) studied the organization of dying by using participant observation in two hospitals: a large, urban West Coast charity institution and a private, general hospital in the Midwest. Most of Sudnow's observations took place in the charity hospital, which he described as a setting for the concentration of death. Three-fourths of the patients were over sixty years old and there was an average of three deaths daily. Most of the deaths occurred on the medicine and surgery wards. The personnel on these wards encountered death so frequently that it was considered routine. The routinization of dying was made easier, both at the charity and the private hospitals, because almost all of the deaths were preceded by a coma. Comatose patients were regarded as

---

[6] The medical and legal definition of death is no longer the traditional criterion of heart stoppage because of the possible restoration of heart action, even when there is no longer the remotest possibility of the patient's recovering consciousness and brain functions (Hirsh, 1974). The new basis for defining death is that of a "flat" or isoelectric electroencephalogram denoting "brain death," which is taken after signs of respiratory and circulatory failure.

being essentially dead and they could be disattended as a social object.[7] Of the some two hundred deaths he witnessed, Sudnow noted that not a single death was of the "Hollywood" variety where the dying person's last sentence was interrupted by a final breath.

Those people having the most contact with death in the hospitals were generally lower echelon employees. Once a patient died, except for the autopsy, the physician lost interest in the body. The higher one's position in the status hierarchy of the hospital as a nurse or a physician, the less likely was one to witness dead bodies or physically handle corpses. The handling of corpses was considered "dirty work" in the value system of the hospital, and whenever possible ward personnel would leave a body to be processed by the next work shift. Usually the morgue attendants and orderlies performing these unpleasant tasks were blacks.

Sudnow saw the hospital as an environment of occurrences, with death being an occurrence mainly definable in reference to its similarity to other deaths experienced by the personnel. Although any given death could give pause for retrospective comment by staff members, the mention of deaths was usually routine except for those involving unusual events, such as obtrusive settings or styles of dying, accidents, diagnostic or treatment errors, or the high social status of a patient. The age of the dead person could also cause comment, especially the deaths of children. General philosophical consideration by the staff of death and dying did not naturally occur.

While the staff sought to minimize and routinize death as much as possible for themselves, the organization of dying was constructed in such a way as to hide the fact of dying from patients and visitors. Most hospitals, for example, locate the morgue in a relatively inaccessible part of the hospital basement. Sudnow (1967:51) quotes a text in hospital administration: "The hospital morgue is best located on the ground floor and placed in an area inaccessible to the general public. It is important that the unit have a suitable exit leading onto a private loading platform which is concealed from hospital patients and the public." Often the patient whose death was imminently expected was moved to a private room to avoid troubling other patients, and bodies were not removed from these rooms during visiting hours to avoid upsetting visitors.

There was, however, a difference between the charity and private hospitals in regard to the presence of family and friends at the dying patient's bedside. At the private hospital, relatives were considered entitled to be present at the bedside at the moment of death. The dying person did not preside over the gathering as in the traditional death ritual; nonetheless, the experience of death was not as solitary as it was in the charity hospital. Dying patients were shielded from relatives at the charity hospital in order to

[7] As suggested by Erving Goffman, Sudnow (1967:74–75) has made a distinction between "clinical death" (signs of death based upon physical examination), "biological death" (cessation of cellular activity), and "social death" (the point at which a person is treated like a corpse although still alive clinically or biologically). "Social death" was not simply the asocial treatment of a dying patient by the hospital staff, but was the beginning of social activities commonly associated with death: planning the autopsy, grieving, preparing obituary notice, contacting insurance companies, disposing of personal effects, arranging for the funeral, etc.

minimize disruption of hospital routine and processing of the body. The justification for this action was to protect the relatives from the "unpleasantness of seeing someone die." Family members were urged by the staff to go home and await further news if death was regarded as imminent or, at least, to wait in waiting rooms or in the corridors, not in the patient's room. The result was that relatives were usually not present at the time of death and were summoned only after the staff had completed its processing duties.

Awareness Contexts

Glaser and Strauss developed a typology of awareness contexts based upon both participant observation and personal interviews in six hospitals in the San Francisco Bay area. These awareness contexts—closed awareness, suspected awareness, mutual pretense awareness, and open awareness—were all derived from observing the social settings and the control of information about dying in the hospital. Glaser and Strauss found that the physicians were reluctant to disclose impending death to the patient, and nurses were not expected to do so without the consent of the responsible physician. Thus, patients were generally required to take action to get information about the extent of their illness and were often prevented from asking questions about dying by the staff. Awareness contexts were not relevant if the patient was comatose, an infant, someone whose knowledge of death was not important to the staff, or in emergency situations. Awareness contexts pertained when the patient was conscious and the staff managed knowledge of the patient's dying.

Closed awareness is a social condition where the staff knows the patient is dying but the patient is unaware of that fact. It is based on the following structural conditions: (1) inability of the patient to recognize the signs of dying; (2) reluctance of the staff to discuss dying with the patient; (3) reluctance of family members to discuss the patient's condition with the patient; (4) organization of the hospital itself, which is designed to conceal information and records, and the skill of the hospital staff at not disclosing information; and (5) lack of anyone to help the patient find out the facts, including other patients. When any of the above conditions was lacking, other awareness contexts were possible. *Suspected awareness* is a situation in which the patient is suspicious but does not know that an illness is terminal. The patient is then forced to draw information from whatever sources are available to confirm his or her suspicions. *Mutual pretense* is a somewhat more comfortable situation; the patient is aware of a terminal condition and refuses to talk about it, and the staff is under no obligation to discuss dying. This arrangement usually worked to contain emotions unless either party to the interaction broke down while trying to maintain the pretense. *Open awareness* is a condition in which everyone knows and openly acknowledges the terminal situation. The patient is held responsible for his or her behavior and is expected by the staff to face death with dignity, to sustain responsibilities to family and friends, and to cooperate with the staff. This last condition was most acceptable to the staff. Although there are no formal norms for the "ideal" death, Glaser and Strauss make the important point that people just can't help judging other people.

The Glaser and Strauss study differs somewhat from Sudnow's research because most of the patients observed by Glaser and Strauss were not comatose, paid for their own hospital care, and were of a higher social status. Unlike patients in the Sudnow study, they were in a better position to negotiate the dying process. Nevertheless, in both studies the staff saw death as inconvenient and managed interaction with the dying patient so as to minimize disruption.

Desensitizing Death: Coroners and Physicians

The implications of the Sudnow and the Glaser and Strauss studies contribute to an understanding of the social psychology of those people whose occupations and professions require routine exposure to death. The findings of other attitudinal studies should also be noted. For example, Kathy Calkins Charmaz (1975) reported that county coroner's deputies employed self-protective strategies to avoid the emotion of the death scene and to maintain the routine character of their work (ascertaining the cause of death, establishing the identity of the deceased, protecting the property of the deceased, and locating the relatives of the deceased to whom the announcement of death could be made). In making the announcement to relatives, most deputies expressly avoided using the word "dead" and substituted the words "fatally injured" or "passed away," if they made any direct reference to death at all. Sometimes they just gave progressively meaningful cues in the conversation so that the relatives would realize what had happened and would themselves say the word "dead." The deputies were also prompt to turn the situation around by asking about funeral and burial arrangements, so that the responsibility for the occasion was thus symbolically shifted to the relatives.

According to Charmaz, one of the most striking features of the attitudes shown by the deputies was the extent to which they reflected typical cultural taboos. The deputies demonstrated an avoidance of death, were uncomfortable during the expression of grief by survivors, and showed an absence of personal philosophy either about death in general or about their own deaths in particular. Instead, they subjectively interpreted death as being a by-product of their work rather than the focus of it. This approach was exemplified by the comment of one deputy (Charmaz, 1975:304), who stated: "That's not a body lying there. It's an *investigation.* You have to look at it as an investigation, not as a person lying there." The deputies supported an occupational ideology that worked against their becoming involved in the situation on the grounds that they would then be unable to perform their job properly.

Studies of physician attitudes have found a similar reluctance to deal with the emotions surrounding death. In a study of over two hundred physicians on the staff of Michael Reese Hospital in Chicago, Donald Oken (1961) found that 90 percent of the doctors stated a preference for not telling cancer patients that their condition was terminal. In discussing their diagnosis with the patient, the use of euphemisms was the general rule. Patients would be told they had a "lesion," a "mass," or perhaps a "tumor," but terms like "cancer" and "malignancy" were avoided. Yet regardless of the patient's condition or the doctor's mode of discussing that condition, the doctor would invariably try to sustain and bolster the patient's hope of a recovery.

Despite this strong reluctance to level with a cancer patient, there was essentially unanimous agreement among the physicians that some family member must be told. Not only were legal and ethical considerations important in disclosing the diagnosis to some relevant person, but Oken believed that the physician had a strong need to share the burden of knowledge that someone was going to die.

The primary reason cited by the doctors for not wanting to tell the patients they had terminal cancer was "clinical experience." "Clinical experience" consisted of the physicians' opinion that most people did not want to know, that they know already, or that they should not be told so that they would not give up or become depressed. However, Oken found that the real determinant for avoiding the disclosure of a terminal diagnosis was an emotion-laden, a priori judgment related to a fear of how the patient would react to the information (become angry, commit suicide) and the physician's underlying feelings of pessimism and futility about cancer.

Oken further explained that the physicians interviewed generally agreed that patients feared cancer because its diagnosis was equated with suffering and certain death. What was impressive was that the physicians themselves felt very much the same way and these feelings were in conflict with their strong desire to prevent suffering and save lives. Oken stated:

> Situations of this kind, associated with intense charges of unpleasant emotions, call forth a variety of psychological defenses which reduce the intensity of feelings to manageable proportions. Among such defenses are those which involve the avoidance, negation, or denial of the existence of some unpleasant fact, and acting as if it were not real.[8]

Robert Coombs and Pauline Powers (1975) have characterized medical school and the teaching hospital as the locale in which medical students and physicians learn to cope with death in an objective manner (while at the same time denying its subjective implications). Coombs and Powers identified five developmental stages in this process: (1) idealizing the doctor's role, (2) desensitizing death symbols, (3) objectifying and combating death, (4) questioning the medical model, and (5) dealing with personal feelings. In the initial stage, medical students tend to demonstrate the same emotional attitudes toward death that are common among laypersons; for example, they found the "coolness" of the qualified physician's approach to death to be "offensive." Nevertheless, they generally realized that they themselves needed to control their emotions about death if they were to become good physicians. In the second stage, they began to become desensitized to the symbols of death as a result of their experience dissecting cadavers, attending autopsies, and working in the pathology laboratory. In addition, they began to acquire the knowledge and medical terminology that allowed them

[8] Donald Oken, "What to Tell Cancer Patients: A Study of Medical Attitudes," *Journal of the American Medical Association*, 175 (April 1961), 1127.

to adopt an intellectual perspective toward disease. The third stage of objectifying and combating death came when the medical students started working in the hospital and were exposed to dead and dying patients. They realized more fully at this time the necessity of detaching themselves from the trauma associated with death in order to protect themselves from their own personal feelings and be able to work effectively as a doctor. An important desensitizing technique at this time, which was modeled by the clinical faculty, was the student's denial of the subjective features of death. Coombs and Powers explained it this way:

> In other words, the clinician learns to view dying patients not as people with feelings, but as medical entities, specimens, or objects of scientific interest. By adopting a scientific frame of mind, utilized so effectively in their previous work with dead bodies, clinicians can effectively avoid the uncomfortable inner feelings which occur when they are exposed to dying patients.[9]

Some (but apparently not all) of the medical students and physicians in the Coombs and Powers study experienced a fourth stage of socialization to death which questioned the medical model. As they perceived it, the medical (scientific) model of treatment tended to dehumanize patients and to define doctors as little more than technicians. From this perspective, it became unrealistic to think that all patients could be cured; thus in some cases it might be inappropriate to prolong life unnecessarily. Some physicians apparently did not experience this fourth stage; their ego was easily inflated when they were cast in the role of a healer who had powers over death. "When his self-esteem was involved," stated Coombs and Powers (1975:262–263), "it is imperative that he prevent death from occurring, for death makes him feel vulnerable. But if he can keep the 'corpse' alive for a few more days or weeks, his mastery over death is demonstrated." This so-called "God complex," regarded by many physicians as incompatible with good medical practice, was nonetheless an observable phenomenon.

What socialization had generally accomplished up to the time of the fifth stage of dealing with their own personal feelings about death was that the doctors had been conditioned to repress their personal anxieties and fears. However, Coombs and Powers (1975:263–264) found: "Our interviews with physicians revealed rather dramatically how much repressed emotionality exists among medical practitioners." When pressed to discuss their own feelings about death, several of the physicians revealed serious psychological problems. One interviewer noted that the interviews were becoming increasingly difficult because the physicians were having a "horrible time" discussing death and dying, both on a professional and a personal level. The most common strategy employed by the physicians to cope with their own fears was that of avoidance. In a comment reminiscent of the Sudnow (1967) and Glaser and Strauss (1965) studies, Coombs and Powers stated:

> Typically every effort is made in the hospital to shield oneself from mourning relatives. In the emergency room quiet crying is tolerated, but if any kind of emotional outburst occurs, relatives are usually hustled off to the chapel as fast as possible. "We isolate them so that their grief is not so obvious," a physician

[9] Robert H. Coombs and Pauline S. Powers, "Socialization for Death: The Physician's Role," *Urban Life*, 4 (October 1975), 258.

said. "It isn't done cruelly, but, frankly, it is done more to protect the emergency room staff than to help the family."[10]

What is suggested by the Charmaz (1975), Oken (1961), and Coombs and Powers (1975) studies is a tendency of people who confront death regularly to develop a self-protective psychology, which consists of a behavioral and cognitive pattern of avoidance and negation of the death experience through the process of objectification. Dead and dying people come to be defined as "cases" or "investigations" rather than as people. Meanwhile, personal fears and anxieties about the subjective meaning of death are suppressed. The objectification of death is justified on the grounds that the professional be able to carry on—"do a good job." Yet despite an outward appearance of control over emotions, both Oken and Coombs and Powers report that the process does not always function smoothly and some physicians do experience a considerable amount of subjective stress about death.

CHANGING ATTITUDES TOWARD DEATH

Death in the wider context of American society has not been socially disruptive because, as Robert Blauner (1966) explained, the impact of death has been controlled through bureaucratization. Hospitals care for the terminally ill and manage the crisis of dying; mortuaries attend to the problem of disposal of the dead and the transition ritual of the funeral. The handling of death by these specialists and the isolation of the dying experience in hospitals and nursing homes has minimized the average person's exposure to death.[11] Blauner describes the modern hospital as a "mass reduction" system because it tends to reduce the individuality of its dying patients. Yet, as Blauner has noted, this system cannot be fully achieved because of the tension between death and a bureaucracy. Bureaucracies are commited to routine and unemotional administrative procedures. Death, on the other hand, is laden with considerable emotionality, not only the deep-rooted fear of one's own dying, but also the grief and bereavement of survivors, which can elicit some of the strongest emotions of human existence. No matter how much effort and control is exerted by a society to contain and routinize death and dying through bureaucratic procedures, such procedures are not in themselves satisfying alternatives for handling a strongly emotional and inevitable event.[12]

[10] Coombs and Powers, "Socialization for Death," p. 265.

[11] Dumont and Foss (1972) estimate that the average American experiences a death in his or her family once every twenty years.

[12] In studies of two retirement communities, Victor Marshall (1975a, 1975b) found that the residents of one particular community (Glen Brae) organized themselves as a community of dying to legitimatize death as an appropriate (although not always positive) event because they had "lived their lives." The residents were able to socialize each other to their impending deaths through frequent conversations about it and the presence of role models with which to anticipate their own dying. All in all, when a death occurred, the residents of Glen Brae managed a "low-key' approach to the way in which that death was observed. Marshall agreed with Arlie Hochschild (1973) that individuals are better able to face their deaths if they can observe, in a kind of a role-modeling process, that the deaths of others take place within a taken-for-granted framework.

Attitudes toward death in American society have reached the point of change. The fundamental cause of this change is the recognition of the failure of efforts to hide and deny the process of dying, which had resulted from death becoming a depersonalizing and lonely experience. The humanistic approach appears to be slowly but steadily returning. Also, as Diana Crane (1975a, 1975b) has observed, there is an increasing desire to exert autonomy in areas where formerly the individual had allowed others to make decisions. Consequently, many individuals desire not only to control their own life but also their own death and the factors contributing to it. Furthermore, Crane notes that the development of certain life-sustaining machines and techniques, such as dialysis for kidney disease and organ transplantation, have stimulated questions about the use of medical technology and the quality of the lives that are thus prolonged.

There is considerable evidence to support the contention that attitudes toward death in American society are changing. In just the last few years a tremendous amount of material on death has been produced and presented in the mass media, particularly in the form of books. Colleges, universities, and schools of medicine, nursing, and public health are adding courses on the social and psychological aspects of death. Ten years ago, practically none of these courses existed; in fact, medical schools offered courses dealing only with clinical facets of death. There has also been recognition in the last few years that large general hospitals have not been very good places to die. To cope with this problem, numerous clinics and seminars have been established to train in-service hospital personnel to handle dying patients more humanely. One particular approach is to encourage physicians and nurses to deal with the reality of their own deaths and their own personal philosophies about life and death. If health practitioners are unable to change the medical outcome of a disease, yet have faced the possibility of their own deaths, it is believed that they can perhaps be supportive of the dying patient in that patient's search for meaning during the remaining portion of his or her life (see also Coombs and Powers, 1975).

Crane (1975a: 10) has summarized changing attitudes toward death as providing the context for the emergence of a loosely coordinated, norm-oriented social movement with two major goals: (1) improvement in the quality of interaction between dying people and those who come into contact with them and (2) enactment of legislation to support the patient's right to refuse treatment. In line with this second goal, there is growing interest in euthanasia, as evidenced by increasing numbers of people who have joined organizations advocating the legality of "mercy killing."

In 1973 the American Hospital Association approved a patient's "bill of rights," which included the provision for the patient to be able to choose death by rejecting lifesaving treatment.[13] A 1974 Gallup Poll showed that 53 percent of those polled, compared to 35 percent in 1950, approved of the

[13]Crane (1975a, 1975b) has found that physicians themselves may decide whether or not to "actively" treat a patient. The criteria used, however, were more social than physiological, since those patients defined as most treatable were those the physicians judged to be capable of engaging in meaningful social interaction.

physician being allowed to induce painless death for an incurable patient if requested by both the patient and the patient's family. Most of the respondents responsible for this shift in public opinion were young and college educated.

However, the legality of directly ending a life is highly questionable. In the widely publicized Karen Ann Quinlan case of 1975–1976, the parents of a comatose girl sued the hospital and physicians attending their daughter to require them to cease their life-prolonging measures in a hopeless situation. There was medical evidence that Miss Quinlan had suffered brain damage thought to be due to the combined effects of alcohol and sleeping pills (exactly what happened has never been fully determined) and was not likely to ever regain consciousness. The hospital staff refused to cease treatment and deliberately allow their patient to die. Eventually the parents won the right to have their daughter removed from the hospital to a nursing home, where the parents had the choice of whether or not to continue extraordinary life-prolonging measures. This case illustrates the moral and legal differences between directly killing a patient or allowing the patient to die by withholding lifesaving treatment. On a moral level there might be a distinction between directly killing a dying patient or simply stopping treatment. But in either case, the result is the same in that the patient dies (Veatch, 1972).

At the core of this dilemma is the position of the physician, who has a special ethical duty to preserve life. So long as the patient is legally competent to make a decision to die, it is arguable that the patient has the right to do so. But what happens when the patient is not legally competent because he or she is comatose or insensible due to pain or drugs? At the present time there is no answer to this question and no policy, other than the decision of a physician to terminate treatment made on a case-by-case basis. Robert Veatch (1972) suggests that the best policy would be legislation based upon the right of a patient to refuse treatment. If the patient is not competent, an agent, such as the next-of-kin, could be appointed to make the decision on the patient's behalf to authorize cessation of treatment. The physician would therefore be protected from having to make a moral (and nonmedical) judgment about what is best for the patient, and the responsibility would rest instead on the family or some court-appointed agent who would be regarded as representing the patient's interest. Veatch (1972:10) says, "At some time the decision must be made that the dying process has been tampered with long enough and that there is nothing more that man can or should do."

Jan Hendrick van den Berg (1978), a Dutch psychiatrist, argues, however, that physicians themselves often lose sight of the patient's interest when they resort to technical procedures—new surgical measures, drugs, and artificial organs—to prolong life when the chance for a genuine recovery is nonexistent and results in endless suffering for the patient and the patient's family. The impact of van den Berg's message is derived from case histories of people suffering terrible physical and mental damage who are kept alive by artificial means simply because the doctor is *able* to do it. One case involved a boy who should have died at birth from a *spina bifida* (exposed spinal membrane). Instead, the child was kept alive for five years through six operations while suffering from hydrocephalus, which caused extensive brain damage and an enlarged head, paralysis of both legs, impaired kidney function, severe bed sores, infection, and eventually blindness as well as other problems. Another example is that of a man who had the lower half of his body amputated below the waist because of a massive infection and later the development of a malignant tumor. His body was "saved" from the waist up. This latter case was hailed as an example of a "successful" lumbosacral operation. But van den Berg asks whether this operation was truly successful because of the type of existence to which the patient was doomed. He states:

> The doctor who published the report and the photograph had to omit every-
> thing concerning the patient personally; otherwise his article would not have
> been plausible, or even readable . . . for I must insist that it was not right to
> perform that operation. The operation consisted of a medico-ethical offense.
> The doctor should have let his patient die.[14]

The image of the physician that van den Berg projects is that of a technician who has become so absorbed in the power of medical procedures for maintaining life that he or she neglects or ignores the morality of the situation. While van den Berg's thesis opens up unanswered philosophical questions, including who should have the ultimate responsibility for making these life and death decisions, he argues that the medical profession has abdicated its ethical responsibilities by removing itself from involvement with patients as people. Medicine is portrayed as rather mindlessly pursuing the preservation of all human life, unconditionally and regardless of the consequences. What is needed is a code of medical ethics in which patients and their families are (if possible) given the right to know the existence they will face if modern medical technology is applied in its fullest extent to extend the patient's life. Such people, in van den Berg's view, should not be hostages to medical power. They should have the right to die if that is their desire and they are capable of making an informed decision.

In contrast, supporters of the "hospice" concept insist that the right to die involves a corresponding duty to kill and that euthanasia should not be allowed. Instead, the hospice, a hospital that specializes in the care of the terminally ill, offers an alternative approach. Tried with some success in Great Britain and currently being introduced in the United States, the hospice involves a complete change in the priorities of the physician and nurse. The aim is no longer to cure the patient, but to make the patient more comfortable and his or her dying days more meaningful. The hospice stresses companionship, sense of security, and control of physical symptoms through medical and nursing techniques. The control of pain is very important in order to allow the patient to be as active as possible for as long as possible.

Because modern society has attempted to be more open and intellectual concerning death does not mean that the fear and anxiety of dying can be rationalized away. It simply suggests that the process of dying may become

[14]Jan Hendrick van den Berg, *Medical Power and Medical Ethics* (New York: W. W. Norton, 1978), pp. 44–45.

less impersonal and dehumanizing. Perhaps death in the future will return to a modern version of Ariés' notion of "tamed death." In the final analysis, however, death will probably remain an experience characterized by various forms of fear.

SUMMARY

This chapter has examined death and dying from the perspective of both the individual and society. The primary problem death presents for society is that of coping with the fear of death, particularly fear of the experience itself and of its consequences. While everyone has difficulty in managing these fears, most people eventually reach a stage of acceptance of death.

At present, death is contained by the larger social system in hospitals, nursing homes, and mortuaries by specialists who ensure that death is not disruptive for society. The result of these practices has been the dehumanization of death in modern society; evidence is now beginning to mount, however, that attitudes in American society are evolving toward a more humanistic interpretation of the dying experience.

EPILOGUE

This book has discussed basic social issues confronting American medicine today. By necessity, much of the material was framed within a social problems context. The reason for this, quite simply, is two-fold: *medicine is both a solution and a cause of many social and individual problems.*

The paradox inherent in this statement derives from the medical profession (with society's blessing) having assumed an ever increasing responsibility for control of a wide variety of social concerns. Physicians not only actively intervene in identifiable disease processes such as atherosclerosis, cancer, and diabetes, but they also deal with complaints not necessarily associated with disease—for example, dangerousness, hyperactive behavior in school, anxiety related to being in love, and television programming for children. There are few areas of daily life not touched by a medical opinion intended to make that life better. Conversely, medicine itself is a social problem as a result of a combination of several negative factors—failure to provide quality care or even adequate care to all segments of society, high cost of health services, maldistribution of these services, and a tendency toward impersonalization in the physician–patient relationship.

Attempts to change the existing structure of health care delivery in the United States have met with strong resistance from organized medicine. Such change threatens not only the fee-for-service or profit-making aspect of medical practice in a free enterprise system, but also might diminish the professional control physicians currently enjoy over their own work and the work of a vast health care industry. Unfortunately, an adversary relationship between the medical profession and some elements of the general public has developed, as evidenced by the rise in malpractice litigation, public demand for national health insurance, and public outrage over the high cost of health care. This has been exacerbated by cases of fraud perpetrated by physicians in Medicare and Medicaid overpayments. Statements such as one made as recently as 1977 by a leading official of the American Medical Association that physicians alone should make decisions regarding health care delivery because the public is unable to understand the complexity of the situation, only serve to underscore a growing credibility gap between the medical profession and the lay public.

Regardless of the position of organized medicine, current trends (as noted in Chapter Six) point toward substantial modification of the physician's role in the future. The power–dependency role of the physician and patient will most likely be changed into more of a provider–consumer relationship. The emergence of paramedical practitioners like the physician's assistant and the nurse practitioner may further modify the physician's professional dominance as these occupations assume an increasing share of responsibility for primary medical care. However, it is unlikely that any radical change is forthcoming that would limit the physician's ability to perform effectively in the provision of medical services.

By and large, physicians appear to be dedicated, hard-working individuals whose highest priority is the welfare of their patients. American medicine has produced technology and expertise second to none in the quality and quantity of health care it is capable of delivering to society. Disenchantment with the medical profession refers not so much to the quality of its work (although errors are sometimes made—as they are in all professions), but to the inequality and expense of existing services and the growing suspicion that organized medicine does not always place the public interest ahead of professional interest.

On the other hand, even if quality health care becomes readily available to all Americans, we may be reaching a point of diminishing returns in health care expenditures. At present, much of the money invested in medical research is spent on ailments like heart disease, cancer, and stroke, which are primarily diseases of old age. If, in fact, these diseases could be eliminated from society, how much would life expectancy be increased? Some estimates are that, at most, only one or two years would be added to the average life span. The human body supposedly has a natural limit on longevity, thought to be about seventy-seven years for most people—even if optimal health conditions exist. Thus, there is a point when the body is going to succumb to the degenerative effects of aging, whether cancer or otherwise; that is, the body just wears out.

Assuming that quality health care is available, what may become more significant for increasing life expectancy in the future than medical technology alone is the effect of lifestyle (urbanization, interpersonal relations, occupational pressures) and physical environment (pollution) on health. This confirms the inescapable notion that medicine is indeed a social science, as advocated by the eminent nineteenth-century German pathologist Rudolf Virchow.

Good health is one of the most cherished benefits available to humankind and good health is based on an intricate relationship between mind, body, and the social and physical environment. This is why knowledge of the principles of sociology, psychology, and anthropology is essential in the practice of contemporary medicine. Accordingly, the contribution of the social sciences to medicine represents tremendous potential for the improvement of life and the treatment of socially related disorders. What makes people sick, how they experience being sick, and what they do about it are all bound up in the prevailing social and cultural expectations of behavior and definitions of disease. Research and theory development are needed. The medical sociologist is in the enviable position of participating in and influencing the course of an exciting, challenging, and important field whose application to human life can provide beneficial results.

BIBLIOGRAPHY

ADAY, LUANN.
   1976 "The impact of health policy on access to medical care." *Milbank Memorial Fund Quarterly*, 54:215–233.
ADAY, LUANN, and RONALD ANDERSEN.
   1975 *Development of indices of access to medical care.* Ann Arbor: Health Administration Press.
ADLER, ISRAEL, and JUDITH T. SHUVAL.
   1978 "Cross pressures during socialization for medicine." *American Sociological Review* 43:693–704.
ALLEN, GILLIAN, and ROY WALLIS.
   1976 "Pentecostalists as a medical minority," pp. 110–137 in *Marginal medicine*, R. Wallis and P. Morley (eds.). New York: Free Press.
ALEXANDER, FRANZ G., and SHELDON T. SELESNICK.
   1966 *The history of psychiatry.* New York: Mentor.
ALFORD, ROBERT R.
   1975 *Health care politics.* Chicago: University of Chicago Press.
ALLEN, MICHAEL A., and MICHELLE TOLLIVIER.
   1974 "Medical delivery system for urban Indians: Consumer and providers' perceptions." Paper presented to the Southwestern and Rocky Mountain Division of the American Association for the Advancement of Science Meeting, April, 1974, Laramie, Wyoming.
ALSOP, STEWART.
   1973 *Stay of execution.* Philadelphia: J. B. Lippincott.
ALVAREZ, W. C.
   1931 "How early do physicians diagnose cancer of the stomach in themselves?" *Journal of the American Medical Association*, 97 (July 11):77–83.
AMERICAN MEDICAL ASSOCIATION.
   1951 *Guide to services.* Chicago: AMA.

ANDERSEN, RONALD, and LUANN ADAY.
    1978 "Access to medical care in the U.S.: Realized and potential." *Medical Care*,
    16:533–546.
ANDERSEN, RONALD, and ODIN W. ANDERSON.
    1979 "Trends in the use of health services," pp. 371–391 in *Handbook of medical
    sociology*, 3rd ed., H. Freeman, S. Levine, and L. Reeder (eds.). Englewood
    Cliffs, N.J.: Prentice-Hall, Inc.
ANDERSEN, RONALD, JOANNA KRAVITS, and ODIN W. ANDERSON (eds.).
    1975 *Equity in health services: Empirical analyses in social policy.* Cambridge, Mass.:
    Ballinger.
ANDERSEN, RONALD, and J. JOEL MAY.
    1972 "Factors associated with increased costs of hospital care." *The Annals of the
    American Academy of Political and Social Science*, 401:62–72.
ANDERSON, JAMES G., and DAVID E. BARTKUS.
    1973 "Choice of medical care: A behavioral model of health and illness be-
    havior." *Journal of Health and Social Behavior*, 14:348–362.
ANDERSON, O. W., and P. B. SHEATSLEY.
    1967 *Hospital use—A survey of patients' and physicians' decisions.* Research Series
    No. 24. Chicago: University of Chicago Center for Health Administration
    Studies.
ANTHONY, SYLVIA.
    1968 "The child's idea of death," pp. 315–328 in *The world of the child*, Toby
    Talbot (ed.). New York: Anchor.
    1972 *The discovery of death in childhood and after.* New York: Basic Books.
ANTONOVSKY, AARON.
    1972 "Social class, life expectancy and overall mortality," pp. 5–30 in *Patients,
    physicians and illness*, 2nd ed., E. Gartly Jaco (ed.). New York: Free Press.
    1979 *Health, stress, and coping.* San Francisco: Jossey-Bass.
APPEL, JAMES Z.
    1970 "Health care delivery," pp. 141–166 in *The health of Americans*, B. Jones
    (ed.). Englewood Cliffs, N.J.: Prentice-Hall, Inc.
APPLE, DORRIAN.
    1960 "How laymen define illness." *Journal of Health and Social Behavior*, 1:219–
    225.
ARIÉS, PHILIPPE.
    1974 *Western attitudes toward death.* Trans. P. M. Ranum. Baltimore: Johns
    Hopkins University Press.
ARLUKE, ARNOLD, LOUANNE KENNEDY, and RONALD C. KESSLER.
    1979 "Reexamining the sick-role concept: An empirical assessment." *Journal of
    Health and Social Behavior*, 20:30–36.
ASKENASY, ALEXANDER R., BRUCE P. DOHRENWEND, and BARBARA S. DOHRENWEND.
    1977 "Some effects of social class and ethnic group membership on judgments
    of the magnitude of stressful life events: A research note." *Journal of Health and
    Social Behavior*, 18:432–439.
ATCHLEY, ROBERT C.
    1976 "Selected social and psychological differences between men and women
    in later life." *Journal of Gerontology*, 31:204–211.
    1977 *The social forces in later life.* 2nd ed. Belmont, Cal.: Wadsworth.
ATKINSON, PAUL, ROBERT DINGWALL, and ANNE MURCOTT.
    1979 *Prospects for the National Health Service.* London: Croom Helm.
AUSUBEL, D. P.
    1912 "Personality disorder is a disease." *American Psychologist*, 16:69–74.

BANDURA, ALBERT.
1969 *Principles of behavior modification.* New York: Holt, Rinehart, and Winston.

BARRON M. L. (ed.).
1961 *The aging american.* New York: Crowell.

BATES, BARBARA.
1970 "Doctor and nurse: Changing roles and relations." *New England Journal of Medicine,* 283:129–134.

BAUMANN, BARBARA.
1961 "Diversities in conceptions of health and physical fitness." *Journal of Health and Social Behavior,* 2:39–46.

BAUWENS, ELEANOR.
1977 "Medical beliefs and practices among lower-income Anglos," pp. 241–270 in *Ethnic medicine in the Southwest,* E. Spicer (ed.). Tucson: University of Arizona Press.

BECKER, HOWARD S.
1973 *Outsiders: Studies in the sociology of deviance.* 2nd ed. New York: Free Press.

BECKER, HOWARD S., and BLANCHE GREER.
1958 "The fate of idealism in medical school." *American Sociological Review,* 23:50–56.

BECKER, HOWARD S., BLANCHE GREER, EVERETT C. HUGHES, and ANSELM STRAUSS.
1961 *Boys in white: Student culture in medical school.* Chicago: University of Chicago Press.

BECKER, MARSHALL H. (ed.).
1974 *The health belief model and personal health behavior.* San Francisco: Society for Public Health Education, Inc.

BECKER, MARSHALL H.
1979 "Psychosocial aspects of health-related behaviors," pp. 253–274 in *Handbook of medical sociology,* H. Freeman, S. Levine, and L. Reeder (eds.). Englewood Cliffs, N.J.: Prentice-Hall, Inc.

BECKER, MARSHALL H., and LOIS A. MAIMAN.
1975 "Sociobehavioral determinants of compliance with health and medical care recommendations." *Medical Care,* 13:10–24.

BECKER, MARSHALL H., LOIS A. MAIMAN, JOHN P. KIRSCHT, DON P. HAEFNER, and ROBERT H. DRACHMAN.
1977 "The health belief model and prediction of dietary compliance: A field experiment." *Journal of Health and Social Behavior,* 18:348–366.

BECKER, S., and G. GORDON.
1966 "The entrepreneurial theory of formal organizations, part I: Patterns of formal organization." *Administrative Science Quarterly,* 2, no. 3:315–344.

BELLIN, SEYMOUR S., and H. JACK GEIGER.
1972 "The impact of a neighborhood health center on a patient's behavior and attitudes relating to health care: A study of low income housing." *Medical Care,* 10:224–239.

BENGTSON, VERN L.
1973 *The social psychology of aging.* New York: Bobbs-Merrill.

BENHAM, LEE, and ALEXANDRA BENHAM.
1975 "Utilization of physician services across income groups, 1963–1970," pp. 97–103 in *Equity in health services: Empirical analyses in social policy,* R. Andersen, J. Kravits, and O. Anderson (eds.). Cambridge, Mass.: Ballinger.

BENOLIEL, JEANNE Q.
1975 "The realities of work: Commentary on Howard Leventhal's information-processing model," pp. 175–188 in *Humanizing health care*, J. Howard and
A. Strauss (eds.). New York: Wiley-Interscience.
BEN-SIRA, ZEEV.
1976 "The function of the professional's affective behavior in client satisfaction: A revised approach to social interaction theory." *Journal of Health and
Social Behavior*, 17:3–11.
1980 "Affective and instrumental components in the physician-patient relationship: An additional dimension of interaction theory." *Journal of Health and
Social Behavior*, 21:170–180.
BERGER, EDWARD J.
1974 "Health and health services in the United States: A perspective and
discussion of some issues." *Annals of Internal Medicine*, 80:645–650.
BERGER, PETER L., and THOMAS LUCKMANN.
1967 *The social construction of reality*. New York: Anchor.
BERKANOVIC, EMIL.
1972 "Lay conceptions of the sick role." *Social Forces*, 51:53–63.
BERKANOVIC, EMIL, and LEO G. REEDER.
1973 "Ethnic, economic, and social psychological factors in the source of medical care." *Social Problems*, 21:246–259.
1974 "Can money buy the appropriate use of services? Some notes on the
meaning of utilization data." *Journal of Health and Social Behavior*, 15:93–99.
BERRY, RALPH E., JR.
1974 "Cost and efficiency in the production of hospital services." *Milbank
Memorial Fund Quarterly*, 52:291–314.
BICE, T. W., R. L. EICHHORN, and P. D. FOX.
1972 "Socioeconomic status and use of physician services: A reconsideration."
Medical Care, 10:261–271.
BINGER, C. M., A. R. ABLIN, R. C. FEUERSTEIN, J. KUSHNER, S. ZOGER, and C.
MIKKELSEN.
1969 "Childhood leukemia: Emotional impact on patient and family." *New
England Journal of Medicine*, 280:414–418.
BIRREN, JAMES F.
1964 *The psychology of aging*. Englewood Cliffs, N.J.: Prentice-Hall, Inc.
BLACKWELL, LOUISE.
1967 "Upper middle class adult expectations about entering the sick role for
physical and psychiatric dysfunctions." *Journal of Health and Social Behavior*,
8:83–95.
BLAUNER, ROBERT.
1966 "Death and social structure." *Psychiatry*, 29:378–394.
BLOOM, SAMUEL W.
1963 *The doctor and his patient*. New York: Free Press.
1973 *Power and dissent in the medical school*. New York: Free Press.
BOOCOCK, SARANE S.
1972 *An introduction to the sociology of learning*. New York: Houghton Mifflin.
BOSK, CHARLES L.
1979 *Forgive and remember: Managing medical failure*. Chicago: University of
Chicago Press.
BOURNE, PETER.
1970 *Men, stress, and Vietnam*. Boston: Little, Brown.
BOWDEN, CHARLES L., and ALVIN G. BURSTEIN.
1974 *Psychosocial basis of medical practice*. Baltimore: Williams & Wilkins.

BOWMAN, ROSEMARY AMASON, and REBECCA CLARK CULPEPPER.
    1974 "Rx for change." *American Journal of Nursing*, 74:1054–1056.
BRADY, JOHN P.
    1975 "Behavior therapy," pp. 1824–1831 in *Comprehensive textbook of psychiatry*, Vol. II, 2nd ed., A. Freedman, H. Kaplan, and B. Sadock (eds.). Baltimore: Williams & Wilkins.
BRAGINSKY, B. M., D. BRAGINSKY, and K. RING.
    1969 *Methods of madness: The mental hospital as a last resort*. New York: Holt, Rinehart, and Winston.
BRENNER, M. HARVEY.
    1973 *Mental illness and the economy*. Cambridge, Mass.: Harvard University Press.
BROOKS, CHARLES H.
    1980 "Social, economic, and biologic correlates of infant mortality in city neighborhoods." *Journal of Health and Social Behavior*, 21:2–11.
BROWN, E. RICHARD.
    1979 *Rockefeller medicine men: Medicine and capitalism in America*. Berkeley: University of California Press.
BROWN, ESTHER L.
    1966 "Nursing and patient care," pp. 176–203 in *The nursing profession*, F. Davis (ed.). New York: Wiley.
BROWN, G. W., J. L. T. BIRLEY, and J. K. WING.
    1972 "Influence of family life on the course of schizophrenic disorders." *British Journal of Psychiatry*, 121:241–258.
BROWN, GEORGE W., and TIRRIL HARRIS.
    1978 *Social origins of depression: A study of psychiatric disorder in women*. New York: Free Press.
BROWN, JULIA S., and MAY E. RAWLINSON.
    1977 "Sex differences in sick role rejection and in work performance following cardiac surgery." *Journal of Health and Social Behavior*, 18:276–292.
BULTENA, GORDON L., and EDWARD A. POWERS.
    1978 "Denial of aging: Age identification and reference group orientations." *Journal of Gerontology*, 33:748–754.
BUNKER, JOHN P.
    1970 "Surgical manpower: A comparison of operations and surgeons in the United States and in England and Wales." *New England Journal of Medicine*, 282:135–144.
BURGER, EDWARD J.
    1974 "Health and health services in the United States." *Annals of Internal Medicine*, 80:645–650.
BURROW, JAMES G.
    1963 *AMA: Voice of American medicine*. Baltimore: Johns Hopkins University Press.
CAMPBELL, JOHN D.
    1978 "The child in the sick role: Contributions of age, sex, parental status, and parental values." *Journal of Health and Social Behavior*, 19:35–51.
CANNON, WALTER B.
    1932 *The wisdom of the body*. New York: Norton.
CARP, FRANCES M.
    1968 "Some components of disengagement." *Journal of Gerontology*, 23:382–386.
CARTWRIGHT, ANN.
    1964 *Human relations and hospital care*. London: Routledge and Kegan Paul.

CASTLE, M., C. M. WILFERT, T. CATE, and S. OSTERHOUT.
1977 "Antibiotic use at Duke University Medical Center." *Journal of the American Medical Association*, 237:2819–2820.

CATALANO, RALPH, and C. DAVID DOOLEY.
1977 "Economic predictors of depressed mood and stressful life events in a metropolitan community." *Journal of Health and Social Behavior*, 18:292–307.

CHALFANT, H. PAUL, and RICHARD KURTZ.
1971 "Alcoholics and the sick role: Assessments by social workers." *Journal of Health and Social Behavior*, 12:66–72.

CHARMAZ, KATHY C.
1975 "The coroner's strategies for announcing death." *Urban Life*, 4:296–316.

CLARK, MARGARET.
1959 *Health in the Mexican-American culture.* Berkeley: University of California Press.

CLAUSEN, JOHN A., and CAROL L. HUFFINE.
1975 "Sociocultural and social/psychological factors affecting social responses to mental disorder." *Journal of Health and Social Behavior*, 16:405–420.

COCKERHAM, WILLIAM C.
1975 "Drinking attitudes and practices among Wind River Reservation Indian youth." *Journal of Studies on Alcohol*, 36:321–326.
1977 "Patterns of alcohol and multiple drug use among rural white and American Indian adolescents." *International Journal of the Addictions*, 12 (2-3):271–285.
1978 "Attitudes toward combat among U.S. Army paratroopers." *Journal of Political and Military Sociology*, 6:1–15.
1981 *Sociology of mental disorder.* Englewood Cliffs, N.J.: Prentice-Hall, Inc.

COCKERHAM, WILLIAM C., MORTON C. CREDITOR, UNA K. CREDITOR, and PETER B. IMREY.
1980 "Minor ailments and illness behavior among physicians." *Medical Care*, 18:164–173.

COCKERHAM, WILLIAM C., MORRIS A. FORSLUND, and ROLLAND M. RABOIN.
1976 "Drug use among white and American Indian high school youth." *International Journal of the Addictions*, 11 (2):209–220.

COE, RODNEY M.
1978 *Sociology of medicine.* 2nd ed. New York: McGraw-Hill.

COE, RODNEY M., and LEONARD FICHTENBAUM.
1972 "Utilization of physician assistants: Some implications for medical practice." *Medical Care*, 10:497–504.

COHEN, J. B., S. L. SYME, C. D. JENKINS, A. KAGAN, and S. J. ZYZANSKI.
1979 "Cultural context of type A behavior and risk for CHD: A study of Japanese American males." *Journal of Behavioral Medicine*, 2:375–384.

COHEN, ROSALIE.
1974 "Neglected legal dilemmas in community psychiatry," pp. 69–82 in *Sociological perspectives on community mental health*, P. Roman and H. Trice (eds.). Philadelphia: F. A. Davis.

COLE, STEPHEN, and ROBERT LeJEUNE.
1972 "Illness and the legitimation of failure." *American Sociological Review*, 37:347–356.

COLUMBOTOS, JOHN.
1969 "Social origins and ideology of physicians: A study of the effects of early socialization." *Journal of Health and Social Behavior*, 10:16–29.

COOLEY, CHARLES H.
1962 *Social organization.* New York: Schocken.
1964 *Human nature and the social order.* New York: Schocken.

COOMBS, ROBERT H.
   1978 *Mastering medicine: Professional socialization in medical school.* New York: Free Press.
COOMBS, ROBERT H., and PAULINE S. POWERS.
   1975 "Socialization for death: The physician's role." *Urban Life,* 4:250–271.
CORDES, LESTER G., and DAVID W. FRASER.
   1980 "Legionellosis." *Medical Clinics of North America,* 64:395–416.
COSER, ROSE L.
   1956 "A home away from home." *Social Problems,* 4:3–17.
   1958 "Authority and decision-making in a hospital." *American Sociological Review,* 23:56–63.
CRANE, DIANA.
   1975a *The sanctity of social life: Physicians' treatment of critically ill patients.* New York: Russell Sage.
   1975b "Decision to treat critically ill patients: A comparison of social versus medical considerations." *Milbank Memorial Fund Quarterly,* 53:1–34.
CREDITOR, MORTON C.
   1971 "If doctors owned the hospitals." *New England Journal of Medicine,* 284:134–139.
CROOG, SYDNEY H., and DONNA F. VER STEEG.
   1972 *"The hospital as a social system,"* pp. 274–314 in *Handbook of medical sociology,* 2nd ed., H. Freeman, S. Levine, and L. Reeder (eds.). Englewood Cliffs, N.J.: Prentice-Hall, Inc.
CUMMING, ELAINE, and WILLIAM E. HENRY.
   1961 *Growing old: The process of disengagement.* New York: Basic Books.
DANIELS, M. J.
   1960 "Affect and its control in the medical intern." *American Journal of Sociology,* 61:259–267.
DAVIDSON, LAURIE, and LAURA KRAMER GORDON.
   1979 *The sociology of gender.* Chicago: Rand McNally.
DAVIS, FRED.
   1966 "Problems and issues in collegiate nursing education," pp. 138–175 in *The nursing profession,* F. Davis (ed.). New York: Wiley.
   1972. *Illness, interaction, and the self.* Belmont, Cal.: Wadsworth.
DAVIS, FRED, and VIRGINIA OLESEN.
   1963 "Initiation into a women's profession: Identity problems in the status transition of coed to student nurse." *Sociometry,* 26:89–101.
DAVIS, KAREN.
   1975a *National health insurance.* Washington, D.C.: The Brookings Institution.
   1975b "Equal treatment and unequal benefits: The Medicare Program." *Milbank Memorial Fund Quarterly,* 53:449–488.
DAVIS, KINGSLEY, and WILBERT MOORE.
   1945 "Some principles of stratification." *American Sociological Review,* 10:242–249.
DAWBER, THOMAS R., WILLIAM B. KANNEL, and LORNA P. LYELL.
   1963 "An approach to longitudinal studies in the community: The Framingham study." *Annals of the New York Academy of Sciences,* 107:539–566.
DEBUSKEY, M. (ed.).
   1970 *The chronically ill child and his family.* Springfield, Ill.: Thomas.
DECKER, DAVID L.
   1980 *Social gerontology: An introduction to the dynamics of aging.* Boston: Little, Brown.
DENTON, JOHN A.
   1978 *Medical sociology.* Boston: Houghton Mifflin.

DENZIN, NORMAN K.
1968 "The self-fulfilling prophecy and patient-therapist interaction," pp. 349–358 in *The mental patient: Studies in the sociology of deviance*, S. Spitzer and N. Denzin (eds.). New York: McGraw-Hill.

DEWOLFF, P., and J. MEERDINK.
1954 "Mortality rates in Amsterdam according to profession," pp. 53–55 in Proceedings of the World Population Conference, Vol. I. New York: United Nations.

DODGE, DAVID L., and WALTER T. MARTIN.
1970 *Social stress and chronic illness*. South Bend, Ind.: University of Notre Dame Press.

DOHRENWEND, BARBARA S.
1973 "Life events as stressors: A methodological inquiry." *Journal of Health and Social Behavior*, 14:167–175.
1975 "Group differences in the anticipation and control of stressful life events." Paper presented at the Conference of the Society for Life History Research in Psychopathology, University of Rochester Medical School, Rochester, New York, May 21–23.

DOHRENWEND, BARBARA S., LARRY KRASNOFF, ALEXANDER R. ASKENASY, and BRUCE P. DOHRENWEND.
1978 "Exemplification of a method for scaling life events: The PERI life events scale." *Journal of Health and Social Behavior*, 19:205–229.

DOHRENWEND, BRUCE P.
1974 "Problems in defining and sampling the relevant population of stressful life events," pp. 275–310 in *Stressful life events: Their nature and effects*, B. S. Dohrenwend and B. P. Dohrenwend (eds.). New York: Wiley.
1975 "Sociocultural and social-psychological factors in the genesis of mental disorders." *Journal of Health and Social Behavior*, 16:365–392.

DOHRENWEND, BRUCE P., and BARBARA SNELL DOHRENWEND.
1969 *Social status and psychological disorders*. New York: Wiley.
1974 "Social and cultural influences on psychopathology." *Annual Review of Psychology*, 25:417–452.
1975 "The conceptualization and measurement of stressful life events: An overview of the issues." Paper presented at the Conference of the Society for Life History Research in Psychopathology, University of Rochester Medical School, Rochester, New York, May 21–23.
1976 "Sex differences and psychiatric disorder." *American Journal of Sociology*, 81:1447–1454.

DOZIER, E.
1966 "Problem drinking among American Indians." *Quarterly Journal of Studies on Alcohol*, 27:72–87.

DREVENSTEDT, JEAN.
1976 "Perceptions of onsets of young adulthood, middle age, and old age." *Journal of Gerontology*, 31:53–57.

DUBOS, RENÉ.
1959 *Mirage of health*. New York: Harper & Row.
1969 *Man, medicine, and environment*. New York: Mentor.

DUFF, RAYMOND S., and AUGUST B. HOLLINGSHEAD.
1968 *Sickness and society*. New York: Harper & Row.

DUMONT, RICHARD G., and DENNIS C. FOSS.
1972 *The American view of death*. Cambridge, Mass.: Schenkman.

DURBIN, RICHARD L., and W. HERBERT SPRINGALL.
1974 *Organization and administration of health care*. St. Louis, Mo.: Mosby.

DURKHEIM, EMILE.
     1950 *The rules of sociological method*. New York: Free Press.
     1951 *Suicide*. New York: Free Press.
     1956 *The division of labor in society*. New York: Free Press.
     1961 *The elementary forms of religious life*. New York: Collier.
DUTTON, DIANA B.
     1978 "Explaining the low use of health services by the poor: Costs, attitudes, or delivery systems?" *American Sociological Review*, 43:348–368.
     1979 "Patterns of ambulatory health care in five different delivery systems." *Medical Care*, 17:221–241.
EASSON, W. M.
     1970 *The dying child: The management of the child or adolescent who is dying*. Springfield, Ill.: Thomas.
EATON, WILLIAM W., JR.
     1974 "Medical hospitalization as a reinforcement process." *American Sociological Review*, 39:252–260.
EHRENREICH, BARBARA, and DEIRDRE ENGLISH.
     1979 "The 'sick' women of the upper classes," pp. 123–143 in *The cultural crisis of modern medicine*, J. Ehrenreich (ed.). New York: Monthly Review Press.
EHRENREICH, JOHN.
     1978 "Introduction: The cultural crisis of modern medicine," pp. 1–35 in *The cultural crisis of modern medicine*, J. Ehrenreich (ed.). New York: Monthly Review Press.
EITINGER, L.
     1964 *Concentration camp survivors in Norway and Israel*. London: Allen & Unwin.
     1973 "A followup of the Norwegian concentration camp survivors." *Israel Annals of Psychiatry and Related Disciplines*, 11:199–209.
ELAM, L.
     1969 "What does the ghetto want from medicine?" pp. 33–42 in *Medicine in the ghetto*, J. C. Norman (ed.). New York: Meredith.
ELDER, R. G.
     1963 "What is the patient saying?" *Nursing Forum*, 2:25–37.
ELLING, RAY H.
     1980 *Cross-national study of health systems*. New Brunswick, N.J.: Transaction.
ELLING, RAY, and SANDOR HALEBSKY.
     1961 "Organizational differentiation and support: A conceptual framework." *Administrative Science Quarterly*, 6:185–209.
ENGEL, GEORGE L.
     1977 "The need for a new medical model: A challenge for biomedicine." *Science*, 196:129–135.
EVANS, A. E., and S. EDIN.
     1968 "If a child must die." *New England Journal of Medicine*, 278:138–142.
EYSENCK, HANS J.
     1961 "The effects of psychotherapy," pp. 697–725, *Handbook of abnormal psychology*, H. Eysenck (ed.). New York: Basic Books.
FAIRBANK, JOHN KING.
     1979 *The United States & China*, 4th ed. Cambridge, Mass.: Harvard University Press.
FARIS, ROBERT E., and H. WARREN DUNHAM.
     1939 *Mental disorders in urban areas*. Chicago: University of Chicago Press.
FBI.
     1979 *Crime in the United States*. Washington, D.C.: U.S. Department of Justice.
FEIFEL, HERMAN, and ALLAN B. BRANSCOMB.
     1973 "Who's afraid of death?" *Journal of Abnormal Psychology*, 81:282–288.

FEIFEL, HERMAN, SUSAN HANSON, ROBERT JONES, and LAURI EDWARDS.
   1967 "Physicians consider death." *Proceedings*, 75th Annual Convention, American Psychological Association.
FELDMAN, J.
   1966 *The dissemination of health information.* Chicago: Aldine.
FIELD, MARK G.
   1967 *Soviet socialized medicine: An introduction.* New York: Free Press.
FISHBEIN, MORRIS.
   1947 *A history of the American Medical Association, 1847–1947.* Philadelphia: W. B. Saunders.
FLOOD, ANN BARRY and W. RICHARD SCOTT.
   1978 "Professional power and professional effectiveness: The power of the surgical staff and the quality of surgical care in hospitals." *Journal of Health and Social Behavior*, 19:240–254.
FORBES, WILLIAM H.
   1967 "Longevity and medical costs." *New England Journal of Medicine*, 277:71–78.
FOX, RENÉE.
   1957 "Training for uncertainty," pp. 207–241 in *The student-physician*, R. K. Merton, G. Reader, and P. L. Kendall (eds.). Cambridge, Mass.: Harvard University Press.
   1974 "Is there a new medical student," pp. 197–220 in *Ethics of health care*, L. R. Tancredi, Washington, D.C.: National Academy of Sciences.
FREDERICKS, MARCEL A., PAUL MUNDY, and JOHN KOSA.
   1974 "Willingness to serve: The medical profession and poverty programs." *Social Science and Medicine*, 8:51–57.
FREEBORN, DONALD K., and BENJAMIN J. DARSKY.
   1974 "A study of the power structure of the medical community." *Medical Care*, 12:1–12.
FREEMAN, HOWARD E., SOL LEVINE, and LEO G. REEDER.
   1972 "Present status of medical sociology," pp. 501–522 in *Handbook of medical sociology*, 2nd ed., H. Freeman, S. Levine, and L. Reeder (eds.). Englewood Cliffs, N.J.: Prentice-Hall, Inc.
FREEMAN, HOWARD E., and OZZIE G. SIMMONS.
   1961 "Feelings of stigma among relatives of former mental patients." *Social Problems*, 8:312–321.
   1963 *The mental patient comes home.* New York: Wiley.
FREIDSON, ELIOT.
   1960 "Client control and medical practice." *American Journal of Sociology*, 65:374–382.
   1970a *Profession of medicine.* New York: Dodd, Mead.
   1970b *Professional dominance.* Chicago: Aldine.
   1975 *Doctoring together.* New York: Elsevier.
FREUD, SIGMUND.
   1953–1966 *Standard edition of the complete psychological works of Sigmund Freud.* London: Hogarth Press.
FRITZ, C. E., and E. S. MARKS.
   1954 "The NORC studies of human behavior in disaster." *Journal of Social Issues*, 10:26–41.
FUCHS, VICTOR R.
   1974 *Who shall live?* New York: Basic Books.
FUNKENSTEIN, DANIEL H.
   1971 "Medical students, medical schools, and society during three eras," pp. 229–281 in *Psychosocial aspects of medical training*, R. H. Coombs and C. E. Vincent (eds.). Springfield, Ill.: Thomas.

GALVIN, MICHAEL L., and MARGARET FAN.
1975 "The utilization of physician's services in Los Angeles County, 1973." *Journal of Health and Social Behavior*, 16:75–94.
GEERTSEN, REED, MELVILLE R. KLAUBER, MARK RINDFLESH, ROBERT L. KANE and ROBERT GRAY.
1975 "A re-examination of Suchman's views on social factors in health care utilization." *Journal of Health and Social Behavior*, 16:226–237.
GEIGER, H. JACK.
1975 "The causes of dehumanization in health care and prospects for humanization," pp. 11–36 in *Humanizing health care*, J. Howard and A. Strauss (eds.). New York: Wiley-Interscience.
GEORGOPOULOS, BASIL F., and FLOYD C. MANN.
1972 "The hospital as an organization," pp. 304–311 in *Patients, physicians and illness*, 2nd ed., E. Jaco (ed.). New York: Macmillan.
GERSHON, ELLIOT S.
1979 "Genetics of the affective disorders." *Hospital Practice*, 14:117–122.
GERSTEN, JOANNE C., THOMAS S. LANGNER, JEANNE G. EISENBERG, and ORA SIMCHA-FAGAN.
1977 "An evaluation of the etiologic role of stressful life events in psychological disorders." *Journal of Health and Social Behavior*, 18:228–244.
GERTH, H. H., and C. WRIGHT MILLS (ed.).
1946 *From Max Weber: Essays in sociology*. New York: Oxford University Press.
GIBBS, JACK.
1971 "A critique of the labeling perspective," pp. 193–205 in *The study of social problems*, Earl Rubington and Martin S. Weinberg (eds.). New York: Oxford University Press.
GIBSON, GEOFFREY, GEORGE BUGBEE, and ODIN W. ANDERSON.
1970 *Emergency medical services in the Chicago area*. Chicago: University of Chicago, Center for Health Administration.
GLASER, BARNEY G., and ANSELM M. STRAUSS.
1965 *Awareness of dying*. Chicago: Aldine.
1968 *Time for dying*. Chicago: Aldine.
GOCHMAN, D. S.
1971 "Some correlates of children's health care beliefs and potential behavior." *Journal of Health and Social Behavior*, 12:148–154.
GODDARD, JAMES L.
1973 "The medical business," pp. 121–125 in *Life, death, and medicine*, San Francisco: W. H. Freeman.
GOFFMAN, ERVING.
1959 *The presentation of self in everyday life*. New York: Anchor.
1961 *Asylums*. New York: Anchor.
GOLDMAN, LEE.
1974a "Doctor's attitudes toward national health insurance." *Medical Care*, 12:413–423.
1974b "Physicians' medical and political attitudes." *Journal of Health and Social Behavior*, 3:177–187.
GOLDMAN, LEE, and A. EBBERT, JR.
1973 "The fate of medical student liberalism: A prediction." *Journal of Medical Education*, 48:1095–1103.
GOLDSTEIN, ABRAHAM S.
1967 *The insanity defense*. New Haven: Yale University Press.
GOODE, WILLIAM J.
1957 "Community within a community." *American Sociological Review*, 22:194–200.

1960 "Encroachment, charlatanism, and the emerging profession: Psychology, sociology, and medicine." *American Sociological Review*, 25:902–914.

GORE, SUSAN.
1978 "The effect of social support in moderating the health consequences of unemployment." *Journal of Health and Social Behavior*, 19:157–165.

GORDON, GERALD.
1966 *Role theory and illness.* New Haven: College and University Press.

GORTMAKER, STEVEN L.
1979 "Poverty and infant mortality in the United States." *American Sociological Review*, 44:280–297.

GOSS, MARY E.
1963 "Patterns of bureaucracy among hospital staff physicians," pp. 170–194 in *The hospital in modern society*, E. Freidson (ed.). New York: Free Press.

GOVE, WALTER A.
1970 "Societal reaction as an explanation of mental illness: An evaluation." *American Sociological Review*, 35:873–884.
1975 "The labelling theory of mental illness: A reply to Scheff." *American Sociological Review*, 40:242–248.

GOVE, WALTER R., and PATRICK HOWELL.
1974 "Individual resources and mental hospitalization: A comparison and evaluation of the societal reaction and psychiatric perspectives." *American Sociological Review*, 39:86–100.

GOVE, WALTER R., and JEANNETTE F. TUDOR.
1973 "Adult sex roles and mental illness." *American Journal of Sociology*, 78:812–835.

GRAHAM, DAVID, J. D. KABLER, and FRANCIS K. GRAHAM.
1962 "Physiological responses to the suggestion of attitudes specific for hives and hypertension." *Psychosomatic Medicine*, 24:159–169.

GRAHAM, SAXON.
1972 "Cancer, culture, and social structure," pp. 31–39 in *Patients, physicians and illness*, 2nd ed., E. Jaco (ed.). New York: Free Press.

GRAHAM, SAXON, and LEO G. REEDER.
1972 "Social factors in the chronic illness," pp. 63–107 in *Handbook of medical sociology*, 2nd ed., H. Freeman, S. Levine, and L. Reeder (eds.). Englewood Cliffs, N.J.: Prentice-Hall, Inc.

GREENLEY, JAMES R.
1979 "Familial expectations, posthospital adjustment, and the societal reaction perspective on mental illness." *Journal of Health and Social Behavior*, 20:217–227.

GREENWALD, BRUCE C. N., and MARNIE W. MUELLER.
1978 "Medical malpractice and medical costs," pp. 65–86 in *The economics of medical malpractice*, S. Rottenberg (ed.). Washington, D.C.: American Enterprise Institute for Public Policy.

GRINKER, ROY.
1953 *Psychosomatic research.* New York: Norton.

HAAS, JACK, and WILLIAM SHAFFIR.
1977 "The professionalization of medical students: Developing competence and a cloak of competence." *Symbolic Interaction*, 1:71–88.

HALL, OSWALD.
1946 "The informal organization of the medical profession." *Canadian Journal of Economics and Political Science*, 12:30–44.
1948 "The stages of a medical career." *American Journal of Sociology*, 53:327–336.

HARE, A. PAUL.
1976 *Handbook of small group research*, 2nd ed. New York: Free Press.

HARRIS, DANIEL M., and SHARON GUTEN.
 1979 "Health-protective behavior: An exploratory study." *Journal of Health and Social Behavior*, 20:17–29.
HAVIGHURST, ROBERT A.
 1963 "Successful aging," pp. 299–320 in *Processes of aging*, R. Williams, C. Tibbitts, and W. Donahue (eds.). New York: Atherton.
HAVIGHURST, ROBERT J., and RUTH ALBRECHT.
 1953 *Older people*. New York: Longmans, Green.
HAYES-BAUTISTA, DAVID E.
 1976 "Termination of the patient-practitioner relationship: Divorce, patient style." *Journal of Health and Social Behavior*, 17:12–21.
HEALTH INSURANCE INSTITUTE.
 1980 *Source book of health insurance data, 1978–79*. New York: Health Insurance Institute.
HEINZELMANN, F.
 1962 "Determinants of prophylaxis behavior with respect to rheumatic fever." *Journal of Health and Human Behavior*, 3:73–81.
HENRY, JULES.
 1954 "The formal structure of a psychiatric hospital." *Psychiatry*, 17:139–151.
 1957 "Types of institutional structure." *Psychiatry*, 20:47–60.
HEYDEBRAND, WOLF V.
 1973 *Hospital bureaucracy*. New York: Dunellen.
HINES, RALPH.
 1972 "The health status of black Americans: Changing perspectives," pp. 40–50 in *Patients, physicians and illness*, 2nd ed., E. Jaco (ed.). New York: Free Press.
HIRSH, HAROLD L.
 1974 "Death: A medical status or legal definition." *Case & Comment*, (Sept.–Oct.):27–30.
HOCHSCHILD, ARLIE RUSSELL.
 1973a *The unexpected community*. Englewood Cliffs, N.J.: Prentice-Hall, Inc.
 1973b "A review of sex role research." *American Journal of Sociology*, 78:1011–1029.
HOLLINGSHEAD, AUGUST B.
 1973 "Medical sociology: A brief review." *Milbank Memorial Fund Quarterly*, 51:531–542.
HOLLINGSHEAD, AUGUST B., and FREDERICK C. REDLICH.
 1958 *Social class and mental illness*. New York: Wiley.
HOLLOWAY, ROBERT G., JAY W. ARTIS, and WALTER E. FREEMAN.
 1972 "The participation pattern of 'economic influentials' and their control of a hospital board of trustees," pp. 312–324 in *Patients, physicians, and illness*, 2nd ed., E. Jaco (ed.). New York: Macmillan.
HOLMES, THOMAS.
 1962 "Psychosocial and psychophysiological studies of tuberculosis," pp. 239–255 in *Physiological correlates of psychological disorders*, R. Roessler and N. Greenfield (eds.). Madison: University of Wisconsin Press.
HOLMES, T. H., and M. MASUDA.
 1974 "Life change and illness susceptibility," pp. 45–72 in *Stressful life events: Their nature and effects*, B. S. Dohrenwend and B. P. Dohrenwend (eds.). New York: Wiley.
HOLMES, T. H., and R. H. RAHE.
 1967 "The social readjustment rating scale." *Journal of Psychosomatic Research*, 11:213–225.
HOLOHAN¿ ANN.
 1977 "Diagnosis: The end of transition," pp. 87–97 in *Medical encounters: The*

experience of illness and treatment, A. Davis and G. Horobin (eds.). New York: St. Martin's Press.

HOOK, ERNEST.
1973 "Behavioral implications of the human XYZ genotype." *Science*, 179:139–150.

HOUGH, RICHARD L., DIANNE TIMBERS FAIRBANKS, and ALMA M. GARCIA.
1976 "Problems in the ratio measurement of life stress." *Journal of Health and Social Behavior*, 17:70–82.

HOUSE, JAMES S.
1974 "Occupational stress and coronary heart disease." *Journal of Health and Social Behavior*, 15:12–27.

HOUSE, JAMES S., ANTHONY J. MCMICHAEL, JAMES A. WELLS, BERTON H. KAPLAN, and LAWRENCE R. LANDERMAN.
1979 "Occupational stress and health among factory workers." *Journal of Health and Social Behavior*, 20:139–160.

HOWARD, JAN, and BARBARA L. HOLMAN.
1970 "The effects of race and occupation on hypertension mortality." *Milbank Memorial Fund Quarterly*, 48:263–296.

HOWARD, JAN, and ANSELM STRAUSS (eds.).
1975 *Humanizing health care*. New York: Wiley-Interscience.

HOWELL, MARY C.
1979 "Pediatricians and mothers," pp. 201–211 in *The cultural crisis of modern medicine*, J. Ehrenreich (ed.). New York: Monthly Review Press.

HUFFINE, CAROL L., and JOHN A. CLAUSEN.
1979 "Madness and work: Short- and long-term effects of mental illness on occupational careers." *Social Forces*, 57:1049–1062.

HUGHES, EVERETT C., HELEN MACGILL, and IRWIN DEUTSCHER.
1958 *Twenty thousand nurses tell their story*. Philadelphia: Lippincott.

HUNTINGTON, MARY J.
1957 "The development of a professional self-image," pp. 179–187 in *The student-physician*, R. K. Merton, G. Reader, and P. L. Kendall (eds.). Cambridge, Mass.: Harvard University Press.

HURLEY, ROGER.
1971 "The health crisis of the poor," pp. 83–112 in *The social organization of health*, P. Dreitzel (ed.). New York: Macmillan.

HYDE, DAVID R., and PAYSON WOLFF.
1954 "The American Medical Association: Power, purpose and politics in organized medicine." *Yale Law Journal*, 63:938–1022.

ILLICH, IVAN.
1976 *Medical nemesis: The expropriation of health*. New York: Pantheon.

INGALLS, A. J., and M. C. SALERNO.
1971 *Maternal and child health nursing*. St. Louis, MO.: Mosby.

JANIS, IRVING L.
1958 *Psychological stress*. New York: Wiley.

JENKINS, C. D.
1971 "Psychologic and social precursors of coronary disease." *New England Journal of Medicine*, 284:244–255, 307–317.

JESSOR, R., T. GRAVES, R. HANSON, and S. JESSOR.
1968 *Society, personality and deviant behavior: A study of a tri-ethnic community*. New York: Holt, Rinehart, and Winston.

KAPLAN, HAROLD I.
1975 "History of psychophysiological medicine," pp. 1624–1631 in *Comprehensive textbook of psychiatry*, Vol. II, 2nd ed., A. Freedman, H. Kaplan, and B. Sadock (eds.). Baltimore: Williams & Wilkins.

KASER, MICHAEL.
1976 *Health care in the Soviet Union and Eastern Europe.* Boulder, CO: Westview Press.
KASL, S., and S. COBB.
1966 "Health behavior, illness behavior, and sick role behavior." *Archives of Environmental Health,* 12:246–266.
KASS, LEON R.
1976 "Medical care and the pursuit of health," pp. 1–22 in *New directions in public health care: An evaluation of proposals for national health insurance.* San Francisco: Institute for Contemporary Studies.
KASSEBAUM, G., and B. BAUMANN.
1965 "Dimensions of the sick role in chronic illness." *Journal of Health and Social Behavior,* 6:16–27.
KASTELER, JOSEPHINE, ROBERT L. KANE, DONNA M. OLSEN, and CONSTANCE THETFORD.
1976 "Issues underlying prevalence of 'doctor-shopping' behavior." *Journal of Health and Social Behavior,* 17:328–339.
KASTENBAUM, ROBERT.
1971 "Age: Getting there." *Psychology Today,* 5:53–54, 82–83.
KAUFMANN, WALTER.
1959 "Existentialism and death," pp. 39–69 in *The meaning of death,* H. Feifel (ed.). New York: McGraw-Hill.
KEGELES, S. S.
1963 "Why people seek dental care: A test of a conceptual formulation." *Journal of Health and Social Behavior,* 4:166–173.
KENDALL, PATRICIA L., and HANAN C. SELVIN.
1957 "Tendencies toward specialization in medical training," pp. 153–174 in *The student-physician,* R. Merton, G. Reader, and P. Kendall (eds.). Cambridge, Mass.: Harvard University Press.
KESSLER, RONALD A.
1979 "Stress, social status, and psychological distress." *Journal of Health and Social Behavior,* 20:259–272.
KETY, SEYMOUR S.
1975 "Biochemistry of the major psychoses," pp. 178–187 in *Comprehensive textbook of psychiatry,* Vol. I, 2nd ed., A. Freedman, H. Kaplan, and B. Sadock (eds.). Baltimore: Williams & Wilkins.
KIEV, ARI.
1968 *Curanderismo: Mexican-American folk psychiatry.* New York: Free Press.
KIRSCHT, JOHN P.
1974 "The health belief model and illness behavior," pp. 387–408 in *The health belief model and personal health,* M. H. Becker (ed.). San Francisco: Society for Public Health Education, Inc.
KNOWLES, JOHN H. (ed.).
1963 *Hospitals, doctors, and the public interest.* Cambridge, Mass.: Harvard University Press.
1973 "The hospital," pp. 91–102 in *Life and death and medicine,* San Francisco: W. H. Freeman.
1979 "Introduction," pp. vii–xi in *Handbook of medical sociology,* 3rd ed., H. E. Freeman, S. Levine, and L. G. Reeder (eds.). Englewood Cliffs, N.J.: Prentice-Hall, Inc.
KNUDSON, A. G., and J. M. NATTERSON.
1960 "Participation of parents in the hospital care of their fatally ill children." *Pediatrics,* 26:482–490.
KOHN, MELVIN L.
1969 *Class and conformity: A study in values.* Homewood, Ill.: Dorsey Press.

1972 "Class, family, and schizophrenia." *Social Forces*, 50:295–304.

1974 "Social class and schizophrenia: A critical review and a reformulation," pp. 113–137 in *Explorations in psychiatric sociology*, P. Roman and H. Trice (eds.). Philadelphia: F. A. Davis.

Koos, Earl.

1954 *The health of Regionsville*. New York: Columbia University Press.

Kosa, J., and L. S. Robertson.

1969 "The social aspects of health and illness," pp. 35–68 in *Poverty and health*, John Kosa, Aaron Antonovsky, and K. Zola (eds.). Cambridge, Mass.: Harvard University Press.

Kosa, John, Aaron Antonovsky, and Irving K. Zola (eds.).

1969 *Poverty and health*. Cambridge, Mass.: Harvard University Press.

Krause, Elliott A.

1971 *The sociology of occupations*. Boston: Little, Brown.

1977 *Power & illness*. New York: Elsevier.

Kravits, Jonna, and John Schneider.

1975 "Health care need and actual use by age, race and income," pp. 169–187 in *Equity in health services: Empirical analyses in social policy*, R. Andersen, J. Kravits, and O. Anderson (eds.). Cambridge, Mass.: Ballinger.

Kronenfeld, Jennie J.

1978 "Provider variables and the utilization of ambulatory care services." *Journal of Health and Social Behavior*, 19:68–76.

Kübler-Ross, Elisabeth.

1969 *On death and dying*. New York: Macmillan.

LaRocco, James M., James S. House, and John R. P. French, Jr.

1980 "Social support, occupational stress, and health." *Journal of Health and Social Behavior*, 21:202–218.

Larson, Donald E., and Irving Rootman.

1976 "Physician role performance and patient satisfaction." *Social Science and Medicine*, 10:29–32.

Larson, Reed.

1978 "Thirty years of research on the subjective well-being of older Americans." *Journal of Gerontology*, 33: 109–125.

Lauer, Robert.

1974 "Rate of change and stress." *Social Forces*, 52:510–516.

LeShan, L.

1966 "An emotional life history pattern associated with neoplastic diseases." *Annals of the New York Academy of Sciences*, 125:780–793.

Leventhal, Howard.

1975 "The consequences of personalization during illness and treatment: An information-processing model," pp. 119–162 in *Humanizing health care*, J. Howard and A. Strauss (eds.). New York: Wiley-Interscience.

Leventhal, H., G. Hochman, and I. Rosenstock.

1960 "Epidemic impact on the general population in two cities," pp. 14–23 in *The impact of Asian influenza on community life*. Washington, D.C.: U.S. Department of Health, Education and Welfare.

Lever, Janet.

1978 "Sex differences in the complexity of children's play and games." *American Sociological Review*, 43:471–483.

Levine, Sol, and Norman Scotch.

1970 *Social stress*. Chicago: Aldine.

Levinson, Richard M., and M. Zan York.

1974 "The attribution of 'dangerousness' in mental health evaluations." *Journal of Health and Social Behavior*, 15:328–335.

LEVY, JERROLD, and STEPHEN KUNITZ.
1973 "Indian drinking: Problems of data collection and interpretation," pp. 217–235 in *Proceedings* of the First Abuse Alcoholism Conference of the National Institute on Alcohol Abuse and Alcoholism, M. Chafetz (ed.). Washington, D.C.: U.S. Government Printing Office.
1974 *Indian drinking: Navajo practices and Anglo-American theories.* New York: Wiley-Interscience.

LIEBER, CHARLES S.
1971 "The magnitude of the problem," pp. 3–5 in *Proceedings* of the First Annual Alcoholism Conference of the National Institute on Alcohol Abuse and Alcoholism, M. Chafetz (ed.). Washington, D.C.: U.S. Government Printing Office.

LIEF, HAROLD I.
1971 "Personality characteristics of medical students," pp. 44–87 in *Psychosocial aspects of medical training*, R. H. Coombs and C. E. Vincent (eds.). Springfield, Ill.: Thomas.

LIEM, RAMSAY, and JOAN LIEM.
1978 "Social class and mental illness reconsidered: The role of economic stress and social support." *Journal of Health and Social Behavior*, 19:139–156.

LIGHT, DONALD, JR.
1979 "Uncertainty and control in professional training." *Journal of Health and Social Behavior*, 20:310–322.

LIN, N., R. S. SIMEONE, W. M. ENSEL, and W. KUO.
1979 "Social support, stressful life events, and illness: A model and an empirical test." *Journal of Health and Social Behavior*, 20:108–119.

LINDESMITH, ALFRED, ANSELM STRAUSS, and NORMAN DENZIN.
1975 *Social psychology*, 4th ed. Hinsdale, Ill.: Dryden Press.

LIPOWSKI, Z. J.
1970 "Physical illness, the individual and the coping process." *Psychiatry in Medicine*, 1:91–101.

LONGINO, CHARLES F., KENT A. MCCLELLAND, and WARREN A. PETERSON.
1980 "The aged subculture hypothesis: Social integration, gerontophilia, and self-conception." *Journal of Gerontology*, 35:758–767.

LOPATA, HELENA Z.
1973 "Social relations of black and white widowed women in a northern metropolis." *American Journal of Sociology*, 78:1003–1010.

LORBER, JUDITH.
1975 "Good patients and problem patients: Conformity and deviance in a general hospital." *Journal of Health and Social Behavior*, 16:213–225.

LOWENTHAL, M. F., and C. HAVEN.
1968 "Interaction and adaptation: Intimacy as a critical variable." *American Sociological Review*, 13:20–30.

LUDWIG, ALFRED O., BENJAMIN J. MURAWSKI, and SOMERS H. STURGIS.
1969 *Psychosomatic aspects of gynecological disorders.* Cambridge, Mass.: Harvard University Press.

MCGRATH, JOSEPH E. (ed.).
1970 *Social and psychological factors in stress.* New York: Holt, Rinehart, and Winston.

MCGRAW, R. M.
1966 *Ferment in medicine: A study of the essence of medical practice and of its new dilemmas.* Philadelphia: W. B. Saunders.

MCINTOSH, JIM.
1974 "Processes of communication, information seeking and control associated with cancer: A selective review of the literature." *Social Science and Medicine*, 8:167–187.

McKINLAY, JOHN B.
1971 "The concept 'patient career' as a heuristic device for making medical sociology relevant to medical students." *Social Science and Medicine,* 5:441–460.
1972 "Some approaches and problems in the study of the use of services—an overview." *Journal of Health and Social Behavior,* 13:115–152.
1973 "Social networks, lay consultation and help-seeking behavior." *Social Forces,* 51:275–291.

McNEIL, ELTON B.
1970 *Neuroses and personality disorders.* Englewood Cliffs, N.J.: Prentice-Hall, Inc.

MACCOBY, ELEANOR (ed.).
1966 *The development of sex differences.* Stanford: Stanford University Press.

MADDOX, GEORGE L.
1962 "Some correlates of differences in self-assessment of health status among the elderly." *Journal of Gerontology,* 17:180–185.

MADSEN, WILLIAM.
1973 *The Mexican-Americans of south Texas,* 2nd ed. New York: Holt, Rinehart, and Winston.

MAGRAW, RICHARD M.
1975 "Medical specialization and medical coordination," pp. 588–606 in *Medical behavioral science,* T. Millon (ed.). Philadelphia: W. B. Saunders.

MAJOR, RALPH A.
1954 *A history of medicine,* Vols. I and II. Springfield, Ill.: Thomas.

MAKOFSKY, DAVID.
1977 "Malpractice and medicine." *Society,* 14:25–29.

MARMOR, THEODORE R.
1973 *The politics of Medicare.* Chicago: Aldine.

MARSHALL, ROBERT J., JR., JOHN P. FULTON, and ALBERT F. WESSEN.
1978 "Physician career outcomes and the process of medical education." *Journal of Health and Social Behavior,* 19:124–138.

MARSHALL, VICTOR W.
1975a "Socialization for impending death in a retirement village." *American Journal of Sociology,* 80:1124–1144.
1975b "Organizational features of terminal status passage in residential facilities for the aged." *Urban Life,* 4:349–368.

MASON, EVELYN P.
1954 "Some correlates of self-judgments of the aged." *Journal of Gerontology,* 9:324–337.

MATSUMOTO, Y. SCOTT.
1971 "Social stress and coronary heart disease in Japan," pp. 123–149 in *The social organization of health,* H. Dreitzel (ed.). New York: Macmillan.

MAUKSCH, HANS.
1972 "Nursing: Churning for a change?" pp. 206–230 in *Handbook of medical sociology,* 2nd ed., H. E. Freeman, S. Levine, and L. G. Reeder (eds.). Englewood Cliffs, N.J.: Prentice-Hall, Inc.

MAY, PHILIP R. A.
1975 "Schizophrenia: Evaluation of treatment methods," pp. 955–982 in *Comprehensive textbook of psychiatry,* Vol. I, 2nd ed., A. Freedman, H. Kaplan, and B. Sadock (eds.). Baltimore: Williams & Wilkins.

MAYNARD, ALAN.
1975 *Health care in the European community.* Pittsburgh: University of Pittsburgh Press.

MAZUR, ALLAN, and LEON S. ROBERTSON.
1972 *Biology and social behavior.* New York: Free Press.

MEAD, GEORGE HERBERT.
1934 *Mind, self, and society*. Chicago: University of Chicago Press.
MECHANIC, DAVID.
1962a "The concept of illness behavior." *Journal of Chronic Diseases*, 15:189–194.
1962b *Students under stress: A study in the social psychology of adaptation*. New York: Free Press.
1964 "The influence of mothers on their children's health attitudes and behavior." *Pediatrics*, 33:444–453.
1972 *Public expectations and health care*. New York: Wiley-Interscience.
1978 *Medical sociology*. 2nd ed. New York: Free Press.
1979 "Correlates of physician utilization: Why do major multivariate studies of physician utilization find trivial psychosocial and organizational effects?" *Journal of Health and Social Behavior*, 20:387–396.
1980 *Mental health and social policy*. 2nd ed. Englewood Cliffs, N.J.: Prentice-Hall, Inc.
MECHANIC, DAVID, and EDMUND H. VOLKART.
1961 "Stress, illness behavior, and the sick role." *American Sociological Review*, 25:51–58.
MEISSNER, W. W., JOHN E. MACK, and ELVIN V. SEMRAD.
1975 "Classical psychoanalysis," pp. 482–566 in *Comprehensive textbook of psychiatry*, Vol. I, 2nd ed., A. Freedman, H. Kaplan, and B. Sadock (eds.). Baltimore: Williams & Wilkins.
MELICK, D. W.
1959 "What a staff doctor expects of the hospital administrator." *Hospitals*, 33:30–33.
MERENSTEIN, JOEL H., HARVEY WOLFE, and KATHLEEN M. BARKER.
1974 "The use of nurse practitioners in a general practice." *Medical Care*, 12:437–444.
MERTON, ROBERT.
1938 "Social structure and anomie." *American Sociological Review*, 3:672–682.
MERTON, ROBERT K., GEORGE G. READER, and PATRICIA KENDALL.
1957 *The student-physician*. Cambridge, Mass.: Harvard University Press.
METTLIN, CURT, and JOSEPH WOELFEL.
1974 "Interpersonal influence and symptoms of stress." *Journal of Health and Social Behavior*, 15:311–319.
MILLER, DOROTHY H.
1971 "Worlds that fail," pp. 102–114 in *Total institutions*, S. Wallace (ed.). Chicago: Aldine.
MILLER, JUDITH.
1975 "Study of death draws interest of psychologists." *APA Monitor*, 6:1, 5.
MILLER, MICHAEL H.
1973 "Who receives optimal medical care?" *Journal of Health and Social Behavior*, 14:176–182.
1974 "Work roles for the associate degree graduate." *American Journal of Nursing*, 74:468–470.
MILLER, STEPHEN J.
1970 *Prescription for leadership: Training for the medical elite*. Chicago: Aldine.
MILLMAN, MARCIA.
1977a "Masking doctors' errors." *Human Behavior*, 6:16–23.
1977b *The unkindest cut*. New York: William Morrow.
MISHLER, ELLIOT G., and NANCY E. WAXLER.
1968 "Decision processes in psychiatric hospitalization: Patients referred,

accepted, and admitted to a psychiatric hospital," pp. 262–276 in *The mental patient: Studies in the sociology of deviance*, S. Spitzer and N. Denzin (eds.). New York: McGraw-Hill.

MONTEIRO, LOIS.
  1973a "Expense is no object . . .: Income and physician visits reconsidered." *Journal of Health and Social Behavior*, 14:99–115.
  1973b "After heart attack: Behavioral expectations for the cardiac." *Social Science and Medicine*, 7:555–565.

MOODY, RAYMOND.
  1976 *Life after life*. New York: Bantam.

MOORE, JOAN.
  1970 *Mexican-Americans*. Englewood Cliffs, N.J.: Prentice-Hall, Inc.

MORA, GEORGE.
  1975 "Historical and theoretical trends in psychiatry," pp. 1–75 in *Comprehensive textbook of psychiatry*, Vol. I, 2nd ed., A. Freedman, H. Kaplan, and B. Sadock (eds.). Baltimore: Williams & Wilkins.

MORISON, ROBERT S.
  1973 "Dying," pp. 39–45 in *Life and death and medicine*. San Francisco: W. H. Freeman.

MORIWAKI, SHARON Y.
  1973 "Self-disclosure, significant others, and psychological well-being in old age." *Journal of Health and Social Behavior*, 14:226–232.

MORSE, EDWARD V., GERALD GORDON, and MICHAEL MOCH.
  1974 "Hospital costs and quality of care: An organizational perspective." *Milbank Memorial Fund Quarterly*, 52:315–346.

MOSKOS, CHARLES C. JR.
  1970 *The American enlisted man*. New York: Russell Sage.

MOSS, GORDON E.
  1973 *Illness, immunity, and social interaction*. New York: Wiley.

MOUSTAFA, A. TAHER, and GERTRUD WEISS.
  1968 *Health status and practices of Mexican-Americans*, Advanced Report II, Mexican-American Study Project. Los Angeles: University of California.

NATHANSON, C. A.
  1977 "Sex roles as variables in preventive health behavior." *Journal of Community Health*, 3:142–155.

NATIONAL CENTER FOR HEALTH STATISTICS.
  1975 *Health resources statistics*. U.S. Department of Health, Education and Welfare.
  1979a *Advance data—Office visits by black patients—National ambulatory medical care survey: United States, 1975–76*, No. 50 (July 23). U.S. Department of Health, Education and Welfare.
  1979b *Physician visits, volume and interval since last visit, United States—1975*, Series 10, No. 128 (April). U.S. Department of Health, Education and Welfare.

NATIONAL INSTITUTE OF MENTAL HEALTH.
  1975 *Research in the service of mental health: Summary report of the Research Task Force of the National Institute of Mental Health*. Washington, D.C.: Department of Health, Education and Welfare.

NATTERSON, J. M., and A. G. KNUDSON.
  1960 "Observations concerning fear of death in fatally ill children and their mothers." *Psychosomatic Medicine*, 22:456–465.

NAVARRO, VICENTE.
  1974 *National and regional health planning in Sweden*. Washington, D.C.: Department of Health, Education and Welfare.
  1976 *Medicine under capitalism*. New York: Prodist.

NEUGARTEN, BERNICE.
1964 *Personality in middle and later life*. New York: Atherton.
1970 "The old and young in modern societies." *American Behavioral Scientist*, 14:13–24.
1971 "Grow old with me. The best is yet to be." *Psychology Today*, 5:45–48, 79–81.

NEUGARTEN, BERNICE, and JOAN W. MOORE.
1968 "The changing age-status system," pp. 5–21 in *Middle age and aging*, B. Neugarten (ed.). Chicago: University of Chicago Press.

NEW, PETER KONG-MING.
1958 "The osteopathic students: A study in dilemma," pp. 413–421 in *Patients, physicians, and illness*, E. Jaco (ed.). Glencoe, Ill.: Free Press.

NEWMAN, JOHN F., WILLIAM B. ELLIOTT, JAMES O. GIBBS, and HELEN C. GIFT.
1979 "Attempts to control health costs: the United States experience." *Social Science & Medicine*, 13A:529–540.

NICKERSON, RITA J., THEODORE COLTON, OSLER L. PETERSON, BERNARD S. BLOOM, and WALTER W. HAUCK, JR.
1976 "Doctors who perform operations: A study of in-hospital surgery in four diverse geographic areas." *New England Journal of Medicine*, 295:921–926, 982–989.

NISBET, ROBERT A.
1966 *The sociological tradition*. New York: Basic Books.
1974 *The sociology of Emile Durkheim*. New York: Oxford.

NOLEN, WILLIAM A.
1970 *The making of a surgeon*. New York: Random House.

NORTHCOTT, HERBERT C.
1980 "Women, work, and health." *Pacific Sociological Review*, 23:393–404.

NOYES, RUSSELL, JR.
1972 "The experience of dying." *Psychiatry*, 35:174–184.

OKEN, DONALD.
1961 "What to tell cancer patients: A study of medical attitudes." *Journal of the American Medical Association*, 175:1120–1128.

OLESEN, VIRGINIA L., and ELVI W. WHITTAKER.
1968 *The silent dialogue*. San Francisco: Jossey-Bass.

OLMSTED, DONALD W., and KATHERINE DURHAM.
1976 "Stability of mental health attitudes: A semantic differential study." *Journal of Health and Social Behavior*, 17:35–44.

PALMORE, ERDMAN.
1968 "The effects of aging on activities and attitudes." *Gerontologist*, 8:259–263.
1969 "Sociological aspects of aging," pp. 33–69 in *Behavior and adaptation in later life*, E. Busse and E. Pfeiffer (eds.). Boston: Little, Brown.
1971 "Attitudes toward aging as shown by humor." *Gerontologist*, 2:181–186.
1975 *The honorable elders*. Durham, N.C.: Duke University Press.

PARSONS, TALCOTT.
1951 *The social system*. Glencoe, Ill.: Free Press.
1975 "The sick role and role of the physician reconsidered." *Milbank Memorial Fund Quarterly*, 53:257–278.
1979 "Definitions of health and illness in light of American values and social structure," pp. 120–144 in *Patients, physicians, and illness*, 3rd ed., E. Jaco (ed.). New York: Free Press.

PARSONS, TALCOTT, and RENÉE FOX.
1952 "Illness, therapy and the modern urban American family." *Journal of Social Issues*, 8:31–44.

338   Bibliography

PAUL, JOHN R.
    1966 *Clinical epidemiology.* Chicago: University of Chicago Press.
PERROW, CHARLES.
    1963 "Goals and power structures; A historical case study," pp. 112–146 in *The hospital in modern society*, E. Freidson (ed.). New York: Free Press.
PETERSON, MERRILL,
    1970 *Thomas Jefferson and the new nation.* New York: Oxford University Press.
PFLANZ, MANFRED, and JOHANN J. ROHDE.
    1970 "Illness: Deviant behavior or conformity." *Social Science and Medicine*, 4:645–653.
PHILLIPS, DAVID P., and KENNETH A. FELDMAN.
    1973 "A dip in deaths before ceremonial occasions: Some new relationships between social integration and mortality." *American Sociological Review*, 38:678–696.
PIAGET, JEAN.
    1959 *The language and thought of the child*, 3rd. ed. New York: Humanities Press.
PRESTHUS, ROBERT.
    1978 *The organizational society.* Rev. ed. New York: St. Martin's Press.
PRESTON, CAROLINE.
    1967 "Self-reporting among older retired and non-retired subjects." *Journal of Gerontology*, 22:415–418.
    1968 "Subjectively perceived agedness and retirement." *Journal of Gerontology*, 23:201–204.
PRESTON, CAROLINE E., and KAREN S. GUDIKEN.
    1966 "A measure of self-perception among older people." *Journal of Gerontology*, 21:63–67.
PRUGH, D. G., E. M. STAUB, H. H. SANDS, R. M. KIRSCHBAUM, and E. A. LENIHAN.
    1953 "A study of the emotional responses of children and families to hospitalization and illness." *American Journal of Orthopsychiatry*, 23:70–106.
PSATHAS, GEORGE.
    1968 "The fate of idealism in nursing school." *Journal of Health and Social Behavior*, 9:52–64.
RADO, S.
    1949 "Pathodynamics and treatment of traumatic war neurosis (traumatophobia)." *Psychosomatic Medicine*, 43:363–398.
RAINER, JOHN D.
    1975 "Genetics and psychiatry," pp. 89–104 in *Comprehensive textbook of psychiatry*, Vol. I, 2nd ed., A. Freedman, H. Kaplan, and B. Sadock (eds.). Baltimore: Williams & Wilkins.
RANK, STEVEN G., and CARDELL K. JACOBSON.
    1977 "Hospital nurses' compliance with medication overdose orders: A failure to replicate." *Journal of Health and Social Behavior*, 18:188–193.
RASMUSSEN, HOWARD.
    1975 "Medical education—revolution or reaction." *Pharos*, 38:53–59.
RAY, OAKLEY S.
    1978 *Drugs, society, and human behavior.* 2nd ed. St. Louis, Mo.: Mosby.
READER, GEORGE G.
    1976 "Should medical schools require a sociology background?" *AAMC Education News*, 4:3, 8.
REEDER, LEO G.
    1972 "The patient-client as a consumer: Some observations on the changing professional-client relationship." *Journal of Health and Social Behavior*, 13:406–412.

REEDER, LEO G., and EMIL BERKANOVIC.
  1973 "Sociological concomitants of health orientations: A partial replication of Suchman." *Journal of Health and Social Behavior*, 14:134–143.
REINHARDT, UWE E.
  1973 "Proposed changes in the organization of health-care delivery: An overview and critique." *Milbank Memorial Fund Quarterly*, 51:169–222.
REISSMAN, LEONARD, and RALPH PLATOU.
  1960 "The motivation and socialization of medical students." *Journal of Health and Human Behavior*, 1:174–182.
REYNOLDS, ROGER A.
  1976 "Improving access to health care among the poor—the neighborhood health care center experience." *Milbank Memorial Fund Quarterly*, 54:47–82.
RICHTER, LUCRETIA, and ELIZABETH RICHTER.
  1974 "Nurses in fiction." *American Journal of Nursing*, 74:1280–1281.
RILEY, MATILDA WHITE.
  1971 "Social gerontology and the age stratification of society." *The Gerontologist*, 11:79–87.
RILEY, MATILDA W., and ANN FONER.
  1968 *Aging and society*, Vol. I. New York: Russell Sage.
RILEY, M. W., M. E. JOHNSON, and A. FONER (eds.).
  1971 *Aging and society*, Vol. III. New York: Russell Sage Foundation.
ROBBINS, G. F., J. D. MACDONALD, and G. T. PACK.
  1953 "Delay in diagnosis and treatment of physicians with cancer." *Cancer*, 6:624–626.
ROBERTS, ROBERT E., and EUN SUL LEE.
  1980 "Medical care use by Mexican-Americans: Evidence from the human population laboratory studies." *Medical Care*, 43:266–281.
ROEBUCK, JULIAN, and ROBERT QUAN.
  1976 "Health-care practices in the American Deep South," pp. 141–161 in *Marginal medicine*, R. Wallis and P. Morely (eds.). New York: Free Press.
ROEMER, MILTON I.
  1977 *Comparative national policies on health care*. New York: Marcel Dekker.
ROEMER, MILTON I., and WILLIAM SHONICK.
  1973 "HMO performance: The recent evidence." *Milbank Memorial Fund Quarterly*, 51:271–318.
ROGERS, D. E.
  1973 "Shattuck lecture—the American health-care scene." *New England Journal of Medicine*, 288:1377–1383.
ROGLER, LLOYD H., and AUGUST B. HOLLINGSHEAD.
  1965 *Trapped: Families and schizophrenia*. New York: Wiley.
ROGOFF, NATALIE.
  1957 "The decision to study medicine," pp. 109–129 in *The student-physician*, R. K. Merton, G. Reader, and P. L. Kendall (eds.). Cambridge, Mass.: Harvard University Press.
ROMAN, PAUL, and PHILIP TAIETZ.
  1967 "Organizational structure and disengagement: The emeritus professor." *Gerontologist*, 7:147–152.
ROOS, NORALOU P., JOHN R. SCHERMERHORN, and LESLIE L. ROOS, JR.
  1974 "Hospital performance: Analyzing power and goals." *Journal of Health and Social Behavior*, 15:78–92.
ROSE, M. P., and W. A. PETERSON (eds.).
  1965 *Older people and their social world*. Philadelphia: F. A. Davis.

ROSEN, GEORGE.
1963 "The hospital: Historical sociology of a community institution," pp. 1–36 in *The hospital in modern society*, E. Freidson (ed.). New York: Free Press.
1979 "The evolution of social medicine," pp. 23–50, in *Handbook of medical sociology*, 2nd ed., H. Freeman, S. Levine, and L. Reeder (eds.). Englewood Cliffs, N.J.: Prentice-Hall, Inc.

ROSENBERG, EMILY J., and BARBARA S. DOHRENWEND.
1975 "Effects of experience and ethnicity on ratings of life events as stressors." *Journal of Health and Social Behavior*, 16:127–129.

ROSENHAN, DAVID L.
1973 "On being sane in insane places." *Science*, 179:250–258.

ROSENSTOCK, IRWIN.
1966 "Why people use health services." *Milbank Memorial Fund Quarterly*, 44:94–127.

ROSOW, IRVING.
1967 *Social integration of the aged*. New York: Free Press.
1974 *Socialization into old age*. Berkeley, Cal.: University of California Press.

ROSS, CATHERINE E., and JOHN MIROWSKY II.
1979 "A comparison of life-event-weighting schemes: Change, undesirability, and effect-proportional indices." *Journal of Health and Social Behavior*, 20:166–177.

ROTH, J. A.
1963 "Information and the control of treatment in tuberculosis hospitals," pp. 293–318 in *The hospital in modern society*, E. Freidson (ed.). New York: Free Press.
1969 "The treatment of the sick," pp. 214–243 in *Poverty and health*, J. Kosa, A. Antonovsky, and I. Zola (eds.). Cambridge, Mass.: Harvard University Press.

ROTTENBERG, SIMON (ed.).
1978 *The economics of medical malpractice*. Washington, D.C.: American Enterprise Institute for Public Policy.

ROUECHÉ, BERTON.
1967 *Annals of epidemiology*. Boston: Little, Brown.
1978 "Annals of medicine." *The New Yorker* (August 21):63–70.

RUCH, LIBBY O.
1977 "Multidimensional analysis of the concept of life change." *Journal of Health and Social Behavior*, 18:71–83.

RUCH, LIBBY O., SUSAN MEYERS CHANDLER, and RICHARD A. HARTER.
1980 "Life change and rape impact." *Journal of Health and Social Behavior*, 21:248–260.

RUESCHMEYER, DIETRICH.
1972 "Doctors and lawyers: A comment on the theory of professions," pp. 5–19 in *Medical men and their work*, E. Freidson and J. Lorber (eds.). Chicago: Aldine.

RUNDALL, THOMAS G.
1978 "Life change and recovery from surgery." *Journal of Health and Social Behavior*, 19:418–427.

RUNDALL, THOMAS G., and JOHN R. C. WHEELER.
1979 "The effect of income on use of preventive care: An evaluation of alternative explanations." *Journal of Health and Social Behavior*, 20:397–406.

RUSHING, WILLIAM A.
1978 "Status resources, societal reactions, and type of mental hospital admissions." *American Sociological Review*, 43:521–533.

RUTSTEIN, DAVID.
1967 *The coming revolution in medicine*. Cambridge, Mass.: MIT Press.

SADOCK, BENJAMIN J.
    1975 "Group psychotherapy," pp. 1850–1877 in *Comprehensive textbook of psychiatry*, Vol. II, 2nd ed., A. Freedman, H. Kaplan, and B. Sadock (eds.). Baltimore: Williams & Wilkins.
SALLOWAY, JEFFREY C.
    1973 "Medical utilization among urban gypsies." *Urban Anthropology*, 2:113–126.
SAMPSON, HAROLD, SHELDON L. MESSINGER, and ROBERT L. TOWNE ET AL.
    1964 "The mental hospital and marital family ties," pp. 139–162 in *The other side: Perspectives on deviance*, H. Becker (ed.). New York: Free Press.
SATIN, GEORGE D.
    1973 "Help?: The hospital emergency unit patient and his presenting picture." *Medical Care*, 11:328–337.
SATIN, GEORGE, and FREDERICK J. DUHL.
    1972 "Help?: The hospital emergency unit as community physician." *Medical Care*, 10:248–260.
SAWARD, ERNEST W.
    1973 "The organization of medical care," pp. 129–135 in *Life, death, and medicine*. San Francisco: W. H. Freeman.
SAWYER, DARWIN O.
    1980 "Normative conflict and physician use: A latent structure approach." *Journal of Health and Social Behavior*, 21:156–169.
SCHEFF, THOMAS J.
    1964 "The societal reaction to deviance: Ascriptive elements in the psychiatric screening of mental patients in a midwestern state." *Social Problems*, 11:444–452.
    1966 *Being mentally ill*. Chicago: Aldine.
    1974 "The labelling theory of mental illness." *American Sociological Review*, 39:444–452.
    1975 *Labeling madness*. Englewood Cliffs, N.J.: Prentice-Hall, Inc.
SCHEFFLER, RICHARD M., and OLIVIA D. STINSON.
    1974 "Characteristics of physician's assistants: A focus on specialty." *Medical Care*, 12:1019–1030.
SCHULMAN, SAM.
    1972 "Mother surrogate—after a decade," pp. 233–239 in *Patients, physicians and illness*, E. Jaco (ed.). New York: Free Press.
SCHWAB, ROBERT S., and JOHN S. PRITCHARD.
    1950 "Situational stresses and extrapyramidal disease in different personalities," pp. 48–61 in *Life, stress and disease*, Proceedings of the Association for Research in Nervous and Mental Diseases, No. 29. Baltimore: Williams & Wilkins.
SCHWARTZ, ARTHUR, and ROBERT W. KLEEMEIER.
    1965 "The effects of illness upon some aspects of personality." *Journal of Gerontology*, 20:85–91.
SCULLY, DIANA, and PAULINE BART.
    1979 "A funny thing happened on the way to the orifice: Women in gynecology textbooks," pp. 212–226 in *The cultural crisis of modern medicine*, J. Ehrenreich (ed.). New York: Monthly Review Press.
SEGALL, ALEXANDER.
    1976 "The sick role concept: Understanding illness behavior." *Journal of Health and Social Behavior*, 17:162–168.
SEGAL, STEVEN P., and URI AVIRAM.
    1978 The mentally ill in community-based shelter care. New York: Wiley-Interscience.
SELIGMAN, MARTIN E. P.
    1974 "Submissive death: Giving up on life." *Psychology Today*, 7:80–85.

SELTZER, MILDRED M., and ROBERT C. ATCHLEY.
1971 "The concept of old age: Changing attitudes and stereotypes." *Gerontologist*, 11:226–230.
SELYE, HANS.
1956 *The stress of life*. New York: McGraw-Hill.
SHAPIRO, D.
1965 *Neurotic styles*. New York: Basic Books.
SHAPIRO, MARTIN.
1978 *Getting doctored*. Kitchener, Ontario, Canada: Between the Lines.
SHILOH, AÌLON.
1965 "Equalitarian and hierarchial patients: An investigation among Hadassah Hospital patients." *Medical Care*, 3:87–95.
1971 "Sanctuary or prison—responses to life in a mental hospital," pp. 9–24 in *Total institutions*, S. Wallace (ed.). Chicago: Aldine.
SHINDELL, SIDNEY, JEFFREY C. SALLOWAY, and COLETTE M. OBEREMBT.
1976 *A coursebook in health care delivery*. New York: Appleton-Century-Crofts.
SHORTELL, STEPHEN M.
1973 "Patterns of referral among internists in private practice." *Journal of Health and Social Behavior*, 14:335–348.
SIGERIST, HENRY E.
1960 "The special position of the sick," pp. 10–11 in *Henry E. Sigerist on the sociology of medicine*, M. Roemer (ed.). New York: MD Publications.
SIMON, RITA JAMES.
1967 *The jury and the defense of insanity*. Boston: Little, Brown.
SMITH, H. L.
1955 "Two lines of authority: The hospital's dilemma." *Modern Hospital*, 84:59–64.
SMITH, HARVEY L., and JEAN THRASHER.
1963 "Roles, cliques and sanctions: Dimensions of patient society." *Journal of Social Psychiatry*, 9:184–191.
SNOW, LOUDELL F.
1977 "Popular medicine in a black neighborhood," pp. 19–95 in *Ethnic medicine in the Southwest*, E. Spicer (ed.). Tucson: University of Arizona Press.
1978 "Sorcerers, saints, and charlatans: Black folk healers in urban America." *Culture, Medicine, and Psychiatry*, 2:69–106.
SOMERS, HERMAN M.
1970 "Health care cost," pp. 167–203 in *The health of Americans*, B. Jones (ed.). Englewood Cliffs, N.J.: Prentice-Hall, Inc.
SORENSON, JAMES R.
1974 "Biomedical innovation, uncertainty, and doctor-patient interaction." *Journal of Health and Social Behavior*, 15:366–374.
SPARER, GERALD, and LOUISE M. OKADA.
1974 "Chronic conditions and physician use patterns in ten urban poverty areas." *Medical Care*, 12:549–560.
SPINETTA, JOHN J.
1974 "The dying child's awareness of death: A review." *Psychological Bulletin*, 81:256–260.
SPINETTA, JOHN J., DAVID RIGLER, and MYRON KARON.
1974 "Personal space as a measure of a dying child's sense of isolation." *Journal of Consulting and Clinical Psychology*, 42:751–756.
SPITZER, ROBERT L., and PAUL T. WILSON.
1975 "Nosology and the official psychiatric nomenclature," pp. 826–845 in *Comprehensive textbook of psychiatry*, Vol. I, 2nd ed., A. Freedman, H. Kaplan, and B. Sadock (eds.). Baltimore: Williams & Wilkins.

SROLE, LEO, T. S. LANGNER, S. T. MICHAEL, M. K. OPLER, and T. A. C. RENNIE.
1962 *Mental health in the metropolis: The midtown Manhattan study*, Vol. I. New York: McGraw-Hill.

STEIN, LEONARD I.
1967 "The doctor-nurse game." *Archives of General Psychiatry*, 16:699–703.

STEVENS, ROSEMARY.
1971 *American medicine and the public interest.* New Haven: Yale University Press.

STEWART, OMAR.
1964 "Questions regarding American Indian criminality." *Human Organization*, 23:61–66.

STRAUS, ROBERT.
1957 "The nature and status of medical sociology." *American Sociological Review*, 22:200–204.

STRAUSS, ANSELM.
1966 "Structure and ideology of the nursing profession," pp. 60–104 in *The nursing profession*, F. Davis (ed.). New York: Wiley.
1970 "Medical ghettos," pp. 9–26 in *Where medicine fails*, A. Strauss (ed.). Chicago: Aldine.
1971 *Professions, work and career.* San Francisco: The Sociology Press.
1975 *Chronic illness and the quality of life.* St. Louis, Mo.: Mosby.

STRAUSS, ANSELM, LEONARD SCHATZMAN, DANUTA EHRLICH, RUE BUCHER, and MELVIN SABSHIN.
1963 "The hospital and its negotiated order," pp. 147–169 in *The hospital in modern society*, E. Freidson (ed.). New York: Free Press.

STRIMBU, JERRY, LYLE SCHOENFELDT, and O. SIMS.
1973 "Drug usage in college students as a function of racial classification and minority group status." *Research in Higher Education*, 1 (3):263–272.

SUCHMAN, EDWARD A.
1965a "Social patterns of illness and medical care." *Journal of Health and Human Behavior*, 6:2–16.
1965b "Stages of illness and medical care." *Journal of Health and Human Behavior*, 6:114–128.

SUDNOW, DAVID.
1967 *Passing on.* Englewood Cliffs, N.J.: Prentice-Hall, Inc.

SUSSER, M. W., and W. WATSON.
1971 *Sociology in medicine*, 2nd ed. New York: Oxford University Press.

SWANSON, GUY E.
1972 "Mead and Freud: Their relevance for social psychology," pp. 23–43 in *Symbolic interaction*, 2nd ed., J. Manis and B. Meltzer (eds.). Boston: Allyn and Bacon.

SYME, LEONARD.
1975 "Social and psychological risk factors in coronary heart disease." *Modern Concepts of Cardiovascular Disease*, 44:17–21.

SZASZ, THOMAS S.
1963 *Law, liberty, and psychiatry.* New York: Collier.
1964 *The myth of mental illness.* New York: Harper & Row.
1970 *The manufacture of madness.* New York: Dell.
1974 *The myth of mental illness*, rev. ed. New York: Harper & Row.

TAGLIACOZZO, DAISY, and HANS O. MAUKSCH.
1972 "The patient's view of the patient's role," pp. 172–185 in *Patients, physicians and illness*, 2nd ed., E. Jaco (ed.). New York: Macmillan.

TALLER, STEPHEN L., and ROBERT FELDMAN.
1974 "The training and utilization of nurse practitioners in adult health appraisal." *Medical Care*, 12:40–48.

TALLMER, MARGOT, and BERNARD KUTNER.
   1969 "Disengagement and the stresses of aging." *Journal of Gerontology*, 24:70–75.
TESSLER, RICHARD, DAVID MECHANIC, and MARGARET DIMOND.
   1976 "The effect of psychological distress on physician utilization: A prospective study." *Journal of Health and Social Behavior*, 17:353–364.
THOITS, PEGGY, and MICHAEL HANNAN.
   1979 "Income and psychological disorder: The impact of an income-maintenance experiment." *Journal of Health and Social Behavior*, 20:120–138.
THOMAS, ELIZABETH C., and KAORU YAMAMOTO.
   1975 "Attitudes toward age: An exploration in school-age children." *International Journal of Aging and Human Development*, 6:29–40.
TIERNEY, KATHLEEN J., and BARBARA BAISDEN.
   1979 *Crisis intervention programs for disaster victims: A source book and manual for smaller communities*. Rockville, Md.: National Institute of Mental Health.
TOWNSEND, J. MARSHALL.
   1975 "Cultural conceptions, mental disorders and social roles: A comparison of Germany and America." *American Sociological Review*, 40:739–752.
   1976 "Self-concept and the institutionalization of mental patients: An overview and critique." *Journal of Health and Social Behavior*, 17:263–271.
TUBESING, DONALD A., PAUL C. HOLINGER, GRANGER E. WESTBERG, and EDWARD A. LICHTER.
   1977 "The wholistic health center project: An action-research model for providing preventive, whole-person health care at the primary level." *Medical Care*, 15:217–227.
TUBESING, NANCY LOVING.
   1977 *Whole person health care: Philosophical assumptions*. Hinsdale, Ill.: Society for Wholistic Medicine.
TUCHMAN, BARBARA W.
   1978 *A distant mirror: The calamitous 14th century*. New York: Random House.
TUCKMAN, JACOB, and IRVING LORGE.
   1952 "The influence of a course on the psychology of the adult on attitudes toward old people and older workers." *Journal of Educational Psychology*, 43:400–407.
   1953 "Attitudes toward old people." *Journal of Social Psychology*, 37:249–260.
TWADDLE, ANDREW.
   1969 "Health decisions and sick role variations: An exploration." *Journal of Health and Social Behavior*, 10:105–114.
   1973 "Illness and deviance." *Social Science and Medicine*, 7:751–762.
U.S. DEPARTMENT OF HEALTH, EDUCATION and WELFARE.
   1976 *National Health Insurance Proposals*. Washington, D.C.: U.S. Government Printing Office.
   1978 *Health United States, 1978*. Washington, D.C.: U.S. Government Printing Office.
   1980 *Health United States, 1979*. Washington, D.C.: U.S. Government Printing Office.
VAN DEN BERG, JAN HENDRICK.
   1978 *Medical power and medical ethics*. New York: W. W. Norton.
VEATCH, ROBERT M.
   1972 "Choosing not to prolong dying." *Medical Dimensions*, 1:8–10, 40.
VERBRUGGE, LOIS M.
   1976 "Females and illness; Recent trends in sex differences in the United States." *Journal of Health and Social Behavior*, 17:387–403.

VOGEL, EZRA F.
1979 *Japan as number one*. Cambridge, Mass.: Harvard University Press.
VOLKART, E. H. (ed.).
1951 *Social behavior and personality*. New York: Social Science Research Council.
WADDELL, JACK O.
1973 "Drink friend! Social contexts of convivial drinking and drunkenness among Papago Indians in an urban setting," pp. 237–251 in *Proceedings of the First Annual Alcoholism Conference of the National Institute on Alcohol Abuse and Alcoholism*, M. Chafetz (ed.). Washington, D.C.: U.S. Government Printing Office.
WAECHTER, E. H.
1971 "Children's awareness of fatal illness." *American Journal of Nursing*, 71:1168–1172.
WAHL, C. W.
1965 "The fear of death," pp. 56–66 in *Death and identity*, R. Fulton (ed.). New York: Wiley.
WAITZKIN, HOWARD.
1971 "Latent functions of the sick role in various settings." *Social Science and Medicine*, 5:45–75.
WALLIS, ROY, and PETER MORLEY.
1976 "Introduction," pp. 9–19 in *Marginal medicine*, R. Wallis and P. Morley (eds.). New York: Free Press.
WAN, THOMAS T. H., and SCOTT J. SOIFER.
1974 "Determinants of physician utilization: A causal analysis." *Journal of Health and Social Behavior*, 15:100–108.
WARD, RUSSELL A.
1977 "Impact of subjective age and stigma on older persons." *Journal of Gerontology*, 32:227–232.
1979 *The aging experience: An introduction to social gerontology*. New York: J. B. Lippincott.
WARDWELL, WALTER I.
1979 "Limited and marginal practitioners," pp. 230–250 in *Handbook of medical sociology*, 3rd ed., H. Freeman, S. Levine, and L. Reeder (eds.). Englewood Cliffs, N.J.: Prentice-Hall, Inc.
1980 "The present and future role of the chiropractor," pp. 25–41 in *Modern developments in the principles and practice of chiropractic*, S. Haldeman (ed.). New York: Appleton-Century-Crofts.
WARHEIT, GEORGE J., CHARLES E. HOLZER III, and SANDRA A. AREY.
1975 "Race and mental illness: An epidemiologic update." *Journal of Health and Social Behavior*, 16:243–256.
WARHEIT, GEORGE J., CHARLES HOLZER III, and JOHN J. SCHWAB.
1973 "An analysis of social class and racial differences in depressive symptomatology." *Journal of Health and Social Behavior*, 14:291–298.
WARNECKE, RICHARD B.
1973 "Non-intellectual factors related to attrition from a collegiate nursing program." *Journal of Health and Social Behavior*, 14:153–167.
WEEKS, LEWIS E., and ROBERT A. DEVRIES.
1978 "Wholistic health centers: Where are they going?" *Inquiry*, 15:3–9.
WEINER, HERBERT.
1975 "Schizophrenia: Etiology," pp. 866–890 in *Comprehensive textbook of psychiatry*, Vol. I, 2nd ed., A. Freedman, H. Kaplan, and B. Sadock (eds.). Baltimore: Williams & Wilkins.

WEINSTEIN, RAYMOND M.
1979 "Patient attitudes toward mental hospitalization: A review of quantitative research." *Journal of Health and Social Behavior*, 20:237–258.

WELCH, SUSAN, JOHN COMER, and MICHAEL STEINMAN.
1973 "Some social and attitudinal correlates of health care among Mexican-Americans." *Journal of Health and Social Behavior*, 14:205–213.

WESSEN, ALBERT F.
1972 "Hospital ideology and communication between ward personnel," pp. 325–342 in *Patients, physicians and illness*, 2nd ed., E. Jaco (ed.). New York: Macmillan.

WEXLER, MURRAY.
1976 "The behavioral sciences in medical education." *American Psychologist*, 31:275–283.

WHATLEY, CHARLES D.
1959 "Social attitudes toward discharged mental patients." *Social Problems*, 6:313–320.

WHITE, KERR L.
1972 "Health care arrangements in the United States: A.D. 1972," pp. 17–40 in *Medical cure and medical care*, S. Andreopoulos (ed.). *Milbank Memorial Fund Quarterly*, 50:17–40.

WILDMAN, RICHARD C., and DAVID RICHARD JOHNSON.
1977 "Life change and Langner's 22-item mental health index: A study and partial replication." *Journal of Health and Social Behavior*, 18:179–188.

WILSON, ROBERT N.
1963 "The social structure of a general hospital." *Annals of the American Academy of Political Science*, 346:67–76.
1970 *The sociology of health.* New York: Random House.

WING, J. K.
1969 "Institutionalism in mental hospitals," pp. 219–238 in *Mental illness and social processes*, T. Scheff (ed.). New York: Harper & Row.

WOLF, STEWART, and HELEN GOODELL (eds.).
1968 *Harold G. Wolff's stress and disease*, 2nd ed. Springfield, Ill.: Thomas.

WOLF, STEWART, and HAROLD G. WOLFF.
1943 *Human gastric function: An experimental study of a man and his stomach.* New York: Oxford University Press.

WOLINSKY, FREDRIC D.
1980 *The sociology of health: Principles, professions, and issues.* Boston: Little, Brown.

WYSS, DIETER.
1973 *Psychoanalytic school from the beginning to the present.* New York: Aronson.

YARROW, M., C. SCHWARTZ, H. MURPHY, and L. DEASY.
1955 "The psychological meaning of mental illness in the family," *Journal of Social Issues*, 11:12–24.

YAHN, GEORGE.
1979 "The impact of holistic medicine, medical groups, and health concepts." *Journal of the American Medical Association*, 242:2202–2205.

ZBOROWSKI, MARK.
1952 "Cultural components in responses to pain." *Journal of Social Issues*, 8:16–30.

ZOLA, IRVING K.
1966 "Culture and symptoms—An analysis of patients' presenting complaints." *American Sociological Review*, 31:615–630.

AUTHOR INDEX

347

SUBJECT INDEX